COMMENTARY

2020–2021

VOLUME 114

R. H. Boyd, D.D., LL.D., Founder (1896–1922)

H. A. Boyd, D.D. (1922–1959) • T. B. Boyd Jr., D.D. (1959–1979) • T. B. Boyd III, D.D. (1979–2017)

LaDonna Boyd, M.B.A.
President/CEO (2017–Present)

LaDonna Boyd, M.B.A.
President/CEO

David Groves, D.Min., Ph.D.
Director of Publications

EDITORIAL STAFF
Olivia M. Cloud, M.R.E.
Associate Editor

Landon Dickerson, M.T.S.; Monique Gooch, B.A.; Joseph Tribble, M.Div.;
Brittany Batson, B.A.; Sinclaire Sparkman, B.S.; Freida Crawley, B.S.; Carla Davis, B.A.

Dr. Claude Forehand • Dr. Barry Johnson
Dr. Frank Houston • Dr. Bernard Williams
Writers

Jasmine Cole
Cover Design

For Customer Service and Toll-Free Ordering, Call 1-877-4RHBOYD (474-2693) Monday–Friday 8 a.m.–5 p.m. Central Time or Fax Toll-Free (800) 615-1815

www.rhboyd.com

R.H. Boyd Publishing Corporation
6717 Centennial Blvd.• Nashville, Tennessee 37209-1017

C O M M E N T A R Y 2 0 2 0 – 2 0 2 1

A Word from the Publisher

To Our Readers,

Thank you for your continued support through the years. We are so glad you have decided to share in the Lord's Gospel with us through this resource. For more than a century, *Boyd's Commentary for the Sunday School* has been a staple in Christian education. This year's book has been thoughtfully prepared through thorough exegesis, engaging theology, and spiritual meditation and prayer.

As you walk through this year's lessons, we hope they will aid you along with the direction of the Holy Spirit. In trying times such as these, it is important to remain steadfast in calling for effective leadership and maintaining hope for a better future. This year has brought on the COVID-19 pandemic, continued racial unrest, economic turmoil, war and disease running rampant, police brutality taking the lives of our youth, hatred rearing its ugly head, and the ever-present effects of systemic racism. Now, possibly more than ever, building strong leaders with sound biblical knowledge and integrity is vital. Our goal is to equip readers with a solid foundation for making effective change.

Again, thank you for your support. As you enjoy this resource, please visit our website, *www.rhboyd.com*, and follow us on social media @rhboydco to stay abreast of all the resources offered by R.H. Boyd.

Onward,

LaDonna Boyd
Fifth-generation *President/CEO*

A Word from the Director

Greetings!

For well over a century, *Boyd's Commentary* has been a reliable resource for those who desire in-depth theological and biblical exposition. The biblical text for examination has been selected by the Committee of Uniformed Series for International Study. The text has been thoroughly and prudently investigated using the appropriate skills and tools for biblical exegesis in an effort to develop a solid biblical hermeneutic that speaks to the issues of modern-day believers. You also can be assured this commentary has been developed by people of faith who serve as pastors, Bible instructors, seminary professors, Christian writers and editors, associate ministers, and in other capacities. Our goal is to provide you with a commentary that will more than meet your needs as you apply the biblical message to enlighten your congregation, class groups, and others of the will of God for their lives. Our goal, hope, and prayer is that *Boyd's Commentary for the Sunday School* will serve your biblical and theological training needs. Thank you for your continued patronage of our products.

Yours in Christ,

Rev. David Groves, D.Min., Ph.D.

NOTES FROM THE EDITOR

The layout of the *2020–2021 Boyd's Commentary* has been formatted for easy use in the classroom. In keeping with our rich history of publishing quality Christian literature, we have added the Unifying Principle as a feature that will enhance our commentary. Listed below is an explanation of each feature and the intended use of each.

Lesson Setting: Gives the basic time line and place for the events in the lesson.

Lesson Outline: Provides the topics used in the exposition of the lesson.

Unifying Principle: States the main idea for the lesson across age groups. This feature allows the teacher to understand exactly what each lesson is about.

Introduction: Gives the thesis and any background information that will be useful in the study of the lesson.

Exposition: Provides the exegetical study done by the writer, breaking down the text for discussion.

The Lesson Applied: Provides possible life applications of the biblical text for today's learners.

Let's Talk About It: Highlights ideas from the text in a question-and-answer format.

Home Daily Devotional Readings: Located at the end of each lesson, the topics are designed to lead into the following lesson.

Know Your Writers

Rev. Dr. Claude Ellis Forehand II

Dr. Forehand is a native of Lakewood, New Jersey who has been residing in Charlotte, North Carolina for over eighteen years. Throughout the years he has spent as a North Carolina resident, he has served nine years in the United States Marine Corps and earned a Bachelor of Science degree from Johnson C. Smith University and a Masters of Divinity and Doctor of Ministry from Hood Theological Seminary.

He is married to Ulinda V. Forehand (a native of Morristown, Tennessee) and is the pastor of Buncombe Baptist Church in Lexington, North Carolina. In addition, he currently serves as an adjunct professor for Queen City Bible College in Charlotte.

Dr. Barry Johnson

Dr. Barry C. Johnson Sr. is a native of and resides in Louisville, Kentucky. He earned a Bachelor of Music Composition and a Master of Music Composition from the University of Louisville and a Doctor of Musical Arts from the University of Kentucky. In addition, Dr. Johnson earned a Master of Divinity and Doctor of Ministry from The Southern Baptist Theological Seminary in Louisville, Kentucky. Dr. Johnson serves as a tenured associate professor of music composition and theory in the Division of Fine Arts at Kentucky State University in Frankfort. In addition, Dr. Johnson serves as pastor of Evergreen Baptist Church in Lawrenceburg.

Dr. Frank Houston

Dr. Frank Warren Houston is a native of Morristown, Tennessee. He earned a bachelor's degree in English from Carson Newman University and received his Master of Divinity and Ph.D. in New Testament studies from The Southern Baptist Theological Seminary in Louisville, Kentucky.

He currently serves as senior pastor-teacher of First Baptist Church of Georgetown, Kentucky. He is a member of Who's Who of America and the American Academy of Religion.

Dr. Bernard Williams

Dr. Bernard Williams is a native of Nashville, Tennessee. He has pastored churches in Tennessee and Florida. He is a graduate of the University of Tennessee Knoxville and The Southern Baptist Theological Seminary in Louisville, Kentucky. He also holds a Ph.D. in homiletics and church and society. Dr. Williams is a great proponent of small-group Bible study and serves as a teacher in Christian education. He holds numerous revivals, conferences, workshops, and seminars each year. He is a member of the American Academy of Religion and the Academy of Homiletics.

2020–2021 LESSON OVERVIEW

The Fall Quarter (September–November 2020) reminds us we are commanded by God to love one another as God loves us. The first unit, "Struggles with Love," looks at familial love, jealousy, and destruction. Love and reconciliation in the Joseph story prevail in spite of harsh and negative circumstances. Unit II centers on love for the stranger, the poor, and enemies. Jesus' Parable of the Good Samaritan illustrates love for one's neighbor. The third unit explores the abiding love of God through the Holy Spirit and reveals the expression of God's love in the formation of the early church.

The Winter Quarter (December 2020–February 2021) examines God's call in stories from the New Testament. The greatest call came to Jesus; others led to the extension of the Christian ministry. Unit I begins with Jesus' heritage and spends time on the story of Jesus' birth, including the witness of the Magi to Jesus' call as the Messiah. The second unit looks at four events from Jesus' ministry. Jesus received a call to proclamation and ministry and expanded His work by calling followers. Unit III highlights women in ministry. From the Samaritan woman to Mary Magdalene to Priscilla and Lydia, women supported Jesus and carried forth His teachings after the Resurrection.

The Spring Quarter (March–May 2021) introduces the ministry of Old Testament prophets. Unit I looks at why prophets were necessary in Israel's history. Unit II reveals the compassion of God when the people forsook God's ways. Prophecies in Ezra, Nehemiah, and Lamentations further show the faith of the prophets. The third unit shows the boldness of God's prophets in 1 Kings, Jeremiah, Ezekiel, and Jonah. Prophets called the returning exiles to restore their covenant with God.

The Summer Quarter (June–August 2021) looks at God's gift of faith as the source of hope and faith. Unit I focuses on Gospel stories of Jesus' teaching and miracles, while Units II and III explore Paul's letter to the Romans and his understanding of the hope of salvation through faith and look in other epistles at faith as essential for the hope of eternal life.

Boyd's Commentary for the Sunday School (2020–2021)

6717 Centennial Blvd., Nashville, TN 37209–1017

Printed in the United States of America.

PREFACE

The *2020–2021 Boyd's Commentary* has been formatted and written with you in mind. This format is to help you further your preparation and study of the Sunday school lessons.

We have presented a parallel Scripture lesson passage with the *New Revised Standard Version* alongside the *King James Version*. This allows you to have a clearer and more contemporary approach to the Scripture passages each week. This version is reliable and reputable. It will bless you as you rightly divide the word of truth (2 Tim. 2:15, KJV).

These lessons have a new look, but they still have the same accurate interpretation, concise Christian doctrine, and competent, skilled scholarship.

The abbreviations used throughout the commentary are as follows:

KJV — King James Version
NIV — New International Version
NKJV — New King James Version
NLT — New Living Translation
NRSV — New Revised Standard Version
RSV — Revised Standard Version
TLB — The Living Bible
NEB — New English Bible
JB — Jerusalem Bible
ESV — English Standard Version

To the pastor: Our hope is that this commentary will provide context and insight for your sermons. Also, we hope this commentary will serve as a preparatory aid for the message of God.

To the Bible teacher: This commentary also has you in mind. You can use it as a ready reference to the background of the text and difficult terms that are used in the Bible. To be sure, this commentary will provide your lesson study with the historical context that will enable you to interpret the text for your students more effectively.

This text is for anyone who wants to get a glimpse at the glory of God. This commentary seeks to highlight and lift the workings of God with His people and to make God's history with humanity ever present.

We hope and pray God will bless you and keep you as you diligently study His mighty and majestic Word. Remain ever steadfast to our one eternal God. Keep the faith, and pray always.

CONTENTS

FIRST QUARTER

UNIT THEME: STRUGGLES WITH LOVE

UNIT THEME: INCLUSIVE LOVE

UNIT THEME: GODLY LOVE AMONG BELIEVERS

CONTENTS

SECOND QUARTER

CONTENTS

THIRD QUARTER

CONTENTS

FOURTH QUARTER

FIRST QUARTER

September

October

November

Lesson material is based on International Sunday School Lessons and International Bible Lessons for Christian Teaching, copyrighted by the International Council of Religious Education, and is used by its permission.

ISSUES OF LOVE

TOPIC:
WHEN LOVE IS LOST

BACKGROUND SCRIPTURE:
GENESIS 37

GENESIS 37:2–11, 23–24, 28

King James Version

THESE are the generations of Jacob. Joseph, being seventeen years old, was feeding the flock with his brethren; and the lad was with the sons of Bilhah, and with the sons of Zilpah, his father's wives: and Joseph brought unto his father their evil report.

3 Now Israel loved Joseph more than all his children, because he was the son of his old age: and he made him a coat of many colours.

4 And when his brethren saw that their father loved him more than all his brethren, they hated him, and could not speak peaceably unto him.

5 And Joseph dreamed a dream, and he told it his brethren: and they hated him yet the more.

6 And he said unto them, Hear, I pray you, this dream which I have dreamed:

7 For, behold, we were binding sheaves in the field, and, lo, my sheaf arose, and also stood upright; and, behold, your sheaves stood round about, and made obeisance to my sheaf.

8 And his brethren said to him, Shalt thou indeed reign over us? or shalt thou indeed have dominion over us? And they hated him yet the more for his dreams, and for his words.

9 And he dreamed yet another dream, and told it his brethren, and said, Behold, I have dreamed a dream more; and, behold, the sun and the moon and the eleven stars made obeisance to me.

10 And he told it to his father, and to his brethren: and his father rebuked him, and

New Revised Standard Version

THIS is the story of the family of Jacob. Joseph, being seventeen years old, was shepherding the flock with his brothers; he was a helper to the sons of Bilhah and Zilpah, his father's wives; and Joseph brought a bad report of them to their father.

3 Now Israel loved Joseph more than any other of his children, because he was the son of his old age; and he had made him a long robe with sleeves.

4 But when his brothers saw that their father loved him more than all his brothers, they hated him, and could not speak peaceably to him.

5 Once Joseph had a dream, and when he told it to his brothers, they hated him even more.

6 He said to them, "Listen to this dream that I dreamed.

7 There we were, binding sheaves in the field. Suddenly my sheaf rose and stood upright; then your sheaves gathered around it, and bowed down to my sheaf."

8 His brothers said to him, "Are you indeed to reign over us? Are you indeed to have dominion over us?" So they hated him even more because of his dreams and his words.

9 He had another dream, and told it to his brothers, saying, "Look, I have had another dream: the sun, the moon, and eleven stars were bowing down to me."

10 But when he told it to his father and to his brothers, his father rebuked him, and said to

MAIN THOUGHT: And his brethren envied him; but his father observed the saying. (Genesis 37:11, KJV)

Genesis 37:2–11, 23–24, 28

King James Version	*New Revised Standard Version*
said unto him, What is this dream that thou hast dreamed? Shall I and thy mother and thy brethren indeed come to bow down ourselves to thee to the earth?	**him, "What kind of dream is this that you have had? Shall we indeed come, I and your mother and your brothers, and bow to the ground before you?"**
11 And his brethren envied him; but his father observed the saying.	**11 So his brothers were jealous of him, but his father kept the matter in mind.**
• • • • • •	• • • • • •
23 And it came to pass, when Joseph was come unto his brethren, that they stript Joseph out of his coat, his coat of many colours that was on him;	**23 So when Joseph came to his brothers, they stripped him of his robe, the long robe with sleeves that he wore;**
24 And they took him, and cast him into a pit: and the pit was empty, there was no water in it.	**24 and they took him and threw him into a pit. The pit was empty; there was no water in it.**
• • • • • •	• • • • • •
28 Then there passed by Midianites merchantmen; and they drew and lifted up Joseph out of the pit, and sold Joseph to the Ishmaelites for twenty pieces of silver: and they brought Joseph into Egypt.	**28 When some Midianite traders passed by, they drew Joseph up, lifting him out of the pit, and sold him to the Ishmaelites for twenty pieces of silver. And they took Joseph to Egypt.**

LESSON SETTING

Time: Unknown
Place: Egypt

LESSON OUTLINE

I. Hate in the Family (Genesis 37:2–11)
II. The Result of Hate (Genesis 37:23–24, 28)

Unifying Principle

Jealousy, hate, and love are emotions people experience in their families. How do people deal with these emotions? An absence of love for Joseph by his brothers led to envy and finally a plot to kill him.

Introduction

The family is made up of loved ones who know us best, in front of whom our vulnerability is on full display. In this divine institution we are introduced to love for the first time, either by the demonstration of it or by the longing for it in its absence. The family is also where love is tragically tested. Whether by grief, betrayal, unfaithfulness, neglect, and more, the strength of a family's love is measured by its ability to navigate the uncertain waters these inevitable life experiences cause. Family dysfunction is unfortunately the evidence of love failing to do so. But *failed* love doesn't mean *lost* love. At the least, failed love implies an attempt to love was made, and there's hope in that. Lost love, on the other hand, is when love has been buried beneath the layers of pain until the flame of its true expression has been totally deprived of much needed oxygen. Like fertilizer, the decomposition of dying love feeds the root of hate in the wake of its eventual and inevitable demise. A scar flourishes in its place, reminiscent of where love once was and is no more.

Sounds depressing, I know, but its unfortunately indicative of the drama played out in the ancient family of the patriarchs of Israel. As the last of the three great patriarchs, Jacob, whose name was changed by God to Israel, was both a victim and perpetrator of lost love in the family. As the youngest son of Isaac and Rebekah, Jacob was favored by his mother, while Isaac his father favored his older brother Esau. This favoritism played out with tragic results. Rebekah and Jacob conspired to manipulate Isaac into giving Jacob the birthright blessing intended for Esau because he was the firstborn. Because of this, Esau hated his brother and vowed to kill him upon the death of their father (Gen. 27:41).

As if inherited by the next generation, hatred in the family again revealed its ugly head among Jacob and his twelve sons. Similar to the favoritism that plagued his family of origin, Jacob favored his second youngest son, Joseph, more than the rest of his sons. Jacob's older sons hated Joseph like his brother Esau hated him, and their hatred for him resulted in tragedy.

Known by many scholars as Joseph's narrative or Joseph's Novella, Genesis 37 opens with a brief introduction of Joseph as a young man. At the time of the lesson, he was seventeen years old and enjoying the life of entitlement and privilege. But that would soon change.

Exposition

I. Hate in the Family (Genesis 37:2–11)

Joseph was the firstborn of Jacob's favorite wife Rachel. This is why he loved Joseph more than all his other children and also because he was the son born in his old age, the eleventh son. Being favored and showing favoritism was part of Jacob's legacy. He was favored by his mother Rebekah, and his father Isaac favored his older brother Esau over him. Jacob favored his second wife Rachel over his first wife Leah. Actually, Jacob never wanted Leah as a wife but was tricked by the sisters' father, Laban, into marrying her. He then was given Rachel in marriage after a total of fourteen years of labor. This history of parental relationships certainly played out in the way in which their offspring were treated. Thus Jacob favored Joseph heavily for the reasons mentioned above.

Sibling rivalry and parental favoritism are a repeated theme within the stories of the families of Genesis. As mentioned, Jacob was favored by his mother and rivaled with his brother Esau. This pattern, however, was entrenched as it was three generations deep. Abraham favored his son of his wife, Isaac, over his son of his slave, Ishmael, ultimately leading to Ishmael and Hagar's removal from their home. Parental favoritism and sibling rivalry have catastrophic results as forecasted by the stories mentioned above and the Cain and Abel narrative of Genesis 4.

Jacob overtly flaunted his favoritism for his younger son by gifting Joseph a specially-made tunic. This further spurred ire and rage against Joseph when his brothers saw that their father loved him more than them. They hated him and could not speak peaceably to him to the extent that their resentment could not be abated. Their anger toward Joseph was kindled by sight. The Hebrew in this text indicates that as they saw Jacob's bias, as they saw the tunic representing Jacob's favoritism, their hatred for Joseph was renewed each time they saw him. It was a cycle of close quarters—at each turn they saw something so that whenever they saw Joseph, they could not stand the sight of him.

Joseph didn't help matters when he pressed his brothers to hear the dream God gave him. In his artlessness and infantilism, he shared the dream, not to offend or boast but hopefully to impress. His brothers, however, were not impressed. Instead they disdained him all the more. In one of his dreams, the sheaves of Joseph and his brothers were symbols of their lives and what was to come. Joseph's sheaf stood upright while the sheaves of his brothers stood all around and bowed low in symbolic subjection to Joseph's. In the second of Joseph's dreams, the sun, moon, and eleven stars all were bowing to him. Whatever Joseph's intent in telling the dreams, wisdom dictated he should have been quiet.

Joseph's dreams gave evidence to his special purpose, but he was most naive in thinking his brothers would rejoice along with him. This was only another reminder for them. His father rebuked him when Joseph told his dreams again in front of him and his brothers. The content of the second dream undermined Jacob's position as head of household and indicated he and Joseph's mother along with his brothers would bow down before Joseph in subjugation. The end result of the dream episode was the hot jealousy of the brothers. Jacob, however, guarded the conversation without passing judgment and instead kept the matter close to his heart. Ironically the brothers, who reacted in an emotionally charged manner against the dream, were the ones who ended up fulfilling it. While Jacob, who did not react poorly, did not end up being part of its fulfillment in later chapters.

II. The Result of Hate (Genesis 37:23–24, 28)

The brothers carried out a plot against Joseph when he came to them in verse 23. Their plan included forcibly taking the special coat. The brothers stripped Joseph and threw him into a pit. Their initial plan was to kill Joseph, but Reuben thought it better to keep him hostage in a pit. The text reveals he wanted to take Joseph back to their father to restore himself to Jacob's good graces (Gen. 37:21–22). Reuben had slept with Bilhah, Jacob's concubine, and was on the periphery of his father's graces (35:22). When Reuben slept with Bilhah, it was an affront to Jacob's status as head of household. Interestingly, it also may be that Reuben had some sense of kinship with Joseph as he would have understood the boy's ambition. The brothers thought following Reuben's plan was the better of two (plus he was the oldest) and threw Joseph into a pit until they could figure out what to do with him. The aggressive way they stripped the coat off Joseph describes a violent act that infers the forceful removal of a garment. Meaning, they did it with extreme cruelty. The pit where they threw him, though it spared his life, only prolonged his agony, as he was left to rot. When the Midianite traders passed by. Joseph's brothers sold him into slavery. According to the original Hebrew, the way the brothers pulled Joseph up and lifted him out of the pit was with the same aggressive contempt they had throwing him in the pit.

Joseph's selling into slavery is a parallel for many African Americans, as it is understood we were sold to lands and people unknown for personal gain by those later considered our kinsmen and women. It is important to bear in mind a major difference. Even as it was Africans selling Africans, there was no such thing as an African identity. Smaller groups of people were ruled by kings, queens, and chieftains who did what they thought best for themselves, families, people, lands, and kingdoms. They sold their enemies, not kinsmen and women. Joseph's story differs in that the brothers sold their kinsman who was their perceived enemy. Perhaps we can learn who our kinsmen and women are or, as Jesus put it, our neighbor.

The brothers sold Joesph for a mere twenty shekels of silver. According to extrabiblical material, this was the going rate for slaves in the second millennium B.C. According to Leviticus 27:2–7, it was the price for redeeming people/property for a young male of five to twenty years old. Joseph's brothers sold him into slavery, and because of his youth and vitality, there is little doubt the traders believed Joseph would fetch a greater price and profit in Egypt.

Joseph's entrance to Egypt was an interesting turn of the plot. Israelite tension with Egyptian power is well-documented in the Old Testament. That tension was represented well by Joseph's great-grandfather, Abraham. Abraham went to Egypt to escape a famine and while there failed to acknowledge Sarai as his wife. Sarai was then taken for the pharaoh's wife. As a result, a plague came over Pharaoh's household. Then pharaoh dismissed Abraham and Sarai upon learning she was his wife and sister, not just the latter (Gen. 12:10–20). This earlier story intersects with our current lesson in two important ways. First, Abraham was escaping famine in Egypt, which portends the brothers' later descent to Egypt for the same reason. The famine eventually caused Joseph's rise to power in this same Egypt. Second, the Abrahamic story seems to serve as a backdrop to the continued tension between Israelites and Egyptians. By the book of Exodus, the Egyptians had enslaved the Israelites and even after their emancipation were a looming political and military power in the region. This story demonstrates their relative geographic proximity and interconnectedness. Joseph was going to lands known and unknown, where Israelite safety was in question, as shown by Abraham's fear and subsequent statement (Gen. 12:12–13). If the story were to end here, the reader would be left to wonder what happened to Joseph.

The Lesson Applied

In this lesson, the three examples of Jacob, Joseph, and the brothers give light to the complexity of family dysfunction that exists today in many families. Families that are devoid of love inevitably fall apart, as love is the glue that binds all hearts together. God is love, and therefore, a family without it has no room for God to abide in the midst. Because God is love, He can restore it when it's lost. How He chooses to, however, is uncertain, and when He chooses is according to His time. For Joseph, love eventually returned (for those who know the story), but it took time for God to penetrate their hearts. Such is the case for the modern family. For those of us who are experiencing the debilitating effects of lost love, know that in God nothing is ever lost. In Him, whatever is hidden will be revealed and whatever is lost can be found, even if it's love.

Let's Talk About It

It has been said, "Family is where life begins and love never ends." That being the case, who or what is to blame for the love lost between Joseph and his brothers? Clearly the plot to kill Joseph implicates his older brothers as the primary reason for what caused the love to fade. Certainly they are to blame, but are they the only ones? What about Joseph? Though he was the victim, could he also have contributed to his own misfortune?

Most of us grew up learning about Joseph being morally superior to his brothers. This wasn't so. Joseph was not perfect and had flaws like everyone else. For example, Joseph leveraged his father's favoritism in an unwise way. He was a tattletale, if not an outright slanderer of his brothers (Gen. 37:2). He accepted and wore the outward symbol of his father's partiality. Perhaps, the greatest insult was when Joseph chose to tell his brothers, prematurely, of his dreams that seemed to imply he would rule over the family. So, in addition to his brothers, Joseph was also complicit in the love lost in the family.

Consider also the complicity of their father. Though he didn't have a major role in Joseph's narrative, Jacob's contribution to the family's dysfunction and subsequent loss of love among them was just as significant, if not more so. He purposely favored Joseph over the rest of his sons without regard of the consequence in so doing. Instead of addressing the tension between them, Jacob doubled down in his favoritism by making Joseph a special coat. For Joseph, the coat was the physical representation of his father's favor, but for his brothers it was a constant sign that Joseph, not them, would receive the birthright blessing.

They all were responsible for the lost love, though not equally. When love is lost in the family, it is incumbent that everyone involved take ownership and responsibility to address the dysfunction. There usually is enough blame to go around. The good news in this passage is that family dysfunction can be overcome with love as the foundation. Joseph exhibited this type of love and saved his family from total destruction. His relationship with God made all the difference. When we turn to God, He will help us to do what is right.

Home Daily Devotional Readings

September 7–13, 2020

Monday	Tuesday	Wednesday	Thursday	Friday	Saturday	Sunday
Paul and Barnabas Appointed for Ministry	Joseph, Chief Interpreter of Dreams	Dreams of Cows and Corn Explained	Preparing for the Expected Famine	Storing Grain for the Future	Egypt Feeds the Middle East	Leadership During Crisis
Acts 13:1–5	Genesis 41:9–13	Genesis 41:14–24	Genesis 41:34–36	Genesis 41:41–49	Genesis 41:53–57	Genesis 41:25–33, 37–40, 50–52

GOD REWARDS OBEDIENCE

TOPIC:
LOVE VERSUS BITTERNESS

BACKGROUND SCRIPTURE:
GENESIS 41:14–57

GENESIS 41:25–33, 37–40, 50–52

King James Version

AND Joseph said unto Pharaoh, The dream of Pharaoh is one: God hath shewed Pharaoh what he is about to do.
26 The seven good kine are seven years; and the seven good ears are seven years: the dream is one.
27 And the seven thin and ill favoured kine that came up after them are seven years; and the seven empty ears blasted with the east wind shall be seven years of famine.
28 This is the thing which I have spoken unto Pharaoh: What God is about to do he sheweth unto Pharaoh.
29 Behold, there come seven years of great plenty throughout all the land of Egypt:
30 And there shall arise after them seven years of famine; and all the plenty shall be forgotten in the land of Egypt; and the famine shall consume the land;
31 And the plenty shall not be known in the land by reason of that famine following; for it shall be very grievous.
32 And for that the dream was doubled unto Pharaoh twice; it is because the thing is established by God, and God will shortly bring it to pass.
33 Now therefore let Pharaoh look out a man discreet and wise, and set him over the land of Egypt.

• • • • • •

37 And the thing was good in the eyes of Pharaoh, and in the eyes of all his servants.

New Revised Standard Version

THEN Joseph said to Pharaoh, "Pharaoh's dreams are one and the same; God has revealed to Pharaoh what he is about to do.
26 The seven good cows are seven years, and the seven good ears are seven years; the dreams are one.
27 The seven lean and ugly cows that came up after them are seven years, as are the seven empty ears blighted by the east wind. They are seven years of famine.
28 It is as I told Pharaoh; God has shown to Pharaoh what he is about to do.
29 There will come seven years of great plenty throughout all the land of Egypt.
30 After them there will arise seven years of famine, and all the plenty will be forgotten in the land of Egypt; the famine will consume the land.
31 The plenty will no longer be known in the land because of the famine that will follow, for it will be very grievous.
32 And the doubling of Pharaoh's dream means that the thing is fixed by God, and God will shortly bring it about.
33 Now therefore let Pharaoh select a man who is discerning and wise, and set him over the land of Egypt.

• • • • • •

37 The proposal pleased Pharaoh and all his servants.

MAIN THOUGHT: And Pharaoh said unto Joseph, Forasmuch as God hath shewed thee all this, there is none so discreet and wise as thou art: Thou shalt be over my house, and according unto thy word shall all my people be ruled: only in the throne will I be greater than thou. (Genesis 41:39–40, KJV)

GENESIS 41:25–33, 37–40, 50–52

King James Version	*New Revised Standard Version*
38 And Pharaoh said unto his servants, Can we find such a one as this is, a man in whom the Spirit of God is?	**38 Pharaoh said to his servants, "Can we find anyone else like this—one in whom is the spirit of God?"**
39 And Pharaoh said unto Joseph, Forasmuch as God hath shewed thee all this, there is none so discreet and wise as thou art:	**39 So Pharaoh said to Joseph, "Since God has shown you all this, there is no one so discerning and wise as you.**
40 Thou shalt be over my house, and according unto thy word shall all my people be ruled: only in the throne will I be greater than thou.	**40 You shall be over my house, and all my people shall order themselves as you command; only with regard to the throne will I be greater than you."**
• • • • • •	• • • • • •
50 And unto Joseph were born two sons before the years of famine came, which Asenath the daughter of Potipherah priest of On bare unto him.	**50 Before the years of famine came, Joseph had two sons, whom Asenath daughter of Potiphera, priest of On, bore to him.**
51 And Joseph called the name of the firstborn Manasseh: For God, said he, hath made me forget all my toil, and all my father's house.	**51 Joseph named the firstborn Manasseh, "For," he said, "God has made me forget all my hardship and all my father's house."**
52 And the name of the second called he Ephraim: For God hath caused me to be fruitful in the land of my affliction.	**52 The second he named Ephraim, "For God has made me fruitful in the land of my misfortunes."**

LESSON SETTING
Time: Unknown
Place: Egypt

LESSON OUTLINE

I. **Facing Pharaoh (Genesis 41:25–33)**
II. **The Power of a Dream (Genesis 41:37–40)**
III. **Using Family to Heal Fractures (Genesis 41:50–52)**

UNIFYING PRINCIPLE

It may be difficult to hold on to dreams of future success when faced with extreme hardships. What inner resources are needed to continue one's quest for success? Because Joseph loved and obeyed God, he was able to engage in wise and discerning problem-solving that motivated Pharaoh to appoint him second-in-command over all of Egypt.

INTRODUCTION

Family difficulties caused by factors outside of the family, such as sickness, economic failure, or global pandemic that arise naturally, can be challenging to cope with. But when family challenges are caused by and are the symptoms of self-inflicted wounds, the ability to cope may feel like an impossible feat. Truthfully, some of the most egregious offenses we encounter in our lives will be orchestrated, if not perpetrated, by family members who claim to love us. When this is a reality, a person may be inclined to ask the Lord, "Why would You allow me to be born into *this* family?" And His answer: "Because it's necessary to bring out in you what you were made to become in Me."

Just as the character of a plant is determined by the soil in which it grows, so it is with us. Regardless of the condition of the soil from which we are both planted in and grow out of, the composition of our family environment helps determine the shape of our character. The hurt and pain we endure from the family, though difficult to bear, are a part of what God allows to strengthen our resolve in Him.

There is no clearer example of this in the Bible than the life of Joseph—after he was sold into slavery by his brothers. From the time the Midianite traders took him into custody, Joseph was saddled with an ever-growing bitterness for his brothers. (Can you blame him?) The trauma of being forcefully separated from your family by those who claim to love you is pretty hard to fathom, let alone forgive.

What's worse is that this same unfair treatment became a common theme throughout Joseph's experience in Egypt. He was falsely accused of raping Potiphar's wife, which resulted in his imprisonment. After interpreting the dream of the chief cupbearer of his imminent restoration to position, he was forgotten for two years by that same cupbearer to whom he gave hope. So, at the time of today's lesson, Joseph was in prison. And yet, God was still with him. After the baker finally told Pharaoh, king of Egypt, who Joseph was and what he could do, the king summoned him from prison to interpret a puzzling dream he had. Joseph's life was about to change. While his dreams in the beginning of the narrative led to his imprisonment, his interpretation of dreams at the end led to his empowerment. Sometimes our worst experiences can be the seeds that bring the most favorable outcomes in the long run.

Exposition

I. Facing Pharaoh (Genesis 41:25–33)

Joseph responded to Pharaoh's request to interpret both of his dreams by explaining the two were one in meaning. God gave Pharaoh two different dreams with the same message to emphasize the importance of the message the dreams conveyed. According to Joseph, they were a forecast of what God was about to do for and in Egypt. In Pharaoh's first dream, there were two sets of seven cows. The first set was healthy and fat, while the second set was bony and skinny. In his dream, the cows from the second set ate the fat cows from the first and yet were still bony and skinny. Being awakened by the confusion of the dream, he later went back to sleep and dreamed again. The second dream was similar to the first, only it was with grain instead of cows. Seven heads of grain full and plenty were swallowed up by seven ears of withered corn that sprouted later.

Joseph stated the two dreams meant God had decided they would happen soon. This reminds the reader of Joseph's double dreams at the beginning of the narrative. His dreams would come to pass. All that was left to determine was when and how they would be fulfilled.

According to Joseph, the seven good cows and seven full heads of grain typified seven years of great plenty and economic prosperity that Egypt soon would enjoy. However, this seven-year period of plenty immediately would be followed by seven years of extreme famine, symbolized in the dream by the seven thin and ugly cows and the seven empty heads of grain. The devouring of the fat cows and healthy grain by thin and ugly ones was interpreted by Joseph to mean the seven years of great famine would be so severe the memory of the seven years of great plenty would fade in the despair of their scarcity. According to Genesis 41:30–31, the foreshadowed famine would totally deplete the land of all resources, completely decimating Egypt's economy.

Our closest corollary would be a recession. The economy comes to a grinding halt and even basic items may be difficult to purchase. For us, unemployment rises and those living on the fringes of society often fall off the proverbial cliff. Even some who were doing well during better times see major upheaval and catastrophe. These moments tend to make us forget better times or at least long for them.

Joseph exceeded the expectations of the king's initial request when he proceeded to advise him as to what steps should be taken in light of the interpretation. He suggested preventative measures instead of reactionary policy. His proposal to collect one-fifth of the produce of the land during the plentiful years as a reserve for the seven years of famine distinguished him to the pharaoh as the kind of administrator who should lead the nation in coping through this disaster. Though Joseph encouraged the ruler to select someone who was a discerning and wise man who could be trusted to govern over the land of Egypt, he knew within himself that God had positioned him to be that one. It was a kind of backhanded self-promotion and self-deprecation. It worked for Joseph but is not recommended for everyone.

In this way Joseph acted shrewdly. It is likely that in his time in Egypt, Joseph gained a mind for political maneuvering. From Potiphar's house to the prison, Joseph always was able to position himself well, close to those who were in charge. In truth, this may have been something innate, as he also positioned himself well in his family of origin, next to Jacob. Obviously, given his nature, he was not going to let the opportunity go to waste. Slavery and prison sharpened his tools.

II. The Power of a Dream (Genesis 41:37–40)

The plan Joseph proposed to Pharaoh seemed good in his eyes and in the eyes of all his servants. If he followed the strategy, it would guarantee Egypt's economic stability during the imminent famine. The question the king asked next was key to the success of this strategy: "Can we find such a one as this who is competent enough to provide this kind of leadership?" Pharaoh quickly realized that just like the dream, this plan was also from God. Therefore, only one who was familiar with God and in whom the Spirit of God resided needed to apply for the job. Because of his faithfulness to God, Joseph's name was at the top of a short list of possible candidates. In fact, in Pharaoh's eyes, his was the only name. Though the king had the dreams, Joseph was the only one to whom God had shown all this. Prudence demanded he should be the one to oversee the project. The required disposition, according to Pharaoh, was one who was discerning and wise. To him, no other person fits that profile better than Joseph.

To support Joseph's leadership in carrying out this robust economic plan, the pharaoh endowed him with great authority and power limited only by his own throne. Joseph was given the task to oversee both the domestic affairs of the ruler's house and the government of his people. Ultimately, Joseph was invited by the pharaoh to rule alongside him as second-in-command. He was given new clothing, a new chariot, a new position, and a new name. Joseph was given a new identity.

III. Using Family to Heal Fractures (Genesis 41:50–52)

The children who were born to Joseph before the predicted years of the famine were evidence of the economic prosperity Egypt enjoyed. The names of his two sons represented the mind Joseph had regarding his new life in Egypt. The naming formula, which included the explanation for the name, is well-documented in Genesis 3:20; 4:25; 26:20. Commonly, the Israelite mother assigned the name of the child based on her interpretation or sentiment of the event (Gen. 4:25; Ex. 2:10; 1 Sam 1:20). Joseph, however, gave his sons Hebrew names that conveyed his response to his Egyptian experience. The name of his firstborn Manasseh, or "he who makes someone forget," implied that the joy of his son had made him forget the sadness he experienced in his father's house, a sadness he had not forgotten but had carried for a long time. That he made no attempt to learn about his family even after his rise to power confirmed not that he forgot his past but rather was *trying* to forget his past. He also had forgotten the hard trail in Egypt that it took to get to this point. Though his life had changed for the better, his bitterness remained and impeded his ability to forgive those of his past. While he recognized the Lord's faithfulness in making him fruitful in the land of his affliction, the name he gave his second son Ephraim, or "to bear fruit," conveyed his attempt to build a new family on top of the hurt from the past of the old. The names of his sons stood in contrast. Joseph forgot even as he was fruitful. His most difficult moments placed him in position to become his best self. That which he attempted to forget was also what caused him to be fruitful. It was the gift and curse of pain that was both blessing and blight.

Ironically, the births of his sons caused Joseph to consciously remember the pain he had experienced. He did not mention his father's household or allude to his painful experiences until they were born. Even as he forgot, he remembered. The only thing that could heal his wounds were not the trappings of success, but family.

The Lesson Applied

Joseph had legitimate reasons to be bitter, given all he had endured before securing a position in the king's palace. But he also had good reason to be encouraged. Despite the thirteen years of a hardening heart that had become weathered by the toxic winds of betrayal, abandonment, and injustice, the Lord was still with him (Gen. 39:2, 21). His role in Potiphar's house and his service in the king's prison helped prepare Joseph to fulfill his destiny as the instrument of God to preserve and reposition the posterity of His people.

As a slave in Potiphar's house, Joseph learned how to be an administrator, managing the day-to-day operations of the master's household. This prepared him on a smaller level for what he would do for the economy of Egypt on a much bigger scale. Because the prison he was in was the king's prison, Joseph's time was spent interacting with and learning from individuals who would have been knowledgeable of the customs and practices in Egypt. By practicing these, Joseph became a more amenable subject before the king.

For every negative experience, there is a positive to match. We only have to search for it. Through the crucible of life, our gaze can become sharpened to recognize Christ hidden in the midst of a crisis. The love we have for the Savior enables us to see past the haze of bitterness and look toward a hope for something better.

Let's Talk About It

When you examine your life and all of the great things you've been blessed to achieve and accomplish, do you appreciate all it took to get where you are? It's easy to reflect on with delight all of the positive features of your journey. But what about the pitfalls, setbacks, and failures. Do we reflect on them too? Do we celebrate the worth of those experiences with the same enthusiasm?

While we don't like to think about the negative experiences in our lives, sometimes they are what God uses to bring out the best in us. Through Him we learn how to appreciate the purpose for the pain and realize our purpose in the pain. This is part of what it means in Romans 8:28 when it says God works all things out for His good and holy purpose.

The reason our ancestors risked life and limb time and time again to emancipate other enslaved people was not just because they themselves knew the pain of slavery. They were driven by a sense of purpose. Living by the light of our purpose enables us not only to endure the pain from hardship but to grow as a result of it. Hardship helps break up the ground of the heart so we can be exposed before God. At the point of Joseph's deepest despair, he discovered purpose in his pain. While in prison, Joseph encountered and used his gift for the king's chief butler, through whom he eventually was granted an audience with the king. Through the crushing of Joseph's spirit, the gift God planted within was given room to flourish.

We all are born with purpose, though we may not be aware of it. Buried beneath the layers of our hurt from life experiences, we learn to ignore the gift God has put within. Just as it took prison to liberate Joseph toward his destiny, it sometimes takes being broken to be whole in our purpose. Let us come to accept our pain and to use it redemptively.

Home Daily Devotional Readings
September 14–20, 2020

Monday	Tuesday	Wednesday	Thursday	Friday	Saturday	Sunday
Have Mercy on Me, a Sinner	Pilate's Judgment of Jesus, "Not Guilty"	Brothers Sent to Egypt to Buy Grain	Joseph Returns Money with Grain	Joseph Questions Motives of Brothers	Jacob Vows Not to Send Benjamin	Joseph Confronts Brothers for Past Behavior
Psalm 51:1–12	Luke 23:9–15	Genesis 42:1–5	Genesis 42:26–28	Genesis 42:29–34	Genesis 42:35–38	Genesis 42:6–25

LOVE VERSUS GUILT

TOPIC:
HAUNTED BY SHAME?

BACKGROUND SCRIPTURE:
GENESIS 42

GENESIS 42:6–25

King James Version

AND Joseph was the governor over the land, and he it was that sold to all the people of the land: and Joseph's brethren came, and bowed down themselves before him with their faces to the earth.

7 And Joseph saw his brethren, and he knew them, but made himself strange unto them, and spake roughly unto them; and he said unto them, Whence come ye? And they said, From the land of Canaan to buy food.

8 And Joseph knew his brethren, but they knew not him.

9 And Joseph remembered the dreams which he dreamed of them, and said unto them, Ye are spies; to see the nakedness of the land ye are come.

10 And they said unto him, Nay, my lord, but to buy food are thy servants come.

11 We are all one man's sons; we are true men, thy servants are no spies.

12 And he said unto them, Nay, but to see the nakedness of the land ye are come.

13 And they said, Thy servants are twelve brethren, the sons of one man in the land of Canaan; and, behold, the youngest is this day with our father, and one is not.

14 And Joseph said unto them, That is it that I spake unto you, saying, Ye are spies:

15 Hereby ye shall be proved: By the life of Pharaoh ye shall not go forth hence, except your youngest brother come hither.

16 Send one of you, and let him fetch your brother, and ye shall be kept in prison, that

New Revised Standard Version

NOW Joseph was governor over the land; it was he who sold to all the people of the land. And Joseph's brothers came and bowed themselves before him with their faces to the ground.

7 When Joseph saw his brothers, he recognized them, but he treated them like strangers and spoke harshly to them. "Where do you come from?" he said. They said, "From the land of Canaan, to buy food."

8 Although Joseph had recognized his brothers, they did not recognize him.

9 Joseph also remembered the dreams that he had dreamed about them. He said to them, "You are spies; you have come to see the nakedness of the land!"

10 They said to him, "No, my lord; your servants have come to buy food.

11 We are all sons of one man; we are honest men; your servants have never been spies."

12 But he said to them, "No, you have come to see the nakedness of the land!"

13 They said, "We, your servants, are twelve brothers, the sons of a certain man in the land of Canaan; the youngest, however, is now with our father, and one is no more."

14 But Joseph said to them, "It is just as I have said to you; you are spies!

15 Here is how you shall be tested: as Pharaoh lives, you shall not leave this place unless your youngest brother comes here!

16 Let one of you go and bring your brother, while the rest of you remain in prison, in order

MAIN THOUGHT: And Reuben answered them, saying, Spake I not unto you, saying, Do not sin against the child; and ye would not hear? therefore, behold, also his blood is required. (Genesis 42:22, KJV)

Genesis 42:6–25

King James Version

your words may be proved, whether there be any truth in you: or else by the life of Pharaoh surely ye are spies.
17 And he put them all together into ward three days.
18 And Joseph said unto them the third day, This do, and live; for I fear God:
19 If ye be true men, let one of your brethren be bound in the house of your prison: go ye, carry corn for the famine of your houses:
20 But bring your youngest brother unto me; so shall your words be verified, and ye shall not die. And they did so.
21 And they said one to another, We are verily guilty concerning our brother, in that we saw the anguish of his soul, when he besought us, and we would not hear; therefore is this distress come upon us.
22 And Reuben answered them, saying, Spake I not unto you, saying, Do not sin against the child; and ye would not hear? therefore, behold, also his blood is required.
23 And they knew not that Joseph understood them; for he spake unto them by an interpreter.
24 And he turned himself about from them, and wept; and returned to them again, and communed with them, and took from them Simeon, and bound him before their eyes.
25 Then Joseph commanded to fill their sacks with corn, and to restore every man's money into his sack, and to give them provision for the way: and thus did he unto them.

New Revised Standard Version

that your words may be tested, whether there is truth in you; or else, as Pharaoh lives, surely you are spies."
17 And he put them all together in prison for three days.
18 On the third day Joseph said to them, "Do this and you will live, for I fear God:
19 if you are honest men, let one of your brothers stay here where you are imprisoned. The rest of you shall go and carry grain for the famine of your households,
20 and bring your youngest brother to me. Thus your words will be verified, and you shall not die." And they agreed to do so.
21 They said to one another, "Alas, we are paying the penalty for what we did to our brother; we saw his anguish when he pleaded with us, but we would not listen. That is why this anguish has come upon us."
22 Then Reuben answered them, "Did I not tell you not to wrong the boy? But you would not listen. So now there comes a reckoning for his blood."
23 They did not know that Joseph understood them, since he spoke with them through an interpreter.
24 He turned away from them and wept; then he returned and spoke to them. And he picked out Simeon and had him bound before their eyes.
25 Joseph then gave orders to fill their bags with grain, to return every man's money to his sack, and to give them provisions for their journey. This was done for them.

LESSON SETTING

Time: Unknown
Place: Egypt

LESSON OUTLINE

I. **Joseph's Revenge (Genesis 42:6–17)**
II. **Joseph's Mercy (Genesis 42:18–25)**

Unifying Principle

Some people allow guilt from their past to poison their present. Is it ever possible to be free from condemnation for our past actions?

When Joseph saw and remembered his brothers who sold him into Egyptian slavery, he showed compassion while motivating them to recall and take responsibility for their earlier actions.

Introduction

Whether one calls it *revenge, vengeance,* or *reprisal*, all forms of retribution are someone's idea of justice without mercy (which isn't justice, by the way). In a hostile world, redress is a natural response of those who have been offended. According to popular society, it's like a "dish best served cold," referring to the so-called "sweet" benefits of payback. But the sweetness of revenge is bad for our health and fails to deliver the delight one would think it does. Retaliating against one who has wronged us always will result in unsatisfying outcomes. In fact, behavioral scientists have observed that instead of quenching hostility, revenge only prolongs the unpleasantness of the original offense. Merely bringing harm upon an offender is not enough to satisfy a person's vengeful spirit. This is evidence that revenge was never meant for us to dispense but is an act that should be left for God to orchestrate.

Paul wrote to the Christians in Rome, "Never avenge yourselves, but leave room for the wrath of God; for it is written, 'Vengeance is mine, I will repay, says the Lord'" (Rom. 12:19, NRSV). Believers who have been offended need to let God exact vengeance on their behalf, for God is God over both the offended and the offender, and only He knows what justice demands.

From Joseph's perspective, this was easier said than done. At the time of today's lesson, the famine in the land had become so severe that Jacob, Joseph's father, instructed all but one of his sons to go to Egypt to buy grain. This meant they would have to unknowingly face their brother and ultimately the shame they had been living with for thirteen years. The dream Joseph dreamed when he was seventeen was finally coming true—his family was coming to bow down to him.

From a position of power, Joseph had a choice to make. He could give into the seductive urge of revenge or choose to forgive. As for the brothers, they too had a choice to make—face their shame or continue to hide from it.

Exposition

I. Joseph's Revenge (Genesis 42:6–17)

A few years into the famine, verse 6 opens with the indication Joseph's position as governor had become the settled norm in Egypt. Second only to Pharaoh, his power was absolute. One of Joseph's responsibilities was to oversee the allocation of food, especially during the predicted seven-year famine. He sold to all the people in the land who came seeking grain. This was what brought him into contact with his brothers. Being foreigners from Canaan, Joseph's brothers came and bowed down before him. While it was an act that showed deference to the master of the land and was expected of the brothers, bowing down to Joseph said far more than they realized. As they bowed, Joseph remembered his dreams. After many years, they had come to pass. Joseph recognized his brothers but maintained his anonymity. He acted like a stranger to them. He was able to secure the concealment of his identity easily. In addition to the twenty years that had passed, Joseph appeared and sounded like an Egyptian, and they never would have thought he could have risen to this seat of power. He didn't disguise his anger from his brothers as he did his identity. Joseph spoke roughly to them as a prelude to the charges against them.

While reunited with his family, the last memory Joseph had of his brothers was of them selling him off to Egypt. His accusation against them in verse 9, calling them "spies … come to see the nakedness of the land" (NRSV), was Joseph's way of testing their character. He wanted to determine what kind of men they turned out to be twenty years later. In protesting their innocence, they disclosed to Joseph details of their family's current state. They told Joseph they were ten of twelve brothers, the youngest was with their father, and the other was no more, indicating they believed Joseph to be dead. Joseph insisted, despite their denial, that they were spies and rejected the reasoning of their pleas of innocence just as they had once rejected his plea from the pit (42:21).

To examine their claim, Joseph proposed a test to see whether there was any truth to their words. On the surface, this was a test to show if they lied about their family and to confirm to Joseph that they also lied about being spies. Deep down, Joseph knew they were telling the truth. His real intent was to ensure he had an opportunity to see his younger brother Benjamin. He held them all in prison for three days as they decided which one of them would return to Canaan and bring Benjamin, their youngest brother, to Egypt.

Joseph was concerned for his younger brother Benjamin. He most likely wondered if Benjamin was as hated as he was in their household. He may have wanted Benjamin to come to Egypt not simply for emotional reasons, but also to ensure his protection and safety from their older brothers.

II. Joseph's Mercy (Genesis 42:18–25)

For his fear of God, Joseph had a change of heart. The phrase "I fear God" in verse 18 (NRSV) can be interpreted in a couple of ways. But it literally says, "God, I fear," meaning Joseph had a moral code to which he adhered. One of the tenets of that code was not to oppress a weaker person. In the moment, the brothers were powerless and hungry. The tables had turned, and they were now the weaker ones. The brothers clearly had not lived by this same code. It was through their actions that this family drama crescendoed in such a sensational fashion. So instead of holding all of his brothers hostage in prison, Joseph decided to hold only one and let the rest return home on the condition that they still come back to Egypt with Benjamin, their youngest brother. Joseph's new plan was practical in that it ensured more grain could be carried for the family and that he would have an opportunity to see Benjamin, his only full brother.

His scheme also served to put them in a position reminiscent of the one in which they put him. Perhaps this might inspire reflection about what they had done and thought they had gotten away with. After accepting Joseph's proposal, his brothers said to one another, *"We are guilty,"* interpreting their ordeal as God's judgment against them. With deep conviction they believed the distress that had come upon them was the direct result of what they did to Joseph. Reuben was especially outspoken in this regard, believing himself to be more vindicated than the others for the act. He reinforced the shared guilt by reminding his brothers that for what they had done his blood was now required of them.

Unbeknownst to the brothers who were speaking to each other in Hebrew, Joseph understood everything they were saying. He only spoke Egyptian and used an interpreter with them. But overhearing them speak in his native tongue about their remorse, Joseph became emotional and turned away to weep. His emotional turmoil became increasingly evident, despite the façade of his stern demeanor and harsh words. After gathering himself, he returned with greater resolve and took Simeon and bound him before their eyes. K. A. Matthews observes: "Joseph's gracious action of returning the brothers' sacks each filled with grain and further provisions for the journey was ambiguous. It can be interpreted in two opposing ways: one, he did it to trump up evidence to sustain the charge that they were dishonest men, or two, he did it for the benefit of his father and family. This ambiguity reflects the internalized tension and conflict Joseph is having to contend with in general. Outwardly he is a hardened interrogator, but inwardly he is a broken-hearted brother whose emotions he hasn't fully processed and yet must restrain himself" (Matthews, *New American Commentary: Genesis 11–50*, 781).

Beyond his emotions, Joseph had to determine who these men before him were. Most certainly they were his brothers, but they had thrown him into a pit and sold him into slavery. Were they the cold-hearted men of yesteryear or had they changed? Had they learned about brotherhood? Joseph also may have been deciding whether or not he wanted to be a brother. He had done well without them. He did not *need* them, but did he *want* them?

The Lesson Applied

True repentance comes from deep remorse, the kind of remorse Joseph's brothers demonstrated. Though they wanted him gone, the void left by Joseph's absence never was filled and was deeply felt. Their quick acceptance of God's judgment against them gave clear indication of how heavy the twin burdens of guilt and shame had become. But through Joseph, God showed them grace and mercy. Such is the case with us. In exchange for our guilt and shame, through Christ God gives us grace and mercy. This is what true repentance is all about. It begins with the difficult challenge to face the ugliness of our actions, not just what we did but *why* we did what we did. Through deep self-reflection we are able to examine the darkest flaws of our character in the divine light of God's grace. As we become more aware of our true selves, we become more aware of God's abundant love for us despite the truth about ourselves.

Let's Talk About It

How do guilt and shame frame this lesson?

Joseph's brothers each were bound by their collective guilt and shame for the part they played in the attempt to take their younger brother's life. Though similar emotions, guilt and shame are not the same. *Guilt* is the feeling that represents remorse or regret for something done.

Shame is the feeling of worthlessness that one internalizes and by which they define themselves. Guilt says, "I have done something bad." Shame says, "I am bad." Though they are not the same, these dysfunctional conditions of the soul complement each other. When we feel guilty for the bad we've done and start believing we are bad because of it, we get tangled up in the endless loop of disappointment and emotional despair. Those who are bound by shame always feel guilty. Those who are guilty often will feel shame. What is the remedy to such a dramatic condition of the soul? For Joseph's brothers, they had to face both their guilt and shame with humility, ownership, and surrender.

The ten brothers realized their predicament and were moved to face their shame (though unexpectedly) by their desperation and need of grain. From a humbled posture, they bowed before their brother, unwittingly exposing their true identity to him. Such is necessary to overcome our guilt. When we are humbled enough to expose the truth of who we really are in front of those we have offended, we are endowed with the strength of God to break free from the bonds of emotional dysfunction.

Joseph's brothers also addressed their shame by owning their actions. Part of what distorts emotional perception is the assignment of blame. On one hand are those who take no blame whatsoever for their actions. On the other are those who unfairly take all of it. Both are wrong. Owning up to our actions means taking responsibility for what we have done to contribute to the problem and realizing the impact.

Finally, the brothers entrusted their well-being into the hands of the one who had all the power. Despite their uncertainty, the brothers had little choice but to do what Joseph said and play his game. So, they did. Overcoming our guilt and shame requires our surrender to the One who has all the power. When we bare ourselves naked in His presence, recognize our need for His grace, and trust in His ability to deliver us from our broken emotions, we are no longer haunted.

When Joseph and his brothers' paths crossed again, they converged at a point of emotional despair by which all of them were burdened. Joseph's despair stemmed from the lingering bitterness he still had against his family. His brothers were haunted by shame and guilt for their actions. At the point of that convergence, God exchanged their guilt and shame for grace and mercy. Grace and mercy always abound when we live according to His purpose.

Home Daily Devotional Readings

September 21–27, 2020

Monday	Tuesday	Wednesday	Thursday	Friday	Saturday	Sunday
During Trouble, Maintain Hope in God	Benjamin Sent to Joseph with Gifts	Stolen Cup Found in Benjamin's Grain	Brothers Offer to Become Slaves to Joseph	Judah Pleads with Joseph for Benjamin	Jacob Will Die without Seeing Benjamin	Joseph and His Brothers Reconcile Their Differences
Psalm 43	Genesis 43:1–15	Genesis 44:1–13	Genesis 44:14–17	Genesis 44:18–26	Genesis 44:27–34	Genesis 45:1–15

GOD'S PLAN REVEALED

TOPIC:
LOVE PREVAILS OVER ALL

BACKGROUND SCRIPTURE:
GENESIS 45:1–15

GENESIS 45:1–8, 10–15

King James Version

THEN Joseph could not refrain himself before all them that stood by him; and he cried, Cause every man to go out from me. And there stood no man with him, while Joseph made himself known unto his brethren.

2 And he wept aloud: and the Egyptians and the house of Pharaoh heard.

3 And Joseph said unto his brethren, I am Joseph; doth my father yet live? And his brethren could not answer him; for they were troubled at his presence.

4 And Joseph said unto his brethren, Come near to me, I pray you. And they came near. And he said, I am Joseph your brother, whom ye sold into Egypt.

5 Now therefore be not grieved, nor angry with yourselves, that ye sold me hither: for God did send me before you to preserve life.

6 For these two years hath the famine been in the land: and yet there are five years, in the which there shall neither be earing nor harvest.

7 And God sent me before you to preserve you a posterity in the earth, and to save your lives by a great deliverance.

8 So now it was not you that sent me hither, but God: and he hath made me a father to Pharaoh, and lord of all his house, and a ruler throughout all the land of Egypt.

• • • • • •

10 And thou shalt dwell in the land of Goshen, and thou shalt be near unto me, thou, and thy

New Revised Standard Version

THEN Joseph could no longer control himself before all those who stood by him, and he cried out, "Send everyone away from me." So no one stayed with him when Joseph made himself known to his brothers.

2 And he wept so loudly that the Egyptians heard it, and the household of Pharaoh heard it.

3 Joseph said to his brothers, "I am Joseph. Is my father still alive?" But his brothers could not answer him, so dismayed were they at his presence.

4 Then Joseph said to his brothers, "Come closer to me." And they came closer. He said, "I am your brother, Joseph, whom you sold into Egypt.

5 And now do not be distressed, or angry with yourselves, because you sold me here; for God sent me before you to preserve life.

6 For the famine has been in the land these two years; and there are five more years in which there will be neither plowing nor harvest.

7 God sent me before you to preserve for you a remnant on earth, and to keep alive for you many survivors.

8 So it was not you who sent me here, but God; he has made me a father to Pharaoh, and lord of all his house and ruler over all the land of Egypt.

• • • • • •

10 You shall settle in the land of Goshen, and you shall be near me, you and your children

MAIN THOUGHT: Now therefore be not grieved, nor angry with yourselves, that ye sold me hither: for God did send me before you to preserve life. (Genesis 45:5, KJV)

Genesis 45:1–8, 10–15

King James Version	*New Revised Standard Version*
children, and thy children's children, and thy flocks, and thy herds, and all that thou hast:	**and your children's children, as well as your flocks, your herds, and all that you have.**
11 And there will I nourish thee; for yet there are five years of famine; lest thou, and thy household, and all that thou hast, come to poverty.	**11 I will provide for you there—since there are five more years of famine to come—so that you and your household, and all that you have, will not come to poverty.'**
12 And, behold, your eyes see, and the eyes of my brother Benjamin, that it is my mouth that speaketh unto you.	**12 And now your eyes and the eyes of my brother Benjamin see that it is my own mouth that speaks to you.**
13 And ye shall tell my father of all my glory in Egypt, and of all that ye have seen; and ye shall haste and bring down my father hither.	**13 You must tell my father how greatly I am honored in Egypt, and all that you have seen. Hurry and bring my father down here."**
14 And he fell upon his brother Benjamin's neck, and wept; and Benjamin wept upon his neck.	**14 Then he fell upon his brother Benjamin's neck and wept, while Benjamin wept upon his neck.**
15 Moreover he kissed all his brethren, and wept upon them: and after that his brethren talked with him.	**15 And he kissed all his brothers and wept upon them; and after that his brothers talked with him.**

LESSON SETTING

Time: Unknown
Place: Egypt

LESSON OUTLINE

I. An Authentic Exposure (Genesis 45:1–8)
II. The Bigger Picture (Genesis 45:10–15)

Unifying Principle

Sometimes one is overwhelmed by tragic events in his or her life. What can keep hope alive after the struggle ends? Joseph told his brothers what they meant as harm was God's plan for saving them, a remnant of God's people.

Introduction

Love conquers all! Because God is love. And, when love is applied to our life situations, nothing can withstand its power. As Christians we are to master love and be mastered by it, acquiescing completely to its influence. When God's love rules over our hearts, it purges soul stains. It empowers us to love ourselves so we can love God and others. Unfortunately, although it empowers, love can be painful.

Such was the kind of love that eventually liberated Joseph's heart. Incarcerated by the pain of being sold into the hands of a foreign nation by the brothers who stood before him, Joseph's heart finally was freed of its agonizing when it was touched by love. Love was his heart's deliverer. After a passionate plea from Judah that Joseph take his life in place of Benjamin's, Joseph got emotional because of Judah's love for their father and youngest brother. The charade was over. It was time to come clean.

Exposition

I. An Authentic Exposure (Genesis 45:1–8)

At the forefront of this text, the attentive reader will notice this was the first time in the narrative that Joseph's siblings were called his *brothers* by the narrator since their reintroduction in chapter 42 (Gen. 45:1). In the preceding references they were called *the men, the brothers of Judah, the brothers of Benjamin*, and such. Being named as Joseph's brothers signaled a shift in the story. Joseph's emotions had reached a tipping point. He now was ready for them to be his brothers once more.

Moved by Judah's impassioned plea (Gen. 44:18–34), Joseph could not restrain himself. He cleared the room before those who stood with him could see him weep aloud. When he did cry, it was so loud in both agony and sound that the Egyptians and the house of Pharaoh heard it. It probably is more fair to say Pharaoh's house heard of it, unless his house and Joseph's court were extremely close in proximity. Finally, Joseph revealed himself. It was simple and raw, "I am Joseph" (Gen. 45:3, NRSV). At first, his focus was neither on himself nor the injustice he suffered. His attention was on his father and he wanted to know from his brothers if his father was still alive. Though this was the third time Joseph asked about his father's well-being (Gen. 43:7, 27), this time he asked without the mask of his secret. His emotions were freed to rush forward.

Being dismayed in his presence by what would have seemed to be a bizarre claim, Joseph's brothers could not answer him. They had no words. They could not fathom that the boy they sold into slavery was now sitting before them as a ruler. Ancient slavery was not as we imagine it from our familiarity with bondage in the Americas. Slavery obviously was not a racial caste system (Joseph was sold by his brothers), and there were more avenues for freedom, so that one was not perpetually locked into its clutches. As an example, Leviticus 25:39–55 provides that slavery could not be passed down from generation to generation and that all slaves were to be freed during the year of Jubilee. Even with these provisions, it was unlikely for a foreign slave to reach such a high level of importance.

As an attempt to mitigate the shock and convince them of the truth, Joseph invited his brothers to come near to him. On closer review, the brothers would see the subtle hints and overtures of family features that were intact. Again, he told them, perhaps with a gentler tone, "I am Joseph." But with this second proclamation, he added irrefutable evidence of who he was—the one "whom you sold into Egypt" (Gen. 45:4, NRSV). He reminded them of what they did to him to prove his identity. No one else would have known this tidbit about Joseph. And it was even more unlikely that if another did know this fact that they would have recognized the brothers in a world without photographs. No one else would have known to say this to them. After Joseph said this, they had no choice but to reason he was their brother. This forced them to face their shame but also to realize their role in God's larger plan to bring him to Egypt.

Now aware of Joseph's true identity and that he wasn't dead, his brothers understandably were terrified and confused. They could not have known how he would react. The brothers would have had to wonder, *What will he do to us?* Joseph had not been exceedingly kind to his brothers when they first arrived in Egypt. Now that they knew who he was, they were unsure what he would do. The words they spoke among themselves in Genesis 42:21 as they recalled their guilty consciences must have haunted them. But Joseph eased their anxiety when he told them not to be grieved or angry with themselves. Instead, he encouraged them to consider their actions as part of a greater purpose in God's plan to preserve life. The preservation of life was tantamount to Joseph's larger divine purpose. Although it was important that the Egyptians were saved from the famine, in the larger story of the Pentateuch, Jacob's family must survive the famine. These were the ancestors of Israel the nation. It was from the eponymous loins of Jacob that a nation would come. In this way, Joseph was an integral cog in the promise foretold to Abraham. Joseph's brothers were despicable; however, through their actions God's plan was set in motion. Had they not sold Joseph into slavery, God likely would have found another way for Joseph to reach Egypt so that their lives might be preserved.

Joseph continued speaking, telling his brothers there were still five years left in the famine, undoubtedly dooming them to death if it hadn't been for God's intercession and their brother's willingness to forgive their heinous acts.

Joseph stressed with emphasis that his brothers were not responsible (ultimately) for his enslavement. It was God's doing for a purpose that transcended their cruel intent. While Joseph did not absolve them of their actions with his declaration, he instead looked to the higher purpose of God's plan for his life to spare life.

The language Joseph used is particularly interesting. He noted that God was using him to preserve a *remnant*. The meaning of this word in this context has multiple layers to it. This is one of the first times where *remnant* is used in the larger canon of Scripture. This is a theme that was developed more fully in the prophetic books, in particular as those who would return from the Babylonian exile would be considered a remnant of the fallen nation of Judah. Also, a *remnant* by definition is "that which is left behind," or one might say "cast aside." This was Joseph's position as he was left behind by his brothers earlier in the narrative. The one who had been left behind was helping ensure there was something to leave behind amidst the destructive forces of the famine. We should not miss the irony in the choosing of this language. It points to God's omnipotence of choice. God sends the leftovers to preserve that which can be saved. A remnant for the remnant. This is God's prerogative, to use that which is not supposed to be used.

II. The Bigger Picture (Genesis 45:10–15)

Joseph's intent to preserve life extended to providing a place for his father and family to relocate from Canaan to the land of Goshen, a region in Egypt. After twenty-plus years of estrangement, he was determined to keep his family near him for several generations to come. And not to interfere with the economy of grain needed to stave off the effects of the five remaining years of famine, Joseph prepared himself to personally provide for his family when they arrived. Joseph's ability to provide for his family was a fulfillment of his dreams. Though his brothers fulfilled his dreams upon bowing to him, his dreams also demonstrated Joseph would become like the eldest and bear the responsibility for providing for the clan. His provision for the family was tied to his purpose to save lives, and not just the lives of the subjects of Egypt. As the saying goes, "Charity begins at home." Joseph also had to save the lives of those to whom he was most closely related, even if the majority were scoundrels.

Joseph instructed Benjamin, perhaps because he was the youngest and his only full brother, to be the one to convince his father of his existence and glory in Egypt. Joseph likely chose Benjamin because he believed he was the only brother who could be trusted. Benjamin was the only brother who had not betrayed Joseph and presumably had not ostensibly lied to their father. Though time had passed and Joseph had forgiven, it would not be prudent to trust his older brothers fully.

Benjamin was distinguished again from his brothers by the way he reciprocated Joseph's act of affection when he fell on his neck and wept. In response, Benjamin wept as well. When Joseph kissed all his other brothers, the older brothers only talked with him, which may reflect caution, showing that (unlike Benjamin) they were unprepared to accept his benevolence as genuine, which for reasons discussed above makes perfectly good sense.

Reaching this point in the narrative, the structure of the story with its varied parts coming to climax, the picture of resolution comes into fuller focus. This story of familial betrayal, separation, and reunion was replete with tension even as the climax and resolution were reached. Joseph's tension with his older brothers remained even past the death of Jacob (Gen. 50:15–21). His brothers wondered if he would take his revenge upon their father's death. This text points to Joseph's longing to be reconnected with his father and feel the embrace of family once again, a family from which he had some painful memories but of which he was a part and was not a foreigner. Though he had risen to prominence in Egypt, it most likely would have been incredibly difficult to live as a stranger with no family connections since adolescence. Though his brothers had wronged him in the most egregious way, his forgiveness was born from an internal peace that purpose existed beyond the harm they perpetrated.

The Lesson Applied

Though it wasn't directly mentioned in today's text, the love Joseph had for his family was clearly implied. His life typified the difficulty people have in forgiving those who have wronged them. Prior to seeing his brothers, Joseph was becoming settled in his bitterness. But upon sight of them, the love that had been buried under the layers of hurt, pain, and disappointment broke through. As Christians we must not let the ground of our heart become so hardened by pain from the past that the light of God's love can't break through it.

No power in this world is greater than the power of love. When we surrender ourselves to it, love empowers us. Whether it is expressed through our passions and purposes or demonstrated in relationships, the power of love is the universal remedy for what afflicts our relationships in our homes, communities, nation, and world.

Love is so powerful. It gives us strength to have difficult conversations and accept hard truths we may not want to hear. It is through the arduous task of loving those who have wronged us that we are made more complete in Christ and they have the ability to experience the reconciliation of God. We too are able to experience life anew by loving those who are incredibly difficult to love. It is the task those who follow God are given without reprieve.

Let's Talk About It

How could Joseph trust there was a larger plan at work in his life?

We must take Joseph's comments in context. He made the statement after having many years to take a panoramic view of his life. The faith he expressed to his brothers had been in development over the course of many years. We can imagine he performed a type of introspection that gave him clarity. We are not given insight to the kind of relationships he formed while in Egypt, but given human nature, it is fair to say he was not alone. He would have formed meaningful relationships with people in similar predicaments that would have encouraged him and let him know not to forsake the faith of his youth.

Truthfully, we do not know how things are going to work out and whether or not moments of treacherous ground are divinely orchestrated. Perhaps they might be those things that have been sent to destroy us and render us unusable by God. This is why relationships are important, particularly forming relationships with sage individuals who have spiritual insight to the workings of life and who have the heart of God. In moments and perhaps years or decades of being pressed, they are those who can recite with confidence the words of Romans 8:28: "All things work together for good for those who love God, who are called according to his purpose" (NRSV). This simply means there are times when we know what God is doing and there are times when we don't and must trust that God knows what He is doing and He is working it out for our best. This kind of trust comes about through a personal relationship with our Creator, Sustainer, and Redeemer. Matthew 6:33 advises us to seek first the Kingdom of God at all times.

Home Daily Devotional Readings

September 28–October 4, 2020

Monday	Tuesday	Wednesday	Thursday	Friday	Saturday	Sunday
Timothy, My Brother and Coworker	David Slays Philistine with a Stone	David and Jonathan Bond Together	Saul Jealous of and Fears David	Jonathan Asserts David as Next King	David Provides for Jonathan's Son Mephibosheth	Saul Promises to Preserve David's Life
1 Thessalonians 3:1–6	1 Samuel 17:41–51	1 Samuel 18:1–5	1 Samuel 18:12–18	1 Samuel 23:14–18	2 Samuel 9:1–10	1 Samuel 19:1–7

Love and Devotion to Others

Topic:
A True Friend Intervenes

Background Scripture:
1 Samuel 19:1–7; 23:1–18; 2 Samuel 9

1 Samuel 19:1–7

King James Version

AND Saul spake to Jonathan his son, and to all his servants, that they should kill David.

2 But Jonathan Saul's son delighted much in David: and Jonathan told David, saying, Saul my father seeketh to kill thee: now therefore, I pray thee, take heed to thyself until the morning, and abide in a secret place, and hide thyself:

3 And I will go out and stand beside my father in the field where thou art, and I will commune with my father of thee; and what I see, that I will tell thee.

4 And Jonathan spake good of David unto Saul his father, and said unto him, Let not the king sin against his servant, against David; because he hath not sinned against thee, and because his works have been to thee-ward very good:

5 For he did put his life in his hand, and slew the Philistine, and the Lord wrought a great salvation for all Israel: thou sawest it, and didst rejoice: wherefore then wilt thou sin against innocent blood, to slay David without a cause?

6 And Saul hearkened unto the voice of Jonathan: and Saul sware, As the Lord liveth, he shall not be slain.

7 And Jonathan called David, and Jonathan shewed him all those things. And Jonathan brought David to Saul, and he was in his presence, as in times past.

New Revised Standard Version

SAUL spoke with his son Jonathan and with all his servants about killing David. But Saul's son Jonathan took great delight in David.

2 Jonathan told David, "My father Saul is trying to kill you; therefore be on guard tomorrow morning; stay in a secret place and hide yourself.

3 I will go out and stand beside my father in the field where you are, and I will speak to my father about you; if I learn anything I will tell you."

4 Jonathan spoke well of David to his father Saul, saying to him, "The king should not sin against his servant David, because he has not sinned against you, and because his deeds have been of good service to you;

5 for he took his life in his hand when he attacked the Philistine, and the Lord brought about a great victory for all Israel. You saw it, and rejoiced; why then will you sin against an innocent person by killing David without cause?"

6 Saul heeded the voice of Jonathan; Saul swore, "As the Lord lives, he shall not be put to death."

7 So Jonathan called David and related all these things to him. Jonathan then brought David to Saul, and he was in his presence as before.

MAIN THOUGHT: And Jonathan spake good of David unto Saul his father, and said unto him, Let not the king sin against his servant, against David; because he hath not sinned against thee, and because his works have been to thee-ward very good. (1 Samuel 19:4, KJV)

LESSON SETTING

Time: 1000 B.C.
Place: Gibeah

LESSON OUTLINE

I. Saul's Plot to Assassinate David (1 Samuel 19:1–5)
II. Jonathan's Intervention for David's Life (1 Samuel 19:5–7)

Unifying Principle

Although families are important, family dysfunction can skew our priorities and lead us to ruin. Is there a greater priority than family? Jonathan opposed the unjust intentions of his father, King Saul, in order to offer support and protection to David.

Introduction

A true friend is a special gift from God, not a social media status profile on Facebook. In today's society, it's hard for some to tell the difference. The definition of *friendship* has nuanced meanings for different people. A friend for some is one who always will agree with, affirm, validate, and condone. They are loyal companions who never will question but only celebrate. Another word for these types of friends is *sycophants*.

A true friend, in stark contrast, is one who proves their loyalty in love, truth, sacrifice, and courage. They are called by God and equipped to help bring out the best in us. Part of how true friends demonstrate such devotion is by knowing when and how to intervene in our lives, even when we don't want them to.

An intervening friend is one who is quick to pray for us, one who speaks up for us when we can't ourselves, an individual who's willing to sacrifice for our well-being. An intervening friend is not just a true friend but someone who reflects the character of Christ. Jonathan was such a friend to David.

After the slaying of Goliath, David's reputation of being a courageous warrior began to surpass Saul's. Needless to say, it became embarrassing to the king. Being consumed by fear, jealousy, and subsequent rage over David's budding success and acclaim from the kingdom inhabitants, Saul sought to take his life.

Today's lesson explores the way Jonathan's loyalty to David was in tension with his loyalty to his father and was tested. Despite the obvious pressure he was under, Jonathan proved to be a true friend to David when he intervened. Jonathan loved and was devoted to his friend. He proved it even above loyalty to his own father.

Exposition

I. Saul's Plot to Assassinate David (1 Samuel 19:1–5)

Chapter 19 opens with Saul's growing efforts to eliminate David. Although he initially loved David (1 Sam. 16:21), Saul eventually came to fear his growing reputation (18:7–9). Public adoration of David's victory over Goliath became louder than their recognition for Saul their king. His pride couldn't withstand the perceived rejection. His jealously led to the urgent appeal for David's death. Saul's hostility began with a murderous thought, then progressed to awkward homicidal acts hidden from public view (18:11). He had David assigned to military tasks virtually certain to bring about his demise

(18:13, 17, 25). Saul then crafted a wider and more artful plan that involved public lies (18:22) and a small circle of people, including servants and a daughter. The circle of involvement widened when this effort failed. Dropping all ruses, Saul then spoke openly and bluntly to Jonathan and all his servants about killing David (19:1).

The author's statement that Jonathan delighted greatly in David was meant to emphasize the deep bond of friendship he and David had forged. It also highlighted the implied tension of loyalties between Jonathan and his father and his friend. This also pointed to the growing power base David was creating. Jonathan was not the only person in Saul's family who was enamored with David. Michal, Saul's daughter, also loved David so much that she helped him escape the wrath of the king (19:8–17). David's power base was what the king feared, if not for his sake, for the sake of his legacy and possible dynasty. Though David was innocent in that he had done no harm to Saul, Saul understood David was a threat to a familial dynasty and for that reason must be eliminated. At this juncture, it is important to understand Saul was a powerful and shrewd politician rather than a stark raving mad man. His actions, while unjust, were no different than Solomon's when he came to power. Solomon eliminated all political threats upon his ascension to the throne, including his own brother (1 Kings 2:13–46). Though Saul knew of Jonathan's love for David, he never would have imagined his son would put the well-being of his friend over the wealth and power of becoming the monarch. Quite simply, this is what was done to consolidate power. In chapter 19, Saul attempted to kill David on four separate occasions. This was just the first.

Saul, while acting shrewdly, was not aware of the happenings in his own house. He knew David was a threat, but not to what degree. Though he knew Jonathan loved David, it does not seem he was aware they had made a covenant with one another. Moreover, he did not know Jonathan had given David his royal vestments to solidify that covenant (1 Sam. 18:3–4). Jonathan's gifting of vestments to David was symbolic of his releasing all claims to royal succession. Thus, as Jonathan acted to protect David, he not only acted as friend but as a man of integrity. He made a covenant and then kept it. He stood in stark contrast to his father who broke his word on several occasions throughout this narrative (he tried to kill David three more times in this chapter after promising not to do so in 19:6).

Interestingly, as Saul attempted to remove David's threat to his kingdom, he was partially the cause of David's rise to power. In 1 Samuel 18:13, Saul made David a commander of a thousand troops. This would have given David a larger power base and men who may have been more loyal to their military leader than the throne. Saul also gave his daughter Michal to David in marriage. This would have given David legitimacy if he ever challenged for the throne. Technically, this made David a member of the royal family even if he was not the crown prince. It seems Saul lived by the motto, "Keep your friends close and your enemies closer." He kept David close by giving him positions so he might control him, but David was larger than the king.

Wisely, Jonathan said nothing publicly to oppose his father's directives, but knowing there always were men eager to commit the most heinous crimes at the king's bidding, he wasted no time in informing David of the impending danger. With sorrowful desperation and urgency, Jonathan revealed to David that his father was seeking to kill him and proceeded to formulate a plan to spare his life, telling him to be on guard until the morning and stay in a secret place and hide. With reckless abandonment, Jonathan put himself between his father, the king of Israel, and David, his true and trusted friend.

Jonathan spoke well of David to Saul as an attempt to dissuade him from killing him. The plan was to steer his father into the field where David was hiding so David might overhear the conversation in his hiding place and Jonathan might more easily report to him the result of his conversation without having to track him down. The first-person pronoun in 1 Samuel 19:3 is emphatic, as if Jonathan was saying, "Leave this to me. I will assume the responsibility of being your advocate."

In speaking well of David, Jonathan provided his father several reasons why he should relent from his campaign of violence. The first was because David was innocent. He hadn't committed any crime against the king or the nation that warranted his death. Second, David had been good to Saul. More than a great help to defeat the dreaded Philistine army, God's hand was clearly on his life and by proxy the lives and well-being of the nation. Jonathan's third reason for sparing David's life was poised in a question, "Why would you sin by killing an innocent person?"

Jonathan may have been trying to keep his father from incurring bloodguilt. Bloodguilt covers a variety of offenses within the Old Testament. One could incur bloodguilt for slaughtering an animal in the field and failing to bring it to the priest (Lev. 17:3–4) or by killing a thief during the day (Ex. 22:3–4). But most recognizably, one would incur bloodguilt for murder—killing with provocation, not in defense, and outside the confines of war. For varying offenses within the Old Testament, there are substitutes for guilt. For bloodguilt, however, there is no substitute. Blood must be shed. Death must occur. In this sense, Jonathan was not only a friend of David but also a friend to his father. He was trying to keep a curse from falling on their household from which they would not be released until a life was lost. If Saul succeeded in killing David, a set of events would have been set in motion from which they would not be able to recover.

In this way, Jonathan taught his father a valuable lesson. Saul stood as king, meaning his power was absolute in his kingdom. Jonathan reminded Saul that though he might be sovereign within the kingdom, there was another to whom he was to be accountable. Saul at times lost sight of this seemingly minor detail, but there was a divine law that was to rule the land beyond the word of the king.

II. Jonathan's Intervention for David's Life (1 Samuel 19:5–7)

Because of Jonathan's respectful demeanor, cogent logic, and impassioned appeal to his father to spare his friend's life, Saul heeded his son's voice and swore an oath before God that he would not kill

David. Oaths were statements by which a person promised or guaranteed a vow would be kept or that a statement was, in fact, true. In the Old Testament, the name of God was invoked as the One who would guarantee the results or veracity of a statement. So, Saul's oath was in fact invoking God's hand to ensure David's protection, even when Saul eventually changed his mind.

One who has read the text knows Saul was a man who broke oaths made to God (1 Sam. 14:24–46). Saul had made an oath for the entire army to fast during a battle against the Philistines. Jonathan did not know his father had made an oath and ate some honey. The penalty for breaking the fast was supposed to be death, thus Saul was supposed to kill his son. Saul did not follow through on his word. Instead he acquiesced to the crowd that pressured him to let Jonathan live. Saul gave in and they ransomed an animal in Jonathan's place. This earlier story gives us insight to the current story in two ways. (1) As was mentioned, Saul was not a man of integrity. He broke his word. (2) Saul was a leader who lived for the approval of the crowd. He needed the praise of his people even if that caused him to be unfaithful to the oaths he swore in the name of God.

Having negotiated the reconciliation, Jonathan went at once to inform David of his success and completed his mission by escorting him back to Saul. Because of Jonathan's intervention, David was restored to court. David's service to the king also was restored as in times past. David resumed his post as a military chieftain and lived within the court of the king. He also continued to be Saul's son-in-law.

The interaction between Saul and Jonathan demonstrated Saul had no clue Jonathan had pledged his loyalty to David. This moment between the two showed how much Saul had lost touch with the reality that the kingdom truly had been torn from his hands. Even his own son had defected to his rival. The text is fraught with tension because as Saul had no idea about his son, Jonathan still had his father's trust. This is but one possibility.

The other possibility is that Saul knew Jonathan and David were close friends. With his knowledge of their friendship, by agreeing to relent from his pursuit of David, he was hoping Jonathan would report back to David. Once the report reached David, David would return to the royal court, making it easier to kill David. Given the narrator's absence of details regarding the inner worlds of the protagonists, either theory can be supported. What is clear is that David and Saul were on opposing sides with Jonathan stuck in the middle.

The Lesson Applied

Jesus is our true friend. As believers we recognize Jesus Christ as our Savior, our Mediator, the ultimate sacrifice for all of humanity. But do we also see Him as a friend? It's easy to lose sight of the more practical nature of Jesus' humanity in the light of His great works and sacrifices for the world. But regarding Him as friend implies a more intimate connection, one that involves the heart. When we consider Jesus as a friend, He makes Himself available for us to experience Him at the deepest levels of our greatest need. In other words, when we make Jesus our true friend, He intervenes in the most complex chaos of our lives and brings order. Like Jonathan intervened on David's behalf, Christ has done so on ours. He is our true friend. The question is, are we a true friend to Him?

Think about how you might be a better friend to Jesus. He stated in John 15:14, "You are my friends if you do what I command you" (NRSV). Friendship with Jesus is simple, but we must desire, like Jonathan, to be people of integrity and loyalty. We should be able to sing along with the hymnologists, "What a friend we have in Jesus" or "There's not a friend like the lowly Jesus."

Let's Talk About It

What was Jonathan's motive for his friendship with David?

Further evidence of Jonathan's devotion to his friendship with David is implied when one considers what he gave up to spare David's life. Being the rightful heir to the throne of Israel, Jonathan had more reason than his father to get rid of David as he was a more imminent threat to his future claim to the throne. Whether it was his sincere love for David or that deep down he knew God had anointed David as the next king, Jonathan's motivation to be a true friend to David was pure. He had no ulterior motives for befriending David outside of wanting to see David do well in life. Real friends are more concerned about what's best for you even at the expense, at times, of their own well-being. The love of a friend can and should be sacrificial. Jesus taught that a man can have no greater love than to lay down his life for his friend (John 15:13).

This story should be able to give us some insight to our own relationships. Jonathan was loyal to David not only when it was easy to do so but also when it was to his own detriment. In our friendships, we should evaluate whether or not we have ulterior motives when engaging others. Furthermore, we should take others at their words and actions. It would have been easy for David to dismiss Jonathan simply because he was Saul's son. But David trusted Jonathan because through his words and actions, Jonathan proved himself trustworthy. The question becomes, what is our friendship worth?

Lastly, we should delight in our friends. Friendship is essential to human flourishing and necessary for the difficult journey of life. The depth of our friendships rests solely on our ability not just to be nice, but to be people whom our friends can count on and who will hold their darkest secrets. We are to love them and they us. The secret to real friendship is to love God first as a priority and then to love one another. It is the more excellent way (1 Cor. 13).

Home Daily Devotional Readings

October 5–11, 2020

Monday	Tuesday	Wednesday	Thursday	Friday	Saturday	Sunday
The Lord Is Merciful and Gracious	Responding to Unwanted Demands	Handling Family Difficulties	Home Life of the Faithful	Forgiving the Ignorant	Blessed and Rewarded	Love and Forgive Your Enemies
Psalm 103:1–14	Matthew 5:38–42	Leviticus 25:35–39	Psalm 128	Luke 23:32–36	Matthew 5:1–12	Luke 6:27–36

Love Your Enemies

Topic:
Overcoming Self-Interest

Background Scripture:
Luke 6:27–36

Luke 6:27–36

King James Version

BUT I say unto you which hear, Love your enemies, do good to them which hate you,

28 Bless them that curse you, and pray for them which despitefully use you.

29 And unto him that smiteth thee on the one cheek offer also the other; and him that taketh away thy cloak forbid not to take thy coat also.

30 Give to every man that asketh of thee; and of him that taketh away thy goods ask them not again.

31 And as ye would that men should do to you, do ye also to them likewise.

32 For if ye love them which love you, what thank have ye? for sinners also love those that love them.

33 And if ye do good to them which do good to you, what thank have ye? for sinners also do even the same.

34 And if ye lend to them of whom ye hope to receive, what thank have ye? for sinners also lend to sinners, to receive as much again.

35 But love ye your enemies, and do good, and lend, hoping for nothing again; and your reward shall be great, and ye shall be the children of the Highest: for he is kind unto the unthankful and to the evil.

36 Be ye therefore merciful, as your Father also is merciful.

New Revised Standard Version

"BUT I say to you that listen, Love your enemies, do good to those who hate you,

28 bless those who curse you, pray for those who abuse you.

29 If anyone strikes you on the cheek, offer the other also; and from anyone who takes away your coat do not withhold even your shirt.

30 Give to everyone who begs from you; and if anyone takes away your goods, do not ask for them again.

31 Do to others as you would have them do to you.

32 "If you love those who love you, what credit is that to you? For even sinners love those who love them.

33 If you do good to those who do good to you, what credit is that to you? For even sinners do the same.

34 If you lend to those from whom you hope to receive, what credit is that to you? Even sinners lend to sinners, to receive as much again.

35 But love your enemies, do good, and lend, expecting nothing in return. Your reward will be great, and you will be children of the Most High; for he is kind to the ungrateful and the wicked.

36 Be merciful, just as your Father is merciful.

MAIN THOUGHT: But I say unto you which hear, Love your enemies, do good to them which hate you, Bless them that curse you, and pray for them which despitefully use you. (Luke 6:27–28, KJV)

LESSON SETTING

Time: A.D. 24
Place: Galilee

LESSON OUTLINE

I. **Love Your Enemies (Luke 6:27–28)**
II. **Responding to Offense (Luke 6:29–31)**
III. **The Reward of Selflessness (Luke 6:32–36)**

Unifying Principle

We often wonder how we should treat our enemies. How should we respond to them? Jesus taught His disciples to love their enemies by forgiving them, responding to their needs, and by being nonjudgmental.

Introduction

Doing the right thing for people who do wrong against you is difficult to embrace. It is hard even for those who claim a heritage in God. Christians should take comfort in remembering the time when we were enemies of God. It was God's all-consuming love for us and His Son's sacrifice as a demonstration of that love that we are no longer God's enemies. God's selfless act through Jesus Christ changed the narrative.

God's love for us establishes the fundamental example of how we can be selfless in our dealings with others, even when they are selfish. God calls us to be selfless as a contrast to the selfishness of this world, creating a difference that reveals the grace and glory of God. How do we do this in the face of contradictive actions and attitudes? Jesus provides the answer in today's lesson.

Jesus completed the paralleled Beatitudes and woes in Luke 6:20–26. At the beginning of our lesson passage (v. 27), Luke turned his attention to the last Beatitude: "Blessed are you when people hate you, and when they exclude you, revile you, and defame you on account of the Son of Man" (6:22, NRSV). The ensuing section is devoted to further developing this theme and contains the following subdivisions: (1) four commands concerning love of one's enemies (6:27–28); (2) four examples of the commands (6:29–30); (3) a summary (6:31); (4) three further examples of the commands (6:32–34); (5) three commands concerning love of enemies (6:35a); (6) a divine promise (6:35b); (7) a concluding summary (6:36). The notion of loving one's enemies is so strong in Jesus' teachings that many of these words are paralleled in Matthew's Gospel as well (Matt. 5:38–48). It is simple. Jesus commands us to love our enemy and friend alike.

Exposition

I. Love Your Enemies (Luke 6:27–28)

After the four Beatitudes in verses 20–23 and the four woes in verses 24–26, Jesus then included in His sermon commands regarding how believers should address their enemies. While He was addressing the crowd, He gave specific attention to those *who listen*, referring to followers in the crowd who were open and sincerely willing to receive His teaching. His first command to love your enemies was Jesus' attempt to challenge His followers' attitudes about their adversaries. While the enemies Jesus referred to included those whom His followers were in personal conflict with, the wider scope of His directives involved individuals or groups of individuals whose hostility was instigated by those who were committed to following Christ. Coming from the perspective of His hearers, this type of discipline to love is difficult to accept, let alone practice.

To mitigate the challenge of loving their enemies, Jesus offered an approach for carrying out His command. He said to do good to those who hate you. For those who curse and spitefully use you, Jesus told His listeners to bless and pray for them. Jesus' intentional specificity of the offenses was meant to emphasize the contrast between egregious acts of hatred when juxtaposed to aggressive corresponding actions of love.

These actions point to the will as opposed to the emotional landscape. Whereas it is nearly impossible to enforce a change in one's emotions, one can be given to new actions. The notion to love one's enemies is an actionable display of the will. As an example consider the words of Exodus 23:4–5 (NIV): "If you come across your enemy's ox or donkey wandering off, be sure to return it. If you see the donkey of someone who hates you fallen down under its load, do not leave it there; be sure you help them with it." This excerpt from the ancient law of Israel demonstrates what is meant by love and what it means to do good. In this sense, goodness is not understood as an inherent quality or something that is internal. Rather, goodness is tied to deed. Love is not so much about *feelings* but *doings*.

II. Responding to Offense (Luke 6:29–31)

Continuing His discourse on loving one's enemies, Jesus encouraged His followers to answer the hostile actions of offenders with extreme kindness. Jesus said, "If anyone strikes you on the one cheek offer the other also" (Luke 6:29, NRSV). While this directive may seem extreme, not to mention a little naive, there is a deeper meaning to it. When an offender in Jesus' day struck someone on the face, they would have used only their right hand to do so as it was considered the more dominant of the two. By turning the other cheek and allowing the offender to strike again, they would be forced to reorient themselves accordingly so as to again use their right hand. Going through the trouble of having to change their position may have dissuaded the offender from doing it at all. Therefore, though it is by violent means, turning the other cheek, according to Jesus, was a way to passively promote change in both the action and attitude of the offender. Jesus commanded His followers to act out of love rather than retaliation.

Jesus furthered His discourse by telling His disciples that if someone stole or took away their cloak, they should give them their tunic as well. This implied that if someone was desperate enough to steal a cloak, the outer garment, they may need the tunic, the inner garment worn under the cloak, as well. This is rooted in part in Exodus 22:26–27 (NRSV): "If you take your neighbor's cloak in pawn, you shall restore it before the sun goes down; for it may be your neighbor's only clothing to use as cover; in what else shall that person sleep? And if your neighbor cries out to me, I will listen, for I am compassionate." Obviously the notion of divine compassion and wrath were not new. Jesus however, inverted the command. In the Old Testament reference, the one who borrowed the tunic was to return it. By inverting the command, Jesus convicted the one who had taken the tunic or coat and not returned it. He or she had already violated the law by doing so. By giving up the tunic, one is able to demonstrate both love and righteousness that is unparalleled by the offender.

Jesus' instruction to give to anyone who asks in Luke 6:30 was a reference to the common practice of lending and borrowing. Instead of lending your possessions to those who are in need and charging interest until its paid off or given back, Jesus implored His disciples to not ask back what was loaned or borrowed—in selfless love, just let them have it. Jesus' directive on borrowing and lending was a strengthening of Exodus 22:25 (NRSV): "If you lend money to my people, to the poor among you, you shall not deal with them as a creditor; you shall not exact interest from them." This emphasis was reiterated in Leviticus 25:35–37. These Old Testament references only specified that interest could not be charged to other Israelites. Outsiders could be charged interest. Additionally it was expected to repay that which was borrowed. Jesus strengthened the command in that interest was not allowed to be charged to anyone, whether they belonged to the same grouping or not. Also, He advocated for generosity as opposed to expected repayment. Jesus built on the Word of God and took the invocation of love further than it was previously known.

In verse 31, Jesus reinforced a common ideology that would be known to the more devoted disciples, to do to others what you would want them to do to you. Known as the golden rule, this last command of Jesus in this passage served as a summation of all He had said. It typified the kind of corresponding action to God's character of mercy and promoted a demonstration of love independent of others' behavior.

III. The Reward of Selflessness (Luke 6:32–36)

Verse 31 set the table for the next unit of Jesus' discourse beginning in verse 32. His disciples were instructed to do unto others what they wanted to be done to them. Jesus asked, "If you love those who love you, what credit is that to you?" (Luke 6:32, NRSV). He was comparing the degree of difficulty to love when it is reciprocated versus showing love when it's not. According to Jesus, anyone can do the former, even sinners. The golden rule, however, goes beyond this in that it seeks nothing in return for its love. Jesus made the same argument in verses 33–34 when He again asked, "If you do good to those who do good to you, what credit is that to you? … If you lend to those from whom you hope to receive, what credit is that to you?" (NRSV). Again even sinners do this.

The three commands are reemphasized in verse 35: "Love your enemies, do good, and lend, expecting nothing in return" (NRSV). These conditional acts of love, according to Jesus, will yield for the believer a great reward. Though Jesus was opposed to His followers doing good deeds only for an expected reciprocation, He motivated His listeners to instead expect blessings from God for their faithfulness. Believers are not to focus on the things this world provides but on the inexhaustible treasures only God can provide. Those who hear and heed His voice, Jesus said, will be sons and daughters of the Most High. Because God is kind even to the unthankful and evil, Jesus assured His followers the grace they show to others (though undeserving) is reflective of God's character and orientation to His people. So, He ended this section of His sermon by telling His followers to "be merciful, just as your Father is merciful" (6:36, NRSV).

The Lesson Applied

This lesson deals with love as deliberate self-sacrificial goodwill toward another. It especially points out loving one's enemy, those who are not in good standing with us. Jesus' declaration to love in this way is an illustration of what God did in relationship to humanity. God created human beings and by doing so, took a risk that the creature would turn against the Creator. Yet, He revealed the extent of His love for His them by sending His own Son, Jesus Christ to redeem human beings from sin. Jesus' actions on the cross was the supreme act and expression of God's great love. As Christians we are called to demonstrate this type of love to others as well. We are called to love those who would use us for their own advantage. We cannot love only those who love us. We must love those who stand in oppositions to our efforts to bring about God's righteousness and will in the world.

Let's Talk About It

How do we overcome self-interest so we can love our enemies?

Jesus was attempting to get His listeners to drop self-interest, self-protection, and self-preservation for a larger principle, that principle being love. Losing self-interest is as difficult as getting lost in love. While getting lost in love is not as simple as it appears, it is not as difficult as we often make it to be.

The key is a level of discipline that one's principles will not waver from. It requires uncompromising integrity. Loving one's enemies is not an esoteric or unattainable level of perfection. It is rooted in the real desire to do what is right. Jesus asks no more or less from His followers. Do right and do what is expected from you without reacting to what is done to you. Jesus taught that we have the ability to control what we do, not what happens to us or what others do. But we choose each moment, each day, and under every circumstance whether we will react or will predetermine what action will we take. Love chooses on the front end to do what is right, not what may be convenient. That is to say, love takes the initiative to set things on their proper course.

Home Daily Devotional Readings
October 12–18, 2020

Monday	Tuesday	Wednesday	Thursday	Friday	Saturday	Sunday
Help Your Neighbor in Need	Love God and Brothers and Sisters	Adopt the First Commandment	Jesus Accepts Thanks from Healed Samaritan	Samaritan Village Refuses to Welcome Jesus	Jesus Offers Samaritan Woman Living Water	Follow the Samaritan's Example
Deuteronomy 15:7–11	1 John 4:16–21	Mark 12:28–34	Luke 17:11–19	Luke 9:51–56	John 4:1–15	Luke 10:25–37

LOVING YOUR NEIGHBOR

TOPIC:
MEETING THE NEEDS OF OTHERS

BACKGROUND SCRIPTURE:
LEVITICUS 19:18, 34; LUKE 10:25–37

LUKE 10:25–37

King James Version

AND, behold, a certain lawyer stood up, and tempted him, saying, Master, what shall I do to inherit eternal life?
26 He said unto him, What is written in the law? how readest thou?
27 And he answering said, Thou shalt love the Lord thy God with all thy heart, and with all thy soul, and with all thy strength, and with all thy mind; and thy neighbour as thyself.
28 And he said unto him, Thou hast answered right: this do, and thou shalt live.
29 But he, willing to justify himself, said unto Jesus, And who is my neighbour?
30 And Jesus answering said, A certain man went down from Jerusalem to Jericho, and fell among thieves, which stripped him of his raiment, and wounded him, and departed, leaving him half dead.
31 And by chance there came down a certain priest that way: and when he saw him, he passed by on the other side.
32 And likewise a Levite, when he was at the place, came and looked on him, and passed by on the other side.
33 But a certain Samaritan, as he journeyed, came where he was: and when he saw him, he had compassion on him,
34 And went to him, and bound up his wounds, pouring in oil and wine, and set him on his own beast, and brought him to an inn, and took care of him.

New Revised Standard Version

JUST then a lawyer stood up to test Jesus. "Teacher," he said, "what must I do to inherit eternal life?"
26 He said to him, "What is written in the law? What do you read there?"
27 He answered, "You shall love the Lord your God with all your heart, and with all your soul, and with all your strength, and with all your mind; and your neighbor as yourself."
28 And he said to him, "You have given the right answer; do this, and you will live."
29 But wanting to justify himself, he asked Jesus, "And who is my neighbor?"
30 Jesus replied, "A man was going down from Jerusalem to Jericho, and fell into the hands of robbers, who stripped him, beat him, and went away, leaving him half dead.
31 Now by chance a priest was going down that road; and when he saw him, he passed by on the other side.
32 So likewise a Levite, when he came to the place and saw him, passed by on the other side.
33 But a Samaritan while traveling came near him; and when he saw him, he was moved with pity.
34 He went to him and bandaged his wounds, having poured oil and wine on them. Then he put him on his own animal, brought him to an inn, and took care of him.

MAIN THOUGHT: Which now of these three, thinkest thou, was neighbour unto him that fell among the thieves? And he said, He that shewed mercy on him. Then said Jesus unto him, Go, and do thou likewise. (Luke 10:36–37, KJV)

Luke 10:25–37

King James Version	*New Revised Standard Version*
35 And on the morrow when he departed, he took out two pence, and gave them to the host, and said unto him, Take care of him; and whatsoever thou spendest more, when I come again, I will repay thee.	**35 The next day he took out two denarii, gave them to the innkeeper, and said, 'Take care of him; and when I come back, I will repay you whatever more you spend.'**
36 Which now of these three, thinkest thou, was neighbour unto him that fell among the thieves?	**36 Which of these three, do you think, was a neighbor to the man who fell into the hands of the robbers?"**
37 And he said, He that shewed mercy on him. Then said Jesus unto him, Go, and do thou likewise.	**37 He said, "The one who showed him mercy." Jesus said to him, "Go and do likewise."**

LESSON SETTING

Time: A.D. 27
Place: Galilee

LESSON OUTLINE

I. **The Question of Our Eternal Life (Luke 10:25–29)**
II. **The Example of a Neighbor (Luke 10:30–35)**
III. **Go and Do Likewise (Luke 10:36–37)**

Unifying Principle

Selfish desires, self-gratification, and self-interests are highly valued in our time. How can we become better neighbors to one another? Jesus challenged us to address the needs and welfare of everyone, including perceived enemies.

Introduction

God's people prosper when instead of living to be blessed we endeavor to be a blessing. This requires that we take seriously the needs of others. With attention on only what we can get from God, it's easy to overlook this chief objective of believers—how we can show God to the world. This has always been and must always be our great commission.

Jesus creatively explained this in today's lesson. In Luke 10:21 He asserted that the so-called wise lack true understanding. Shortly following in verse 25, one who was considered an expert in Mosaic Law, a wise one, asked Jesus one of the most basic religious questions: "What must I do to inherit eternal life?" (NRSV). Though asked in insincerity, the lawyer's query revealed the need of divine understanding. The two engaged in a series of questions and answers that led to Jesus being able to answer the question, "And who is my neighbor?" (10:29, NRSV). This question served nicely to demonstrate what God requires of us—to love God and our neighbor as ourselves.

Exposition

I. The Question of our Eternal Life (Luke 10:25–29)

Verse 25 opens with a question for Jesus from a lawyer in the crowd. While the occasion is unknown, it easily can be inferred Jesus was teaching a small group of people. This lawyer stood out in the group as a man with excellent religious credentials, one who studied God's law continually to interpret it for the people who desired to obey it. He had garnered respect among the people as an expert in the law. When he asked Jesus what he must do to inherit eternal life, it was clear he was seeking validation more than an answer to his question. The text shows the lawyer's motivation was malevolent. The word used is *εκπειραζω* (*ekpeirazo*). It comes from the word *πειραζω* (*peirazo*) meaning "to trap, test, or tempt." This same family of words is used in the narrative of Satan's temptation of Jesus. This man stood as an emissary for the devil.

Beyond being an attempt to trip up Jesus, the lawyer's question was not a very good question. Noted New Testament scholar Amy-Jill Levine in her book *Short Stories by Jesus* points out that the language used by the lawyer indicates he wanted to do something to gain possession of eternal life, as if one might earn the gratuitous gift of God. Secondly, he asked what he could do to *inherit* eternal life. To inherit something is to gain by possession something that is owned and/or controlled by the future possessor. Eternal life is not to be possessed or gained. It can only be participated in.

Jesus, knowing the lawyer's true intent, created an opportunity for the lawyer to flaunt his expertise. Rather than answering his question directly, Jesus bounced it back to him and asked, "What is written in the law?" (10:26, NRSV). Given he was an expert of the law, Jesus invited him to share his interpretation or his reading of it. As expected, the lawyer answered by quoting the most sacred law in Judaism—Deuteronomy 6:5. Known as the *Shema*, this law is both a prayer and a law because it is upon this prayer that all the Law of Moses rests. A devout Jew would pray it twice each day. It consists of three prepositional phrases that describe the total response of love toward God: the heart (emotions), the soul (consciousness), and strength (motivation). Further validating his answer, the lawyer also quoted Leviticus 19:18 (NRSV), "You shall love your neighbor as yourself." Agreeing with the lawyer's answer, Jesus told him, "Do this, and you will live" (Luke 10:28, NRSV). To justify himself as a pious Jew in front of Jesus and the surrounding crowd, the lawyer further asked, "And who is my neighbor?" (10:29, NRSV).

This was the problem with the lawyer. He wanted to justify himself or appear righteous. Justification is a gift that comes only from God. As he attempted to justify himself, he dug a deeper hole that would be harder for him to get out.

II. The Example of a Neighbor (Luke 10:30–35)

Jesus answered the lawyer's second question with a parable about a man who fell among thieves. He was stripped of his clothing, wounded, and left half-dead. To draw contrast, Jesus introduced a priest who came down that road and encountered the wounded man. By identifying the priest, Jesus made the implication that if anyone should be concerned for the well-being of a suffering person it should be the priest. But in Jesus' parable, the priest did the opposite of what was expected. He passed by on the other side. Jesus added that a Levite came, looked, and passed by on the other side as well. Regardless of the various speculations as to why they chose to disregard the wounded man, the point of the lesson was to not ignore religious responsibility. When Jesus introduced the Samaritan in the parable, he remedied the actions of the priest and Levite. Jesus deliberately chose an outsider, a hated one at that, to be His example to emphasize what it means to be a neighbor. Being a neighbor is not a matter of nationality, race, religious affiliation, or any of the identity markers we use to separate ourselves. By contrast, when the Samaritan came to the wounded man, he had compassion and bandaged his wounds. In addition to treating his wounds, the Samaritan furthered his commitment to helping the wounded man by setting him on his own animal and taking him to an inn to take care of him.

Jesus' depiction of the Samaritan's kindness was further stressed by indicating the Samaritan stayed with the wounded man throughout the night, then as he departed the next day, paid for the man's lodging and care throughout his recovery. He even promised to repay any debt incurred while taking care of the man upon his return to the area.

The Samaritan's care for the man who fell among the thieves would have stuck out to the law expert. Samaritans and Jews were not friendly. Through a long history of rivalry, Jews and Samaritans regarded each other as enemies even as they were partially of common ancestry both in terms of ethnicity and religion (Samaritans were bound by the Torah). Because of their common religious background, the Samaritan would have been under similar compulsion to help a man hurt on the road. Though the Old Testament Law does not specifically mention a case like this, Exodus 23:4–5 (NRSV) states, "When you come upon your enemy's ox or donkey going astray, you shall bring it back. When you see the donkey of one who hates you lying under its burden and you would hold back from setting it free, you must help to set it free." By deductive reasoning, as the Torah compels one to help an enemy with his or her ox or donkey, why would one not be compelled to help the enemy? The Samaritan was bound to the Torah and simply fulfilled his duty to the Law, a duty the priest and Levite chose to ignore for reasons unknown.

III. Go and Do Likewise (Luke 10:36–37)

Confirming the lawyer understood the main point of His parable, after Jesus finished the story He asked him, "Which of these three, do you think, was a neighbor to the man who fell into the hands of the robbers?" (Luke 10:36, NRSV). Jesus asked this to indicate one should not worry about who our neighbor is as much as about being a good neighbor. Jesus' counter question reversed the roles so that just as Jesus answered the lawyer's question (10:29), the lawyer had to answer Jesus'. While the lawyer's answer indicated he understood the point of the story, it also showed his reluctance to fully accept it. His hidden contempt for the Samaritan people was revealed by his avoidance of associating a good deed with one of them. Rather than just saying "the Samaritan," he instead referred to him as "the one who showed mercy." Knowing the challenge comparing himself to a

Samaritan presented to the lawyer's pride, Jesus told him to go and do likewise. The point is simple but profound, a profundity we have been wrestling with ever since.

The Lesson Applied

One of the fundamental features of Black culture that has preserved the African American community throughout the years of enduring racism and discrimination is our shared understanding of struggle. The systems of this country were not made to accommodate the needs of people of color; therefore, if you are a person of color, just surviving one day to the next can be stressful.

Our shared understanding of struggle is what strengthens the bond of our fellowship. Under the weight and pressure of lack, we are naturally brought together by the same unifying desire to meet the needs of the other. This philosophy has undergirded the primary mission of the Black Baptist church. In the early years of all Black congregational gatherings, our distant fathers and mothers assembled for worship with a love for God expressed through meeting the needs of one another. This passage challenges the Black Church to meet needs beyond the membership of the Black Church. This story encourages us beyond the Black community, even into "enemy territory."

Let's Talk About It

What happens if I choose not to help?

Martin Luther King Jr. in his last speech delivered on April 3, 1968 in Memphis, Tennessee raised this parable as a parallel to the struggle for rights by the Black sanitation workers. In his explication, he stated that the priest and Levite asked, "What will happen to *me* if I stop?" This was predicated on their understanding that the road from Jerusalem to Jericho was quite dangerous. King said they wondered whether the robbers were close or if the bloodied man was faking and a part of the band of thieves. They were afraid. King changed the question the Samaritan asked himself. He said the Samaritan asked, "What will happen to *him* if I do *not* stop?" The inversion of the question demonstrates a willingness to picture oneself in the ditch. The answer, if the Samaritan did not stop, was the man in the ditch most likely dies. The world will not stop, but what will become of his wife and children? This is the question we should ask ourselves when we see even an enemy in distress. *What will happen to him or her if I do not stop?* Most likely further harm may come to those who need our help. We are neighbors in as much as we decide to stop and help those in the ditch. Jesus was clear we should be those who go and do likewise, developing a "dangerous unselfishness."

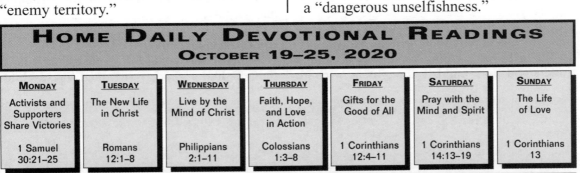

Home Daily Devotional Readings

October 19–25, 2020

Monday	Tuesday	Wednesday	Thursday	Friday	Saturday	Sunday
Activists and Supporters Share Victories	The New Life in Christ	Live by the Mind of Christ	Faith, Hope, and Love in Action	Gifts for the Good of All	Pray with the Mind and Spirit	The Life of Love
1 Samuel 30:21–25	Romans 12:1–8	Philippians 2:1–11	Colossians 1:3–8	1 Corinthians 12:4–11	1 Corinthians 14:13–19	1 Corinthians 13

Love Divine

Topic:
The Most Excellent Way

Background Scripture:
1 Corinthians 12:27–14:1

1 Corinthians 13:1–13

King James Version

**THOUGH I speak with the tongues of men and
of angels, and have not charity, I am become as
sounding brass, or a tinkling cymbal.
2 And though I have the gift of prophecy, and
understand all mysteries, and all knowledge;
and though I have all faith, so that I could
remove mountains, and have not charity, I
am nothing.
3 And though I bestow all my goods to feed
the poor, and though I give my body to be
burned, and have not charity, it profiteth
me nothing.
4 Charity suffereth long, and is kind; charity
envieth not; charity vaunteth not itself, is not
puffed up,
5 Doth not behave itself unseemly, seeketh
not her own, is not easily provoked, thinketh
no evil;
6 Rejoiceth not in iniquity, but rejoiceth in
the truth;
7 Beareth all things, believeth all things, hop-
eth all things, endureth all things.
8 Charity never faileth: but whether there
be prophecies, they shall fail; whether there
be tongues, they shall cease; whether there be
knowledge, it shall vanish away.
9 For we know in part, and we prophesy
in part.
10 But when that which is perfect is come, then
that which is in part shall be done away.
11 When I was a child, I spake as a child, I
understood as a child, I thought as a child:**

New Revised Standard Version

**IF I speak in the tongues of mortals and of
angels, but do not have love, I am a noisy gong
or a clanging cymbal.
2 And if I have prophetic powers, and understand all mysteries and all knowledge, and if I
have all faith, so as to remove mountains, but
do not have love, I am nothing.
3 If I give away all my possessions, and if I
hand over my body so that I may boast, but do
not have love, I gain nothing.
4 Love is patient; love is kind; love is not envi-
ous or boastful or arrogant
5 or rude. It does not insist on its own way; it
is not irritable or resentful;
6 it does not rejoice in wrongdoing, but rejoic-
es in the truth.
7 It bears all things, believes all things, hopes
all things, endures all things.
8 Love never ends. But as for prophecies, they
will come to an end; as for tongues, they will
cease; as for knowledge, it will come to an end.
9 For we know only in part, and we prophesy
only in part;
10 but when the complete comes, the partial
will come to an end.
11 When I was a child, I spoke like a child, I
thought like a child, I reasoned like a child;**

MAIN THOUGHT: And now abideth faith, hope, charity, these three; but the greatest of these is charity. (1 Corinthians 13:13, KJV)

but when I became a man, I put away childish things.
12 For now we see through a glass, darkly; but then face to face: now I know in part; but then shall I know even as also I am known.

13 And now abideth faith, hope, charity, these three; but the greatest of these is charity.

when I became an adult, I put an end to childish ways.
12 For now we see in a mirror, dimly, but then we will see face to face. Now I know only in part; then I will know fully, even as I have been fully known.
13 And now faith, hope, and love abide, these three; and the greatest of these is love.

LESSON SETTING

Time: A.D. 53–54
Place: Corinth

LESSON OUTLINE

I. **Ministry without Love (1 Corinthians 13:1–3)**
II. **What Is Love? (1 Corinthians 13:4–7)**
III. **It's All About Love (1 Corinthians 13:8–13)**

Unifying Principle

Special gifts such as knowledge and wisdom easily can make us lose sight of our obligations to others. How can we avoid being pleased with ourselves? Paul suggested love is the best way to relate to others and forget one's own status.

Introduction

People in general understand the need for love, but rarely do you find many living their lives according to it. Before we recognize our call to preach, the gift to teach, the passion to serve, or even the desire to worship, God asks us, "Do you love Me?" The love we have for God is what connects us to God and enables us to be used by God. Sometimes this fundamental idea gets lost in the prestige of spiritual gifts.

God endows us with spiritual gifts not to inflate the ego but to empower us to create an environment where love can be nurtured, grown, and developed in the heart of every believer. God's will for us is that we reflect the light of His glory and love in the world. The way we do this is through the use of our spiritual gifts. However, without love, our spiritual gifts are rendered of no effect. Which means, it's not about what kind of gifts we get or who is more gifted. Instead, it's a question of love and our commitment to live the more excellent way.

Paul used this phrase to encourage the Christians living in Corinth to choose love as the more excellent way. After receiving prior correspondence from them and learning about disagreements and divisions that had arisen over spiritual gifts among the people in the community, Paul wrote back. He encouraged believers to live and serve God based on the conviction of love rather than any other gift. Love is the only sure thing to last.

Exposition

I. Ministry without Love (1 Corinthians 13:1–3)

According to Paul, only one thing matters when it comes to spiritual gifts—love. Without it, one's gifts, no matter how elaborate and divine, are as useless as sounding brass or clanging cymbals. As an example, exercising the gift of speaking in tongues without love is like a band of expensive instruments playing out of sync with each other. It disrupts rather than creating harmony amid the community of believers. In hypothetical fashion, Paul continued with his insistence of love. He intentionally exaggerated his position. He wrote, "If I have prophetic powers, and understand all mysteries and all knowledge, and if I have faith, so as to remove mountains, but do not have love, I am nothing" (1 Cor. 13:2, NRSV). This stressed his point that without love those spectacular feats of faith are meaningless. He further argued that even the most noble acts of personal sacrifice, such as giving away personal possessions or surrendering the body to be burned, count for nothing when love is not the reason for doing them.

First Corinthians 13 is couched between two chapters that explain Paul's understanding of spiritual gifts. The reality of spiritual gifts has never been in question, but only their implementation. Paul wrote in 14:26 (NRSV), "What should be done then, my friends? When you come together, each one has a hymn, a lesson, a revelation, a tongue, or an interpretation. Let all things be done for building up." The notion of love is that whatever is done must be done in and for a spirit of collective blessing.

Tongues without love are of no help to any but the speaker. They produce cacophony. Love tempers its gifts so they are used in an appropriate manner for the moment and setting. Anything less is self-aggrandizement and given to produce division, strife, and power struggles. Nothing is gained from this. Paul wrote repeatedly in 13:1–3 that "I am nothing" or "I gain nothing." An appropriate translation would be, "I am no one, and I accomplish nothing."

These latter phrases get at the heart of the matter. Because spiritual gifts can be a matter of pride, those who possessed them within the Corinthian church needed a reminder the gifts were not a matter of pride. The gifts' expression and reason for use should take center stage.

II. What Is Love? (1 Corinthians 13:4–7)

Verse 1–3 are designed to teach the emptiness of gifts not controlled by love. Verses 4–7 show the characteristics of love. Paul's ideas of love were especially relevant to the congregational and liturgical problems evident within the life of the believers in Corinth. Paul drew attention to those characteristics of love most important for harmonious relationships because of the Corinthians' misunderstanding of spiritual matters, which lay primarily in their failure to live as a body.

First, Paul said love suffers long or is patient, a quality he had developed by default in his dealings with the people of Corinth and their slow surrender to the principles of Christ. Having to handle them with a firm tenderness made Paul realize love is also kind and gentle. The love he felt for them was so fulfilling, so satisfying, there was little room for anything else and, therefore, it did not envy. Because of his many humbling encounters throughout his journey, Paul had discovered love is not puffed up, meaning love isn't fueled by pride but by conviction.

He continued in his commentary on love in verse 5 where he said love does not behave rudely, in reference to social decorum. Though the definitions of *rude* vary from culture to culture, at the heart of rudeness is a disregard for the social customs others have adopted. When one does not concern themselves with the likes and dislikes of others, they show a disrespect. A perfect example is taken from the Pauline corpus. In 1 Corinthians 8, Paul said stronger believers should not eat meat if it offended their weaker brothers or sisters. This was an issue that was constrained by culture, but it's lesson still rings true for modern believers. Rudeness is relegated to culture, and for that matter, love takes the time to learn the culture of another so as not to offend. Proper regard indicates love for another. Nevertheless, love does not always require a person to go along with the crowd. When the customs of a culture contradict the higher ideals of the Christian faith, it is not unloving to break these social mores. In fact, it actually may show Christlike love to break with such cultural norms. For instance, every loving Christian bears the responsibility to break the customs that perpetuate racial, gender, and other forms of discrimination.

According to Paul, love does not seek its own, meaning it's not self-serving and therefore is not easily provoked. Those who love others are slow to anger. Anger is slow to develop in love because love seeks to understand rather than to be understood. Understanding the other gives over to patience because it gives another perspective that may not have been previously considered. Love considers that each person has something to contribute. In doing so, it takes the opinions and feelings of others seriously. To not seek one's own is to consider others before self, such as is stated in Philippians 2:3. Selfishness is the product of a belief in entitlement or privilege. Acting in love essentially means to think of the other as one thinks of the self. As I am beautiful, smart, worthy, and made in the image of God, so is the other. This produces patience.

Love thinks no evil in that those who are controlled by love don't keep meticulous records of wrongdoing or offenses against them. Instead they offer forgiveness time and time again. Love does not rejoice in iniquity but contrasts it in truth. The term that is translated as *wrongdoing* is ἀδικία (*adikia*) or *unrighteousness*. Often when this word is used in the New Testament, it is used to contrast with *righteousness* or another term that emphasizes the waywardness or violation of God's Word. The *Theological Dictionary of the New Testament* says this of its usage in verse 6: "The antithesis is conceived in such a way that we see the relation between ἀλήθεια (aletheia, truth) and δικαιοσύνη (diakaiosune, righteousness); for obedience to the truth is ἀγάπη (agape, love), which is the direct opposite of ἀδικία " (Vol. 1, 156). Truth and the embracing of that truth is equated to love. It is the obedience to God's truth that love lives within. And in this truth love endures all without fail.

III. It's All About Love (1 Corinthians 13:8–13)

Pressing his argument of what love is, Paul described three other spiritual gifts as being temporary when compared with love. Prophecies, tongues, or divine knowledge all will pass away long before love does because love is eternal and never fails. As Paul talked about the perfect nature of love in verse 9, he was referencing the moment in which love matures in us. When that time comes, dependency on spiritual gifts will not be as necessary as it once was.

Paul supported his view with two analogies. First, he appealed to a parallel of the natural experience of maturation, explaining that when he was a child, he spoke, understood, and thought as a child. When he became a man or matured in love, he put away childish things. Because they are limited by the constraints of this life, the gifts of prophecy, tongues, and knowledge, when compared to love, were considered by Paul to be childish things. As a subtle rebuke to the Christians in Corinth, Paul was saying that fighting over spiritual gifts is childish and something one outgrows when they have matured in love.

Each one of the listed gifts only appears in part. Though this appears to be obvious, it is important to note for it is not uncommon for gifted people to behave as if their gifts are final and complete. Paul was simply arguing that as good as a prophecy or knowledge might be, neither represents the fullness of God or His vision for the world and His people. An example is the prophecies of the Old Testament that represented the coming of the Messiah. Each one held merit in itself. However, none of them represented the fullness of the Christ in the person of Jesus. Jesus was the end of those prophecies, but each only provided a snippet of the totality of His character, beauty, grandeur, and wisdom. Love, however is the fullness of the deity, for God is love and love is from God (1 John 4:7–8).

Paul's second analogy involved the experience of looking dimly in a mirror. In Paul's day, Corinth was well-known for its mirrors. Because their mirrors were made of polished brass, some interpreters have argued Paul referred to the fact that metal mirrors reflected one's image only imperfectly. Corinth, however, made high-quality mirrors that probably provided good reflections. Yet even the reflection of those mirrors was no substitute for a real person. A modern parallel would be a photograph. Modern believers enjoy clear photographs of loved ones, but those pictures barely begin to portray the wonderful people they depict. For Paul, the gifts of the Spirit are like photographs for the community for now. When love is made complete in us, everyone will experience the God in the photographs from a more intimate face-to-face disposition. At this point a full knowledge can be recognized. Only through experiencing the being and *is*ness of God is this made complete. This is differentiated from a simple viewing, as in a mirror or a picture. It's being in the presence of and seeing, feeling, touching. Quite simply, *experiencing* something is quite different than *observing* something.

Paul closed his discussion of the most excellent way with a summary of what should be most important for the believer—faith, hope, and love. These three remain when all else is gone. The language used here was intentional as Paul argued that all other gifts will pass away. Faith, hope, and love will stand the test of time, trial, and—given Paul's predilection to eschatological thought—even the *parousia* (the second coming). These virtues will survive and be necessary even as the world fades away. Thus they each stand above all other spiritual gifts, displacing the Corinthians' favorites, such as prophecy, tongues, and knowledge. Love is raised even higher. Out of the three, it is the greatest. Love completes all other gifts and is what has been demonstrated by God and through God.

The Lesson Applied

Love is defined differently for different people. Depending on their most frequent and impacting experiences with love, love can mean many things. One side of love that is important is passion. Passion is a form of love we overlook because it doesn't directly involve another person. It isn't meant to. Passion isn't affirmed by things outside, but rather those things inside of us. Our passion leads us to discover and fuel our purpose in God.

Living our lives on purpose through passion is how we reveal His love in the world. Those things and people we are passionate about are what we love most completely. Passion is what gives us the ability to move from the head knowledge of love to the fullness of the application of love. Passion drives our work and lives in God and brings out the best of our spiritual gifts to the service of God and His people. Find your passion and live into it, loving God and His people every step of the way.

Let's Talk About It

If this passage is not specifically about the love between a man and a woman, why is it read so often at weddings?

This passage is a favorite at weddings. Even though it is somewhat philosophical, it also is practical in what perfect love should look like. For many the list is not complete, but Paul did not write this as an exhaustive list or definition of love. Rather, this text serves as a baseline for what love should look like. These are the basics. Even though it was written for a local body of believers, what better way to celebrate the love between two people than to set a biblical precedent on the ground rules in the relationship.

To read this passage at a wedding is in essence to invoke a biblical blessing in the future marital relationship by stating this is who we will be to each other. *We will be kind. We will be patient. We will not be boastful nor assume to know it all.* The reading of this passage is not only beautiful, but it's spiritually sound. Its reading reflects the couple's bond is deeper than physical attraction and mutual respect flows from lives that are ultimately rooted in the Almighty. These are two who have decided to walk together in love. Since God is the Creator, this passage provides the groundwork for the building of a relationship, and the beauty of it all is that it is the formula of success for all relationships, not just familiar ones. Godly love should be the foundation for all life.

Home Daily Devotional Readings

October 26–November 1, 2020

Monday	Tuesday	Wednesday	Thursday	Friday	Saturday	Sunday
Laban Arranges to Wash Servant's Feet	Brothers Provided Water to Wash Feet	Servants and Masters, but Same Lord	Peter Denies Jesus Three Times	Jesus Betrayed by a Trusted Disciple	Mary Anoints Jesus' Feet with Perfume	Jesus Loved Disciples; Washed Their Feet
Genesis 24:24–33	Genesis 43:20–25	Ephesians 4:1–8	John 13:36–38; 18:15–18, 25–27	Psalm 41:8–10; John 13:21–30	John 12:1–7	John 13:1–15, 34–35

LOVING BY SERVING

TOPIC:
UPSIDE-DOWN LOVE

BACKGROUND SCRIPTURE:
JOHN 13:1–35

JOHN 13:1–15, 34–35

King James Version

NOW before the feast of the passover, when Jesus knew that his hour was come that he should depart out of this world unto the Father, having loved his own which were in the world, he loved them unto the end.

2 And supper being ended, the devil having now put into the heart of Judas Iscariot, Simon's son, to betray him;

3 Jesus knowing that the Father had given all things into his hands, and that he was come from God, and went to God;

4 He riseth from supper, and laid aside his garments; and took a towel, and girded himself.

5 After that he poureth water into a bason, and began to wash the disciples' feet, and to wipe them with the towel wherewith he was girded.

6 Then cometh he to Simon Peter: and Peter saith unto him, Lord, dost thou wash my feet?

7 Jesus answered and said unto him, What I do thou knowest not now; but thou shalt know hereafter.

8 Peter saith unto him, Thou shalt never wash my feet. Jesus answered him, If I wash thee not, thou hast no part with me.

9 Simon Peter saith unto him, Lord, not my feet only, but also my hands and my head.

10 Jesus saith to him, He that is washed needeth not save to wash his feet, but is clean every whit: and ye are clean, but not all.

11 For he knew who should betray him; therefore said he, Ye are not all clean.

New Revised Standard Version

NOW before the festival of the Passover, Jesus knew that his hour had come to depart from this world and go to the Father. Having loved his own who were in the world, he loved them to the end.

2 The devil had already put it into the heart of Judas son of Simon Iscariot to betray him. And during supper

3 Jesus, knowing that the Father had given all things into his hands, and that he had come from God and was going to God,

4 got up from the table, took off his outer robe, and tied a towel around himself.

5 Then he poured water into a basin and began to wash the disciples' feet and to wipe them with the towel that was tied around him.

6 He came to Simon Peter, who said to him, "Lord, are you going to wash my feet?"

7 Jesus answered, "You do not know now what I am doing, but later you will understand."

8 Peter said to him, "You will never wash my feet." Jesus answered, "Unless I wash you, you have no share with me."

9 Simon Peter said to him, "Lord, not my feet only but also my hands and my head!"

10 Jesus said to him, "One who has bathed does not need to wash, except for the feet, but is entirely clean. And you are clean, though not all of you."

11 For he knew who was to betray him; for this reason he said, "Not all of you are clean."

MAIN THOUGHT: For I have given you an example, that ye should do as I have done to you. (John 13:15, KJV)

John 13:1–15, 34–35

King James Version	*New Revised Standard Version*
12 So after he had washed their feet, and had taken his garments, and was set down again, he said unto them, Know ye what I have done to you?	**12 After he had washed their feet, had put on his robe, and had returned to the table, he said to them, "Do you know what I have done to you?**
13 Ye call me Master and Lord: and ye say well; for so I am.	**13 You call me Teacher and Lord—and you are right, for that is what I am.**
14 If I then, your Lord and Master, have washed your feet; ye also ought to wash one another's feet.	**14 So if I, your Lord and Teacher, have washed your feet, you also ought to wash one another's feet.**
15 For I have given you an example, that ye should do as I have done to you.	**15 For I have set you an example, that you also should do as I have done to you.**
••••••	••••••
34 A new commandment I give unto you, That ye love one another; as I have loved you, that ye also love one another.	**34 I give you a new commandment, that you love one another. Just as I have loved you, you also should love one another.**
35 By this shall all men know that ye are my disciples, if ye have love one to another.	**35 By this everyone will know that you are my disciples, if you have love for one another."**

LESSON SETTING

Time: A.D. 27
Place: Jerusalem

LESSON OUTLINE

I. Washing the Disciples' Feet (John 13:1–11)
II. Why Jesus Washed His Disciples' Feet (John 13:12–15)
III. The New Command for Christ's Community (John 13:34–35)

Unifying Principle

Multiple definitions of love leave people confused about how to love. What is the bottom line when it comes to love? Jesus taught that our love for one another should be manifested in our service to others.

Introduction

It goes without saying, love can sometimes be confusing. Growing up when my mother would physically chastise me, she often would remind me it hurt her more than it did me. As I got older, I understood such is the nature of love. When we let it rule the heart, love sometimes can make those for whom we care the most feel uncomfortable. In addition to the preferred favorable emotions that are usually associated with love, as we mature, love is also about having hard conversations, knowing how to accept criticism, and holding one another accountable. These expressions of love are just as, if not more so, painful to convey as they are to receive. And yet this too is love, though an upside-down version of it.

Jesus demonstrated this type of love to His disciples in today's lesson. During the time of Passover, He and His disciples were gathered together enjoying supper. This night was to be memorable as it was Jesus' last meal with them. The mood was notably somber as the time of Jesus' departure was at hand. As a part of His farewell discourse, Jesus exemplified to His disciples how they were expected to live as a community bound together by love—a love for each other that would, at times, feel awkward, uncomfortable and require sacrifice.

Exposition

I. Washing the Disciples' Feet (John 13:1–11)

Verse 1 opens with the description of the scene of Jesus and His disciples before the Feast of the Passover. Knowing His hour had come and it was time for Him to depart from this world and go back to the Father, Jesus was having a final meal with His disciples.

Knowing who Jesus was, where He was from, and where He was going was central to John's depiction of Jesus throughout the Gospel. Jesus was mission-driven and had been given authority by His status as the Word who had been enfleshed (John 1:14). The restatement of Jesus' status helped to further set the shock experienced by His disciples as even more understandable. Verse 3 makes clear Jesus was operating according to a divine plan and timing. It further pressed the claim that He was God in the flesh or that He and the Father were one (10:30). Jesus was moving and thinking in a dimension in which normal human beings are unable to operate. He was not operating according to the rules of time or space but rather on a divine plane that demands His essence more than the world to which He had come to offer salvation.

Confident of His identity coming from God and in His intent to go back to God, Jesus rose from supper, laid aside His garments, and wrapped Himself with a towel. This He did to prepare Himself for what He was going to do next—He began to wash the disciples' feet.

While it isn't clear if Peter was the first disciple Jesus came to, Peter's protest was clear. "Lord, are you going to wash my feet?" (13:6, NRSV) exemplified the shock and wonderment of all of the disciples in regard to Jesus' actions. In ancient Near Eastern culture, being at someone's feet, being stepped on, or even being struck by someone's shoe was a tremendous insult. Washing someone's feet was a humbling and humiliating act of domestic servitude, relegated to those who were considered of a lower subservient class. It's no wonder Peter and the rest of the disciples were apprehensive about Jesus washing their feet. To them, the prestige and pedigree of Jesus absolved Him of ever having to be subject to such lowly duties. Nevertheless, Jesus washed their feet and offered a disclaimer while doing so, "You do not know what I am doing, but later you will understand" (10:7, NRSV). This was Jesus' way of assuring the disciples they could trust everything would be made clear in due time. This He said to address their confusion with both His current actions and what would happen to Him later.

This did nothing, however, to settle Peter's resistance to the Lord relegating Himself to the status of a servant. In disgust, he expressed his discomfort by telling Jesus, "You will never wash my feet" (13:8, NRSV). Jesus' rebuttal to Peter was quick and firm, "Unless I wash you, you have no share with me" (13:8, NRSV). Either Peter would be washed by Jesus or he would be excluded from being an heir to the Kingdom. The force of His words of consequence was devastating to Peter. In reaction to Jesus' ultimatum, Peter took the extreme opposite position. Almost with the same breath of saying "You will never wash my feet," he instructed Jesus to wash not just his feet but his hands and head as well. Once again, Peter missed the point, so Jesus corrected him saying, "One who has bathed does not to wash, except for the feet" (13:10, NRSV). Because the popular footwear during that time was open-toe sandals, the feet always were dirty and in need of washing. Through Jesus' act of washing His disciples' feet, He demonstrated the example of humility, servitude, and love. While washing the disciples' feet, Jesus used the analogy of being clean to affirm that because of their acceptance of Him as their Lord, they were clean, though not all of them. This referred to Judas of Iscariot, the disciple who betrayed Jesus the Christ.

Amazingly, even as Jesus demonstrated servanthood by washing the disciples' feet, He also showed redemptive love. Even as He acknowledged Judas's future betrayal, He presumably washed his feet. Judas did not leave the gathering until later in the passage at verse 30. Judas even participated in the final meal! Instead of singling Judas out, Jesus offered a cleansing before the ultimate act of sinful activity, betrayal of the Son of God. Jesus understood that more than most, Judas needed a cleansing not only of his feet but of his soul.

Later in the passage, Jesus gave a new command to love one another, excluding outsiders and enemies. Much scholarship has been devoted as to why John's Gospel does not include some form of Jesus' words found in the Synoptic Gospels to love one's enemies and outsiders. However, if we read this passage in light of the pericope's context, even though Jesus did not say to love your enemies, He showed what it is to love your enemies. He loved Judas even in his betrayal. While making this point, the text illuminates there is always a choice in response to divine love or any form of love. Though Jesus showed Judas love by including him in the foot washing, Judas did not cease his plans to hand Jesus over to those who would later crucify Him. Jesus loved him anyway.

II. Why Jesus Washed His Disciples' Feet (John 13:12–15)

After Jesus washed the disciples' feet, He sat down again. Focusing attention on what He just did, Jesus asked rhetorically, "Do you know what I have done to you?" (13:12, NRSV). After reaffirming His position of authority as Teacher and Lord, He explained the intent of the act. "If I, your Lord and Teacher, have washed your feet, you also ought to wash one another's feet" (13:14, NRSV). His point was to set an example of the relationships He expected in the future community of His believers. If He, the greatest of them, willingly served them, then there was no excuse for any of them to disdain service. "Whoever wishes to become great among you must be your servant, and whoever wishes to be first must be slave of all" (Mark 10:43–44, NRSV).

This passage exemplifies a technique called *greater to lesser.* In other words, as Jesus was the greater, the lesser disciples should follow suit. In as much as this text points to the servanthood of Jesus, it also notes His Lordship. Verse 14 reverses the order of *Teacher* and *Lord* from verse 13 to emphasize Jesus is Lord before He is Teacher. It is a question of the derivation of authority. Jesus' authority did not come from His ability to teach or correctly explicate the teachings of the Scriptures. Jesus' authority was placed in His position as Lord. His ability to teach was derived from His status as Lord. This breeds a type of circular thought that continuously emphasizes the magnanimity of His choice toward service.

Jesus' choice of service to His disciples pointed forward to His new command of verses 34–35. As love is to be displayed amongst His followers, service to one another is to be a distinguishing mark of that love. Service is to then point to and be a reminder for humility within the community. This community is to be free from the kind of pridefulness that runs rampant in the context of the greater society and the world. "One of the ways human pride manifests itself in a stratified society is in refusing to take the lower role" (Carson, 467). Jesus took the lower role. His followers are to do the same.

To take the lower position is a type of self-sacrifice. This of course was the greatest act of Jesus as He gave over His life for the world. Washing the disciples' feet was only symbolic for a greater sacrifice that would come later. Foot washing can be a wonderful expression of solidarity in the community of believers. However, it is not the act so much as it is the spirit behind the act. In this way, foot washing is an act of preparation. It prepares one for greater acts of service that require humility and a spirit of a selflessness.

III. The New Command for Christ's Community (John 13:34–35)

After the departure of Judas, Jesus gave His farewell speech to the remaining disciples. He instructed them to maintain the kind of community that exemplified His character in His absence. Jesus gave them a new command to love one another as He had loved them. Jesus assured them that by showing love for one another, all would know that in the absence of Jesus' physical presence, His disciples were a reminder that He's always near.

It is important to note this new commandment was not new in some ways. The Shema of the Old Testament commanded Yahweh's people to love the Lord your God and to love your neighbor. This command was new not so much through the words but in its birth and application. The command to love one another as a distinctive mark for the community of believers is to be a derivative and reflection of the love shared between the Father and Son and also their love for the world. It is in recognition of that love that believers are commanded to love each other. Therefore, it is a modeling of the bestowal of divine love on us.

Secondly, as a new command, it is to be birthed from love both divine and human. Through divine love, God calls believers together through His sacrifice of His beloved Son, for God gave His Son for the world (3:16). Even as God gave His Son, the Son also willingly was given (15:13). Therefore believers or disciples are to be given to this same level of commitment and covenant in their gathering. The community's continued gathering in love and through love points back to God's extravagant love for humanity. This is to be the identifying mark of the Church. It is love.

The Lesson Applied

To be ruled by love is to be governed by the heart, a heart that has surrendered to the will of God. Love is the fuel that directs our actions toward serving God and God's people, which is why the love we show can be measured by the service we render. This is the primary message Jesus was stressing with His disciples. If their love and respect for Him was sincere, then Jesus' example of serving them by taking on the role of a servant and washing their feet would serve as the model they were to follow upon His departure from them.

Jesus' example for the disciples is ours as well. As believers we are to lead the world in service, kindness, and justice. In doing so, we confirm God's presence through the expressions of our love. The more matured our growth in God, the more humbled we ought to be in our willingness to serve God's people.

Let's Talk About It

Are there consequences to service?

Jesus washed His disciples feet even as He realized there are consequences to service. Even as Peter abandoned his position that Jesus would never wash his feet, Peter did not fully understand that service at a certain level may demand more of us than we want to give. Foot washing is not commanded by Scripture; however, following Jesus' lead of service is very much a part of the dutiful Christian's journey. Service as shown here can be both humbling and humiliating. Whereas we lift up this example as the perfect example, often we are faced with the dilemma to choose rank or humiliation. We often choose wrongly because we do not want to appear to be less than we are. Once there was a youth pastor who was charged with leading a community cleanup for his church. On the day of the cleanup, a good number of members showed up ready to work. They began to walk through the neighborhood picking up trash. One of the people who showed up was the senior pastor. Noticing his pastor leading the charge, the youth pastor walked up to him and said, "Pastor, thank you for coming out here with us today. Not many pastors would volunteer to pick up trash." The senior pastor responded, "It's all about your theology." In other words, if you believe a task is beneath you, you will be humiliated by performing it, but if you know who you are, there is no task too low. Jesus knew who He was and His purpose. So should you!

Home Daily Devotional Readings

November 2–8, 2020

Monday	Tuesday	Wednesday	Thursday	Friday	Saturday	Sunday
God Is Disappointed with Israel	God Will Redeem Israel	Believers Continue God's Work	Jesus Freely Lays Down His Life	Facing the World as Jesus Did	Jesus Tends to His Vineyard	Always Love One Another
Isaiah 5:1–7	Isaiah 27:2–6	John 14:8–14	John 10:11–18	John 15:18–25	John 15:1–3	John 15:4–17

ABIDING LOVE

TOPIC:
THE LOVE CONNECTION

BACKGROUND SCRIPTURE:
JOHN 15:4–17

JOHN 15:4–17

King James Version

ABIDE in me, and I in you. As the branch cannot bear fruit of itself, except it abide in the vine; no more can ye, except ye abide in me.

5 I am the vine, ye are the branches: He that abideth in me, and I in him, the same bringeth forth much fruit: for without me ye can do nothing.
6 If a man abide not in me, he is cast forth as a branch, and is withered; and men gather them, and cast them into the fire, and they are burned.
7 If ye abide in me, and my words abide in you, ye shall ask what ye will, and it shall be done unto you.
8 Herein is my Father glorified, that ye bear much fruit; so shall ye be my disciples.
9 As the Father hath loved me, so have I loved you: continue ye in my love.
10 If ye keep my commandments, ye shall abide in my love; even as I have kept my Father's commandments, and abide in his love.
11 These things have I spoken unto you, that my joy might remain in you, and that your joy might be full.
12 This is my commandment, That ye love one another, as I have loved you.
13 Greater love hath no man than this, that a man lay down his life for his friends.
14 Ye are my friends, if ye do whatsoever I command you.
15 Henceforth I call you not servants; for the servant knoweth not what his lord doeth: but

New Revised Standard Version

ABIDE in me as I abide in you. Just as the branch cannot bear fruit by itself unless it abides in the vine, neither can you unless you abide in me.
5 I am the vine, you are the branches. Those who abide in me and I in them bear much fruit, because apart from me you can do nothing.

6 Whoever does not abide in me is thrown away like a branch and withers; such branches are gathered, thrown into the fire, and burned.

7 If you abide in me, and my words abide in you, ask for whatever you wish, and it will be done for you.
8 My Father is glorified by this, that you bear much fruit and become my disciples.
9 As the Father has loved me, so I have loved you; abide in my love.
10 If you keep my commandments, you will abide in my love, just as I have kept my Father's commandments and abide in his love.
11 I have said these things to you so that my joy may be in you, and that your joy may be complete.
12 "This is my commandment, that you love one another as I have loved you.
13 No one has greater love than this, to lay down one's life for one's friends.
14 You are my friends if you do what I command you.
15 I do not call you servants any longer, because the servant does not know what the master is

MAIN THOUGHT: I am the vine, ye are the branches: He that abideth in me, and I in him, the same bringeth forth much fruit: for without me ye can do nothing. (John 15:5, KJV)

JOHN 15:4–17

King James Version	*New Revised Standard Version*
I have called you friends; for all things that I have heard of my Father I have made known unto you.	**doing; but I have called you friends, because I have made known to you everything that I have heard from my Father.**
16 Ye have not chosen me, but I have chosen you, and ordained you, that ye should go and bring forth fruit, and that your fruit should remain: that whatsoever ye shall ask of the Father in my name, he may give it you.	**16 You did not choose me but I chose you. And I appointed you to go and bear fruit, fruit that will last, so that the Father will give you whatever you ask him in my name.**
17 These things I command you, that ye love one another.	**17 I am giving you these commands so that you may love one another.**

LESSON SETTING

Time: A.D. 27
Place: Jerusalem

LESSON OUTLINE

I. Connected to the Vine (John 15:4–8)
II. Connected to One Another (John 15:9–13)
III. From Servant to Servant-Friend (John 15:14–17)

UNIFYING PRINCIPLE

We try to love, but we feel beaten down by the world's greed and jealousy. How can we love one another in the face of the world's selfishness? Jesus declared we will be able to love one another if we abide in Him, keep the commandments, and abide in His love as the Holy Spirit abides in us.

INTRODUCTION

The value of love can be measured by the strength of its bonding power. Have you ever examined the connections you have with others and wondered how strong they really are they? How supportive are they to you? How supportive are you to them? Both who we are connected with and how strong those connections are determine the kind of fruit we ultimately will bear. God has purposed all of us to produce fruit for the Kingdom—if we stay connected.

This is what Jesus was stressing in today's lesson to His disciples. According to Jesus, the key to surviving the turbulence that would begin upon His departure was to stay connected to both Him and each other. Because vineyards were common then, He used the analogy of the vine, Jesus being the true vine and the disciples His branches. With this He began His discourse to emphasize the need for them to stay connected.

EXPOSITION

I. CONNECTED TO THE VINE (JOHN 15:4–8)

To stress the importance of His disciples' relationship with Him, Jesus employed the use of metaphor by incorporating the natural orientation between the vine and its branches. "Abide in me as I abide in you" (John 15:4, NRSV). The key word in these next few verses, and indeed the entire passage, is translated as *abide* in both the KJV and NRSV or *remain* in the NIV. The Greek word is μενω (*meno*) meaning "to remain or abide." The sense of the word is to continue a certain state, condition, or activity. "John seeks to express the immutability and inviolability of the relation of immanence" (*Theological Dictionary of the New Testament*, vol. 4, 576). John used μενω to demonstrate both the closeness of God to the believers through the indwelling of the Spirit and the believers dwelling within the Word of Christ. The contingency of believers ultimately is expressed in one's ability to stay true to the teachings and Spirit of Jesus. To remain in Him is to not only live within orthodox praxis but to believe and behave as if one has his or her life, breath, and being within God.

Jesus instructed the disciples to remain in Him as the branch abides in its own vine. Referencing His earlier proclamation of being the true vine in verse 1, Jesus furthered His metaphor by implying the disciples were branches that needed to remain in Him, the vine. Just as a branch that's not connected to the vine cannot bear fruit, without Jesus, the disciples could do nothing. A branch is not a self-contained entity, and neither is a disciple. Separated and deprived of the supply of nourishment, both eventually will die. Fruit-bearing for the disciple is totally dependent on a direct connection to Jesus

The fruit disciples are expected to bear is contingent on their utter dependence in relation to Jesus. Fruit comes through that entire relationship and encompasses everything that comes forth from that relationship. Therefore, *fruit* may mean a great many things as long as it is consistent with the Word of Jesus. It can be recruitment and development of new disciples, personal behavioral changes, or a continued commitment to good works that bring glory to the Father.

Failure to produce fruit, according to Jesus, brings about severe consequences. "Whoever does not abide in me is thrown away like a branch and withers; such branches are gathered, thrown into the fire, and burned" (15:6, NRSV). Jesus knew allowing the branches that don't produce fruit to remain on the vine compromises the distribution of nourishment for the branches that are producing. Dried up branches on a vine-producing tree sends conflicting messages as to the integrity of the fruit produced by the tree. The branches that are cut off eventually are gathered and thrown into the fire. Through this metaphor, Jesus forcefully endorsed the need for His disciples to remember their source of strength so as to prevent losing their usefulness to the vinedresser, the Father.

In contrast to the consequences of not abiding in the vine, Jesus furthered His argument with a conditional promise. He said, "If you abide in me, and my words in you, ask for whatever you wish, and it will be done for you" (15:7, NRSV). In this Jesus revealed how His disciples are expected to abide in Him—through His words and prayer. The more they reflect on the lessons from, experiences with, and demonstrations of Jesus' love, what God wants for them will be what they desire. Abiding through prayer is reiterative in that as one asks because of one's connection to Jesus through His words, one only asks for that which is His will. The more one abides through prayer, coming close to Him, the less one desires that which may be selfish and desires only what God would have her or him to desire.

In verse 8, Jesus presented three overall objectives for His disciples to consider. Staying connected to Jesus guarantees they will bear much fruit, and their fruitfulness confirms their spiritual status of being Jesus' disciples. But more important, by staying connected to Jesus and producing fruit, the Father is glorified. Only through connection to Jesus can the Father be glorified. The actions of disciples do not bring glory to the Father by themselves. Rather, it is through the connection to Jesus that the Father is glorified as the Father is glorified by the Son.

II. Connected to One Another (John 15:9–13)

The theme of abiding in Jesus is continued in verse 9, but with a stronger appeal by first enunciating the depth of His love and how it flows from God to Him to the disciples. "As the Father has loved me, so I have loved you" (15:9, NRSV). Accepting this truth presented a theological challenge, however. To embrace Jesus' idea of God as Father, when traditionally God was revered as the One who transcends all human relationships, would have been a difficult concept to consider. God is too holy to be associated within a domesticated context. In fact, just the mention of His name was considered taboo for the observant Jew. It came to be seen as imbued with spiritual force, so they prohibited the pronunciation of it.

The orientation between Himself and God as Father and Son created the perception that God is both accessible and relatable. By abiding in His love, Jesus promised the disciples the same love that binds Him to the Father would bind them to Him. Jesus told them how to abide in Him: "Keep my commandments" (15:10, NRSV). Ironically, in 14:15 Jesus implied that loving him is how the disciples were to keep His commandments, but in this text the order is reversed. Keeping His commandments (first) will result in abiding in Jesus' love. "The only natural conclusion from these virtually reversible statements, therefore, is that they are so interrelated and inseparable that one cannot exist without the other" (Borchert, *The New American Commentary*, 146). To love Jesus is to follow His commandments, and to follow His commandments is to love Jesus.

In verse 11 Jesus offered another benefit for those disciples who abide in His love through following His commandments. He said, "So that my joy may be in you, and that your joy may be complete" (15:11, NRSV). This is a joy the world cannot give or take away. Jesus offered this promise as an encouragement for the disciples upon His departure from them. If they remained in His love, even in His absence, His love would remain in them. The joy disciples experience is related to fulfillment. Their joy can be complete in the realization of Jesus and the fullness of His mission and time. Their joy is directly related to His glorification. Following His words and commands further increases His glory and, therefore, the glory of the Father. Disciples take joy in the glory of the Father and the Son.

All of the commands Jesus gave to His disciples to this point are encapsulated into one core directive: "Love one another as I have loved you" (15:13, NRSV). This command is a restatement of the "new command" Jesus presented in 13:34–35 as the mark of authentic discipleship. The strategy of Jesus' discourse is disclosed in this verse. His admonishment to the disciples to remain in His love was what would enable them to sincerely abide in love with one another. To emphasize the measure of love He had for them, Jesus explained, "No one has greater love than this, to lay down one's life for one's friends" (15:13, NRSV). As a forecast for what was to come, Jesus described the disciples as friends for whom He would demonstrate His love through offering Himself as the ultimate sacrifice.

This ultimate sacrifice is His glorification. His glorification is born of love He desires His disciples to experience and participate in. As He loves them, they are to love each other. As the Father loves the Son, the Son loves the disciples. Disciples therefore are to love each other, the Son, and the Father, perfecting the bond of love—a love that may require sacrifice.

III. From Servant to Servant-Friend (John 15:14–17)

The relationship status between Jesus and the disciples was upgraded when He referred to them as His friends. However, this friendship status was conditional. They would only remain friends with Jesus if they did whatever He commanded them to do, suggesting that friendship with Him is negotiated through the faithfulness of His followers. Their upgrade to friend also changed their status of importance. When Jesus said He no longer called them servants in verse 15, this was not to suggest they were absolved from serving but that their faithfulness evolved into a servant-friend status. This idea of being a servant-friend of Jesus is distinguished by divine insight. A servant does not know what his master is doing. A servant is expected to obey even though the master doesn't explain the reason for any given command. A servant or a slave (the Greek word in this verse is *δουλος*. *Doulos* (or *slave*) is simply to be the extension of the will of his or her master. A servant has no mind of his or her own and follows without question or knowledge. A servant-friend of Jesus is viewed in a completely different light. A servant-friend is an object of divine revelation and is given access to all things from the Father made known through his or her relationship with Jesus, a relationship based on knowing and accepting His divine purpose.

Though they were now servant-friends of Jesus, He reminded the disciples, "You did not choose me but I chose you" (15:16, NRSV). Just as a branch cannot choose its vine, those who would be servant-friends of Jesus must be chosen by Jesus and appointed so they can go and bear fruit. The divine insight that has been made known to them by Jesus now obligates them to be fruit bearers for Jesus. They are not left without a resource, however. Jesus reassured that whatever His servant-friends ask from the Father in His name will be provided for them (15:16).

Jesus concluded this section of His sermon with the reassertion to His now servant-friends to love one another (15:17). Jesus restated this command from 15:12 to reinforce what mattered most among them.

True discipleship is defined and measured by their love for one another.

The Lesson Applied

No stronger force than love is in this world. In addition to making us feel more complete, love, when harnessed properly, can fuel ambitions, heal deficiencies, and define purpose. This, however, is contingent upon how well we develop and keep a connection with God and in God. Since God is love, He is the source of love and all of its expressions. Our intimate connection with God directly exposes us to the light and power of this love, in that we become slaves to its influence.

It is of the utmost importance for us to remain in Him so we can properly love those around us. When we keep this in mind, we are able to better love those whom God has placed in our lives. Our love for them stems from our love for God. Acceptance of God's love is what completes us and makes us be the men and women He has made and called us to be in fullness.

Let's Talk About It

Why is prayer central to remaining connected to Jesus in God?

Prayer is our key to remaining connected to Jesus in God. Often we believe prayer is simply asking God for what we want. Whereas this is true, prayer is so much more. Prayer is not the cessation of action but understanding what direction one should take. Prayer thereby allows us to experience God sufficiently so the lives we live are born of His continued presence. Brother Lawrence, a seventeenth century monk, invented a helpful phrase and way of life for Christians. He wrote a book entitled *The Practice of the Presence of God*. Essentially, this means we are consistently and fully in God's presence even through the ordinariness of quotidian existence. To practice the presence of God is to remain full of prayer so one is able to live in and out of the will of God. Prayer, therefore, as opposed to a distinctive activity, is the totality of one's life.

Prayer is in this way transformative as opposed to only being a directed plea or supplication born of selfish desire. This is our connection to God. That our lives are so transformed through the consistent practice of His presence that we begin to walk after the Spirit without regard to our own will or desire. Our desire is God and God alone. Prayer then keeps us close to Jesus in God, for we are always in communication with Him. And the Good News is that through prayer He is always in communication with us. Prayer then is a two-way street.

Home Daily Devotional Readings
November 9–15, 2020

Monday	Tuesday	Wednesday	Thursday	Friday	Saturday	Sunday
Example of Faith and Obedience	Then Darkness, Now Light	Live by the Light	Children of God Love One Another	Walking Faithfully in the Truth	Imitate What Is Good, Not Evil	Believe Jesus Christ; Love One Another
1 Thessalonians 2:1–10	Ephesians 5:8–16	John 3:16–21	1 John 2:28–3:10	3 John 1–4	3 John 9–12	1 John 3:11–24

LESSON 11

NOVEMBER 15, 2020

CONFIDENT LOVE

TOPIC:
LOVING OTHERS

BACKGROUND SCRIPTURE:
1 JOHN 3:11–24; 2 JOHN 4–11; 3 JOHN 5–8

1 JOHN 3:11–24

King James Version

FOR this is the message that ye heard from the beginning, that we should love one another.

12 Not as Cain, who was of that wicked one, and slew his brother. And wherefore slew he him? Because his own works were evil, and his brother's righteous.

13 Marvel not, my brethren, if the world hate you.

14 We know that we have passed from death unto life, because we love the brethren. He that loveth not his brother abideth in death.

15 Whosoever hateth his brother is a murderer: and ye know that no murderer hath eternal life abiding in him.

16 Hereby perceive we the love of God, because he laid down his life for us: and we ought to lay down our lives for the brethren.

17 But whoso hath this world's good, and seeth his brother have need, and shutteth up his bowels of compassion from him, how dwelleth the love of God in him?

18 My little children, let us not love in word, neither in tongue; but in deed and in truth.

19 And hereby we know that we are of the truth, and shall assure our hearts before him.

20 For if our heart condemn us, God is greater than our heart, and knoweth all things.

21 Beloved, if our heart condemn us not, then have we confidence toward God.

New Revised Standard Version

FOR this is the message you have heard from the beginning, that we should love one another.

12 We must not be like Cain who was from the evil one and murdered his brother. And why did he murder him? Because his own deeds were evil and his brother's righteous.

13 Do not be astonished, brothers and sisters, that the world hates you.

14 We know that we have passed from death to life because we love one another. Whoever does not love abides in death.

15 All who hate a brother or sister are murderers, and you know that murderers do not have eternal life abiding in them.

16 We know love by this, that he laid down his life for us—and we ought to lay down our lives for one another.

17 How does God's love abide in anyone who has the world's goods and sees a brother or sister in need and yet refuses help?

18 Little children, let us love, not in word or speech, but in truth and action.

19 And by this we will know that we are from the truth and will reassure our hearts before him

20 whenever our hearts condemn us; for God is greater than our hearts, and he knows everything.

21 Beloved, if our hearts do not condemn us, we have boldness before God;

MAIN THOUGHT: And he that keepeth his commandments dwelleth in him, and he in him. And hereby we know that he abideth in us, by the Spirit which he hath given us. (1 John 3:24, KJV)

1 John 3:11–24

King James Version	*New Revised Standard Version*
22 And whatsoever we ask, we receive of him, because we keep his commandments, and do those things that are pleasing in his sight.	**22 and we receive from him whatever we ask, because we obey his commandments and do what pleases him.**
23 And this is his commandment, That we should believe on the name of his Son Jesus Christ, and love one another, as he gave us commandment.	**23 And this is his commandment, that we should believe in the name of his Son Jesus Christ and love one another, just as he has commanded us.**
24 And he that keepeth his commandments dwelleth in him, and he in him. And hereby we know that he abideth in us, by the Spirit which he hath given us.	**24 All who obey his commandments abide in him, and he abides in them. And by this we know that he abides in us, by the Spirit that he has given us.**

LESSON SETTING

Time: A.D. 90–100
Place: Ephesus

LESSON OUTLINE

I. Love and Hate (1 John 3:11–15)
II. Love by Sacrifice (1 John 3:16–18)
III. Love Is Action (1 John 3:19–24)

Unifying Principle

Hatred toward others sometimes seems far easier than love. How can we show love for others? The willingness of Jesus to die for us and His command that we live for others brings that confidence.

Introduction

All Christians know we're supposed to love one another. At times that's part of the problem. We only "know" as oppose to acting on what we know and doing it. Loving one another can be an exercise of human expediency. It nurtures the hidden virtues of our greatness. The way we advertise Christ and His character in this world is through the actions of love by His followers. God is love, and Christ is the greatest demonstration of that love for the world in that while we were yet sinners, He died for us.

But what do we do when loving one another isn't easy? We remember the love God has for us. When we embrace our unworthiness of being loved by God, we're humbled by the weight of His grace that has kept and covered us throughout our lives. God's love is patient, persistent, and personal. No matter how far we may drift from the shore of His presence, He remains available to be received and to restore us to Him.

Why is His love so abundant toward us? So the grace He has shown us might be reflected as empathy for another. The more love we have been freely given and shown, the more we do unto others.

This is the message of John's letter. It was written to a church or group of churches in crisis—churches that were being attacked by false teaching (2:18–28; 4:1–6). The false teachers went so far as to organize and send out missionaries who moved among and throughout the churches with the goal of converting others to their beliefs. This theological assault created confusion and crisis within the believing community. In response to this situation, John wrote to combat the propaganda and reassure believers in the faith of the faith.

Exposition

I. Love and Hate (1 John 3:11–15)

A natural parallel is drawn between 1:5 and 3:11, a link connected by the phrase, "For this message you have heard from the beginning" (NRSV). This was to validate the end of one section and the start of a new. From 1:5–3:10, greater attention is given to the theme of God as light, but in 3:11–5:12 the focus is more on God as love. The implication of the author is that because of what his readers had been exposed to regarding the children of God, they should automatically love one another. To further illustrate the imperative to love one another, the author cited the contrast of Cain, who was from the evil one and murdered his brother. According to him, Cain's murderous actions against his brother were precipitated by jealousy and resentment born from God accepting his brother's sacrifice as righteous and rejecting his as evil. In short, the righteous acts of Abel provoked hatred in Cain. The reference to Cain's hatred introduces another conflict between good and evil, namely, God-prompted love and Satan-inspired hatred. The tension between righteousness and sinfulness, typified in the account of Cain and Abel, will never end in this world.

The use of the Cain and Abel story also gives another helpful narrative in the light of John's focus on loving one another. Cain and Abel were the first brothers in the Bible. The strife between the two highlights the difficulty of loving family properly or, for that matter, at all. With 1 John's focus on loving one another, this text is a dark reminder of what can happen when love is not at the forefront of the minds of people living in close proximity and in relationship with one another. John used this story to reemphasize this message—to love one another—is from the beginning, not just the beginning of the Jesus movement, but *the* beginning, as in the genesis of human existence. God has called His children to love our brothers and sisters, biological and Christian.

This is why John instructed his readers not to marvel if the world hated them. The evil of the world has the potential to distract, as it apparently had for some of his readers. It's likely that believers of John's time were enduring mistreatment from docetic teachers who challenged the integrity of their belief. Docetism was an early system of beliefs, deemed heretical, that emphasized Jesus was not truly flesh but only appeared to be human and did not suffer on the cross. This is why 1 John 4:2 (NRSV) states, "Every spirit that confesses that Jesus Christ has come in the flesh is from God." His readers may have been influenced and were being dissuaded from their initial convictions. John sought to remind his readers that as believers, they should expect to be hated, as evil is an ever-present reality fighting against good. The Johannine community was to be different from that which they experienced from outside the confines of itself. The message is clear: The world hates, but amongst yourselves is to be love.

With the use of the emphatic *we*, John included himself with his readers in verse 14 when he appealed to their personal knowledge and assurance of a new life in Christ. This *we* also gives some indication that the writer of this letter was a part of the community himself. As opposed to an outsider writing to this church or churches, he was one of their number. As a part of the community, he regarded himself as one of those who have passed from death to life. Evidenced by the love for the brethren, living in this new life is based on a practice of loving one another. In contrast, he who does not love his brother abides in death. In verse 15 John paralleled those individuals with the murderous action of Cain. This sweeping indictment provides no exceptions and offers no middle ground. Whoever hates is, in essence, a murderer. The verse parallels Jesus' words of Matthew 5:21–22 (NRSV): "You have heard that it was said to those of ancient time, 'You shall not murder'; and 'whoever murders shall be liable to judgment.' But I say to you that if you are angry with a brother or sister, you will be liable to the council; and if you say, 'You fool,' you will be liable to the hell of fire." Both of these texts highlight the divisiveness of anger and hate and their ability to produce irreparable damage. The destructive nature of hatred can be equivalent to the act of murder itself.

II. Love by Sacrifice (1 John 3:16–18)

Having shown that love is the evidence of life in the child of God, John pressed his argument by providing the ultimate demonstration of love: Jesus Christ's sacrifice as He laid down His life for us. Just as Christ died for all, believers ought to be prepared, according to the author, to do the same for one another. While the necessity of laying down their lives for one another was rare, the necessity of helping meet one another's needs was not. So, from the grand example of love demonstrated through Christ's sacrifice, John moved to a more practical example of what love is not. Those who have the resources and see their brother in need and shut up their hearts have no room for God's love to abide in them, according to John. The question he asked rhetorically was meant to challenge his readers to evaluate the callous response of such an individual so as to elicit from them the opposite reaction.

Laying down one's life typically is understood in the sense of death. However, it can be nuanced so that it does not require death. The laying down of life also is to take from what one needs to give to another. This is why the sacrifice of death is so beyond what we might hope for another to do for us. But to share of one's resources for which one has need is also a laying down of one's life. Instead of thinking about sharing from one's abundance, it is sharing from what one needs. This also is a laying down of life. Consider the Old Testament story in 1 Kings 17 of the widow of Zarephath and Elijah. She made bread for the prophet instead of herself and her son. Though she did not die, this was an ultimate sacrifice, or a laying down of her life, for the improvement of another. This is what it means to demonstrate love by laying down one's life for another—not to give just from abundance but from possible lack.

As a final exhortation to his readers, John contended in verse 18 (NRSV), "Let us love, not in word or in speech, but in truth and action." Including himself in this challenge, the author established a distinction between so-called love expressed through empty words and love expressed in deed and in truth. The objective lesson for John's readers was that the true expression of love is observed in the behavior and overall conduct of the believer. Love is not relegated to emotions; rather, love without action is mere affection.

III. Love Is Action (1 John 3:19–24)

John reassured both himself and his readers that the revelations they had been given were the truth and no other could compare. He confirmed to them in the face of opposing beliefs systems that their hearts could be assured before God in His presence. Using *we know* in verse 19 set up what he proved in verses 20–21 as what defines the people of truth—that they are people who are governed by the heart. The heart condemns God's children when they transgress against Him. But God, who knows all things and is greater than our heart, still allows us to approach Him in confidence for forgiveness and restoration.

When the heart does not condemn, however, believers are free to approach God's throne of grace in prayer, being assured that whatever we ask, we receive from Him. This guarantee is based on our commitment to keep His commandments and do those things that are pleasing in His sight. This also reinforces the idea that the believer through obedience only asks for that which is pleasing in God's sight. This text points to the necessity for believers to live in complete obedience to God to align their wills with His own. At this point, prayer reflects only God's own character. Therefore, God has no reason to say no for our requests reflect His wishes.

Having spoken of the need to obey God's commands, John established the central command, summing up all previous instruction: We should believe on the name of Jesus Christ and love one another. Really, only one command is conveyed in a dual form—an explicit belief in the Son, Jesus Christ, and an active love for one another. The two parallel verbs *believe* and *love* work together to form one primary command. You cannot believe without loving. This introduces the notion that belief is not true without formidable action that buttresses it. For ancient people, the idea that one could believe without action was absurd. This is at least in part demonstrated in Leviticus 19:18, which commands Israel to love its neighbor. This command is in a litany of commands that outline a code of morality and acceptable behavior. The surrounding verses can be read as actions that should or should not be taken constituting love. Love, therefore, is constitutional to certain actions without which it does not exist.

This reinforces the conditional promise Jesus gave to His disciples in John 15:10. John told his readers that he who keeps God's commandments abides in Him and He in him. As it was with Jesus and His disciples, this mutually abiding relationship is predicated on obedience to God's will. The one who lives in obedience to God experiences a reciprocal fellowship with Him, one indicative of a close and intimate communion. Believers who enjoy such a connection with God are distinguished by the Spirit that abides in Him.

The Lesson Applied

In order to live our lives from a conviction of love, it's important to understand the nature of its influence. Love starts with God because God is love. In fact, our first encounter with God is also our initial introduction to love. By discovering and accepting God's love for us, we are taught how to love ourselves in return. Out of our gratitude, we love God back through loving one another.

One of the easiest ways for us to accept the task of loving as God would have us to is to concentrate on loving those who are closest to us. Through the discipline of choosing to love our closest family members, friends, and community members, we are able to reflect the love of God in our lives. We should choose to love those in close proximity even when it is difficult to do so, through their difficult moments and even as they may choose not to love us in return. Love, therefore, is a spiritual discipline. We choose it each and every day, or we choose to do something else for which we will be held accountable. So, from a practical standpoint, choose to be generous, peaceable, kind, faithful, and accepting to those whom God has placed in your life.

Let's Talk About It

What does is it mean to pass from death to life?

To pass from death to life means we no longer adhere to those things that produce death in our bodies and spirits. Our reality is that we live in a world that engages in that which produces death. However, lives that are lived unto Christ no longer participate in the death-dealing circumstances, institutions, and cultural phenomena. This is not simply at the level of personal piety but raises the consciousness and spirit to have a communal code of morality and responsibility.

True love is that which has the ability to move us beyond self and personal hedonistic desires to that which presses us and those around us into abundant, flourishing, and productive life. So, yes, we live in the "holiness" of personal discipline by leaving behind those things Paul characterized as walking after the flesh, but we also are concerned with destroying those entities that destroy life.

In other words, as Christians who have passed from death to life, we should actively work toward securing a better world from a systemic standpoint for the marginalized and locked out. We don't just give alms. We figure out how to make alms unnecessary, so that each person walks in dignity.

Home Daily Devotional Readings

November 16–22, 2020

Monday	Tuesday	Wednesday	Thursday	Friday	Saturday	Sunday
Preparing to Become a Deacon	Healing Ministry Grows the Church	Church Sharing Plan Enlarged	Stephen's Ministry Opposed	Sharing All of Life Together	Prayer for Boldness and Signs	Sharing All Possessions Challenges the Church
1 Timothy 3:8–13	Acts 5:12–16	Acts 6:1–7	Acts 6:8–15	Acts 2:42–47	Acts 4:23–31	Acts 4:32–5:11

SHARING LOVE

TOPIC:
SHARING LOVE IN TRUTH

BACKGROUND SCRIPTURE:
ACTS 4:32–5:11

ACTS 4:32–5:11

King James Version

AND the multitude of them that believed were of one heart and of one soul: neither said any of them that ought of the things which he possessed was his own; but they had all things common.
33 And with great power gave the apostles witness of the resurrection of the Lord Jesus: and great grace was upon them all.
34 Neither was there any among them that lacked: for as many as were possessors of lands or houses sold them, and brought the prices of the things that were sold,
35 And laid them down at the apostles' feet: and distribution was made unto every man according as he had need.
36 And Joses, who by the apostles was surnamed Barnabas, (which is, being interpreted, The son of consolation,) a Levite, and of the country of Cyprus,
37 Having land, sold it, and brought the money, and laid it at the apostles' feet.

• • • Acts 5:1–11 • • •

1 But a certain man named Ananias, with Sapphira his wife, sold a possession,
2 And kept back part of the price, his wife also being privy to it, and brought a certain part, and laid it at the apostles' feet.
3 But Peter said, Ananias, why hath Satan filled thine heart to lie to the Holy Ghost, and to keep back part of the price of the land?

New Revised Standard Version

NOW the whole group of those who believed were of one heart and soul, and no one claimed private ownership of any possessions, but everything they owned was held in common.
33 With great power the apostles gave their testimony to the resurrection of the Lord Jesus, and great grace was upon them all.
34 There was not a needy person among them, for as many as owned lands or houses sold them and brought the proceeds of what was sold.
35 They laid it at the apostles' feet, and it was distributed to each as any had need.
36 There was a Levite, a native of Cyprus, Joseph, to whom the apostles gave the name Barnabas (which means "son of encouragement").
37 He sold a field that belonged to him, then brought the money, and laid it at the apostles' feet.

• • • Acts 5:1–11 • • •

1 But a man named Ananias, with the consent of his wife Sapphira, sold a piece of property;
2 with his wife's knowledge, he kept back some of the proceeds, and brought only a part and laid it at the apostles' feet.
3 "Ananias," Peter asked, "why has Satan filled your heart to lie to the Holy Spirit and to keep back part of the proceeds of the land?

MAIN THOUGHT: And the multitude of them that believed were of one heart and of one soul: neither said any of them that ought of the things which he possessed was his own; but they had all things common. (Acts 4:32, KJV)

Acts 4:32–5:11

King James Version

4 Whiles it remained, was it not thine own? and after it was sold, was it not in thine own power? why hast thou conceived this thing in thine heart? thou hast not lied unto men, but unto God.

5 And Ananias hearing these words fell down, and gave up the ghost: and great fear came on all them that heard these things.

6 And the young men arose, wound him up, and carried him out, and buried him.

7 And it was about the space of three hours after, when his wife, not knowing what was done, came in.

8 And Peter answered unto her, Tell me whether ye sold the land for so much? And she said, Yea, for so much.

9 Then Peter said unto her, How is it that ye have agreed together to tempt the Spirit of the Lord? behold, the feet of them which have buried thy husband are at the door, and shall carry thee out.

10 Then fell she down straightway at his feet, and yielded up the ghost: and the young men came in, and found her dead, and, carrying her forth, buried her by her husband.

11 And great fear came upon all the church, and upon as many as heard these things.

New Revised Standard Version

4 While it remained unsold, did it not remain your own? And after it was sold, were not the proceeds at your disposal? How is it that you have contrived this deed in your heart? You did not lie to us but to God!"

5 Now when Ananias heard these words, he fell down and died. And great fear seized all who heard of it.

6 The young men came and wrapped up his body, then carried him out and buried him.

7 After an interval of about three hours his wife came in, not knowing what had happened.

8 Peter said to her, "Tell me whether you and your husband sold the land for such and such a price." And she said, "Yes, that was the price."

9 Then Peter said to her, "How is it that you have agreed together to put the Spirit of the Lord to the test? Look, the feet of those who have buried your husband are at the door, and they will carry you out."

10 Immediately she fell down at his feet and died. When the young men came in they found her dead, so they carried her out and buried her beside her husband.

11 And great fear seized the whole church and all who heard of these things.

LESSON SETTING

Time: A.D. 28
Place: Jerusalem

LESSON OUTLINE

I. Community of Believers (Acts 4:32–37)
II. Ananias Confronted (Acts 5:1–6)
III. Sapphira Confronted (Acts 5:7–11)

Unifying Principle

In every community, there are people who have less than they need to maintain healthy lives. How can we best meet the needs of everyone in our communities? As the first believers in Jesus shared everything in common, the needs of everyone were satisfied.

Introduction

Love and truth are two sides of the same coin. In a healthy relationship, you can't have one without the other. While this might seem obvious to most, it's not to everyone. Many individuals, couples, families, friendships, and even faith communities have become upended because of the lack of one or both of these fundamental virtues. While essential for our spiritual formation, being grounded in the love and truth of God isn't automatic for the believer. It takes work to sustain such an orientation—a lot of work.

The viable assimilation of love and truth in relationship requires an authentic personality, one that encompasses a disposition of reflection, accountability, honesty, and humility. When any of these is absent, it compromises the integrity of the relationship at large.

This was the setting for today's lesson. After the experience of Pentecost, a new community of faith was born. Though it was still in its infancy, the endowment of the Holy Spirit enabled the young community to grow by the thousands. In the attempt to manage its growth, which later turned into a movement and eventually a religious tradition, the community had to ensure certain expectations of truth and love among its members were being observed.

Exposition

I. Community of Believers (Acts 4:32–37)

Verse 32 opens with a description of the community's spiritual unity. They were a multitude of people who believed and were of one heart and one soul. This was the fundamental characteristic that fostered growth in the early Christian church. Unified believers coalesced around a common conviction in Christ. That they were of the same heart and soul spoke of their familiarity with one another. They enjoyed a oneness that extended to a natural concern for the practical needs of the believers in the community. Possessions were shared so they had all things in common. The word used for *common* is κοινος (*koinos*). Κοινος is the root word for κοίνωνια (koinonia: *fellowship*) and κοιωνος (koionos: *partner; sharer*). This indicated their closeness and that they literally shared all. Given the closeness of the meaning of the Greek words defined above, it is fair to write that they fellowshipped through holding their possessions as one. The idea of commonness served two important points of separation from the general culture. (1) The community was not stratified, but it was egalitarian. One would not possess more than another or one would have enough or more than enough and another not enough. It was an affront to the cultural values of their historical situation, as the Roman Empire was a highly stratified society and was the world's largest slavocracy prior to the American South of the eighteenth and nineteenth centuries. (2) It ensured all needs were met within the community by the community. In many ways it helped the fledging community get off the ground because they did not need outside help. They could do ministry and make sure the Word of God went forth because all needs were met.

The leaders of this new community were the apostles in whom God endowed great power and authority to give witness to the resurrection of the Lord Jesus. The grace of God upon them all proved His abiding presence in their midst and is what guaranteed the subsequent successes of the growing church.

Because of their commitment to each other, the believers in this community of faith lacked nothing as they developed a system to ensure all needs were being met. Details of this new economy of sharing resources is explained further in verse 34. All who possessed lands or houses sold them, then brought the proceeds of what was sold and laid them at the apostles' feet. Though this wasn't a required exercise, their voluntary compliance to the practice was no doubt motivated by the believers' deep conviction to the virtues of love and truth in the community of Christ. After surrendering the proceeds to the apostles, the apostles in turn systematically redistributed those resources to each as anyone had need.

Barnabas was singled out as a positive example of how this system worked in verses 36–37. After selling his land, he brought the money and laid it at the apostles' feet.

At the beginning of the nation of Israel, the tribe of Levi was not allotted land as an inheritance. By the time the church began, however, Joseph of Cyprus (called Barnabas) was a landowner. The selfless nature of Joseph that caused him to be known as the "son of encouragement" is evident in the following chapters of Acts. He reconciled Saul of Tarsus with the church that Saul once persecuted (Acts 9:26–27); led one of the first churches to have both Jewish and Gentile believers (11:19–24); and played a key role in the first major missionary campaign of the church (Acts 13–14).

Barnabas's example also serves to emphasize the voluntary nature of this communal practice. There was no transfer of ownership, no control of production or income, no requirement to surrender one's property, but his willingness to do so illustrates the kind of attitude indicative of a fully functional community of believers.

II. Ananias Confronted (Acts 5:1–6)

Like Barnabas, Ananias and his wife Sapphira made an agreement to sell a possession or a piece of property and turn the profits over to the apostles. They conspired together, however, to keep back part of the proceeds, disguising their dishonesty in front of Peter as if it were the whole amount. Peter's quick response in verse 3 revealed the truly deceptive agent of whose influence they were under. He asked Ananias first, "Why has Satan filled your heart to lie to the Holy Spirit?" (5:3, NRSV). This indicated Peter not only knew the portion they were giving wasn't the full amount, but that his knowledge of the plot was made known to him supernaturally. The implication of lying to the Holy Spirit, as opposed to the apostles, leads one to believe it was the Holy Spirit who informed them of Ananias's deceit. Peter reminded Ananias in verse 4 (NRSV), "While it remained unsold, did it not remain your own?" Ananias had been under no compulsion to sell his land. And if he did, he could have chosen to retain all of the proceeds for himself. The act of dedicating the land to the community was strictly voluntary. Once pledged, however, it became a wholly different matter. It had been dedicated to the community. Lying about the amount of money turned in undermined the integrity of the process, not to mention the sacred trust in the community. According to Peter, Ananias didn't just lie to them, but to God.

Upon hearing these words, Ananias fell down and breathed his last. While the cause of his death is unknown, the meaning behind his tragic ending is clear. It served as a warning for those who heard and witnessed what happened. The great fear that came upon all the believers inspired a collective reverence for the sacredness of the community. The manner in which Ananias's funeral was handled emphasized the intensity of divine judgment against him. Young men wrapped him up, carried him outside the city, and buried him. They wasted no time in ceremony, as they were back only three hours later (5:7). Burials usually lasted much longer than three hours, but when the death was under unusual circumstances, such as suicide, criminal activity, or judgment from God, ceremony was streamlined to the barest of practical measures taken to dispose of the deceased (Polhill, *The New American Commentary*, 158).

III. Sapphira Confronted (Acts 5:7–11)

When Sapphira, Ananias's wife, came in, not knowing what had happened, she too was met with the same interrogation as her husband. Peter confronted her about the sales price of the property and asked her to confirm the amount they said they sold the land for. "Is this the price you got for the land?" is another way of understanding Peter's question. Though there are not many details regarding the amount given and what was held back, it can be implied that Sapphira's response incriminated herself in her futile attempt to maintain the deception.

As with her husband prior, Peter exposed her lack of integrity by asking, "How is it that you have agreed together to put the Spirit of the Lord to the test?" (5:9, NRSV). The phrase *testing the Spirit of the Lord* referred to the couple's efforts to challenge the limits of God's tolerance and grace. Peter asked this of Sapphira to emphasize the weight of their offense. If left unaddressed, their duplicity would have compromised the overall integrity of the community and Christian movement. Being just informed of her husband's death, Sapphira was directed to look at the feet of the men responsible for burying him, as they would also be the ones to carry her out. And like her husband before her, Sapphira too immediately fell down and breathed her last.

Verse 11 begins with the same ending epitaph of her husband's in verse 5—great fear came upon those who heard these things. The repetition was intentional, as it's meant to emphasize the spiritual nature and necessity of the church. It should be noted this is the first time the word *church* occurs in the book of Acts, further confirming the people of God began to identify themselves as a religious community.

The Lesson Applied

To be a champion for civic and human rights, understanding the nature of love and truth is essential for success. Love is the basis for understanding the plight of the oppressed and disenfranchised. Truth is what we speak to power on behalf of those we love.

As such, perhaps we should take more seriously holding more in common or fellowship through possessions. Truth is not only what we speak, but what we act as well. Our text confirms what we already know: Within the community of believers, there is more than enough, so there should be none who are in lack. This story teaches us we cannot "fake the funk." Ananias and Sapphira wanted to act as though they had given their all to the cause. They had not. We may condemn them—and rightly so—but many of us fit into this same category. We should be able to answer in the affirmative, "Is your all on the altar?" If we cannot, we should reconsider if we are lying to ourselves and the Holy Spirit.

Let's Talk About It

The NRSV states that Ananias sold the property with the consent of his wife. Does that tell us anything about marital relations in the first-century Christian community?

Unfortunately it does not. The NRSV at this juncture does not represent the true meaning of the oldest Greek manuscripts. The KJV and NIV translate that Ananias sold the piece of property *with* his wife Sapphira, which hits the nail on the head. The NRSV uses the phrase *with the consent* because it is implied by the direct knowledge she demonstrated of the sale later in the text at verse 8. However, this little phrase changes the meaning of the text ever so slightly. The danger is that as modern Bible readers we may become guilty of performing anachronistic readings on the text. Simply put, when we see a text like this, we might think, *Of course he checked with his wife and got her consent before making a major decision. This is the right thing to do*. However, this would be a reading of our culture back into the text. The prevalent culture of the day would not have required her consent. The one exception under Roman law was if the property was a gift from her family to ensure her financial well-being. Then it would be her property, and he would need her consent. However, there is no indication the property was Sapphira's. It simply says they sold property, meaning it was property held within the communal bond of marriage. Because of their cultural constraints, this meant for all intents and purposes it was his property. She had knowledge of the sale and had agreed with him to hold back money. She also may have been present at the time of the sale and thus was also accountable for the act of deception.

Even though Ananias did not need Sapphira's consent, it does tell us something about the inner workings of their relationship. Sapphira knew of the property sale and the details of the deal. Thus, it says she had some level of agency within their relationship and that perhaps Ananias respected her mind and counsel. This couple is by no means a Kingdom example of honesty, but they may give us some insight into how best to conduct business with each marital partner being in full knowledge of any kind of major decision.

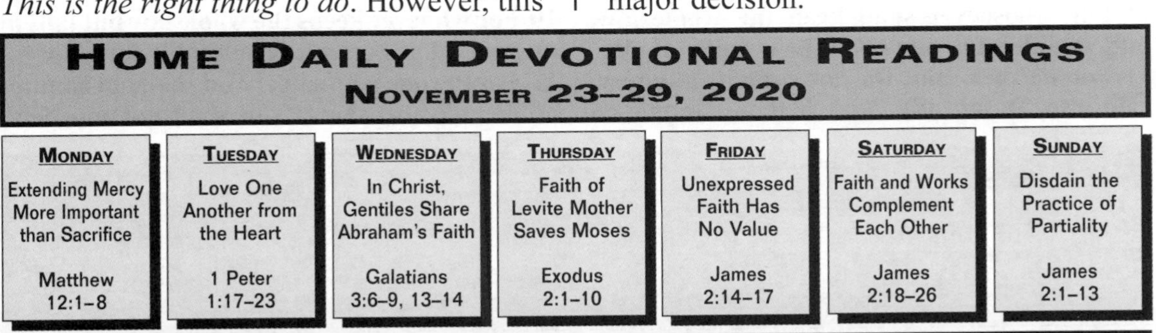

Home Daily Devotional Readings

November 23–29, 2020

Monday	Tuesday	Wednesday	Thursday	Friday	Saturday	Sunday
Extending Mercy More Important than Sacrifice	Love One Another from the Heart	In Christ, Gentiles Share Abraham's Faith	Faith of Levite Mother Saves Moses	Unexpressed Faith Has No Value	Faith and Works Complement Each Other	Disdain the Practice of Partiality
Matthew 12:1–8	1 Peter 1:17–23	Galatians 3:6–9, 13–14	Exodus 2:1–10	James 2:14–17	James 2:18–26	James 2:1–13

LESSON 13 NOVEMBER 29, 2020

IMPARTIAL LOVE

TOPIC:
A COMMUNITY OF EQUALS

BACKGROUND SCRIPTURE:
JAMES 2

JAMES 2:1–13

King James Version

MY brethren, have not the faith of our Lord Jesus Christ, the Lord of glory, with respect of persons.

2 For if there come unto your assembly a man with a gold ring, in goodly apparel, and there come in also a poor man in vile raiment;

3 And ye have respect to him that weareth the gay clothing, and say unto him, Sit thou here in a good place; and say to the poor, Stand thou there, or sit here under my footstool:

4 Are ye not then partial in yourselves, and are become judges of evil thoughts?

5 Hearken, my beloved brethren, Hath not God chosen the poor of this world rich in faith, and heirs of the kingdom which he hath promised to them that love him?

6 But ye have despised the poor. Do not rich men oppress you, and draw you before the judgment seats?

7 Do not they blaspheme that worthy name by the which ye are called?

8 If ye fulfil the royal law according to the scripture, Thou shalt love thy neighbour as thyself, ye do well:

9 But if ye have respect to persons, ye commit sin, and are convinced of the law as transgressors.

10 For whosoever shall keep the whole law, and yet offend in one point, he is guilty of all.

11 For he that said, Do not commit adultery, said also, Do not kill. Now if thou commit no

New Revised Standard Version

MY brothers and sisters, do you with your acts of favoritism really believe in our glorious Lord Jesus Christ?

2 For if a person with gold rings and in fine clothes comes into your assembly, and if a poor person in dirty clothes also comes in,

3 and if you take notice of the one wearing the fine clothes and say, "Have a seat here, please," while to the one who is poor you say, "Stand there," or, "Sit at my feet,"

4 have you not made distinctions among yourselves, and become judges with evil thoughts?

5 Listen, my beloved brothers and sisters. Has not God chosen the poor in the world to be rich in faith and to be heirs of the kingdom that he has promised to those who love him?

6 But you have dishonored the poor. Is it not the rich who oppress you? Is it not they who drag you into court?

7 Is it not they who blaspheme the excellent name that was invoked over you?

8 You do well if you really fulfill the royal law according to the scripture, "You shall love your neighbor as yourself."

9 But if you show partiality, you commit sin and are convicted by the law as transgressors.

10 For whoever keeps the whole law but fails in one point has become accountable for all of it.

11 For the one who said, "You shall not commit adultery," also said, "You shall not murder."

MAIN THOUGHT: Hearken, my beloved brethren, Hath not God chosen the poor of this world rich in faith, and heirs of the kingdom which he hath promised to them that love him?. (James 2:5, KJV)

James 2:1–13

King James Version	*New Revised Standard Version*
adultery, yet if thou kill, thou art become a transgressor of the law.	**Now if you do not commit adultery but if you murder, you have become a transgressor of the law.**
12 So speak ye, and so do, as they that shall be judged by the law of liberty.	**12 So speak and so act as those who are to be judged by the law of liberty.**
13 For he shall have judgment without mercy, that hath shewed no mercy; and mercy rejoiceth against judgment.	**13 For judgment will be without mercy to anyone who has shown no mercy; mercy triumphs over judgment.**

LESSON SETTING

Time: A.D. 50s
Place: Jerusalem

LESSON OUTLINE

I. Community of Believers (James 2:1–4)
II. The Poor of This World (James 2:5–7)
III. The Royal Law (James 2:8–13)

Unifying Principle

Favoring one person or group over others is a common occurrence in human relationships. Why is it unacceptable to show partiality to certain people or groups? James reminded us that love requires us to treat everyone equally.

Introduction

Many people fail to understand the difference between equality and equity. *Equality* is when all things are equal. *Equity* is when all things are equal and fair. Understanding this difference is essential to knowing how to address the persistent stain of racism in this country. We live in a society that defines itself by economic status—by what is owned and by the power one has. Unfortunately, the social construct of race denies many in this country the basic needs for one to become a productive citizen in this society. The burden of oppression and racism is one that has been carried on the backs and shoulders of people of color for more than four hundred years in this broken Republic. That said, we have learned to expect and cope with the evils of inequality within the world. However, it is disconcerting when this kind of conduct is reflected in the Church. The Church is to be the place where equity is not only practiced but nurtured—at least it's supposed to be.

Not much information is available regarding the contextual setting of James's audience. But from what is written, one can surmise that throughout the Christian community, the tension between the wealthy and the poor began to warp perceptions of what it means to live like Christ. In today's lesson, James addressed this contradiction head on. Cautioning against favoring the rich over the poor, James admonished believers to live out their faith in relation to others because real faith plays no favorites.

Exposition

I. Community of Believers (James 2:1–4)

Verse 1 opens with a warning for the believers of the Christian community

James was writing to: Do not hold the faith of our Lord Jesus Christ with partiality. According to the author, if they were to stand equal to each other before the presence of God, then there must be no unfair discrimination among themselves. As an example of this discrimination, James invited a hypothetical scenario drawn from everyday life with which the audience would have been familiar, The scenario consisted of two imaginary visitors who came into the assembly. The first was a man with gold rings and fine apparel that was suggestive of his wealth. The plurality of rings he wore meant he wore more than one on several different fingers to advertise his wealth. Shops during that time customarily would rent rings to those wanting to give this impression. This was in stark contrast, however, to the appearance of the other visitor, a poor man who was perhaps coming from work and as a result came dressed in filthy clothes stained by the evidence of his labor. The attractive apparel of the rich man earned special treatment for him in verse 3, as the greeter gave him a place of special honor inviting him to sit in a good place. Conversely, the soiled clothing of the poor man earned him shame and indifference to his comfort or feelings. Different than being offered a seat of honor like the rich man, he instead was given an option to either stand or sit at the greeter's footstool, showing no concern for the needs of the poor man. The position given to the poor man may give some indication to his presumed societal status. During the first century, two classes of people were made to sit on the floor—children and slaves. Clearly, the second man was no child, thus he may have been a slave. This gives reasonable explanation for his soiled clothing. As mentioned in a previous lesson, Roman society was a slavocracy. By some estimates, up to a third of the empire's population were slaves; thus, encountering a slave would not be uncommon. By his actions, the greeter was merely giving a reflection of the larger cultural norms.

In verse 4, the author used a question to accuse his readers of two distinct actions of discrimination based on the preceding example. First, they had shown partiality among themselves and were guilty of creating divisions in their midst. Second, they had become judges with evil thoughts, showing prejudicial bias against the poor, which undermined the faith and joy of the church. Their practice of favoritism to the rich at the exclusion of the same treatment being shown to the poor was inconsistent with the faith they claimed to have in the Lord Jesus. The issue was not that of disunity within the Christian fellowship brought about by the visitation of the rich man, but more generally the adoption of the world's values, reflected in their preferential treatment of the rich visitor.

As this church was drawing lines of distinction within the church, James was more concerned that they show distinction from the world. By their actions they demonstrated that instead of transforming the cultural values of the society at large, they had largely adopted a classist approach to meeting within the church. Where this would be fine in some voluntary organizations, the writer argued that the church ought to be different from what was experienced in everyday life.

II. The Poor of This World (James 2:5–7)

With the same force of emphasis regarding the command James gave to his readers in verse 1 in the direct address *My brethren*, he does so again with the added imperative *Listen*. With another rhetorical question he asked, "Has not God chosen the poor of this world to be rich in faith and to be heirs of the kingdom that he has promised to those who love him?" (James 2:5, NRSV). This is reminiscent of Luke 6:20 (NRSV), "Blessed are you who are poor, for yours is the kingdom of God." James, alongside his brother, our Lord, situated the poor at the center of God's saving work and reversed their status in that they will be made wealthy in their faith.

According to James, by not offering the poor man the seat of honor, the believers in the Christian community dishonored him by their actions. The notion of dishonor is mostly a foreign concept to our Western sensibilities. However, for their culture, dishonor would provoke real issues of shame and reinforce cultural stratifications. It was bad enough to be a slave. It was worse to be treated like one in the house of God.

In verses 6–7, James asked more rhetorical questions: "Is it not the rich who oppress you? Is is not they who drag you into court? Is it not they who blaspheme the excellent name that was invoked over you?" (NRSV). These were intended to expose the Christian community for not confronting the wealthy and their ways of exploiting the poor. James' concern, of course, was for what the poor had endured at the hands of the rich. They were being oppressed and defrauded of what little money they had to enrich the coffers of the already rich. The believers' partiality and favoritism shown to the rich, because they were rich, was an indictment to the faith, which was to blaspheme the noble name by which they were called a child of God and follower of Christ.

In a parallel manner, James also was asking these questions with the understanding that those who were members of this church were not considered wealthy. It was akin to Paul's statement to the Corinthian church: "Not many of you were wise by human standards, not many were powerful, not many were of noble birth" (1 Cor. 1:26, NRSV). They were being oppressed and having to deal with the ravages of a system that was designed to keep them down and lock them out. James's question was, *Why are you emulating those who have been horrible to you?* The issue was whether they would have the courage and faith to do something different than that to which they were exposed. They were to choose the egalitarian mores of the early Christian movement and forsake the hierarchy of the imperial culture.

III. The Royal Law (James 2:8–13)

In Verse 8, James reminded his audience that the antidote to the wrong attitude of preferential treatment toward the rich at the expense of the poor was to fulfill or maintain what he called the *royal law* according to the Scripture. He was referencing Leviticus 19:18 (NRSV): "You shall love your neighbor as yourself." This citation was rooted in both the teachings of Jesus and Old Testament requirements. Under this law, there should be no acts of favoritism to anyone because all are equal recipients of the love that's due them. Therefore, as it was established by the law and taught by Jesus Christ, to love your neighbor as yourself goes hand in hand with one's sincere love for God. One is not valid without the other. If the believers did this, according to James, they would do well.

To love completely is to show no partiality. This is the point of godly love, to overcome the deficits of humanity and the ways in which human beings are unequal. Love in this way is the great equalizer. By choosing to follow the example of God in Christ, the poor cannot be differentiated from the rich for each one is a neighbor in need of love. To love thy neighbor is an injunction to impartiality, equity, and justice. To love the neighbor as self is to consider the neighbor's needs as you consider the needs of any, whether rich or poor, as one considers the needs of his or her own self.

However, the conditional conjunction *but* in verse 9 preempts the contrast. If you show partiality, you commit sin and are convicted as transgressors of the law. Some people saw God's law as containing many detached requirements forbidding such actions as murder, adultery, and robbery. They failed to see its unity. They may have felt that strict obedience at one point would compensate for disobedience elsewhere. But according to the author, whoever kept the whole law and yet stumbled in one point was guilty of all. Verse 11 presses James's point with two examples of breaking God's law—adultery and murder—further stressing that sin is never a question of breaking a single law but a matter of violating the integrity of the whole law.

James clearly followed in the thought pattern of Jesus as understanding the royal law to be the heart of the law in its entirety. To love God and to love neighbor are not to be negotiated. To fail to love neighbor by partiality and favoritism is to violate the heart of the law. This, of course, is to violate the One who has given the law, namely God. This is also why if one breaks the law on one point, he or she is guilty of its entirety. The law, therefore, is not seen negatively but as a guide to a life that is unto God.

Lastly in this regard, earlier in the text James alluded to Leviticus 19:15 as he stated they had become unjust judges. "You shall not render an unjust judgment; you shall not be partial to the poor or defer to the great: with justice you shall judge your neighbor" (Lev. 19:15, NRSV). James's claim obviously was not without law precedent. Their indictment was clear. They had violated the law by showing preferential treatment to the rich. According to Leviticus 19:15, no partiality was to be given to rich or poor, but judges were to consider only the facts of a case.

James summarized this section with a final admonition to his readers to treat others both in what was said and done as those whose actions would be judged by the law of liberty. This was a reminder that all will be judged. In particular, those who claim a knowledge of God will be judged according to the Word of God. Those who know better are expected to do better. God will not show mercy to the one who has shown no mercy. Mercy is always better than judgment.

The Lesson Applied

God's love shows no favorites, and yet we all are His favorite. But in the Church today, like James's audience, partiality is shown. People who are considered of a wealthier status and contribute generously to the church often are given preferred attention while those who require attention often are overlooked. Amid the cloud of conferences, conventions, and consecration services meticulously orchestrated by the esteemed apostles, bishops, and so-called prophets, where do the masses gather for missions? If we claim to be children of God and desire to represent His presence in this world, our obligation to the faith is to adopt the mission of Christ: "The Spirit of the Lord God is upon me,because the Lord has anointed me;he has sent me to bring good news to the oppressed, to bind up the brokenhearted,to proclaim liberty to the captives, and release to the prisoners; to proclaim the year of the Lord's favor" (Isaiah 61:1–2 (NRSV, see also Luke 4:16-18). We are called to address the needs of the poor, the disenfranchised, the underserved, and the overlooked because these are the children of God as well.

Let's Talk About It

Are there any examples from history that show the kind of partial unjust treatment referenced by James?

Yes. During the period of American enslavement in the eighteenth and nineteenth centuries, the cultural norm was to force Blacks to sit in the balcony during church service. It was such an ingrained practice that it was the norm even in "free" states such as Pennsylvania. This was the case at Saint George Methodist Episcopal Church of Philadelphia where Richard Allen and Absalom Jones were members and preachers. Their Black membership were not granted the same rights and privileges as white members. They were not even allowed to pray at the altar, during the time for prayer.

Allen described one such event. The two led a walkout in protest, never returned, and formed their own congregations. "We had not been long upon our knees before I heard a considerable scuffling and low talking, I raised my head up and saw one of the trustees, ... having hold of the Rev. Absalom Jones, pulling him up off his knees, and saying, 'You must get up—you must not kneel here.' Mr. Jones replied, 'Wait until prayer is over.' The trustee, 'No, you must get up now or I will call for aid and force you away'" (White, 179). True religion is not based on racial characteristics.

Home Daily Devotional Readings
November 30–December 6, 2020

Monday	Tuesday	Wednesday	Thursday	Friday	Saturday	Sunday
God's Anointed Ruler of All Nations	Blessed and Chosen in Christ	Christ, Head over All People/Things	In the Family Line of David	God Anoints Jesus King	Jesus, Creator and Eternal Ruler	Expectations of Jesus Before His Birth
Psalm 2	Ephesians 1:1–14	Ephesians 1:15–23	Matthew 1:1–15	Hebrews 1:6–9	Hebrews 1:10–14	Hebrews 1:1–5; Matthew 1:1–6, 16–17

Second Quarter

December

January

February

Called through Heritage

Adult Topic: Fulfilling One's Calling

Background Scripture: Hebrews 1; Matthew 1:1–17

Hebrews 1:1–5; Matthew 1:1–6, 16–17

King James Version

GOD, who at sundry times and in divers manners spake in time past unto the fathers by the prophets,
2 Hath in these last days spoken unto us by his Son, whom he hath appointed heir of all things, by whom also he made the worlds;
3 Who being the brightness of his glory, and the express image of his person, and upholding all things by the word of his power, when he had by himself purged our sins, sat down on the right hand of the Majesty on high;
4 Being made so much better than the angels, as he hath by inheritance obtained a more excellent name than they.
5 For unto which of the angels said he at any time, Thou art my Son, this day have I begotten thee? And again, I will be to him a Father, and he shall be to me a Son?

• • • Matthew 1:1–6, 16–17 • • •

THE book of the generation of Jesus Christ, the son of David, the son of Abraham.
2 Abraham begat Isaac; and Isaac begat Jacob; and Jacob begat Judah and his brethren;
3 And Judah begat Phares and Zara of Thamar; and Phares begat Esrom; and Esrom begat Aram;
4 And Aram begat Aminadab; and Aminadab begat Naasson; and Naasson begat Salmon;
5 And Salmon begat Booz of Rahab; and Booz begat Obed of Ruth; and Obed begat Jesse;

New Revised Standard Version

LONG ago God spoke to our ancestors in many and various ways by the prophets,
2 but in these last days he has spoken to us by a Son, whom he appointed heir of all things, through whom he also created the worlds.
3 He is the reflection of God's glory and the exact imprint of God's very being, and he sustains all things by his powerful word. When he had made purification for sins, he sat down at the right hand of the Majesty on high,
4 having become as much superior to angels as the name he has inherited is more excellent than theirs.
5 For to which of the angels did God ever say, "You are my Son; today I have begotten you"? Or again, "I will be his Father, and he will be my Son"?

• • • Matthew 1:1–6, 16–17 • • •

AN account of the genealogy of Jesus the Messiah, the son of David, the son of Abraham.
2 Abraham was the father of Isaac, and Isaac the father of Jacob, and Jacob the father of Judah and his brothers,
3 and Judah the father of Perez and Zerah by Tamar, and Perez the father of Hezron, and Hezron the father of Aram,
4 and Aram the father of Aminadab, and Aminadab the father of Nahshon, and Nahshon the father of Salmon,
5 and Salmon the father of Boaz by Rahab, and Boaz the father of Obed by Ruth, and Obed the father of Jesse,

MAIN THOUGHT: [God] Hath in these last days spoken unto us by his Son, whom he hath appointed heir of all things, by whom also he made the worlds. (Hebrews 1:2, KJV)

Hebrews 1:1–5, Matthew 1:1–6, 16–17

King James Version

6 And Jesse begat David the king; and David the king begat Solomon of her that had been the wife of Urias;

• • • • • •

16 And Jacob begat Joseph the husband of Mary, of whom was born Jesus, who is called Christ.
17 So all the generations from Abraham to David are fourteen generations; and from David until the carrying away into Babylon are fourteen generations; and from the carrying away into Babylon unto Christ are fourteen generations.

New Revised Standard Version

6 and Jesse the father of King David. And David was the father of Solomon by the wife of Uriah,

• • • • • •

16 and Jacob the father of Joseph the husband of Mary, of whom Jesus was born, who is called the Messiah.
17 So all the generations from Abraham to David are fourteen generations; and from David to the deportation to Babylon, fourteen generations; and from the deportation to Babylon to the Messiah, fourteen generations.

LESSON SETTING

Time: *circa* A.D. 60–70 (Hebrews)
***circa* 6 B.C. (Matthew)**
Place: Rome (Hebrews)
Judea (Matthew)

LESSON OUTLINE

I. The Eternal Savior (Hebrews 1:1–5)
II. The Ultimate Savior (Matthew 1:1–6, 16–17)

Unifying Principle

Where we come from often speaks volumes about what we are like. How are people rooted in what has come before? Hebrews affirms the ultimate origins of Jesus in the life of God, and Matthew explains how He was the product of His long biblical heritage.

Introduction

This lesson merges the writings of two authors, Matthew and the anonymous writer of Hebrews, who demonstrated the celestial provision of a Savior to humankind. In both writings, the idea was to confirm the biological lineage through God's chosen humans and the eternal aspect of Jesus from the existence of time to an audience of primarily Jewish believers. These authors provided documentation in the family dynasty of Jesus that was both genetic and cosmic. Matthew's goal was to dispel the thought that Jesus' beginning started with His birth in Bethlehem, to show He was rooted in a past that demonstrated God's plan. The writer of Hebrews hoped to testify to the Son's authority and worthiness above any and all human agents. Together they helped give us a more complete understanding of Jesus the Christ.

Exposition

I. The Eternal Savior (Hebrews 1:1–5)

Fulfilling his desire to cement the superiority of Jesus in the annals of Scripture and the knowledge of believers, the unknown writer of Hebrews began the missive by describing how He had spoken to the many prophets throughout the periods of the world. Although the English verse begins with *God,* the original Greek text begins with *In many parts and in many ways,* which reads like the opening of a formal Greek oration rather than the customary greetings of a letter. The term πολυμερῶς (*polymeros*) is used to mean "in many parts, in many portions, or in many times," and describes the myriad of places and occurrences where God spoke to (and through) His prophets. Additionally, the term πολυτρόπως (*polytropos*), meaning "in many ways or kinds of ways," indicates God's constant aggressiveness in implementing His message. The Scriptures are filled with descriptions of the methods in God's directing of His message to (and through) His chosen leaders. Moreover, although he did not identify any of the prophets by name, the writer made it obvious God spoke from the beginning of creation, establishing a time period: *Long ago God spoke to the fathers, our ancestors, and the prophets.* This opening verse could have read, *In the beginning*, to solidify the time line of this message and to denote the many ways and methods God used to reveal Himself.

The writer of Hebrews moved from his initial message and manner into the rationale of God's series of revelations throughout history, which led to the fulfillment of the gift of His Son. The opening of the Gospel of John is reflected here, as John explained Christ was in existence before time began, stating, "In the beginning was the Word, and the Word was with God, and the Word was God. He was in the beginning with God. All things came into being through him" (John 1:1–3, NRSV). A time line is continued from the beginning of creation to the last days, using the term ἔσχατος (*eschatos*) to describe the furthest distance in time. During this period, God's message is accomplished and achieved in His Son, whom God appointed as Savior of the world. The term used here is τίθημι (*tithemi*), which means God put in place the method through which the gift of Jesus allows us to become beneficiaries of God's love and the gift of eternal life. Because the Son has inherited all elements of the Father, and due to our acceptance and discipleship with Jesus, we are in a position to become inheritors (κληρονόμος, *kleronomos*) of all things of God. Again, John's reference to the Son's (the Word's) existence from the beginning is tantamount to understanding the importance and the supremacy of Christ.

Continuing to bask in the presentation of the Son, the writer of Hebrews was ebullient and mesmerized in the description of the Savior! Notice the descriptions seem to reflect the physical appearance of the Son. The Greek term ἀπαύγασμα (*apaugasma*), meaning "radiance or brightness," was used in verse 3 to embellish the character or attributes of the true representation and nature of the Son. This glory is not restricted to the superficial aspect but serves to describe the spiritual appearances or attributes of the Son. The combination of His nature is best described by the term ὑπόστασις (*hypostasis*), which attempts to explain the essence or substance of which He is made. The important of His radiance cements Him as the Light of the World in an effulgence or flood of resplendent light. This light exudes the power to uphold all of the components and aspects of the world simply by the power of His word. Recall God spoke creation into existence (Gen. 1:1–31), and Jesus healed the lepers through a spoken phrase (Luke 17:12–14). This power allowed Jesus to become the ultimate sacrifice of the remission of sin (or separation of the Son from His people). It led Him to sit at the right or strong hand of the Father, where He advocates for the saved in heaven that they may receive the gift of eternal life.

The author made it clear Jesus cannot be compared or confused with the angels. The angels have their respective functions and positions in God's Kingdom; however, their existence is steeped in assisting God and serving humankind. In both Matthew and Luke, angels served as messengers and a support system at Jesus' birth, to the people, and for the holy family. R. Kent Hughes argues the angels have at least four specific functions:

1. Angels continuously worship and praise the God they serve.
2. Angels communicate God's message to humans.
3. Angels minister to believers.
4. Angels will be God's agents in the final earthly judgments and second coming.

Additionally, certain angels have a checkered history, prompting Augustine to declare they sinned and were thrust down to the lowest parts of this world where they are incarcerated until their final damnation in the Day of Judgment. The Apostle Peter plainly declared that when he said, "God did not spare the angels when they sinned, but cast them into hell and committed them to chains of deepest darkness to be kept until the judgment" (2 Pet. 2:4, NRSV). Therefore, angels have the capacity to sin or become separated from God, which is impossible for Jesus. The writer declared that by His inheritance Jesus has a more excellent name than those of the angels who exist to serve Him.

The author concluded verse 5 with two rhetorical questions that were not meant to display a sense of arrogance or condescension but were intended to dispel some Jewish believers who were in danger of compromising Jesus' superiority. The angels could not be in a position to ask these two questions; therefore, the writer isolated their position in the hierarchy of heaven and their relationship to God. To further demonstrate the position of the angels and allay any possible confusion for these Jewish believers, the original Greek term for *begotten* (*μονογενής, monogenes*), or *only, one and only* (John 3:16), is not used to modify God's relationship to the Son as found in other scriptural passages. Instead, the term used is *γεννάω* (*gennao*), meaning "the parent of, or the father of." P. Ellingworth and E. A. Nida argue, in this strict theological sense, that in the first question, *You* and *Son* are emphasized, and *I have become your Father* avoids the metaphor *begotten,* which could be misleading for various reasons. The first reason is because the English word is archaic. Second, in English, as in some other languages, the verb *beget* is not often used as a metaphor. Third, it could suggest the Son did not exist until the moment at which God said, "I have begotten you." Technically, in verse 5, there should be no complication in this expression, which denies God's relationship to an angel. But indirectly, this statement is to be interpreted as the relation of God to His Son. The argument is for the sake of clarity. There should not be any confusion that Jesus is not the Son through any other means, such as adoption, but the Sonship is eternal. In this idea, the rhetorical question is answered.

II. The Ultimate Savior (Matthew 1:1–6, 16–17)

The Scriptures promised an eternal dynasty of Davidic rule, which was not simply an earthly empire but a continuous line that is of God. Two genealogies are presented in the New Testament, chronicled by Matthew and Luke. However, the names can be different and the direction of the genealogies are opposite. For example, Matthew's genealogy begins with Abraham and ends with Jesus (Matt. 1:1–16), whereas Luke's begins with Jesus and ends with God (Luke 3:23–38). The Greek term *γένεσις* (*genesis*) is used to denote genealogy. However, a more lucid understanding is based on the origin, existence, and lineage of the *Χριστός* (*Christos*), the Anointed One. The Greek texts do not use the term for *Messiah* until Matthew 2:4. In a number of languages, *Χριστός or Μεσσίας* (*Messias*)as a reference to the Messiah occurs in a transliterated form based either on *Χριστός* in Greek or on *Messiah* in Hebrew. Still yet, in some languages, an attempt is made to represent the significance of the terms *Χριστός* and *Μεσσίας* by translating "God's appointed one" or "God's specially chosen one" or "the expected one," in the sense of one to whom everyone was looking for help and deliverance. The name *Jesus* (*Yeshua*) was a popular name of the period and is a form of the name *Joshua*, which in Hebrew means "the Lord is salvation," whereas the Hebrew *Messiah* (*Meshiah*) means "Anointed One." Jesus was called the *son of David*, which was a popular manner in the linkage of a family. This did not indicate David was the father of Jesus but would clearly place the subject in the lineage of the family. Matthew chronicled Jesus' ancestry through Joseph, Jesus' legal (though not natural) father, and it established His claim and right to the throne of David.

Matthew started Jesus' genealogy with Abraham and reminded us of the promise that Abraham and his seed would be a great nation (Gen. 12:2). Matthew emphasized the connection to Abraham in the chronology of these members of the family tree. The registering of this dynasty was complete with the importance of the twelve tribes of Israel and the connection and additional promise to David. Moreover, the importance of the bloodline of lineage in the Jewish family was highlighted in the birthright issue between Jacob and Esau. An interesting aspect of the genealogy was in the manner in which the parent (mostly father) and sons were connected. The NKJV Bible uses the term *begot* to denote the father and his subsequent son, whereas the NASB and the original Greek use *the father of*. It is interesting, however, that four women, plus Mary, are in the genealogy presented by Matthew. The women are listed as Tamar, Rahab, Ruth, and Bathsheba, Solomon's mother. In contrast to the wording of *begat* or *father*, the women were connected to these sons using the terms *of* or *by*, with Judah as the father of Perez and Zerah *by*

Tamar (v. 3). Mary was mentioned (v. 16), and there is a change in the wording from *the father of* to *of whom was born* Jesus. *Of whom* is a feminine relative pronoun (*ex hēs*), clearly indicating Jesus was the physical child of Mary but Joseph was not His physical father.

Joseph was listed as the husband of Mary, of whom Jesus was born. The phrase in verse 16, *ἐκ ὅς γεννάω (ek hos gennao)*, is translated as *of whom was born*. However, *γεννάω* (*gennao*; *parent*) also could mean "father of." This term also indicated the male role as causing the conception and birth of a child—to be the father of, to procreate, to beget. Charles Ryrie notes that Matthew used the phrase *by whom*, which is feminine singular, indicating clearly that Jesus was born of Mary only and not of Mary and Joseph. It is one of the strongest evidences for Jesus' virgin birth. Nonetheless, the Greek term *μήτηρ* (*meter*), meaning "mother," is not used until Matthew noted that "his mother Mary had been engaged to Joseph" (Matt. 1:18, NRSV). Although Joseph and Mary were Jesus' parents, Matthew demonstrated the child was a product of the Holy Spirit.

The Lesson Applied

The genealogy that connects to the beginning of existence and the Davidic promise that a seed of his lineage would forever inherit the throne of God is part of the messianic fulfillment. This act is a gift to all believers and was expressed almost poetically by Matthew. However, the subsequent Hebrew writer also did not refute this concept or dilute its importance. We discover the Hebrews writer explaining the supremacy of God by his argument that the Son has existed from the beginning of time (*χρόνος, chronos*) or eternity.

Let's Talk About It

Why do many demonstrative preachers conclude their sermons by exclaiming, "He came down through forty-two generations"?

This "close out" declared Jesus was given to us as a promise God fulfilled through this successive family group. Matthew stated that all of the generations from Abraham to David were fourteen generations; from David to the deportation to Babylon, fourteen generations; and from the deportation to Babylon to the Messiah, fourteen generations (Matt. 1:17). It is an expression that shows God's patience and care within salvation history. As many families become interested in their genealogy, they will discover prominent historical aspects, such as wars, the election of presidents, and social movements. Knowing who we come from is important as it tells who we have the capacity to be!

Home Daily Devotional Readings
December 7–13, 2020

Monday	Tuesday	Wednesday	Thursday	Friday	Saturday	Sunday
Sign of God's Presence	Called as Light to the Nations	Called to Mission Before Birth	Birth of Jesus Foretold to Mary	Simeon Foretells Jesus' Ministry	Mary, in the Lineage of Ruth	Miracle of the Holy Spirit Conception
Isaiah 7:10–15	Isaiah 42:1–9	Isaiah 49:1–7	Luke 1:26–38	Luke 2:34–38	Ruth 4:9–17	Matthew 1:18–25

CALLED BEFORE BIRTH

ADULT TOPIC:
CALLED TO PARTICIPATE IN A PROMISE

BACKGROUND SCRIPTURE:
MATTHEW 1:18–25

MATTHEW 1:18–25

King James Version

NOW the birth of Jesus Christ was on this wise: When as his mother Mary was espoused to Joseph, before they came together, she was found with child of the Holy Ghost.

19 Then Joseph her husband, being a just man, and not willing to make her a publick example, was minded to put her away privily.
20 But while he thought on these things, behold, the angel of the Lord appeared unto him in a dream, saying, Joseph, thou son of David, fear not to take unto thee Mary thy wife: for that which is conceived in her is of the Holy Ghost.
21 And she shall bring forth a son, and thou shalt call his name JESUS: for he shall save his people from their sins.
22 Now all this was done, that it might be fulfilled which was spoken of the Lord by the prophet, saying,
23 Behold, a virgin shall be with child, and shall bring forth a son, and they shall call his name Emmanuel, which being interpreted is, God with us.
24 Then Joseph being raised from sleep did as the angel of the Lord had bidden him, and took unto him his wife:
25 And knew her not till she had brought forth her firstborn son: and he called his name JESUS.

New Revised Standard Version

NOW the birth of Jesus the Messiah took place in this way. When his mother Mary had been engaged to Joseph, but before they lived together, she was found to be with child from the Holy Spirit.
19 Her husband Joseph, being a righteous man and unwilling to expose her to public disgrace, planned to dismiss her quietly.
20 But just when he had resolved to do this, an angel of the Lord appeared to him in a dream and said, "Joseph, son of David, do not be afraid to take Mary as your wife, for the child conceived in her is from the Holy Spirit.
21 She will bear a son, and you are to name him Jesus, for he will save his people from their sins."
22 All this took place to fulfill what had been spoken by the Lord through the prophet:

23 "Look, the virgin shall conceive and bear a son, and they shall name him Emmanuel," which means, "God is with us."

24 When Joseph awoke from sleep, he did as the angel of the Lord commanded him; he took her as his wife,
25 but had no marital relations with her until she had borne a son; and he named him Jesus.

MAIN THOUGHT: But while he thought on these things, behold, the angel of the Lord appeared unto him in a dream, saying, Joseph, thou son of David, fear not to take unto thee Mary thy wife: for that which is conceived in her is of the Holy Ghost. And she shall bring forth a son, and thou shalt call his name JESUS: for he shall save his people from their sins. (Matthew 1:20–21, KJV)

LESSON SETTING

Time: ***circa*** **6 B.C.**
Place: Judea

LESSON OUTLINE

I. Joseph's Dilemma (Matthew 1:18–19)
II. Joseph's Dream (Matthew 1:20–21)
III. The Message of Joseph's Dream (Matthew 1:22–23)
IV. The Realization of Joseph's Dream (Matthew 1:24–25)

UNIFYING PRINCIPLE

A newborn baby inspires us to wonder about the potential of every human life. How do we understand the designs of our lives? Joseph's call to form a family with Mary suggests God calls us to give hope to the world through our families.

INTRODUCTION

Matthew provided this sequel to the initial introduction or genealogy of Jesus to cement the place of Mary and Joseph in their parentage of the child, born to be the Savior of the world. This backstory sheds light on the human conflicts that are presented when humankind is chosen to serve a cosmic purpose. Although Matthew presented the virgin birth, Mary's perpetual virginity does not serve the same purpose as the initial virgin birth of Jesus. The virginity of Mary was important to underscore because she was impregnated by the Holy Spirit, and her body was special in the carrying and delivering of this baby. Matthew explained how Joseph overcame his reluctance to marry Mary and thus became a servant in God's plan.

EXPOSITION

I. JOSEPH'S DILEMMA (MATTHEW 1:18–19)

In a period of traditional Jewish law that did not accept children born out of wedlock, Matthew was forced to explain the circumstances surrounding the birth of Jesus and the relationship between the parents, Mary and Joseph. The birth or origin of Jesus was a scandal because cohabitation was not acceptable, and the product of a child was even more deplorable. Matthew actually fueled the scandal of their union by noting the couple was not officially married according to Jewish law and custom. He stated that while they were in the engagement period or betrothed, and before they were married, she was found with child. The Greek term *συνέρχομαι* (*synerchomai*), "come together," could be thought of as "before they were married." However, it also could mean that "before they had sexual consummation," Mary discovered she had a child in her womb. One of the keys to accepting the situation presented by Matthew is centered around the meaning of the betrothal period in Jewish marriage customs.

Marriages were arranged for individuals by parents, and contracts were negotiated. After this was accomplished, the individuals were considered married and were called husband and wife. They did not, however, begin to live together. Instead, the woman continued to live with her parents, and the man with his, for one year. The waiting period was to demonstrate the faithfulness of the pledge of purity given concerning the bride. If the one-year waiting period demonstrated the purity of the bride, the husband would then go to the house of the bride's parents and, in a grand processional march, lead his bride back to his home. There they would begin to live together as husband and wife and consummate their marriage physically.

Matthew explained Mary was with child, or that in her womb was the child of the Holy Spirit. She would be called the *christotokos* ("mother of Christ" or "child-bearer"), which would give her credibility in this seemingly shameful situation. The account does focus on the fact Mary and Joseph had not been sexually active—this birth was brought about by God through His Holy Spirit. Matthew's story should be read with this background in mind.

Joseph found himself in a dilemma. According to their customs and laws, his betrothed fiancée was in danger of being disgraced or punished. Although adultery laws seemed to protect the man, these proud Jewish families would have been devastated to learn of Mary's pregnancy. Additionally, there was the aspect of Joseph's sensibilities. As a man, his friends probably would deride and publicly humiliate him, adding to the pressure of how he would handle this situation. Throughout the Scriptures, unmarried pregnancies were frowned upon, and there were many variants of how these situations were adjudicated. Joseph was engaged to Mary; thus, he did not violate the component of the law that decreed a man who violated a virgin who was not engaged must pay the father fifty shekels for the woman and marry her without the provision for divorce (Deut. 22:28–29). Therefore, Joseph's situation may have involved humiliation and social ostracism more so than the danger of Mary being put to death by stoning. Matthew reminded his readers Joseph was a righteous or just man who loved Mary. Joseph had a plan to send her away to shield her from the disgrace of the social ostracism she obviously would face in the clannish village of Nazareth. The Greek term used here is *δειγματίζω* (*deigmatizo*), meaning "to disgrace." However, a better understanding of what Joseph wanted to avoid was putting Mary on public display, knowing the pain and anguish it would cause the young mother-to-be. As Matthew explained Joseph's frame of mind, his intent or wish was to protect Mary. Matthew did not provide any further details of the plan, such as where he would send Mary or if he had made any provisions with family or friends as to whom she would live with during her pregnancy. Matthew only recounted she would be sent away. He also suggested Joseph wished to secretly divorce Mary because of the use of the term *ἀπολύω* (*apoluo*), which means "to release or to set free." Nevertheless, it is obvious Joseph's concern for Mary's safety and well-being, both physically and emotionally, was his primary interest for this teenage girl.

II. Joseph's Dream (Matthew 1:20–21)

Pondering his dilemma, Joseph decided on a plan that could solve this problem, albeit temporary at best. Matthew did not disclose Joseph's innermost thoughts, such as whether he wanted to be with Mary after the baby was born. At this time, Joseph believed Mary had been unfaithful to him and had become pregnant by another man. Joseph knew he had not slept with Mary, and the thought of her betrayal must have been devastating. Matthew, however, provided insight into the issue at hand—what seemed to be a curse was actually a blessing! It was up to Joseph to believe the angel and rely upon his faith in the Lord. Remember, Joseph had been described as a righteous man, but he was also a devout man, a practicing Jew who believed in the God of his fathers. The genealogy of Joseph was provided to place the "spiritual Joseph" in the line of the promised dynasty of David.

Matthew turned the account by explaining that although Joseph was sure of his plans, when he had considered this (*ἐνθυμέομαι, enthymeomai*) or concluded with his solution, God sent an angel to change his mind and course of action. God's solution was not based on protecting Mary from humiliation but was to ensure Joseph believed in what was the most unthinkable, that this child was a product of the Holy Spirit. Joseph needed to stir up his faith to trust the message that both he and Mary were chosen to be instruments of God. Joseph was told, "Do not be afraid or frightened because your union has found favor with God." This angelic assurance to fear not is also found in the message that was given to the frightened shepherds at the announcement of Jesus' birth (Luke 2:8–14).

Continuing the message, Joseph was notified that Mary would bear and give birth to a son. In a period when contemporary medical technology such as an ultrasound (which may be used to determine the gender of a baby still in the womb) was nonexistent, Joseph was told the child would be a male. This was further evidence the dream was from heaven. Additionally, the angel demonstrated the significance of his missive in that the name of the child had been decided by heaven. He would be called Jesus, which was a surprisingly common name. *Jesus* means "Jehovah is his help or Jehovah the Savior." Joseph also was told this precious child would be gifted with the power to save or deliver His people (Israel) from their sin. Israel's sin was an egregious failure that had been a source of damnation for Israel and a basis for their being out of favor with God. God, however, in His gracious nature, decided to bequeath this gift of His Son as a remedy for all of the world's needs. The significance of His common name was that Jesus was to be a gift to the people.

Joseph was commanded to ignore his previous plans and take Mary as his wife. Awakening from his dream, he simply had to believe the message and follow the direction of the Lord, who ultimately would secure the protection and well-being of the holy family. Joseph had to rely on his faith and believe the angelic message! God's messages are not always the easiest to believe.

III. The Message of Joseph's Dream (Matthew 1:22–23)

At this juncture, Matthew (not the angel) was speaking as he explained this all happened to complete what was spoken by the Lord through the prophet Isaiah. The announcement of Mary's pregnancy and what was to take place was a fulfillment of Isaiah's prophecy. In Old Testament literature, the prophets spoke for God and provided direction and warnings about future events. Prophets functioned as emissaries that stood between God and His people. Matthew noted the gift of this child was a prophetic fulfillment by quoting from Isaiah that the virgin's conception of a son was of God. For Isaiah, the name of the child was important. However, Isaiah did not call Him Jesus but prophesied the child would be named Immanuel, which is translated as "God with us" (Isa. 7:14).

During Isaiah's time, the constant threat of invasion by foreign powers affected him deeply. Isaiah tried to assure the people God had not neglected them and their most immediate need was to return their lives back to God. A direct understanding of Isaiah's message was to convince the people that salvation and deliverance were possible through repentance and hope in the coming Messiah. Isaiah's prophecy fit with the kingly motif Matthew highlighted in his Gospel, especially in his birth narrative of Jesus as King, noting the conflict with Herod the Great and the following of the star that led the Wise Men or Magi to the one born King of the Jews. The knowledge and understanding that "God is with us" was crucial for the security and future of the nation of Israel. Isaiah realized the God of deliverance who brought them out of Egypt was their only source of liberation. The Assyrians (722 B.C.) and Babylonians (586 B.C.) would occupy the land, and Isaiah's message was crucial in persuading the people to forsake their godless pride and return to the service of Yahweh. Later the land would be occupied by the Greeks and, in Jesus' day, the Romans. There was an obvious need for the people to know that "God is with us." The child is referred to as Immanuel only in Matthew, but Isaiah's prophecy was a significant reminder and assurance that this child was to be a Savior to His people and God had not forsaken them.

IV. The Realization of Joseph's Dream (Matthew 1:24–25)

Joseph responded to the message by following the command of the angel. When he awakened, Joseph was convinced he had experienced a mandatory directive from God, not just a dream. Matthew did not explain how Joseph took Mary as his wife. There is not an account of a wedding ceremony or the acceptance of the union by the families, which was probably insignificant for Matthew and not crucial to the narrative. The command to marry Mary in verse 20 was the answer to Joseph's fear. What was important was the meaning of the command, "Do not be afraid to take Mary as your wife" (NRSV). The reference, of course, was to the final phase in the marital arrangement, whereby the husband took his wife to his home. William Barclay renders it, "Do not hesitate to marry Mary." The act of Joseph moving Mary into his house signified the conclusion of the betrothal or engagement period, which would allow them to put behind them the fear of the out-of-wedlock pregnancy. The message from God that Joseph understood was the child was not biologically his but was a gift by the Holy Spirit. Therefore, Joseph was to place his trust in God and serve as the earthly father.

Matthew continued the response from Joseph's dream by keeping the virgin concept alive and stating that although Joseph married Mary (he moved her into his house), they did not have any sexual relations. It is probable they could have had sex, depending upon how far along she was in her pregnancy or within the period of her pregnancy. The NASB translates the initial phrase in verse 25 as he "kept her a virgin until she gave birth."It is interesting an emphasis was placed on this restriction, as the original Greek manuscript renders it as, "Joseph did not know her until she gave birth to a son," with the meaning of *knowing her* being a euphemism for sexual relations. Obviously, the emphasis of the text was to relay the awesomeness of Jesus' conception. It would have been a signal for early readers that the child to be born was of notable significance. This is a biblical motif—many of the notable characters of the Old Testament had miraculous circumstances surrounding their births. As examples, consider Samuel and Isaac who were born to women unable to conceive. The virgin conception and subsequent birth takes this motif to the next level. In most circumstances virgins are unable to give birth, obviously. If a virgin gives birth, the child undoubtedly will come forth in great power and significance.

The Lesson Applied

Mary was designated to be the mother of Jesus and, therefore, could not have been touched sexually by a man. A thought exists about the perpetuity of Mary's virginity and the concept that Joseph was a widower with children from his previous marriage. Joseph was a dignified man, filled with the pride of an upstanding Jew; therefore, to be engaged to a woman, pregnant with a child he did not father, created a stressful situation, to say the least. Joseph, however, was to serve a purpose that was created and ordained by God. The couple eventually had other children, who were Jesus' younger brothers and sisters who might not have understood their older brother or have been in a position to influence His ministry.

Let's Talk About It

Is there anything that should be believed about Mary?

Mary was not chosen by God to absolve sin or serve as a pathway to eternal life. Separate from giving birth to Jesus, Mary was not given powers of signs and wonders (that we will witness in Acts) or any other attributes other than her being a good mother to Jesus. In certain churches, images of Jesus are absent (a good thing) but often are replaced with statues of Mary (a bad thing). The Scriptures do not support the idea that Mary is to be prayed to, but do support that as the mother of Jesus, she is to be honored and respected, but not worshiped.

Home Daily Devotional Readings

December 14–20, 2020

Monday	Tuesday	Wednesday	Thursday	Friday	Saturday	Sunday
Midwives Frustrate Pharaoh's Decree	God Answers Solomon's Dream	Insight into the Meaning of Dreams	In Christ No Divisions Allowed	Gracious Ruler to Come from Bethlehem	Successful Return from Egypt	Safe in the Midst of Danger
Exodus 1:15–22	1 Kings 3:5–14	Daniel 1:8–17	Galatians 3:25–29	Micah 5:1–5	Matthew 2:19–23	Matthew 2:7–15

A REGAL RESPONSE TO HOLY LIGHT

ADULT TOPIC:
INTERNATIONAL HONOR FOR THE KING OF THE WORLD

BACKGROUND SCRIPTURE:
MATTHEW 2:7–15

MATTHEW 2:7–15

King James Version

THEN Herod, when he had privily called the
wise men, enquired of them diligently what
time the star appeared.
8 And he sent them to Bethlehem, and said,
Go and search diligently for the young child;
and when ye have found him, bring me word
again, that I may come and worship him also.
9 When they had heard the king, they departed; and, lo, the star, which they saw in the east,
went before them, till it came and stood over
where the young child was.
10 When they saw the star, they rejoiced with
exceeding great joy.
11 And when they were come into the house,
they saw the young child with Mary his mother,
and fell down, and worshipped him: and when
they had opened their treasures, they presented unto him gifts; gold, and frankincense,
and myrrh.
12 And being warned of God in a dream that
they should not return to Herod, they departed
into their own country another way.
13 And when they were departed, behold, the
angel of the Lord appeareth to Joseph in a
dream, saying, Arise, and take the young child
and his mother, and flee into Egypt, and be
thou there until I bring thee word: for Herod
will seek the young child to destroy him.
14 When he arose, he took the young child and
his mother by night, and departed into Egypt:

New Revised Standard Version

THEN Herod secretly called for the wise men
and learned from them the exact time when the
star had appeared.
8 Then he sent them to Bethlehem, saying,
"Go and search diligently for the child; and
when you have found him, bring me word so
that I may also go and pay him homage."
9 When they had heard the king, they set out;
and there, ahead of them, went the star that
they had seen at its rising, until it stopped over
the place where the child was.
10 When they saw that the star had stopped,
they were overwhelmed with joy.
11 On entering the house, they saw the child
with Mary his mother; and they knelt down
and paid him homage. Then, opening their
treasure chests, they offered him gifts of gold,
frankincense, and myrrh.

12 And having been warned in a dream not to
return to Herod, they left for their own country
by another road.
13 Now after they had left, an angel of the
Lord appeared to Joseph in a dream and said,
"Get up, take the child and his mother, and
flee to Egypt, and remain there until I tell you;
for Herod is about to search for the child, to
destroy him."
14 Then Joseph got up, took the child and his
mother by night, and went to Egypt,

MAIN THOUGHT: And when they were come into the house, they saw the young child with Mary his mother, and fell down, and worshipped him: and when they had opened their treasures, they presented unto him gifts; gold, and frankincense, and myrrh. (Matthew 2:11, KJV)

Matthew 2:7–15

King James Version	*New Revised Standard Version*
15 And was there until the death of Herod: that it might be fulfilled which was spoken of the Lord by the prophet, saying, Out of Egypt have I called my son.	**15 and remained there until the death of Herod. This was to fulfill what had been spoken by the Lord through the prophet, "Out of Egypt I have called my son."**

LESSON SETTING

Time: *circa* 7–6 B.C.
Place: Bethlehem

LESSON OUTLINE

I. Herod's Challenge (Matthew 2:7–9)
II. The Visit of the Magi (Matthew 2:10–12)
III. The Flight to Egypt (Matthew 2:13–15)

Unifying Principle

As our world gets smaller, we are more and more exposed to people who differ from us in race, culture, and religious values. Where can we find unity in such a world? By summoning Wise Men from far-off lands to worship Jesus, God demonstrated this newborn King would transcend the differences that divide us.

Introduction

In our previous lesson, we were provided an account of Joseph's dilemma as to how he should respond to a pregnant fiancée carrying a child that was not biologically his. After Joseph acknowledged the indwelling of the Holy Spirit, this account depicted the visit of the Magi, also known as Wise Men; their encounter with an insecure, mad, and despotic ruler of Judea; the plot to murder Jesus; and the relocation of the holy family to Egypt. There was an emphasis on the recurring continuum of dreams that were given to Joseph and to the Magi. These dreams served as both reassurances and warnings to the intended parties that God was in control of all the events they would encounter.

Exposition

I. Herod's Challenge (Matthew 2:7–9)

Herod the Great (*circa* 73–4 B.C.) was furious. An entourage of men known as "Wise Men" arrived in Jerusalem and asked permission to enter Herod's kingdom to search for a newborn child who was to be King of the Jews. These men also were known as Magi (*μάγος, magos*), Wise Men, magicians, or *magus*, and have been identified as kings. However, many scholars believe they were noted for their unusual capacity of understanding based upon astrology (such persons were regarded as possessing a combination of secular and religious aspects of knowledge and understanding). In Matthew 2:1, *μάγοι (magoi)* may be translated as "men of wisdom who studied the stars." It was customary and prudent for a group of foreign pilgrims to seek permission to travel in the lands of a ruling monarch. The Magi had to check in with Herod, who granted their wishes. However, Herod was upset by their visit and the reasons they were in Judah. After all, he was king of the Jews, and any other person who would seek the title was a threat to the king. This menace had to be eliminated. Herod, not wanting anyone but his closest associates to know of his planned treachery, discreetly inquired of the Magi as to their estimate of the exact time the star (which guided the journey of the pilgrims) appeared, or began to shine in the East. An interesting note is that Matthew indicated Herod was not alone in his concern about this revelation—all of Jerusalem was troubled along with Herod. Some people owed their livelihood to the king, and others felt an announcement of a new ruler or coup would signify the beginning of an uprising that would destroy the peace and bring suffering to the common person and those who prayed for Herod's removal. However, they also were afraid of the wrath of the Romans that occupied Judea. Therefore, this announcement, although probably limited to Herod's court and close environs, was probably not so widespread to have had any serious effect on the majority of citizens.

Although Herod was a king who was supported by the Roman government, he knew the Old Testament prophecies that foretold a messiah-king who would redeem His people. Consequently, upon counseling with his chief priests, scribes, and advisers, he inquired about where the child was to be born, which was Bethlehem of Judea. Herod sent the Magi to Bethlehem to inquire about and carefully search for the child and to report their findings back to the king. At this juncture the depth of his treachery and hypocrisy was revealed. Herod lied to the Magi and attempted to convince them his plea was earnest, in that he also wanted to worship and bow down to the child. Translators differ on a common age range when speaking about the child. *παιδίον* (*paidion*) is a term that could imply a young child without providing an idea of the actual age. B. M. Newman and P. C. Stine propose that the context suggests Jesus was no longer a baby at the time the Wise Men arrived. They seem not to have set off from their homeland in the East until the star signifying His birth had appeared, which indicates the star was not leading them to the event of His birth but to the place of His birth.

The Wise Men were polite in the court of Herod and listened to his deception. They could sense something was wrong in the manner Herod presented his desire to join in the worship of the child and that he was scheming, attempting to use the Wise Men as co-conspirators. Remember, these Wise Men or Magi were not defined as kings. It seems as if Herod was not aware of the star as Matthew described it, and they were following the star until it stopped and stood over the place where the child was.

II. The Visit of the Magi (Matthew 2:10–12)

Upon seeing the star, Matthew reported the Magi rejoiced with a great sense of joy when the beacon that had led them appeared in a manner of confirmation that their journey was part of a celestial plan. Finally, their expedition was back on track.

The journey of the Magi from Jerusalem wrought a further miracle. The star they had seen in the East now appeared and led them to a specific house in Bethlehem where they found the child Jesus.

Bethlehem is about five miles south of Jerusalem. L. A. Barbieri argues that stars (or planets) naturally travel from East to West across the heavens, not from North to South (remember, it was a star out of the East). Could it be the star the Magi saw, which led them to a specific house, was the *shekinah* glory of God?

Additionally, Barbieri believes it was the same glory that had led the children of Israel through the wilderness for forty years as a pillar of fire and cloud. Perhaps, this was what the Magi saw in the East and, for want of a better term, they called it a star. All other natural efforts to explain this star are inadequate. The Magi came to their final destination where the star led. Matthew did not provide any detail about the dwelling, its ownership, or its connection to the holy family. Notice, however, that they came into or entered a house, not a barn or stable.

This aspect of the nativity has confused generations because of the convolution of the Matthean and Lukan accounts of Jesus' birth. In most nativity scenes, the Wise Men and the animals are present at Jesus' birth. However, Matthew detailed the presence of the Magi, whereas Luke did not, and Luke wrote that after wrapping the child in cloths, or as in the adjectival use of swaddling cloths, Mary placed the baby in a manger.

The baby having been in a manger, which is an animal feeding trough, suggests the presence of beasts within the structure, since it was an indoor facility. The image of these buildings or houses generally are lost in our contemporary sense of architecture. Both Matthew and Luke were accurate when reporting on the divergent views of Jesus' birth. The house served as both living quarters and a stable for the animals. The living quarters would be on the second floor and the ground floor would consist of the stable and food preparation area. An example of how the stable area of the house was used is found in Exodus 9:19–20, where the need was to get the cattle indoors because of the forthcoming plague of hail. Although Matthew did not mention the manger or animals, the Magi found the baby in a house, where they immediately begin their worship by first falling to the ground, presenting themselves in a prostrate position, which is indicative of ultimate submission and holy worship. Following the recognition of the baby-king, they presented gifts, which was the custom when a visiting monarch or an explorer was given an audience with a king. Upon opening their gifts, the holy family received the offering of gifts they had brought from their lands. Matthew recorded that these gifts consisted of gold, frankincense, and myrrh.

These gifts were acceptable because of their need and usefulness during this period. However, there also exists spiritual imagery associated with these presents. The gift of gold is obvious. This was a precious metal that was probably gold coins that would be redeemable in any country or land. Spiritually, gold represented the greatest status or riches of God. Frankincense is a form of incense that probably reduced the musty smell of the house. Spiritually, however, frankincense was one of the ingredients in the perfume of the sanctuary (Exod. 30:34–37) and was used as an accompaniment to the grain offering (Lev. 2:1, 16; 6:15; 24:7).

When burnt, it emitted a fragrant odor and, hence, the incense became a symbol of the divine name (Mal. 1:11) and an emblem of prayer (Ps. 141:2; Rev. 5:8; 8:3).

Myrrh was used as a perfume and a disinfectant, possibly in the cleaning process of the birth mother, who was considered unclean. Spiritually, it was used in embalming (John 19:39). Myrrh would be present at Jesus' crucifixion as it was a custom of the Jews to give those who were condemned to death by crucifixion wine mingled with myrrh.

God confirmed the treachery of Herod, and the Magi departed without revealing any information about the child. In all probability, they spent the night on the grounds or in the area of the house where they had visited the baby Jesus. Although we are not provided with the time of day in which their visit occurred, it is safe to assume the visit was at night, as they followed the star. The Magi were warned in a dream not to return to Herod or any of his associates and reveal anything about the presence or location of the child. They were to return to their country by another route. In their leaving Bethlehem and the region of Judea, the Magi literally had to escape the area because the duplicitous Herod would have had spies follow or look for them, as verse 16 will reveal, when Herod realized he had been tricked!

III. The Flight to Egypt (Matthew 2:13–15)

Matthew shifted his attention back to the next development in the account of the holy family. They had become the focus of Herod's anger and jealousy and, therefore, must be protected from the wrath of the Judean ruler. Following the departure of the Magi, an angel of the Lord appeared, or better yet reappeared, in a dream to warn Joseph of the impending dangers to his family. Herod had passed a death sentence on the child and was marshaling his forces to find and kill the infant-king. As Herod was looking for their location, Joseph was immediately instructed to escape from Judea and go to live in Egypt (the phrase is *εἰμί ἐκεῖ, (eimi ekei),*" "live in that place," or "remain in Egypt") until it was safe for them to return. The Greek word used is *φεύγω* (*pheugo*), which means "to flee, escape, or run away." There are some issues with the wording here because it suggests God was impotent in protecting the family due to the emphasis on fleeing or running away. This is not an accurate assessment. Matthew's use of the term instead underscored the importance of the death decree that had been placed on the child, with the unfortunate realization some children would be massacred.

The subsequent Slaughter of the Innocents, as it is known, occurred due to Herod's decree that all male children two years and under be slain. Although Jesus escaped the carnage, the theological distinctions and comparisons could not be clearer. Recall that an Egyptian pharaoh decreed that upon giving birth, all male children of Hebrew descent were to be killed by the midwives (who ignored Pharaoh's orders), then he ordered all newborn males be cast into the Nile River. Moses was hidden and became the adopted son of Pharaoh's daughter and lived to lead God's people through the Exodus.

Obeying God's command, Joseph rose immediately and left Judea. It was at night, indicating Joseph did not wait for the morning to travel to Egypt. Joseph did not have an issue following the revelations of the Lord because God had not been inaccurate in His predictions of the child's birth and, therefore, would not lead Joseph astray in His protection of the holy family. Whereas Joseph may have hesitated when warned by God of the circumstances surrounding Mary's pregnancy, here he acted instantaneously and quickly.

In biblical history, there has existed a love-hate relationship between Israel and Egypt, as the latter empire is known for enslaving the Hebrews and later allied themselves with other nations determined to destroy Israel and Judea. God used Egypt, however, as a sanctuary for Joseph to save Israel from a massive famine and starvation and now as protection for the holy family. Although Egypt was a sovereign nation, God created all of the land. Therefore, owning the nation allowed Him to use the country as a haven to preserve the child Jesus. The holy family remained in Egypt until the death of Herod (*circa* 4 B.C.), which was understood as a fulfillment of the prophecy of the Lord spoken by Hosea, "Out of Egypt I called my son" (Hos. 11:1, NRSV). When the news reached the family, they left Egypt and settled in Nazareth in Galilee. Hence, Jesus was called a Nazarene.

The Lesson Applied

Through countless Sunday school lessons, we believe there were three Wise Men who followed the star. How did we arrive at this number? Matthew did not provide a count of the visitors. The reason is quite simple. Three gifts—gold, frankincense, and myrrh—were presented to the child. Who gave each gift was not identified, although we are provided the order of the presentation, which could have been offered by one or by all of them! Three gifts equaled three Wise Men! What is important is that they responded to God's greatest Gift with gifts of their own.

Let's Talk About It

Why were swaddling cloths used?

The use of swaddling cloths was common among newborns in the first century. After the infant was born, the umbilical cord was cut and tied, then the baby was washed, rubbed with salt, and wrapped with strips of cloth. Wrapping a child in these bands provided warmth, protected the extremities, and gave a sense of security. Additionally, wrapping the legs of a child was thought to have prevented rickets, a form of weak or soft bones that would result in the child developing bowed legs. Understanding this first-century practice reveals Jesus' human nature and the ordinary customs of His family.

Home Daily Devotional Readings

December 21–27, 2020

Monday	Tuesday	Wednesday	Thursday	Friday	Saturday	Sunday
A Voice Cries, "Comfort My People"	John the Baptist Is the Greatest	The Baptist's Testimony of Faith	Jesus, the Father's Beloved Son	In John, Elijah Has Come	John Baptizes Jesus in the Jordan	John Prepares the Way for Jesus
Isaiah 40:1–5	Matthew 11:2–15	John 1:19–34	Matthew 17:1–8	Matthew 17:9–13; Malachi 4:4–5	Matthew 3:13–17	Matthew 3:1–12

LESSON 4 DECEMBER 27, 2020

CALLED TO PREPARE THE WAY

ADULT TOPIC:
GET READY

BACKGROUND SCRIPTURE:
MATTHEW 3

MATTHEW 3:1–12

King James Version

IN those days came John the Baptist, preaching in the wilderness of Judaea,
2 And saying, Repent ye: for the kingdom of
heaven is at hand.
3 For this is he that was spoken of by the
prophet Esaias, saying, The voice of one crying
in the wilderness, Prepare ye the way of the
Lord, make his paths straight.
4 And the same John had his raiment of camel's hair, and a leathern girdle about his loins;
and his meat was locusts and wild honey.
5 Then went out to him Jerusalem, and all
Judaea, and all the region round about Jordan,
6 And were baptized of him in Jordan, confessing their sins.
7 But when he saw many of the Pharisees and
Sadducees come to his baptism, he said unto
them, O generation of vipers, who hath warned
you to flee from the wrath to come?
8 Bring forth therefore fruits meet for
repentance:
9 And think not to say within yourselves, We
have Abraham to our father: for I say unto
you, that God is able of these stones to raise up
children unto Abraham.
10 And now also the axe is laid unto the root of
the trees: therefore every tree which bringeth
not forth good fruit is hewn down, and cast into
the fire.
11 I indeed baptize you with water unto repentance. but he that cometh after me is mightier
than I, whose shoes I am not worthy to bear:

New Revised Standard Version

IN those days John the Baptist appeared in the
wilderness of Judea, proclaiming,
2 "Repent, for the kingdom of heaven has
come near."
3 This is the one of whom the prophet Isaiah
spoke when he said, "The voice of one crying
out in the wilderness: 'Prepare the way of the
Lord, make his paths straight.'"
4 Now John wore clothing of camel's hair
with a leather belt around his waist, and his
food was locusts and wild honey.
5 Then the people of Jerusalem and all Judea
were going out to him, and all the region along
the Jordan,
6 and they were baptized by him in the river
Jordan, confessing their sins.
7 But when he saw many Pharisees and
Sadducees coming for baptism, he said to
them, "You brood of vipers! Who warned you
to flee from the wrath to come?
8 Bear fruit worthy of repentance.
9 Do not presume to say to yourselves, 'We
have Abraham as our ancestor'; for I tell
you, God is able from these stones to raise up
children to Abraham.
10 Even now the ax is lying at the root of the
trees; every tree therefore that does not bear
good fruit is cut down and thrown into the fire.
11 "I baptize you with water for repentance,
but one who is more powerful than I is coming
after me; I am not worthy to carry his sandals.

MAIN THOUGHT: For this is he that was spoken of by the prophet Esaias, saying, The voice of one crying in the wilderness, Prepare ye the way of the Lord, make his paths straight. (Matthew 3:3, KJV)

King James Version	*New Revised Standard Version*
he shall baptize you with the Holy Ghost, and with fire:	**He will baptize you with the Holy Spirit and fire.**
12 Whose fan is in his hand, and he will throughly purge his floor, and gather his wheat into the garner; but he will burn up the chaff with unquenchable fire.	**12 His winnowing fork is in his hand, and he will clear his threshing floor and will gather his wheat into the granary; but the chaff he will burn with unquenchable fire."**

LESSON SETTING

Time: *circa* A.D. 24
Place: The Jordan Valley

LESSON OUTLINE

I. John the Baptist (Matthew 3:1–4)
II. John's Message (Matthew 3:5–10)
III. John's Prophecy (Matthew 3:11–12)

UNIFYING PRINCIPLE

Important projects require thoughtful preparation. What endeavors demand our greatest preparation efforts? John called for people to repent of their sins and get ready to welcome the soon-coming Messiah.

INTRODUCTION

A prophet went to the Jordan River region to bring a message from God that the long-awaited Messiah was coming soon. The prophet-preacher John the Baptist delivered a practical message that attacked the sins of the people. His doctrine and manner of life roused the people, and they flocked to him at the Jordan. There, he baptized many to repentance. John's message of repentance could easily be lost in a focus on his baptisms. The two are inseparable, as the call to repentance and the demonstration of baptism were partners in the need for salvation.

EXPOSITION

I. JOHN THE BAPTIST (MATTHEW 3:1–4)

Considered to be aligned with the Old Testament prophets, John the Baptist arrived in the Judean desert a few years prior to the inauguration of Jesus' ministry. John, a Nazarite, was destined to serve Yahweh as one of His great prophets with a simple but profound message of repentance. John received his sobriquet *Baptist* or *baptizer* because of the activity for which he is most noted. As part of his preaching, he carved out a space along the Jordan River where he baptized as a sign of repentance. John was a devout Jew, and the Jewish people had been promised a Messiah. John's message pointed to the fulfillment of that promise.

John's ministry took place in the Jordan River Valley. Although Matthew described John's activities as occurring in the wilderness, John was not far away from civilization. A lot of traffic moved on the road as well as up and down the river connecting Judea with Galilee. John's mobility allowed him to baptize in several locations of the Jordan, not being confined to one place. He could play the role of the ascetic prophet yet interact with sophisticated people. And plenty of people came to him.

All of the Gospels present an account of John as a forerunner of Jesus' ministry. Mark actually began his Gospel with the declaration of Isaiah's prophecy, "See, I am sending my messenger ahead of you" (Mark 1:2, NRSV; Isa. 40:3), noting the task John the Baptist had been given. John's central message was repentance (*μετανοία, metanoia*). The act of repentance is to change one's mind or outlook, especially in the manner of his or her relationship to God. If the people were to receive the blessing of the Messiah, their bond with God must be impeccable. John boldly preached and declared God's Kingdom was at hand. Matthew used the Greek term *ἐγγίζω* (*engizo*), which means "to draw near," indicating the duality of the message: The Kingdom was near, and the people must draw near or be drawn to it.

John's preaching was prior to the institution of Christianity. Much emphasis has been placed on his disciples; however, the centrality of his message was not as much about conversion as it was about bringing a renewal of Judaism. The concept of a coming Kingdom was well-known in Old Testament Scriptures; however, the idea that repentance was necessary in order to enter this Kingdom was new.

Quoting Isaiah, Matthew reinforced the fact that prophecy was central to John's message. John, who was identified with the prophet Elijah, was a fiery speaker who was focused on the power of his message. John's identity was expressed in his style of dress. His spartan clothing, a camel's hair garment accessorized with a leather belt, would not garner any fashion accolades. John may have been aware of Elijah's appearance—a hairy man with a leather belt around his loins (2 Kings 1:8)—and patterned himself accordingly. John's diet of locusts and wild honey seems unfathomable to our tastes but kept with his ascetic lifestyle.

II. John's Message (Matthew 3:5–10)

John's movement was popular. As word spread, prospective converts came out to hear his message and be baptized as a symbol of their repentance. The people of the districts of his base of operation would have included the aforementioned tract of land along the Jordan before it empties into the Dead Sea. However, this does not preclude people from any of the neighboring districts such as Galilee.

The record seems to indicate John kept a busy schedule baptizing his converts in the Jordan as they confessed their sins. Contemporary thought may place a sense of sadness or "doom and gloom" in this scenario. However, the Greek term used to describe the event is *ἐξομολογέω* (*exomologeo*), which means "to confess one's sins" but carries a secondary meaning, "to praise," indicating those who were seeking a return to good standing with the Lord understood their confession to also be an act of praise! The expressed desire of the people was to acknowledge their failures and deficiencies through confession, change their outlook and lifestyles through repentance, and praise the Lord because of His mercy.

Members of the Pharisees, who during this period were the most influential of the Jewish sects, came to be baptized. Another group mentioned was the Sadducees, who also opposed Jesus and who denied the resurrection and the supremacy of Christ. Matthew mentioned that members of both groups came to be baptized, but were they actually coming for baptism or coming to witness the baptisms?

John called them a brood of vipers. John's words are venomous, as he questioned their motives. John asked who had warned them to flee the coming wrath. John was speaking about the impending punishment to those who had rejected God's commandments.

These Pharisees and Sadducees had an opportunity to repent, and if their hearts had been pure, this would have changed the suspicions of their visit. Using an agricultural metaphor, John chastised them, saying that if their lives resembled the fruit worthy of repentance they would be favored by God. However, they rejected John's overtures because they felt they belonged to an exclusive union in that they were sons of Abraham and were granted a right to inhabit a share in God's Kingdom. These men were not interested.

Verse 10 is an ominous reference to Jesus, who later declared, "Every tree that does not bear good fruit is cut down and thrown into the fire" (Matt. 7:19, NRSV). John stated the same! The essence of our lives and the resultant activities, whether physical, attitudinal, or spiritual, will be judged. If our produce is deemed deficient, our lives will be cut down, and we will be cut off from God.

III. John's Prophecy (Matthew 3:11–12)

Distancing himself from the pseudo-righteous Pharisees and Sadducees, John declared, "As for me …" John told the Pharisees and Sadducees he was called to minister and had selected the medium of baptism as a ritual for those who were affirming their relationship to God.

The act of baptizing with water, as in today's practices, would not save the believer. It was a sign of repentance, a changed direction that would positively alter one's lifestyle. The apex of repentance was to be totally devoted to God and to humanity.

John continued his discourse about the Promised One, who was mightier and more powerful and would also appear and use the practice of baptism. The One who was to come would add fire and the Holy Spirit to His baptism. This form of baptism represents a sharper cleansing than that of water and is a biblical symbol for purity. Additionally, the baptism of the Holy Spirit cannot be performed by a human—it can come only from God through Jesus.

In deference to the One who was coming, John explained his position through self-depreciation, stating he was not worthy of removing the sandals from the feet of the One. Recall that one of the duties of servants was to wash the feet of a visitor, and it was necessary to remove or untie the thongs of the sandals. John had grown quite popular; nonetheless, he also was aware of his calling and mission.

In this final verse, John referred to a motif that invoked the act of separation. He declared the winnowing fork, which is a tool for throwing threshed grain into the air in order to let the chaff blow away, would separate the useful part of the grain from that which was not edible. Recall that Jesus further used this motif—as He brings all nations before Him, He will separate the sheep from the goats (Matt. 25:32). Additionally, though John used this idea of separating grain, Jesus declared the wheat and tares, which actually carry poisonous spores, will be burned with a destructive fire. John was explicit in presenting an atmosphere in which these religious leaders would not have a place in the Kingdom unless they repented. He also provided an idea of how Jesus would reveal their false sense of faith and hypocrisy.

John also used another illustration to impress upon his audience that once the separation of the wheat and chaff occurred, only the usable grain would remain. For John, his message was that the Messiah would clean out the sullied and polluted people who are exposed on the threshing floor. Therefore, all of the corruption that soils the world and impedes the worship of the Lord would be ended. The image of the unusable chaff being burned up by fire recalled the use of fire as a cleansing agent.

John ended with a positive message: God will be the victor and conqueror, and in all finality, those who remain faithful to Him and those whom He loves will be gathered to be with Him. The imagery is that He will assemble a throng of believers who have been tested by the wind of the winnowing fork, delivered from the destruction of the fire, and approved to be taken into His barn, which is an obvious reference to His Kingdom.

The Lesson Applied

It is surprising that *repentance* has a negative connotation for believers. This term is nonthreatening in that it simply means to change one's mind or outlook on life. *Repentance* is a term of encouragement instead of derision. In contemporary self-help books, *repentance* would be thought of as *self-reflection* or *self-assessment*. Why do some believers reject the call for repentance as though someone is incriminating them? Self-reflection is necessary in our Christian journey. Can we be better Christians today than we were yesterday? The answer is a resounding yes. But we never will realize our Christian potential if we are afraid of the term *repent*.

Let's Talk About It

Who were the Pharisees and Sadducees?

Historically, Pharisees and Saddducees were sects within Judaism. Truthfully, they were the equivalent to Baptists, Methodists, and Pentecostals—of the same tree but different branches. Unfortunately, many of them got it wrong, Jesus was the Messiah. When they appear in the story, think of them as people who are trying but just don't get it.

Home Daily Devotional Readings

December 28–January 3, 2021

Monday	Tuesday	Wednesday	Thursday	Friday	Saturday	Sunday
Live by God's Word	Jubilee, Year of God's Favor	Miracle of the Meal and Oil	Naaman's Leprosy Healed in Jordan River	Jesus Overcomes the Devil's Temptations	Jesus Driven out of Nazareth	Jesus' Mandate for Ministry Announced
Deuteronomy 8:1–11	Leviticus 25:8–17	1 Kings 17:8–16	2 Kings 5:1–14	Luke 4:1–13	Luke 4:23–30	Luke 4:14–22

LESSON 5 JANUARY 3, 2021

CALLED TO PROCLAIM

ADULT TOPIC:
AN AMAZING MESSENGER

BACKGROUND SCRIPTURE:
LUKE 4

LUKE 4:14–22

King James Version

**AND Jesus returned in the power of the Spirit
into Galilee: and there went out a fame of him
through all the region round about.
15 And he taught in their synagogues, being
glorified of all.
16 And he came to Nazareth, where he had
been brought up: and, as his custom was, he
went into the synagogue on the sabbath day,
and stood up for to read.
17 And there was delivered unto him the
book of the prophet Esaias. And when he had
opened the book, he found the place where it
was written,
18 The Spirit of the Lord is upon me, because
he hath anointed me to preach the gospel to the
poor; he hath sent me to heal the brokenhearted, to preach deliverance to the captives, and
recovering of sight to the blind, to set at liberty
them that are bruised,
19 To preach the acceptable year of the Lord.
20 And he closed the book, and he gave it again
to the minister, and sat down. And the eyes of
all them that were in the synagogue were fas-
tened on him.
21 And he began to say unto them, This day is
this scripture fulfilled in your ears.
22 And all bare him witness, and wondered at
the gracious words which proceeded out of his
mouth. And they said, Is not this Joseph's son?**

New Revised Standard Version

**THEN Jesus, filled with the power of the Spirit,
returned to Galilee, and a report about him
spread through all the surrounding country.
15 He began to teach in their synagogues and
was praised by everyone.
16 When he came to Nazareth, where he had
been brought up, he went to the synagogue on
the sabbath day, as was his custom. He stood
up to read,
17 and the scroll of the prophet Isaiah was
given to him. He unrolled the scroll and found
the place where it was written:
18 "The Spirit of the Lord is upon me, because
he has anointed me to bring good news to the
poor. He has sent me to proclaim release to the
captives and recovery of sight to the blind, to
let the oppressed go free,
19 to proclaim the year of the Lord's favor."
20 And he rolled up the scroll, gave it back to
the attendant, and sat down. The eyes of all in
the synagogue were fixed on him.
21 Then he began to say to them, "Today this
scripture has been fulfilled in your hearing."
22 All spoke well of him and were amazed at
the gracious words that came from his mouth.
They said, "Is not this Joseph's son?"**

MAIN THOUGHT: The Spirit of the Lord is upon me, because he hath anointed me to preach the gospel to the poor; he hath sent me to heal the brokenhearted, to preach deliverance to the captives, and recovering of sight to the blind, to set at liberty them that are bruised, To preach the acceptable year of the Lord. (Luke 4:18–19 , KJV)

LESSON SETTING

Time: ***circa*** **A.D. 24–27**
Place: Nazareth

LESSON OUTLINE

I. The Beginning of Jesus' Ministry (Luke 4:14–15)
II. Jesus Teaching in the Synagogue (Luke 4:16–19)
III. Reaction in the Synagogue (Luke 4:20–22)

Unifying Principle

People hear conflicting messages and proclamations all of the time. What message would provide answers to life's deepest problems? The worshipers at Nazareth listened to Jesus' proclamation of justice and compassion and were amazed.

Introduction

After Jesus was baptized by John the Baptist, He returned from the Jordan River to a remote desert region. While in the wilderness, He faced a series of satanic temptations that challenged His humanity as well as His deity. From a human perspective, Jesus was physically weak, having fasted for forty days. Satan tempted Jesus with items such as bread to satisfy His hunger, kingdoms to check His desire for riches, and His authority as the Son of God to assess His standing with Yahweh. Jesus rejected the traps and traveled back home to Nazareth to launch His ministry.

Exposition

I. The Beginning of Jesus' Ministry (Luke 4:14–15)

Luke reported that Jesus basked in the strength of the Spirit, and this strength was contagious to the people with whom He interacted. Part of this positive contagion reflected the joy of an encounter with and blessing from the Holy Spirit. Jesus recently had been baptized by John in the Jordan. The Spirit compelled Jesus, and the Spirit was evidence of God's approval. The Spirit descended on Jesus in the form of a dove, and a voice spoke from heaven, verifying God's approval. The dove was a symbol of virtue. It also represented that all persons of the Trinity were present at Christ's baptism. Bible scholars have questioned whether the descending Spirit was an actual dove or a theophany representing the attributes and manifestations of the Spirit. Whichever, Matthew said the heavens were opened and the Spirit of God descended on Him as if it were a dove lighting on Him (Matt. 3:16).

After His baptism and temptation, Jesus most likely preached in several villages en route to Nazareth, where He was well-received. Jesus' teaching must have been refreshing and attractive to His audiences, as He was praised by all who heard His messages. The Greek word *δοξάζω* (*doxazo*), meaning "to praise or honor," was used here to describe the feelings the people had for Jesus. The adoration Jesus received must have been a positive sign for the future, which was a phenomenal manner to begin His ministry. By the time Jesus reached His home, word had spread throughout the surrounding districts, and the report preceded His journey.

Luke began this section as the formal announcement of Jesus' ministry and later recorded Jesus' first miracle as the exorcism of demons from a young man (Luke 4:33–36; Mark 1:23–28).

II. Jesus Teaching in the Synagogue (Luke 4:16–19)

As Jesus reached His home in Nazareth of Galilee, He was refreshed and restored despite His encounter with Satan. Throughout His ordeal, He never wavered from His mission as the Christ who had come to save the world. Now, He entered the village where He grew into manhood. Luke used the Greek term *τρέφω* (*trepho*), which can be translated as *reared*. However, a more interesting definition of the expression may be rendered as "nourished or fed," which describes a warm, nurturing hamlet that embraced Jesus as its native son. The Scriptures are silent about His activities growing up. Nonetheless, Jesus was back in His Nazareth, His hometown. As a reflection of His upbringing, Jesus went to the synagogue on the Sabbath because it was His habit. At a certain point while in the assembly, Jesus stood up to read aloud the Scriptures that served as the liturgical reading of the service.

The people in attendance received Jesus as He took the book or what was more likely the scroll of the writings of the prophet Isaiah. R. Kent Hughes details the order of the service as he notes that from the Mishnah's Megillah IV, which supplies numerous details about synagogue worship, we can trace the general flow of the service. There was singing from Psalms 145–150 followed by the recitation of the Shema, which begins, "Hear, O Israel, the Lord is our God, the Lord alone" (Deut. 6:4–9, NRSV). Next, the Eighteen Benedictions, known as the Tefillah, were also recited aloud in succession. Then came the reading of Scripture. An officer went to the holy ark, took out the Torah scroll, removed its cloth covering, opened it to its designated place, and placed it on the table where it was read by various attendees. The Torah was then returned to the ark, and a portion from the prophets, the Haftarah, was read. This was followed by a sermon. The service was closed with the Aaronic benediction with the people pronouncing *Amen* at each of its divisions. "The Lord bless you and keep you [Amen]; the Lord make his face to shine upon you and be gracious to you [Amen]; the Lord lift up his countenance upon you, and give you peace [Amen]" (Num. 6:24–26, NRSV).

What is interesting is that Isaiah foretold the gift of the Messiah to the world, predicting His birth (Isa. 9:6–7) and calling Him Immanuel, "God with us" (Isa. 7:14). Nevertheless, as Jesus unrolled the scroll and spread out its contents, He found the place where these words were written, declaring in the first person, "The Spirit of the Lord is upon me" (Luke 4:18, NRSV), which probably did not register or offend the congregation at this point because Jesus was allowed to complete the reading. They may have missed it; however, Jesus was incredibly accurate when He acknowledged He had been anointed (*χρίω, chrio*) or designated to preach the Gospel or Good News to the poor. The poor represented those without the means of living above the poverty line or lacking sufficient finances to live at a standard set by society, including those who were destitute and marginalized spiritually. Recall Jesus' blessing on the poor in spirit, "for theirs is the kingdom of heaven" (Matt. 5:3, NRSV), while He also blessed those who were physically poor as well (Luke 6:21). Jesus' preaching and encouragement toward the poor who believed in Him would lead to a life of salvation through eternity with Him. Jesus mentioned His mission was of God and He had been sent to proclaim and pronounce the end of captivity to those oppressed by the dark forces of the world. In freeing the enslaved, Jesus would provide freedom or a release to those bound by sin and separation. Additionally, this term indicates a pardon would be provided for those enveloped in the shroud of estrangement, and forgiveness would be granted to those in need. Moreover, Jesus has the power to provide recovery of sight to those who are physically blind and also to those who are spiritually blind to the beauty and glory of the Lord. Through His strength and anointing power, Jesus will restore humanity's natural ability and desire to see Jesus as the Light of the World while ensuring their position in the Kingdom of heaven. Through these blessings, Jesus will break the chains of the oppressed, those whose lives are broken by the world.

An interesting occurrence appeared in verse 19, where Jesus declared He had been sent to proclaim the favorable year of the Lord. The phrase "to proclaim the year of the Lord's favor" (NRSV) has several implications. The Greek term *δεκτός* (*dektos*) can be translated as "the acceptable or proper year of the Lord." Isaiah's prophecies shed light on this meaning. The Messiah will set free those who are oppressed, shackled, or captive, those who will welcome the moment they regain their freedom. Isaiah's message of the year of the Lord is contrasted with Joel's prophecy of the day of the Lord, which will involve God's special intervention in the affairs of human history. Three facets of the day of the Lord are discernible: (1) the historical, that is, God's intervention in the affairs of Israel and heathen nations; (2) the illustrative, whereby a historical incident represents a partial fulfillment of the eschatological day of the Lord, such as Joel's prophecy of a devastating locust invasion as an illustration of an invading army that would destroy the nation; (3) the eschatological day, which includes the time of the Great Tribulation, both a series of Old Testament punishments and deliverances and that of the New Testament, which predicts the fate of the wicked and the glorification and rule of Christ and His believers, the second coming of Christ and the Millennium, the 1000-year era in which the resurrected martyrs reign with Christ on earth. It often is understood as occurring between the destruction of this evil, temporal age ruled by Satan and the creation of a new heaven and earth in a righteous, eternal age indisputably ruled by God. The day of the Lord motif is decreed by several others, such as Zephaniah, who predicted the day of the Lord was near (Zeph. 1:7), and Paul (1 Thess.) and Peter (2 Pet. 3:10), who both declared it will come as a thief in the night. In quoting this passage from Isaiah, Jesus ended His reading with the year of the Lord. He, however, stopped short, not continuing the missive that described the day of vengeance and subsequent comfort of God. The ministry of the Messiah at His first coming is described in Isaiah 61:1–2a and at His second coming in Isaiah 61:2b–3. In claiming to be the Messiah,

Jesus Christ read in the synagogue only that which applied to His ministry during His first coming (Luke 4:18–19). The day of vengeance will bring judgment on nonbelievers. At the same time, the Messiah will comfort the Church, which will have undergone the persecution of the Great Tribulation.

III. Reaction in the Synagogue (Luke 4:20–22)

Satisfied with His presentation, Jesus closed the book or rolled up the scroll and gave it back to the attendant, probably an official placed in charge of maintaining the sacred scrolls of the synagogue. As Jesus returned to His seat, He was more than aware all of the eyes in the assembly were intensely looking at Him and thinking.

Concluding His discourse, Jesus added an epilogue, stating, "Today, this scripture has been fulfilled in your hearing" (Luke 4:21, NRSV), meaning the message that had been placed in the ears was true, a direct reference to John's witness from the angel, "He who has an ear, let him hear what the Spirit says to the churches" (Rev. 2:7, ESV). For Jesus, nothing else had to be added to His reading because in their witness, He serves as the accomplishment of a mission that is completely fulfilled.

At verse 22 Luke reported the congregation began to speak well of Jesus' presentation in His hometown synagogue. The crowd in attendance seemed to actually be in a joyous and receptive mood, creating an atmosphere in which the people were quite proud of Him. Luke described a group that was astonished at His gracious words and marveled at the maturity and wisdom that flowed from His mouth. If we ended our discourse at this juncture, it would provide an impression they "lived happily ever after." However, when Jesus added, "Today this scripture has been fulfilled in your hearing" (Luke 4:21, NRSV), the implication was made. Jesus was claiming to be the Messiah who could bring the Kingdom of God that had been promised for so long, but His initial mission was not for pronouncing judgment.

Yes, the people were amazed at the words He spoke. Mark revealed their pride as they asked, "Is not this the carpenter, the son of Mary and brother of James and Joses and Judas and Simon, and are not his sisters here with us?" (Mark 6:3, NRSV). Clearly, Jesus' teaching in the hometown synagogue attracted neighbors, friends, and family. Nevertheless, all was not well. The assembly became unsettled as they seemed to be initially unsure of what to think of Jesus' interpretation. Both Mark (6:2–6) and Matthew (13:54–57) revealed the reaction of the crowd was to immediately question the authority with which He could say these things, wondering how this man, who grew up before their eyes, could be the long-promised Messiah. Jesus, sensing their opposition (Luke 4:23–24), noted two instances in which God's prophets ministered miraculous acts of grace to Gentiles while Israel was in unbelief—Elijah and the widow of Zarephath (Luke 4:25–26; 1 Kings 17:8–16) and Elisha and Naaman the Syrian leper (Luke 4:27; 2 Kings 5:1–19).

Realizing their joy had turned to anger, Jesus uttered the infamous statement, "No prophet is accepted in the prophet's hometown" (Luke 4:24, NRSV).

This statement indicated Jesus was disappointed in the attitude of His neighbors and friends. At this juncture, Jesus reduced His work in Nazareth, laying His hands on and healing only a few sick people. Otherwise, He could (would) not perform any miracles there because of their unbelief. Jesus left Nazareth and set off on the path of His ministry. He created a base of operations in Capernaum, and although He came to redeem Israel, He brought His mission to the Gentiles throughout the area while also focusing on the lost of Israel. Among the myriad lessons that emanate from this passage is that a failure to recognize Jesus for who He is and for His purpose is devastating. That unbelief and lack of faith will eliminate any rewards and all realization of blessings.

The Lesson Applied

The townspeople of Nazareth were quite proud of their native son who had turned out to be a successful teacher-preacher. As we have witnessed, they marveled at His vocabulary and allegorical pedagogy while commenting on His growth and maturity. They were amazed at the display of wisdom from such a young man (remember, Jesus was approximately thirty years of age) who had been reared in their village. Yes, they were quite proud. But sadly, their pride turned to anger simply because the depth of their faith restricted the belief that He was called by God beyond what they were able to recognize. As believers, we must not allow our prejudices based on age, sex, or a person's history to limit who may respond to the call of God into ministry. Often people have to leave their hometowns to experience their greatest success. Why do you think that is? Is it harder to accept someone with whom something is known or unknown?

Let's Talk About It

Why did Satan come to Jesus?

The wilderness temptation by Satan should not be surprising. Jesus and Satan had a history. They knew each other well. When Satan was thrown out of heaven, Jesus was there. Through all of the evil that Israel faced throughout the centuries, the Savior was there. And later, as probably the first documented healing of His ministry, Jesus exorcised the demoniac as the demons recognized and called Jesus by name because He was known by Satan (Luke 8:26–39).

Satan should have known these temptations would not be successful, and although the attempt was made, Jesus resisted and pleased God. How was Jesus able to successfully defend Himself from Satan? How might we do the same when we are tempted?

Home Daily Devotional Readings

January 4–10, 2021

Monday	Tuesday	Wednesday	Thursday	Friday	Saturday	Sunday
Called to Lead Israelites from Egypt	Called to Deliver Israelites from Midianites	Called and Cleansed for Ministry	Single-Mindedness Required to Follow Jesus	Repentance, Goal of God's Kindness	Jesus Calls Peter to Ministry	Don't Be Afraid to Catch People
Exodus 3:1–12	Judges 6:11–16	Isaiah 6:1–8	Luke 9:57–62	Romans 2:1–11	John 21:15–19	Luke 5:1–11

CALLED TO SIGNIFICANCE

ADULT TOPIC:
THE ULTIMATE FISH STORY

BACKGROUND SCRIPTURE:
LUKE 5:1–11

LUKE 5:1–11

King James Version

AND it came to pass, that, as the people pressed upon him to hear the word of God, he stood by the lake of Gennesaret,

2 And saw two ships standing by the lake: but the fishermen were gone out of them, and were washing their nets.

3 And he entered into one of the ships, which was Simon's, and prayed him that he would thrust out a little from the land. And he sat down, and taught the people out of the ship.

4 Now when he had left speaking, he said unto Simon, Launch out into the deep, and let down your nets for a draught.

5 And Simon answering said unto him, Master, we have toiled all the night, and have taken nothing: nevertheless at thy word I will let down the net.

6 And when they had this done, they inclosed a great multitude of fishes: and their net brake.

7 And they beckoned unto their partners, which were in the other ship, that they should come and help them. And they came, and filled both the ships, so that they began to sink.

8 When Simon Peter saw it, he fell down at Jesus' knees, saying, Depart from me; for I am a sinful man, O Lord.

9 For he was astonished, and all that were with him, at the draught of the fishes which they had taken:

10 And so was also James, and John, the sons of Zebedee, which were partners with Simon.

New Revised Standard Version

ONCE while Jesus was standing beside the lake of Gennesaret, and the crowd was pressing in on him to hear the word of God,

2 he saw two boats there at the shore of the lake; the fishermen had gone out of them and were washing their nets.

3 He got into one of the boats, the one belonging to Simon, and asked him to put out a little way from the shore. Then he sat down and taught the crowds from the boat.

4 When he had finished speaking, he said to Simon, "Put out into the deep water and let down your nets for a catch."

5 Simon answered, "Master, we have worked all night long but have caught nothing. Yet if you say so, I will let down the nets."

6 When they had done this, they caught so many fish that their nets were beginning to break.

7 So they signaled their partners in the other boat to come and help them. And they came and filled both boats, so that they began to sink.

8 But when Simon Peter saw it, he fell down at Jesus' knees, saying, "Go away from me, Lord, for I am a sinful man!"

9 For he and all who were with him were amazed at the catch of fish that they had taken;

10 and so also were James and John, sons of Zebedee, who were partners with Simon. Then

MAIN THOUGHT: And so was also James, and John, the sons of Zebedee, which were partners with Simon. And Jesus said unto Simon, Fear not; from henceforth thou shalt catch men. (Luke 5:10, KJV)

Luke 5:1–11

King James Version	*New Revised Standard Version*
And Jesus said unto Simon, Fear not; from henceforth thou shalt catch men.	**Jesus said to Simon, "Do not be afraid; from now on you will be catching people."**
11 And when they had brought their ships to land, they forsook all, and followed him.	**11 When they had brought their boats to shore, they left everything and followed him.**

LESSON SETTING

Time: *circa* A.D. 27
Place: Gennesaret, Galilee

LESSON OUTLINE

I. Identifying the First Disciples (Luke 5:1–4)
II. Following Jesus' Command (Luke 5:5–8)
III. The Reaction of the Fishermen (Luke 5:9–11)

Unifying Principle

People seek significance and purpose. Are we on earth just to eke out a living, or can we be part of something greater? Jesus called Simon and his cohorts to follow Him and find fulfillment in doing the work of God's Kingdom.

Introduction

Following a mood swing from pride and jubilation to utter rejection and disdain, Jesus left His hometown of Nazareth and went to Capernaum in Galilee. As He did in many other villages and in Nazareth, Jesus began to teach in the local synagogue, which gained Him a new wave of popularity. There, in Gentile territory, Jesus made Capernaum His base of operations.

As an indicator of His movement, Jesus' authority had been proven over demons (Luke 4:31–37), disease (Luke 4:38–44), and now, on this fishing expedition, over the first disciples. At a beach near the lake, the scene displayed the call of the first four disciples to become an integral part of Jesus' mission.

Exposition

I. Identifying the First Disciples (Luke 5:1–4)

In this narrative, Luke noted that Jesus was walking or standing by the Lake of Gennesaret, which is also known as the Sea of Tiberias (John 6:1) or the Sea of Galilee (Matt. 4:18). Jesus was attempting to escape the massive crowds that were searching for Him. Luke indicated Jesus had increased the number of healings, as He did not refuse to lay hands on any of the people who were brought before Him (Luke 4:40). As word spread, many people who could not be cured by the physicians of the area or could not afford a doctor came to Him. It is probable the majority did not seek Jesus for His teaching and preaching, which was necessary to cure their spiritual infections or disorders, but to have their physical maladies alleviated. Notice that among the anonymous restorations that occurred, Luke highlighted the healing of Peter's mother-in-law prior to Simon becoming a disciple of Jesus (Luke 4:38–39). This indicates Jesus had developed a relationship with Simon (who would become known as Peter), probably through Andrew, who was a disciple of John but had switched his allegiance to Jesus. Notice they asked Jesus to help the woman following Jesus' appearance in the synagogue. It is no wonder Simon invited Jesus home after the synagogue incident. Now, the authority of Jesus over those who would be called as disciples was established.

Although Jesus had begun to wind down His activities and found what seemed to be a secluded place to rest and recuperate, Luke indicated the people continued to press against Him, which became an imposition that impeded His movement. As Jesus continued walking along the waterfront, He came upon the dock area where the fishermen were tending to their boats after a night of fishing. These fishermen did not have the elaborate boat docks that would be seen in a wealthy community or the type the navy or a military power would use. Their boats most likely were pulled up to the shore, as Luke described their position at the edge of the waters. These boats probably were secured by tying them to poles or dragging them completely out of the water, which would make it easy to put them out again at Jesus' request. On this morning, these fishermen were cleaning their nets and trying to make up from the possible lackluster catch from the previous night.

Due to Jesus' growing popularity, crowds continued to gather around Him. At some point, Jesus got into one of the boats, which belonged to Simon, and asked the fishermen to return to sea. Luke did not provide any dialogue that occurred between Jesus and Simon; however, it would be difficult to believe Simon did not protest at this stage. Nonetheless, Luke's description was that Jesus sat down in the boat and began to teach the people who had been following Him. It seems as if He wanted some space between the boat (which was pulled up along the shore) and the crowds because He asked Simon to go out a short distance from the banks. This would allow Him to teach and be heard by the crowds without them being able to press against Him.

Simon complied with Jesus' request; and it appears all of Simon's crew, including Andrew, were present aboard the small craft. When Jesus finished or concluded His instruction, He asked Simon to navigate his boat out into the deep water of the sea. What happened next is incredible because Jesus asked Simon to again lower his nets in order to catch or begin to start catching fish. The Scriptures do not provide any information as to whether, prior to this encounter, Simon was aware of Jesus' vocation as a stonecutter or carpenter. Neither did Jesus provide Simon with any evidence that demonstrated His expertise as a seasoned fisherman. From this perspective, it is obvious Simon would not have recognized Jesus as one of the locals who plied their trade along the Gennesaret coastline. Therefore, the insistence to fish during the day, and possibly in an area they had previously fished, must have seemed incredulous or foolish to Simon. However, only the Christ could reverse the designs of that which could be considered irrational or unwise. Jesus, Rabbi, Teacher, and Master of the elements could command Simon to do what Simon believed was impossible!

II. Following Jesus' Command (Luke 5:5–8)

Notice the response from Simon: "Master, we have worked all night long but have caught nothing" (Luke 5:5, NRSV). Remember, these men fished at night because the fish stayed in the depths of the lake during the day to escape the heat, only to surface at night to eat. Fishing at night made it easier to obtain a large catch, although they might not necessarily cast their nets where the fish surfaced. The use of nets was their preferred method of fishing. At this point, we are witness to a great display of Simon's faith in Jesus. As aforementioned, a relationship already had developed between Simon and Jesus, attested by the dinner invitation to Simon's house and the healing of his mother-in-law. Following Jesus' request to lower their nets, Simon replied, "I will do as You say and let down the nets" (Luke 5:5, NASB). Simon, an experienced fisherman did not obey Jesus' command because of Jesus' proficiency in fishing; he displayed a sense of faith that would bring him close to Jesus and endear him to the Master. Simon called Jesus *Master* or *Rabbi* (*ἐπιστάτης, epistates*) because he recognized Jesus as a person of high status. However, a more accurate definition of the Greek term describes Jesus as the One who stands near!

Now, when Simon and his companions followed the command of Jesus, a miracle occurred. When they brought up their nets, they found they had caught such a large quantity of fish—which appear for the first time in verse 6—that their nets began to strain under the weight of the load. The fish literally were breaking through or tearing their freshly washed nets. In the imagery of David's cup running over (Ps. 23:5) and Malachi's praise of God's pouring out blessings that overflow and are impossible to receive (Mal. 3:10), the men on the boat were witnesses to their inability to hold on to or seize the entirety of God's blessings.

The load was so heavy there was a danger of capsizing. Therefore, the men in Simon's boat signaled to their partners and companions who were in other boats. Simon's men probably were screaming to the other boats in both fear and delight. Here, in the heat of the day, at a time when successful fishing was almost nonexistent, the haul of fish filled all of the nets to their capacity, to such a degree even the other boats that had assisted in the catch began to sink beneath the waves. Interestingly, this scene indicates that when Jesus had Simon's boat move out into the depths of the lake, several other boats followed. Although Luke did not say Jesus commanded any of the other boats to cast out with Him, the curiosity or power of His command to Simon demanded the other vessels, and the men aboard, not be left out of the objective.

Simon realized that although he did not say it, he did not totally believe Jesus as he rowed his small boat out into the depths. He had *some* faith, but not *total* faith. Some may believe he responded to Jesus' request to humor Him. However, any skepticism on Simon's part probably was based on his perception that Jesus was not an experienced fisherman. The incredible haul of fish shocked Simon, and at that point, he realized his shortcomings in the presence of the Master. Simon saw that Jesus belonged to a sphere to which he did not belong. "Here in his presence was the Lord of fish and fishermen, the Lord of nature, the Lord of men and of their daily work." If by now, Simon did not fully understand Jesus was the Christ, he did at least understand the divine presence was in Christ, and thus, he called him Lord. Simon knew he was in some way in the presence of God. Humbled, Simon fell down (*προσπίπτω, prospipto*) before the Lord. Interestingly, this term is defined as to "prostrate oneself before another," implying supplication. A strictly literal translation of *προσπίπτω*, "to fall down before," can be entirely misleading in that it may suggest an accident caused by stumbling or tripping. It may, therefore, be necessary to translate it as "to bow down low before" or "to bow down to the ground before." Moreover, in the original text, Luke included the Greek noun *γόνυ* (*gony*), knee, to describe that Simon fell at Jesus' knees while bowing and assumed a prostrate position as he went to his knees. Simon probably felt a horrible twinge of shame and embarrassment at his lack of complete faith in Jesus. Simon's reply in this situation was that he was a sinner or a sinful man. Simon did not actually want Jesus to leave him, but he realized his shortcomings and felt ashamed to be in Jesus' presence.

III. The Reaction of the Fishermen (Luke 5:9–11)

Regardless of the mortification Simon felt, his humiliation soon turned to amazement and excitement. These seasoned fishermen had never experienced anything like this, and they were reeling in a sense of awe. These men, Simon and his companions, now seized the moment, and they could barely contain themselves because of the miracle that had taken place.

Continuing the jubilation, Luke named some of the key players who witnessed Jesus' command over the fishing expedition. After regaining their senses, their joy may have turned to fear. They may have become afraid of the unknown, of what would happen next. The men, who did not really know Jesus, may have been fearful of His reaction to their lack of faith. After some unrecorded conversation, Jesus immediately got to the point. He asked the disciples to join His movement. While familiar with the charge of "follow Me," the language used is *deute* (*δεῦτε*), meaning "to come." Their response to follow Jesus did not occur until the next verse (v. 11). However, we must caution against having a strict literal translation of this phrase. The familiar, "I will make you fishers [or catchers] of men," can be problematic. For example, the verb *poieo* (*ποιέω*) is understood as "to cause or to make." *Fishers of men* is such a well-known phrase to us that we seldom suspect it can provide the basis for considerable misunderstanding in translations. Nonetheless, it does. If the expression used for "catching fish" contains the same verb as is used for those who round up forced labor, or those who arrest people, there inevitably will be misunderstanding. For certain linguists, this traditional wording is understood or implied. However, it also leads to some awkward translations if the wording is taken literally. Obviously, when Jesus encouraged Simon and the others to use their craft in this new movement, He essentially was saying that if they could indeed catch fish, they could (in a spiritual sense) capture the hearts and minds of people who needed rescue from the perils of being outside the will of God. These men, feeling the power of Jesus's invitation, immediately abandoned their nets and vocations. James and John, sons of Zebedee, were fishing partners with Simon and Andrew and formed the quadrant core of Jesus' twelve disciples. Nonetheless, it is in this small space that we find Jesus at His best, as He comforted His future disciples by allaying their apprehension and proverbially embracing them into His movement with these words: "From now on you will be catching people" (Luke 4:10, NRSV).

Concluding the narrative, Luke explained the fishing party brought their boats (and the large catch of fish) to the beach where they docked their boats. After disseminating their catch, probably with their families and Zebedee, they demonstrated their allegiance to Jesus. In this method of calling, they decided to leave everything—their boats, their vocation, and their lifestyles. These new disciples of Jesus committed to follow Him as they pursued a program to catch people, a decision they would not regret by any standard of any time period.

The Lesson Applied

Jesus called these fishermen to leave their profession behind and to begin following Him permanently. This probably was not as easy or as sanitized as the Scriptures reveal. Recall that fishing was their vocation, not their vacation. Their immediate concern was to put food on the table and care for their families. The question as to how they would live and exist probably weighed heavily on their minds. Nonetheless, placing their faith in Jesus proved to be invaluable, as the Lord provided whatever they needed. Believers now have a scriptural record of the flow of provision for those who believed in Him.

Let's Talk About It

What makes the fish such a significant symbol in Christian history?

The symbol of fish preceded the cross as the symbol for Christianity and will be forever linked with Peter more than the other disciples. The Galilean setting of Jesus' ministry created rich a metaphor, as Jesus called at least seven fishermen to be His disciples. The imagery of fish is ripe in the New Testament, such as the feeding of the five thousand and Jesus providing breakfast for His disciples (John 21:11–13). Paul and other New Testament writers used the imagery in their respective literature, and it became a prominent image of the early church. While the symbol of the boat represented safety and salvation, the fish represented Jesus Christ, Son of God.

Home Daily Devotional Readings

January 11–17, 2021

Monday	Tuesday	Wednesday	Thursday	Friday	Saturday	Sunday
Peace and Healing Will Come	Healed by Christ's Wounds	Canaanite Daughter Healed by Mother's Faith	Anoint Sick with Oil and Prayer	Woman Healed by Her Faith	The Sick Need a Physician	Jesus Heals and Forgives the Paralytic
Isaiah 57:14–21	1 Peter 2:18–25	Matthew 15:21–28	James 5:13–16	Mark 5:21–34	Mark 2:13–17	Mark 2:1–12

CALLED TO HEAL

ADULT TOPIC:
HEALING FOR THE WHOLE PERSON

BACKGROUND SCRIPTURE:
MARK 2:1–12

MARK 2:1–12

King James Version

AND again he entered into Capernaum after some days; and it was noised that he was in the house.

2 And straightway many were gathered together, insomuch that there was no room to receive them, no, not so much as about the door: and he preached the word unto them.

3 And they come unto him, bringing one sick of the palsy, which was borne of four.

4 And when they could not come nigh unto him for the press, they uncovered the roof where he was: and when they had broken it up, they let down the bed wherein the sick of the palsy lay.

5 When Jesus saw their faith, he said unto the sick of the palsy, Son, thy sins be forgiven thee.

6 But there were certain of the scribes sitting there, and reasoning in their hearts,

7 Why doth this man thus speak blasphemies? who can forgive sins but God only?

8 And immediately when Jesus perceived in his spirit that they so reasoned within themselves, he said unto them, Why reason ye these things in your hearts?

9 Whether is it easier to say to the sick of the palsy, Thy sins be forgiven thee; or to say, Arise, and take up thy bed, and walk?

10 But that ye may know that the Son of man hath power on earth to forgive sins, (he saith to the sick of the palsy,)

11 I say unto thee, Arise, and take up thy bed, and go thy way into thine house.

New Revised Standard Version

WHEN he returned to Capernaum after some days, it was reported that he was at home.

2 So many gathered around that there was no longer room for them, not even in front of the door; and he was speaking the word to them.

3 Then some people came, bringing to him a paralyzed man, carried by four of them.

4 And when they could not bring him to Jesus because of the crowd, they removed the roof above him; and after having dug through it, they let down the mat on which the paralytic lay.

5 When Jesus saw their faith, he said to the paralytic, "Son, your sins are forgiven."

6 Now some of the scribes were sitting there, questioning in their hearts,

7 "Why does this fellow speak in this way? It is blasphemy! Who can forgive sins but God alone?"

8 At once Jesus perceived in his spirit that they were discussing these questions among themselves; and he said to them, "Why do you raise such questions in your hearts?

9 Which is easier, to say to the paralytic, 'Your sins are forgiven,' or to say, 'Stand up and take your mat and walk'?

10 But so that you may know that the Son of Man has authority on earth to forgive sins"—he said to the paralytic—

11 "I say to you, stand up, take your mat and go to your home."

MAIN THOUGHT: Whether is it easier to say to the sick of the palsy, Thy sins be forgiven thee; or to say, Arise, and take up thy bed, and walk? (Mark 2:9, KJV)

MARK 2:1–12

King James Version	*New Revised Standard Version*
12 And immediately he arose, took up the bed, and went forth before them all; insomuch that they were all amazed, and glorified God, saying, We never saw it on this fashion.	**12 And he stood up, and immediately took the mat and went out before all of them; so that they were all amazed and glorified God, saying, "We have never seen anything like this!"**

LESSON SETTING

Time: *circa* A.D. 27
Place: Capernaum, Galilee

LESSON OUTLINE

I. Unknown Men Driven by Faith (Mark 2:1–4)
II. Healing of the Paralytic (Mark 2:5–10)
III. All Authority Is in My Hands (Mark 2:10–12)

UNIFYING PRINCIPLE

The limitations of human existence make genuine wholeness an elusive goal. Where can we find true healing? By declaring a paralyzed man's sins forgiven and restoring his physical health, Jesus demonstrated that God called Jesus to heal infirmities of the soul as well as the body.

INTRODUCTION

Jesus proved His authority over leprosy, over disease, over a demon, over His disciples, and now over the crippling effects of paralysis of both the body and mind. What is interesting in this account is that He encountered a man who exhibited a powerful faith, whose paralyzed body was healed because of the realization of Jesus' identity. The scene is almost unbelievable, and the story of this healing is one of the most famously quoted commands in Scripture. None of this could have been possible without the massive amount of faith demonstrated by the man and his friends.

EXPOSITION

I. UNKNOWN MEN DRIVEN BY FAITH (MARK 2:1–4)

Jesus returned to Capernaum after spending time in what Mark described as a desert region. Because of the widespread acclaim of His healing, Jesus' popularity had become so intense He could not spend time in any of the surrounding cities or villages. Therefore, He sought refuge in desolate, unpopulated areas that provided some sense of isolation and respite from the people. Despite Jesus' attempts at sequestration, Mark recorded that the people continued to come from everywhere, seeking Him (Mark 1:45). It is interesting that Jesus returned home to this fishing village located on the northwest coast of the Sea of Galilee. Mark recorded Jesus' home as Capernaum and not Nazareth (His childhood city), where He was rebuffed. This identified Capernaum as Jesus' base of operations for His movement and ministry. Even after spending some days away from this area, the people of Capernaum heard Jesus had returned. As word spread, it became known Jesus could be found there, and the people were determined to press Him to solve their needs, so much so that they sought the place where He was staying.

As the narrative continues, it becomes painfully obvious the people found Jesus at home, only to discover the crowd had grown so large they were spilling out of the house and into the courtyard. Mark described the scene as a quasi-mob spectacle, saying there was no room for the people to assemble, using the Greek adverb *μηκέτι* (*meketi*), "no more" or "no longer" (any room), to illustrate the situation in the house. Although Mark did not relate the details of the message, due to their unruliness, all the crowd could do was listen as Jesus continued to speak the word to them.

The focus shifted to several men who were approaching the house. Not all of the men were in the same or equal physical shape. These men were carrying a man to seek a blessing from Jesus. The Scripture describes the nature of the man's illness as a paralytic. It is not known whether he had been crippled from birth. Nonetheless, these four men must have been family members or dedicated friends to have borne, or taken up, his pallet to the now overly crowded house. The phrase *they came* must in many languages be rendered as "some people came." If this is not done, an impression may be given that the crowd that was gathered (the last third person plural referent) brought the man. An interesting parallel to Mark's account is that Luke 5:18 reads, "And behold, some men were bringing…" (ESV). Who "they" are is a matter of conjecture. Some theologians believe they were the relatives of the paralytic, as distinct from the bearers. To the degree Mark's version is presented, the man on the stretcher was being brought to Jesus for grace and mercy.

As the party carrying the man reached the house, they realized that because of the crowd, it was going to be impossible to get to Jesus. Not realizing all things are possible with God (Mark 10:27), the party was resigned they could not and were not able or capable to help their friend and brother by presenting his situation to Jesus. Suddenly, someone had an idea: "Let's find another opening into the house where we don't have to fight the crowd." More than likely, they had tried the back door and any windows only to find them blocked, but there was another way. In a manner our contemporary culture could not imagine, their access to Jesus would be through the roof!

Mark revealed the method of how these men executed their plans as they reached the flat roof by an outside stairway. Mark continued to describe their mission using the Greek term *ἀποστεγάζω* (*apostegazo*), which means "unroof" or "to remove the roof from the house." In Mark 2:4, ἀποστεγάζω refers to only a part of the roof; therefore, in a number of languages, it may be necessary to translate as, "They made a hole in the roof." In view of the types of houses built in Palestine in New Testament times, the roof would have been flat, held up by heavy beams over which were laid planks or sticks that were covered with sunbaked clay. They were then able to dig out an area in the flat roof by breaking the planks and digging through the branches and clay to create an opening that allowed them to lower the pallet on which the paralytic was lying.

II. Healing of the Paralytic (Mark 2:5–10)

As a hole was being created in the roof, it probably interrupted Jesus' teaching because the attention would have shifted to the commotion above their heads. There would have been a combination of anger, such as the homeowners decrying the destruction of the property, and the insults of the people who could not get to Jesus (as we are frustrated by people who cut line). Jesus, however, was not disturbed by this breach, what would have been considered improper conduct, but saw the faith that drove their mission. Rather than scold the men who had destroyed a portion of the roof and disrupted Jesus' discourse, Jesus said to the paralytic, "Son, your sins are forgiven" (Mark 2:5, NRSV). Notice that Mark used the Greek term *τέκνον* (*teknon*), which is translated as "child." Although this is written as "son," it is not the same term used in John 3:16 where John uses *υἱός* (*huios*), meaning "son," but specifically "offspring." In a number of languages, it is impossible to translate *τέκνον* as "child," since this might immediately suggest Jesus was declaring Himself to be the father of this man. Furthermore, the paralytic was evidently an adult male. A more satisfactory equivalent would be "my dear man" or "my dear fellow."

A careful understanding of Jesus' proclamation that the man's sins were forgiven should not be misconstrued as indicating the man's sickness was the direct result of sin. Some Jews speculated such was always the case. Sickness and suffering commonly were held to be the consequences of one's sin. This idea became troublesome, however, when the victim was born with a disability such as blindness. Jesus corrected this false idea and then focused on the purpose of this particular suffering, which provided an occasion for revealing God's glory (John 9:1–3).

As an opposing reaction to God's glory, evil penetrated the hearts of the scribes who were present in the crowded home. Jesus noticed they began to discuss the situation and consider the implications of what they had heard from Jesus' lips. It quickly became obvious the scribes were not pleased with Jesus' reaction to the drastic measures of the men. Mark stated they contemplated in their hearts, and their demeanor probably turned to anger as they argued among themselves as to how they should interpret Jesus' pronouncement. These pseudo-holy men seemed to always show up where Jesus taught and preached because His reputation drew both the common people and those who sought to discredit Him. Because of their positions as the religious authorities of the people, they would be afforded the best seats in any gathering, whether in a synagogue or this house. So they came looking for one false move.

Nevertheless, the appearance of these religious authorities was only going to end in a disagreement. They asked, loudly, why Jesus was saying these things. For these men, Jesus was committing blasphemy, which meant "to revile, to slander, or to speak irreverently" about God or sacred things. Moreover, and most seriously, a blasphemer would claim to be God, which Jesus was later accused of doing by declaring He was the Son of God. In the minds of these scribes, Jesus was wrong because only God can forgive sins, as Daniel declared, "To the Lord our God belong mercy and forgiveness" (Dan. 9:9, NRSV). In the Old Testament, the forgiveness of sins never was attributed to the Messiah. Therefore, the scribes regarded such talk by this fellow as a pretentious affront to God's power and authority, which was a serious offense punishable by death from stoning (Lev. 24:15–16). Such a charge became the basis for a formal condemnation later when Jesus spoke about the concept and the ability to forgive. The religious leaders later challenged Jesus by asking who gave Him the authority to do these things or define forgiveness (Mark 11:28). These men had gathered to find fault with Jesus and missed that Jesus was the authority who was filled with power from the same God they were attempting to limit!

Immediately, Jesus knew these men were plotting against Him. Mark spoke of the center or place of the reasoning as "in their hearts" (Mark 2:6, NRSV). The heart often was used to relate to such things as personality, memory, emotions, desires, and the will in the imagery of biblical lore.

The heart can be imbued with moral qualities, as in hearts that can be proud (Ps. 131:1) or evil (1 Sam. 17:28). It is because the heart stands for human personality that God looks there rather than at our actions to see whether we are faithful or not. Therefore, Mark's emphasis was on the heart, not any possible quizzical expressions that may have been on the men's faces. Through their hearts, Jesus saw their real intent and malicious thoughts.

Jesus turned His objective to the authorities. He challenged them by setting up questions that were complex but quite simple. As an example, Mark later reported that Jesus challenged these same religious leaders by asking them if the baptism of John was from heaven or from humans. The leaders knew they had been outmaneuvered because if they responded that John's baptism was from heaven, Jesus' reply would have been, "Yet you refused to believe him." But if they said it was from humans, the people would turn against them because John was regarded as a prophet (Mark 11:30–32). In the same way Jesus forced them to determine whether John the Baptist had been sent from God, the apex of Jesus' questions was whether the paralytic's sins could be forgiven or his body healed. If the men answered that it was easier to say to the paralytic his sins were forgiven, they would be guilty of the same blasphemy of which they had accused Jesus, as they thought no one could forgive sins but God. Likewise, if they said to the paralytic, "Take up your bed and walk," they would look foolish, knowing they did not have the authority to heal the paralytic!

III. All Authority Is in My Hands (Mark 2:10–12)

As the challenge came to a conclusion, Jesus revealed He, the Son of Man, had the authority, better yet the power, on earth to forgive sins. This statement seemed to be lost to the leaders. If these men had any idea of some of the attributes of the Messiah they were awaiting, they should have recognized Jesus' proclamation was not idle speech but a declaration of His persuasion, His power, and His position!

In one of the more famous phrases of the New Testament, Jesus commanded the paralytic man to pick up his bed and go home! The Greek term *ὑπάγω* (*hypago*) also could mean "go away," the purpose of which was not to insinuate the man should simply depart but to realize he was healed. The compassion of Jesus and the glory of God was witnessed in the healing of this formerly paralyzed man.

The man got up immediately, picked up the pallet that was once his stretcher, and left the house and the amazed crowd. Mark did not report that anyone was concerned about the damage to the roof of the house. They were too dazzled at what they had witnessed. No one was upset about losing their place in line to speak to Jesus, as it seemed they now were hopeful their collective and individual situations could be changed by Jesus. The people had never seen anything like this, and that was the objective of this public healing—that they might witness the authority, compassion, and mercy of Jesus. The reaction of the people was to begin to glorify God. The Greek term used by Mark is *δοξάζω* (*doxazo*), which means "to praise or glorify God." From this, we get our term *doxology*, which is defined as "the study of the glorification of God." However, doxology is also a liturgical formula for praise to God. An example of further use may be found in Pauline doxologies that frequently take on the form, "To [God] be the glory forever and ever. Amen" (Gal. 1:5; Phil. 4:20; 2 Tim. 4:18, NRSV). Paul often ended his letters with a note of praise to God.

The Lesson Applied

During His ministry, Jesus was the supreme authority on earth and had authority and power designated from the Father in heaven. The religious leaders did not recognize the long-awaited Messiah because of spiritual blindness. Their lack of faith was based on their desire to retain position and status. Their lack of faith was in their misinterpretation of the mission of Jesus. Because of their obstinacy, they were blinded. They had problems seeing God because they held to the wrong appropriations.

Let's Talk About It

Why did Jesus use the title *Son of Man* to refer to Himself?

Jesus used the term *Son of Man* to describe who He was and did not refer to Himself as the Messiah. This was His favorite self-descriptive method of identification, which is found fourteen times in Mark and was based on Daniel 7:13–14. The title *Son of God* is Jesus' divine name (Matt. 8:29), while *Son of David* is His Jewish name (Matt. 9:27). However, *Son of Man* is the name that links Him to the earth and to His mission. The use of the *Son of Man* title emphasized His lowliness and humanity (Matt. 8:20), His suffering and death, (Matt. 20:28), and His future reign as King (Matt. 24:27).

Home Daily Devotional Readings
January 18–24, 2021

Monday	Tuesday	Wednesday	Thursday	Friday	Saturday	Sunday
Prayer for Peter in Prison	Pray for a Successful Ministry	Pray for Inner Strength and Power	Pray the Prayer of Our Lord	Pray for Your Abusers	Pray to Avoid Trials	Jesus Prays for His Disciples
Acts 12:5–11	Romans 15:22–33	Ephesians 3:14–21	Matthew 6:7–13	Luke 6:22–33	Luke 22:39–46	John 17:13–24

LESSON 8 JANUARY 24, 2021

CALLED AS THE INTERCESSOR

ADULT TOPIC:
STANDING IN THE GAP

BACKGROUND SCRIPTURE:
JOHN 17:14–24

JOHN 17:14–24

King James Version

**I HAVE given them thy word; and the world
hath hated them, because they are not of the
world, even as I am not of the world.
15 I pray not that thou shouldest take them out
of the world, but that thou shouldest keep them
from the evil.
16 They are not of the world, even as I am not
of the world.
17 Sanctify them through thy truth: thy word
is truth.
18 As thou hast sent me into the world, even so
have I also sent them into the world.
19 And for their sakes I sanctify myself, that
they also might be sanctified through the truth.
20 Neither pray I for these alone, but for
them also which shall believe on me through
their word;
21 That they all may be one; as thou, Father,
art in me, and I in thee, that they also may be
one in us: that the world may believe that thou
hast sent me.
22 And the glory which thou gavest me I have
given them; that they may be one, even as we
are one:
23 I in them, and thou in me, that they may be
made perfect in one; and that the world may
know that thou hast sent me, and hast loved
them, as thou hast loved me.
24 Father, I will that they also, whom thou hast
given me, be with me where I am; that they
may behold my glory, which thou hast given
me: for thou lovedst me before the foundation
of the world.**

New Revised Standard Version

**I HAVE given them your word, and the world
has hated them because they do not belong to
the world, just as I do not belong to the world.
15 I am not asking you to take them out of the
world, but I ask you to protect them from the
evil one.
16 They do not belong to the world, just as I do
not belong to the world.
17 Sanctify them in the truth; your word
is truth.
18 As you have sent me into the world, so I
have sent them into the world.
19 And for their sakes I sanctify myself, so that
they also may be sanctified in truth.
20 "I ask not only on behalf of these, but
also on behalf of those who will believe in me
through their word,
21 that they may all be one. As you, Father, are
in me and I am in you, may they also be in us,
so that the world may believe that you have
sent me.
22 The glory that you have given me I have
given them, so that they may be one, as we
are one,
23 I in them and you in me, that they may
become completely one, so that the world may
know that you have sent me and have loved
them even as you have loved me.
24 Father, I desire that those also, whom you
have given me, may be with me where I am,
to see my glory, which you have given me
because you loved me before the foundation of
the world.**

MAIN THOUGHT: Neither pray I for these alone, but for them also which shall believe on me through their word. (John 17:20, KJV)

LESSON SETTING

Time: *circa* A.D. 29
Place: Capernaum, Galilee

LESSON OUTLINE

I. **The Glory of God's Word (John 17:14–16)**
II. **The Glory of Sanctification (John 17:17–21)**
III. **The Glory of Oneness (John 17:22–24)**

Unifying Principle

People often look for ways to appeal for assistance on the behalf of others. How can people respond to the urge to intercede in a meaningful manner? Jesus' prayer for His disciples serves as a call to use intercessory prayer for the sake of others.

Introduction

The basic definition of intercessory prayer is that the source is someone other than the one for which it is intended—it is a prayer lifted for the benefit of another. In the Bible, petition and intercession are primary, though adoration, thanksgiving, and confession also have roles. Yet, the petitionary element is present in all these forms of prayer. Intercessory prayer is a gift to both the believer and to those for whom the prayer is directed. Intercessory prayer comes from Jesus because it was given to Him from the Father. The following example is Jesus' intercessory prayer for us!

Exposition

I. The Glory of God's Word (John 17:14–16)

Jesus began His discourse by saying He had given His followers the word of God, not to be misunderstood as the Scriptures but a bond, a covenantal commitment, a guarantee. Jesus bestowed this promise to the believers because they had a special connection with Him. He considered His faithful as those who were beyond the world because He is beyond the world. To understand this concept is to realize Jesus is a gift, even in His human form, to humanity and to the world. Although many will reject Him, to those who receive Him, He remains special. Sadly, evil forces have hampered the gift of God from the beginning of creation. To be certain, John used the term *world* (*κόσμος, kosmos*) to define those who oppose the mission of Jesus and the loyalty of His followers. Therefore, understanding John, the world hates and detests the believers of the Lord. In the manner the Old Testament account of Joseph was used to preserve a remnant in the earth, a protected remainder of God's people, by keeping them alive for posterity (Gen. 45:7), Jesus echoed the protection that will be granted to His believers. Jesus gave His followers the word of God's protection because He knew about the jealousy and dangerous forces allied against the mission of the Lord.

Under these circumstances, there should be the appearance of panic. However, God's plan was not to remove the disciples and fellow believers from danger and opposition by taking them out of the world, but to preserve them in the midst of conflict. In His prayer, Jesus requested His Father leave them in the world but provide His protection that would keep them for their contribution to the movement. As history moves forward, the intercessory prayer of protection will observe the snares of the evil one (*πονηρός, poneros*), whose wickedness has been inserted in the devotees of Satan. In some languages, one may use such an expression as "keep them safe from the one who is truly evil" or "is really evil." Unfortunately, much of humanity does not believe in the struggle between the moral goodness of Jesus and the dark forces of Satan. Their disbelief and apathy become a snare that lures the nonbeliever into being a satanic disciple who does his bidding by committing ethical crimes or ignoring the plight of the common people. As Martin Luther King Jr. so eloquently stated, "Injustice anywhere is a threat to justice everywhere. We are caught in an inescapable network of mutuality, tied in a single garment of destiny. Whatever affects one directly, affects all indirectly" (King, "Letter From Birmingham Jail," 1). To be effective, Satan's minions do not always have to do something; they simply can disregard the ability to right a wrong. Therefore, Christians are protected by God's ability to intercede in all facets of life, and the followers of Jesus must remain in this world and believe this concept through a display of their faith.

One of the issues presented at this point is there was a lack of understanding as to where Jesus was from, since He was not of the world. John previously recorded an account of a debate between Jesus and a faction of Pharisees in which Jesus scolded them on their lack of knowledge of the Father and Son and heaven. They did not know of His origin, nor did they understand His destination once His earthly mission concluded. Jesus told these men He would be leaving and that where He was going, they could not follow (John 8:13–23). John wrote that He who comes from above is above all, but he who is of the earth is from the earth and speaks with or has earthly understanding. However, He (Jesus) who comes from heaven is above all (John 3:31). Additionally, after telling the disciples He was going away to prepare a place for them so they could be with Him also, Jesus had to remind the disciples they should know the way to where He was going. However, Thomas said to Him, "Lord, we do not know where you are going. How can we know the way?" (John 14:5, NRSV). The disciple's failure was to understand Jesus eventually would be resurrected from the world but they and other generations of believers would remain behind in the world to become testimonies of His glory, make disciples, and further the mission until He comes back for His Church. Again, this is the emphasis of the famous, "If I go and prepare a place for you, I will come again and will take you to myself, so that where I am, there you may be also" (John 14:3, NRSV). Thankfully, because of their special status, *all* believers have been removed from the nonspiritual part of the world. Although we physically may live in the world, believers are not part of it. We are part of the Kingdom.

II. The Glory of Sanctification (John 17:17–21)

Jesus asked God to sanctify all believers and dedicate the full protection of heaven to them. Jesus' prayer to sanctify them in truth was appropriate because Jesus is also the truth (and the light). To sanctify them in truth means to "sanctify them in Me!"

This also indicated Jesus would be responsible for the believers who remained faithful to the mission and the movement. Since God's word is indisputable and unquestionable, His promises will never be abated or diluted but are pure and eternal. The holiness of the community of believers will remain secure because of the promises and power of the Lord. However, such security is predicated on our faithfulness.

Again referring to the gift God gave in His only begotten Son, Jesus was sent into the world for the redemption of humankind. As a Jew, Jesus was born into a Jewish family, raised in Jewish culture, and derisively crucified as "King of the Jews." The irony here is that God had been pleading with His chosen people Israel to return to His sanctuary and become the ideal representatives of the Kingdom. Remember, God continuously directed the prophets to remind a disobedient Israel the Lord had brought them out of Egypt as a loving God. He was not willing to give up on His people. Recall, Paul reminded his followers there was no distinction between Jew and Greek, for the same Lord is Lord of all (Rom. 10:12). This was not to disqualify the Gentiles but to remind humanity of the prominence of Jesus' mission of redemption toward Israel, many of whom rejected Him. Jesus' mission among the Gentiles substantiated that although the gift of the Son was for the redemption of Israel, the gift also was for the saving of everyone from their separation from God (sin).

Continuing His prayer, Jesus intoned that for their sakes He had sanctified Himself. A better understanding may be that although Jesus was holy, His sanctification was dedicated to His mission, which was the cross and the subsequent resurrection. Jesus did not have to reinvent Himself to undergo self-sanctification as the One who throughout His earthly sojourn was sinless. Nonetheless, the object and target of His consecration were the disciples and all believers. The importance of the declaration of sanctifying Himself was the extension of sanctifying His followers in a specialized manner. This sanctification refers to His being separated and dedicated to His death. The purpose of His death was that His followers also may be sanctified in truth.

Jesus' prayer was not selfish or contained to a certain group, although it may seem to be focused on the disciples. Jesus was not interceding for this group only. The prayer and gift are for all who are committed to Jesus. Moreover, Jesus was looking forward to include a future period that forecasts the needs of the Church. Evil will attack the Church and seek to divide believers by using the body to divide itself through things such as jealousies, envy, class warfare, and false teachers. In this final portion of the prayer, Jesus wished for all believers to embrace the realization the Church never will fail. Recall Jesus' words when He declared He would build the Church, and although issues and problems may arise, the gates of hell will not prevail against it (Matt. 16:18). Jesus knew the remnant will need the protection of heaven but also that they will prevail because the mission will be secure.

As Jesus continued, He raised the concept of oneness, or Christian unity. Jesus prayed the effect of this prayer was the believers (and the future Church) will all be one, as the Father, Jesus, and the Holy Spirit are one. The basic definition of the adjective *one* (εἷς, *eis*) is "a single unit made of the same kind of matter." To echo this definition, the Godhead is composed of the same matter spiritually and also in a metaphysical component, such as is realized in the various theophanies in which God may manifest Himself. In an earlier portion of the prayer, Jesus asked the Father keep them "in your name that you have given me, so that they may be one, as we are one" (John 17:11, NRSV). This was another continuation of the desire for the disciples and all believers to emulate the oneness of heaven, as they also were taught to imitate the attributes of Jesus so they may become holy. In this prayer for oneness, Paul later wrote of only a single body of believers, which we are dedicated to in one Lord, one faith, and one baptism (Eph. 4:4–5). Jesus' prayer for the unity of His disciples became obvious because through unity there is also strength; therefore, the pattern to be followed is the unity of the Father, Son, and the Holy Spirit, that all in heaven and earth may become one. The unity here seems to be that of will and purpose, as all believers will only understand and adapt this sense of unity because of their belief and trust in the fact Jesus has been sent from heaven. Believers are from the world, and they will be unified in their desires to serve and glorify the Son.

III. The Glory of Oneness (John 17:22–24)

The aspect of oneness changes the paradigm of the divisions of humanity that Jesus came to redeem. Although it has been aforementioned that His primary mission was to emancipate Israel, the rest of humanity was never an afterthought. Remember, God so loved the entire world that He gave the gift of Jesus so that all of humanity will be reunited with the Creator in an eternal union. In this future unification, the Church will demonstrate its willingness to embrace those who seek Him as well as those who are called according to His purpose. Jesus intoned that the goal of oneness will be realized because of the glory of God, by the power of God. All will share in the total and complete victory over Satan and anything or anyone that would seek to divide God's creation.

The goal of this portion of the prayer is futuristic—that all believers be perfected and made complete when we are at the mountaintop, which stands as a gateway to the Promised Land. Jesus' prayer was that believers demonstrate His glory and love for humanity and that the world will realize all have the ability to be saved because in the unity of the body of Christ, differences of race, status, and gender lose their significance.

Charles Ryrie notes that spiritual position is the same for all, but that does not mean distinctions cease to exist, nor that all have the same functions within the body. Nonetheless, all who are baptized into Christ have clothed themselves with Christ. The result is there is neither Jew nor Greek, neither slave nor free, and neither male nor female, for we all are one in Christ Jesus (Gal. 3:27–28). The theme of God's love is echoed here, as God loves the faithful with the same spirit as God loves the Son! We are reminded Jesus is able to keep us from stumbling and will present us blameless in a perfected state of oneness when we are presented to the Lord. Based on this concept of shared love, it is imperative all believers realize the only way to the Father is through the Son.

In the conclusion of this section on intercessory prayer, Jesus expressed His desire for the oneness of believers and the unity of the mission by reinforcing the people He is to redeem, Jews and Gentiles, have been given over to Him. His petition was that through His mission, the glory of the Lord will be seen by a world that seems to choose to be unrepentant. Not to be lost on this concept is that His believers should not fail to see His glory. However, it is also because of the power element of His glory that His splendor will be revealed and all flesh will acknowledge Jesus is the Messiah. Moreover, if we recall John's teaching that Jesus was there in the beginning (John 1:2), the foundation of the world is defined as the Father's love superseding all boundaries of time, which reflects that God's love and glory has been in place even prior to creation. The final expression of cause—"You loved Me before the foundation of the world"—may then be introduced as a separate sentence by saying, "You gave it to Me because You loved Me before the world was made."

The Lesson Applied

We should not confuse our petitions as a method to change the mind of God. When we consider that James wrote we should pray for one another (James 5:16) and Jesus taught us to pray for those who persecute us (Matt. 5:44), we are able to witness a Christian who is filled with power and has a relationship with the Lord. Intercessory prayer is a gift granted to believers who must first recognize personal prayer works and plays a prominent role in their daily lives. From the realization of personal prayer, intercessory prayer simply becomes an extension of the greatness and glory of God.

Let's Talk About It

What does "in your truth" mean?

The purpose of Christ's death was to dedicate or separate believers to God and His program. B. M. Newman and E. A. Nida explain that "by means of the truth" in John 17:17 is literally "in the truth." If the phrase *in truth* appeared in isolation, it would be natural to translate it as the adverb *truly*. However, in the context of verse 19, it seems best to translate it "by means of the truth." Jesus, as the supreme Gift, extends His sanctification to believers, but this bestowal must be understood by means of the truth that their sanctification is established in Him.

Home Daily Devotional Readings

January 25–31, 2021

Monday	Tuesday	Wednesday	Thursday	Friday	Saturday	Sunday
Jesus Supports Mary's Choice	Jesus Responds to Sisters' Call	Jesus Raises Lazarus; Mary Believes	Women Carry Resurrection Message to Apostles	Jesus' Final Words and Ascension	Simeon Sees Impact of Jesus' Ministry	The Spirit Empowers Daughters to Prophesy
Luke 10:38–42	John 11:1–11	John 11:38–45	Luke 24:5–10	Luke 24:44–53	Luke 2:28–35	Luke 2:36–38; Acts 2:16–21; 21:8–9

PROPHESYING DAUGHTERS

ADULT TOPIC:
WOMEN SPEAK OUT

BACKGROUND SCRIPTURE:
LUKE 2:36–38; ACTS 1:12–14; 2:16–21; 21:8–9

LUKE 2:36–38; ACTS 2:16–21; 21:8–9

King James Version

AND there was one Anna, a prophetess, the daughter of Phanuel, of the tribe of Aser: she was of a great age, and had lived with an husband seven years from her virginity;
37 And she was a widow of about fourscore and four years, which departed not from the temple, but served God with fastings and prayers night and day.
38 And she coming in that instant gave thanks likewise unto the Lord, and spake of him to all them that looked for redemption in Jerusalem.

• • • Acts 2:16–21 • • •

BUT this is that which was spoken by the prophet Joel;
17 And it shall come to pass in the last days, saith God, I will pour out of my Spirit upon all flesh: and your sons and your daughters shall prophesy, and your young men shall see visions, and your old men shall dream dreams:
18 And on my servants and on my handmaidens I will pour out in those days of my Spirit; and they shall prophesy:
19 And I will shew wonders in heaven above, and signs in the earth beneath; blood, and fire, and vapour of smoke:
20 The sun shall be turned into darkness, and the moon into blood, before the great and notable day of the Lord come:
21 And it shall come to pass, that whosoever shall call on the name of the Lord shall be saved.

New Revised Standard Version

THERE was also a prophet, Anna the daughter of Phanuel, of the tribe of Asher. She was of a great age, having lived with her husband seven years after her marriage,
37 then as a widow to the age of eighty–four. She never left the temple but worshiped there with fasting and prayer night and day.
38 At that moment she came, and began to praise God and to speak about the child to all who were looking for the redemption of Jerusalem.

• • • Acts 2:16–21 • • •

NO, this is what was spoken through the prophet Joel:
17 'In the last days it will be, God declares, that I will pour out my Spirit upon all flesh, and your sons and your daughters shall prophesy, and your young men shall see visions, and your old men shall dream dreams.
18 Even upon my slaves, both men and women, in those days I will pour out my Spirit; and they shall prophesy.
19 And I will show portents in the heaven above and signs on the earth below, blood, and fire, and smoky mist.
20 The sun shall be turned to darkness and the moon to blood, before the coming of the Lord's great and glorious day.
21 Then everyone who calls on the name of the Lord shall be saved.'

MAIN THOUGHT: And it shall come to pass in the last days, saith God, I will pour out of my Spirit upon all flesh: and your sons and your daughters shall prophesy, and your young men shall see visions, and your old men shall dream dreams. (Acts 2:17, KJV)

King James Version	*New Revised Standard Version*
• • • Acts 21:8–9 • • •	**• • • Acts 21:8–9 • • •**
8 And the next day we that were of Paul's company departed, and came unto Caesarea: and we entered into the house of Philip the evangelist, which was one of the seven; and abode with him.	**8 The next day we left and came to Caesarea; and we went into the house of Philip the evangelist, one of the seven, and stayed with him.**
9 And the same man had four daughters, virgins, which did prophesy.	**9 He had four unmarried daughters who had the gift of prophecy.**

LESSON SETTING

Time: ***circa*** **6 B.C. (Luke), A.D. 30 and A.D. 55 (Acts)**
Place: Jerusalem (Luke and Acts 2) and Caesarea (Acts 21)

LESSON OUTLINE

I. Anna's Confirmation of Jesus (Luke 2:36–38)
II. Peter's Greatest Sermon (Acts 2:16–21)
III. The Failure of Philip's Daughters (Acts 21:8–9)

UNIFYING PRINCIPLE

All people have a unique purpose in life. How do we affirm each individual's purpose? The Gospels of Luke and John and the book of Acts provide examples of women responding to God's call.

INTRODUCTION

The lesson is a three-part series of vignettes presented by Luke in both his Gospel and in Acts. *Prophecy* is the theme in all three stories. The first reveals how the prophetess Anna used her gift in a positive manner as she played a dominant role in confirming the arrival of the baby Messiah. The second emanates from Peter's sermon, which was based on the prophecy of Joel (*circa* sixth century B.C.). Peter's Pentecost message was a link from Joel to future events and taught that prophecy always can be available as God gives it. The final story, unfortunately, reveals the issues when those with the gift of prophecy ignore the perils of a certain situation.

EXPOSITION

I. ANNA'S CONFIRMATION OF JESUS (LUKE 2:36–38)

Jesus had been circumcised on the eighth day of His birth according to the Law of Moses (Gen. 17:12). It was then He officially was named Jesus, the name given by the angel before He was conceived in the womb. According to the customs of the period, Mary was unclean after giving birth, but especially to a male child. Following the law, she had to undergo a series of ritual baths and allow the impurities of post-childbirth to depart from her body. When she completed this cleansing, which consisted of thirty-three more days, she presented a burnt offering and a sin offering for her restoration. As the holy family came to the temple to present Jesus, they encountered a man named Simeon and a woman named Anna. Simeon was a devout man who lived in Jerusalem but had a special relationship with God, who promised Simeon he would physically see the Messiah before God closed Simeon's eyes. Luke recorded the special verses where Simeon was able to pray for and bless the baby and the parents in the temple (Luke 2:25–35).

In addition to Simeon, another person also was in the temple. She often is overlooked in the account of this particular blessing of the baby Jesus. An elderly widow by the name of Anna (which means "grace") of the tribe of Asher devoutly served daily at the temple and was there at the presentation of the infant Jesus. Luke listed Anna as the daughter of Phanuel, who is listed only in these passages. Additionally, Luke called Anna a prophetess, to distinguish her from any male counterpart. This designation did not regulate Anna to a lower status. However, the suffix of the former is feminine, which serves to differentiate between the two. Luke identified Anna in the vein of Miriam, Deborah, and Huldah (2 Chr. 34:22). After seven years of married life, her husband died. During her long widowhood she daily attended the temple services. At eighty-four years old, she entered the temple at the moment when the aged Simeon uttered his memorable words of praise and thanks to God that He had fulfilled His promise in sending His Son into the world.

We are not provided any information of Anna's age when she became a widow. Luke emphasized that Anna lived with her husband for only seven years to demonstrate her years of service and dedication to the temple. Interestingly, if reading the KJV, you will notice language surrounding her virginity. She was not a virgin by the time the reader comes across her in Scripture. Luke was emphasizing that she lost her virginity to her husband as she consummated her marriage. This was to demonstrate she lived righteously before she entered the service of the temple. Anna reminds one of Samuel because she literally lived in the temple, as Luke indicated she never left. She constantly dedicated herself to worship and service to the Lord. Anna gained a reputation for her strict regimen of fasting, prayer, and supplication to God. Anna could be considered a female Nazirite, which is possible, as Numbers describes it as, "When a man or woman makes a special vow, the vow of a Nazirite, to dedicate himself to the Lord" (Num. 6:2, NASB). The law in Numbers implies that living as a Nazirite was a matter of personal choice. In other Old Testament texts, this is not as clear. Samson was consecrated as a Nazirite while still in his mother's womb (Judg. 13:4–14), and Samuel's mother made the consecration for him (1 Sam. 1:11). Amos 2:11 implies that living as a Nazirite was a divine gift rather than a personal choice. Nonetheless, Luke indicated the appearance by Anna was special and ordained, as both she and Simeon confirmed the baby was the consolation of Israel.

Luke recorded Anna's exuberance as she approached the child being held by Simeon. Anna's entrance to the scene is important, not only from the standpoint that she affirms Simeon's role in identifying the baby Jesus, but because of their reputation and standing in the community, which added to the spread of the news of the Christ. Remember, although news of the baby's birth had been shared by the shepherds, the people may not have been likely to believe them because of their lowly societal status. The word of Anna and Simeon, however, would reach the upper echelons of the Jewish religious community, which would include Pharisees, Sadducees, the scribes, and the entire Sanhedrin. This child would grow into the man who would serve as a ransom for humankind. For her position and God's grace in selecting her for this moment, Anna began to praise and give thanks to the Lord. As such, Anna continued to spread the news to the nation and speak to all who were looking forward to and had been waiting for the redemption of Jerusalem.

II. Peter's Greatest Sermon (Acts 2:16–21)

During the Festival of Pentecost, the Holy Spirit was gifted to the believers who were gathered in Jerusalem. This blessing was part of the promise Jesus gave His disciples prior to His ascension, and now it had arrived and filled the believers with a new sense of holiness and hope. Several spectators declared the actions of these believers were occurring because they were under the influence of too much wine. Peter, however, defended their exuberance as being under the fire and influence of the Holy Spirit.

Not to be confused with the demonstrations of an energized man, Peter was standing before this gathering in Jerusalem. This is the same Peter who was hindered by failing faith that denied Jesus. He told Jesus he would die for Him but wilted when the possibility of arrest seized him. At this point, a refreshed Peter was on full display. In what has become known as Peter's greatest sermon, Peter reflected on the words spoken several centuries prior by the prophet Joel, quoting the motif of the last days (*ἔσχατος, eschatos*), in that God will pour out (*ἐκχέω, ekcheo*), literally, "pour out from (*ἀπό: apo*) the Spirit"! In this time, sons and daughters will accept the gift of prophecy, with young men receiving visions and appearances of heavenly foretellings, while the older men will be able to dream again. The ages of the youth were not given and are not necessary for inclusion in receiving these spiritual gifts because their ability is based on spiritual maturity. The future dreams (*ἐνύπνιον, enypnion*) of the elders are based on communication with heaven being revealed while they are asleep!

Continuing the impact on prophecy, Peter detailed the Spirit will be granted to those who are enslaved, both male and female, and the Lord will not discriminate between those He selects for the receipt of His gifts. Peter noted that Joel spoke for God, who said He will grant wonders from the heavens above while providing signs, or even miracles, to the earth below. These signs will be blood, actually, lifeblood fire, accompanied by vapor and smoke. These symbols are important because the Old Testament was concerned with the use of blood in the expression of worship. Additionally, fire served as the primary medium for theophanies and other divine manifestations. Several examples are seen as Yahweh was represented in Abram's dream in the form of a smoking fire pot and flaming torch (Gen. 15:17), and Yahweh spoke to Moses out of a burning bush (Exod. 3:2) and descended to Mount Sinai in fire (Exod. 19:18).

In what can be seen as an impending series of gloom and doom during the last days, the sun will refuse to shine and turn to darkness, and the moon, to blood. This also was a prediction of the condition of the earth between the sixth and ninth hours, when darkness clothed the land while Jesus was on the cross (Matt. 27:45). This period will not be joyous, and Joel predicted it will come before the arrival of the glorious and splendid day of the Lord. Appealing to the faith of the believers, Peter explained that everyone who calls on the name of the Lord shall be saved!

In a moment of connection, in his letter to the Philippians, Paul later declared that at the name of Jesus, every knee will bow in submission and call upon Him while confessing and acknowledging He is Lord. Therefore, instead of being drunk, the believers in Acts 2 were experiencing what was described in Joel 2. In Peter's words, the phrase, "This is what was spoken through the prophet Joel" (Acts 2:16, NRSV), does not mean, "This is like that." It means Pentecost fulfilled what Joel had described. The prophecies of Joel quoted in Acts 2:17–18 were being fulfilled. The implication was the remainder would be fulfilled as Israel and all people repented. Peter was on full display as one who was filled with the Holy Spirit, and in his excitement, he hinted Jesus' disciples believed they would live to see His return.

III. The Failure of Philip's Daughters (Acts 21:8–9)

At this point in the lesson, the scene shifts to Paul and his companions who were completing the third missionary journey (A.D. 52–55). This expedition had taken them from Antioch to Greece, with many stops in Asia Minor, such as Ephesus, Athens, and Corinth. The return trip, however, included cities such as Troas and Miletus, which would be prominent in the intrigue and drama that played out in the final stages of Paul's life. Continuing, Paul and his companions traveled through the cities of Cos, Rhodes, and Patara before securing passage on a ship that took them across the Mediterranean Sea, past the island of Cyprus. Finally, they disembarked at Tyre and then traveled by land through Ptolemais, Caesarea, and to their final destination of Jerusalem. Paul and his group stayed in Tyre for seven days and while there, he was warned not to set foot in Jerusalem. Paul's group then stayed in Ptolemais for a day before arriving in Caesarea on the following day. Paul and his group did not return to Antioch, which was the city where the journey had originated, but went to Jerusalem to deliver an offering that was sent by the churches in Macedonia and Achaia for the poor in Jerusalem (Rom. 15:25–27). Paul faced severe challenges while in Jerusalem when at the Feast of Pentecost he was almost murdered by a Jewish mob in the temple.

While in Caesarea during this journey, Paul stayed in the home of Philip the evangelist. This Philip is not to be confused with the Philip who was one of Jesus' twelve disciples. This Philip, along with Stephen, was introduced in Acts 6:1–7 as a member of the seven appointed by the apostles to care for the Hellenist widows. Luke noted that Philip expanded the Gospel outside of Jerusalem, first to Samaria (Acts 8:5–13) and then to the "ends of the earth" (Acts 8:26–40), represented in the person of an

Ethiopian convert. Early in Church history, many confused the two Philips. However, in this story Luke was talking about Philip the evangelist, not the Apostle Philip.

Luke noted Philip had four daughters who were described as virgins. A number of commentators and translators understand Luke's phrase "virgin daughters" to mean simply unmarried daughters. Luke included this information about Philip's daughters to note they had the gift of prophecy.

Although the focus seemed to highlight the status of females who had the gift of prophecy, it was a male, Agabus, who foretold of events that were to change Paul's life and hinder his mission. Agabus, who possibly predicted a great famine that would befall Jerusalem during the reign of Claudius, foresaw that Paul would be bound and delivered to Gentiles who would seek his death. This was the warning Paul received while staying in Caesarea with Philip.

Again, this spiritual gift of prophecy, evident in the early church, was not limited to men. The daughters' apparent silence, however, in view of all the other prophecies regarding Paul's suffering in Jerusalem was quite surprising. In comparison with the account of Anna, Philip's daughters woefully underperformed.

The Lesson Applied

Each passage supports the idea of women having the gift of prophecy. Anna's desire to follow the lifestyle of a Nazirite and her dedication to the temple placed her in a direct position to confirm the baby Jesus. Some think the use of the term *prophet* versus *prophetess* somehow dilutes the importance of the women's gifts. In actuality, the two terms are simply the context designations of masculine and feminine.

Let's Talk About It

Women prophesied in the Bible. Why is it difficult for women to be accepted as ministers in today's society?

The mood is changing today, but many churches do not believe in women receiving the call and gift of preaching. At a time when certain denominations are struggling to attract men into pastoral ministry, there are openings for women to fill those roles, but the key text which has caused some question of women being called to ministry is I Timothy 2:11-12. Here the writer refuses to grant authority for the women to teach men. However, the Scriptures are filled with many other examples of the contributions of great women who were dedicated to the Lord and the mission of Jesus. We are not privy to whom the Lord calls into ministry. The call to ministry is an individual one.

Home Daily Devotional Readings

February 1–7, 2021

Monday	Tuesday	Wednesday	Thursday	Friday	Saturday	Sunday
Receive the Water of Life	Jesus Declares, "I Am from Above"	God's Children Led by the Spirit	Simon and Andrew, First Disciples	Philip and Nathaniel Become Disciples	Jesus Heals Son of Galilean Official	Samaritans Come to Jesus
Revelation 21:1–7	John 8:21–30	Romans 8:12–17	John 1:35–42	John 1:43–51	John 4:43–54	John 4:25–42

Called to Evangelize

Adult Topic:
No Insignificant Witnesses

Background Scripture:
John 1:37–51; 4:25–42

John 4:25–42

King James Version

THE woman saith unto him, I know that Messias cometh, which is called Christ: when he is come, he will tell us all things.
26 Jesus saith unto her, I that speak unto thee am he.
27 And upon this came his disciples, and marvelled that he talked with the woman: yet no man said, What seekest thou? or, Why talkest thou with her?
28 The woman then left her waterpot, and went her way into the city, and saith to the men,
29 Come, see a man, which told me all things that ever I did: is not this the Christ?
30 Then they went out of the city, and came unto him.
31 In the mean while his disciples prayed him, saying, Master, eat.
32 But he said unto them, I have meat to eat that ye know not of.
33 Therefore said the disciples one to another, Hath any man brought him ought to eat?
34 Jesus saith unto them, My meat is to do the will of him that sent me, and to finish his work.
35 Say not ye, There are yet four months, and then cometh harvest? behold, I say unto you, Lift up your eyes, and look on the fields; for they are white already to harvest.
36 And he that reapeth receiveth wages, and gathereth fruit unto life eternal: that both he that soweth and he that reapeth may rejoice together.

New Revised Standard Version

THE woman said to him, “I know that Messiah is coming” (who is called Christ). “When he comes, he will proclaim all things to us.”
26 Jesus said to her, “I am he, the one who is speaking to you.”
27 Just then his disciples came. They were astonished that he was speaking with a woman, but no one said, “What do you want?” or, “Why are you speaking with her?”
28 Then the woman left her water jar and went back to the city. She said to the people,
29 “Come and see a man who told me everything I have ever done! He cannot be the Messiah, can he?”
30 They left the city and were on their way to him.
31 Meanwhile the disciples were urging him, “Rabbi, eat something.”
32 But he said to them, “I have food to eat that you do not know about.”
33 So the disciples said to one another, “Surely no one has brought him something to eat?”
34 Jesus said to them, “My food is to do the will of him who sent me and to complete his work.
35 Do you not say, ‘Four months more, then comes the harvest’? But I tell you, look around you, and see how the fields are ripe for harvesting.
36 The reaper is already receiving wages and is gathering fruit for eternal life, so that sower and reaper may rejoice together.

MAIN THOUGHT: And many of the Samaritans of that city believed on him for the saying of the woman, which testified, He told me all that ever I did. (John 4:39, KJV)

JOHN 4:25–42

King James Version	*New Revised Standard Version*
37 And herein is that saying true, One soweth, and another reapeth.	**37 For here the saying holds true, 'One sows and another reaps.'**
38 I sent you to reap that whereon ye bestowed no labour: other men laboured, and ye are entered into their labours.	**38 I sent you to reap that for which you did not labor. Others have labored, and you have entered into their labor."**
39 And many of the Samaritans of that city believed on him for the saying of the woman, which testified, He told me all that ever I did.	**39 Many Samaritans from that city believed in him because of the woman's testimony, "He told me everything I have ever done."**
40 So when the Samaritans were come unto him, they besought him that he would tarry with them: and he abode there two days.	**40 So when the Samaritans came to him, they asked him to stay with them; and he stayed there two days.**
41 And many more believed because of his own word;	**41 And many more believed because of his word.**
42 And said unto the woman, Now we believe, not because of thy saying: for we have heard him ourselves, and know that this is indeed the Christ, the Saviour of the world.	**42 They said to the woman, "It is no longer because of what you said that we believe, for we have heard for ourselves, and we know that this is truly the Savior of the world."**

LESSON SETTING

Time: Circa A.D. 26
Place: Sychar, Samaria

LESSON OUTLINE

I. The Samaritan Woman Meets Jesus (John 4:25–30)
II. The Lesson of the Harvest (John 4:30–38)
III. The Results of the Harvest (John 4:39–42)

UNIFYING PRINCIPLE

Some people wonder if they are good enough to give direction to others. How can they share or witness to others? The woman at the well was considered an outcast, but after meeting Jesus she eagerly became a witness and brought others to Him.

INTRODUCTION

While traveling through Samaria, Jesus met a woman at a well, and they had a poignant conversation about the number of husbands she'd had. Another issue in the conversation was the comparison of drawing physical water from a well and spiritual or living water from heaven. The woman was astonished at Jesus' revelations and believed He is the Christ. The disciples also were taught a lesson about the true nature of God's human harvest. The woman's witness drew the people of her community to Jesus, who was well-received in this country where Samaritans and Jews did not like each other and had different places of worship—Mount Gerizim and Jerusalem.

EXPOSITION

I. THE SAMARITAN WOMAN MEETS JESUS (JOHN 4:25–30)

Jesus and His disciples traveled through the dreaded territory of Samaria. When they reached the city of Sychar, Jesus met a Samaritan woman at Jacob's well. She was there to draw water. However, they met around noon, an unusual time to go to the well because it was during the most intense heat of the day. This woman was ostracized because of both her past and present. However, after her encounter with Jesus, her future looked bright. In her conversation with Jesus, the woman revealed she was looking for the coming of the Messiah. This showed Samaritan linkage to Judaism. However, the Samaritan concept of Messiah differed from the Judaic understanding. It was more about the restoration of proper worship of God. The confidence of the woman was revealed when she declared to Jesus she knew the Messiah was coming. The Samaritans expected a coming messianic leader but did not expect Him to be an anointed king of the Davidic line since they rejected all of the Old Testament except the Pentateuch. They expected a Moses-like figure based on Deuteronomy 18:15–18. The woman, who was a believer in the Messiah, declared that when He came, He would disclose all the secrets, truths, and promises that had been handed down.

Jesus then revealed He is the Messiah, which He rarely confirmed because of the political and spiritual backlash. Jesus usually referred to Himself as the *Son of Man* because of the issues that occurred when using the title *Son of God*, especially among many of the religious leaders and His other critics. Additionally, Jesus wanted to avoid the charges of blasphemy that would occur during the final stages of His ministry. He did not want to create controversy that would impede His present mission. Consequently, He did something He usually did not do. He did not use the full term but simply said that the One she was speaking with was He.

The disciples had left Jesus by the well and gone into the city to buy food. However, at some time during the conversation between Jesus and the woman, the disciples returned. They were flabbergasted He was out in the open speaking to a single woman. They had not been there to witness Jesus asking the woman for a drink, which was traditionally strange since a rabbi would not have had any public conversation with a woman. Furthermore, Jews would not have had *any* dealings with Samaritans. The normal well-drawing time was morning or evening, when it was cooler. But because the woman was ostracized, she came to the well when likely no one else would be there. Although the disciples were shocked to find Jesus alone with this woman, none of them challenged Him, criticized Him, or even asked what He was looking for that would generate any conversation with her. But they must have wondered why He was speaking with her.

The woman could feel the unspoken disdain from these men but was so excited about her encounter with Jesus that she forgot her original intent for coming to the well, left her water pot, and went into the city to witness to what she had experienced. Although several translations read that she spoke to the men of the city, John used the Greek term *ἄνθρωπος* (*anthropos*), which can denote "men" but also can mean "people" or "persons." A better understanding would be that she spoke to the people, which was probably a combination of both men and women.

She urged the people to go and meet Jesus, who spoke to her in a manner she had never experienced. It was not just His tone of voice, it was also His mannerisms and compassion that she obviously was not privy to in her world. She declared that this man, this stranger, was able to tell her all she had done. Although this statement uses the term *all*, it was not possible in the given time for Jesus to provide a commentary on her entire life. In her utter excitement, she spoke in hyperbolic terms. The people of this era were accustomed to fortune-tellers and soothsayers whose revelations about a person's history were a fundamental component of their gimmicks. But Jesus was different. In her excitement, she stepped out of the shadows of her existence and mistakes and into a whole-hearted effort to persuade the people to meet the Messiah, Jesus from Nazareth.

In the last phrase of the verse, she asked a question, "This is not the Christ, is it?" (John 4:29, NASB). Several biblical theorists believe this utterance revealed there remained some doubt as to whether she believed Jesus was the Christ. However, the statement must be understood that she was stating that because of what Jesus had shown her, He must be the Christ!

II. The Lesson of the Harvest (John 4:30–38)

Recall earlier, the disciples had gone into the city to purchase food and possibly drink because they had become hungry. As the woman was talking with the townspeople, the disciples had plenty of food and now urged Jesus to eat, but Jesus was not concerned about their food.

Instead, in a perplexing comment, Jesus declared He already had food of which they were unaware. The disciples had purchased food because they all were hungry, and now Jesus was telling them He had food they did not know about. So, they inquired among themselves, asking if anyone had brought any food to Jesus and not told the others.

Sensing their anxiety, Jesus explained His food was to do the will, or the desire, of the One (the Father) "who sent Me" to accomplish (*τελειόω, teleioo*), or finish, His work, that it may be complete and perfected. The disciples misunderstood the food metaphor Jesus was using, not realizing Jesus was comparing food to the tasks that were imperative, knowing the success of the mission was more important than anything. Jesus had been sent to finish the work God had started, which was the redemption of all humanity.

Jesus moved to an agrarian metaphor to exemplify the completed work. Jesus framed this example in the form of a question but answered it Himself by noting it is apparent when it is time for reaping. He implored them to lift up their eyes, but also to raise up their sensibilities, to understand the fields are white for the ingathering. In the phrase *they are white for the harvest*, Jesus may have been alluding to the imminent encounter with the Samaritans who would believe in Him. *White for the harvest* can mean "ripe for harvest," as the tops of crops signify the time at which they are ready for reaping, having completed their cycle of fruitfulness. The fields represented the communities or lands, and the souls of the people were ready to be gathered in for the harvest. The metaphor of the harvest also revealed a severe need. Recall that Jesus said the harvest was plentiful but the workers were few while encouraging they pray for the Lord to send out workers into His harvest (Matt. 9:37–38).

Jesus noted that the one who reaps is directly rewarded. John used the Greek term *μισθός* (*misthos*) to signify that the reaper receives wages for his labor. Moreover, both the reaper and the sower will receive the earnings of what is yielded from the soil. However, Jesus spoke of the fruit of the ground that is gathered at the harvest, in preparation for eternal life. This fruit will never become spoiled but will last forever. This imagery is a forecast. Jesus will gather all who have remained in the faith for a final ingathering of the harvest, and all who have been part of the mission will rejoice. In this case, the saying is true, that one may sow while another reaps. Jesus, however, pointed out that the one who sows is not necessarily the one who reaps. The first one to tell someone about salvation may not be the person who actually brings him/her to salvation, but no matter who does the work, God deserves the credit!

When Jesus mentioned He sent the disciples to reap that for which they had not labored, He provided a glimpse into the fact that it is God who provides the gift of grace and power. Additionally, this may have had future implications in that it was Jesus who went to the cross for the redemption of humanity, not the disciples. When He spoke of the labor of others, He may have been talking about the prophets who had preceded them. Now the disciples were entering into the fields of their labor.

III. The Results of the Harvest (John 4:39–42)

Notice there was an emphasis on the woman's declaration that Jesus had told her about all that she had done, which is an actual recalling of the conversation in which Jesus questioned her about her husband. Throughout the centuries, much has been made about this sequence to degrade those who are considered "loose" women. There may be, however, a plausible understanding of this issue from what has been historically portrayed. The woman replied she had no husband, and Jesus said, "You are right when you say you have no husband. The fact is, you have had five husbands, and the man you now have is not your husband" (John 4:17–18, NIV). She did not say she was a widow, but the explanation does not indicate she was not legally married. Therefore, the implications are that the man was either someone else's husband or she was living with someone illegally. There is a possible twist here, as the Greek word *ἀνήρ* (*aner*) can mean "man" or "husband." If the woman had five previous husbands that either died or divorced her, she would have exceeded the traditional limit of three husbands in Jewish law (according to the rabbinic Babylonian Talmud Yebamot 64; Niddah 64a). However, the ambiguity of the word suggests the possibility that none of the five was a legal husband, just as the current man was not her husband. This comment also revealed a reason why Jesus chose to speak with her about her place before God. It is an incredible testament to the power of God and the human witness of one who has sincerely been converted because many in the city believed in the testimony of this woman. That they trusted the word of this woman has serious implications as to the power of the human spirit. The testimony of a woman, especially this woman, should have had little credibility because of the condescending nature and attitude toward women in general. And because of her reputation, the testimony of this particular woman should have ensured her declaration would receive scant consideration. Yet the testimony of the woman was effective. Jesus' comprehensive knowledge of one's life is an indication of His deity. Because of her witness of Jesus' revelation of her life, the people believed!

The excitement began to spread, and the new believers among the Samaritans asked Jesus to stay with them. So, He remained for two more days, and many more were converted. To demonstrate the impact of the woman's account, many more or a great many, a majority of the inhabitants, believed Jesus was the Christ.

In an almost celebratory mood, the people told the woman they no longer believed because of what she had told them, but because they had heard the words of Jesus for themselves and were convinced He was the Anointed One. The salvation of a large group of Samaritans provides a glimpse into the universal nature of God's plan of salvation. The entire earth is God's domain, and there are no geographical limitations to Jesus' ministry. Luke recorded Jesus as saying the disciples would be His witnesses both in Jerusalem, and in all Judea and Samaria, and even to the remotest part of the earth (Acts 1:8).

The Lesson Applied

The Samaritans were actually brothers or cousins to the Jewish people of Judea, as the country of Samaria was the central region of Palestine that was located between Judea and Galilee. This area had been the heart of the Northern Kingdom of Israel until the Assyrians conquered the area in 722 B.C. and deported those they had not murdered. When the Assyrians imported their native-born and intermarriage occurred, the result was a severe hatred between the Jews and the Samaritans. Here, Jesus' mission was successful and revealed His desire to embrace the entire world unto Him.

Let's Talk About It

What is the biggest lesson in this story?

Jesus' parable of the Good Samaritan serves as an example of compassion and love for a fellow human. The hated Samaritan did not have to help or provide for the beaten man; however, he was driven by a spirit of oneness with humanity. When we read Jesus' command that we should pray for our enemies, this is not an idle challenge. While difficult, Jesus has given us the ability and power to pray for and care about those with whom we may have disagreement. In Jesus, we pray that enemies can become friends. The Samaritan shows we all are human.

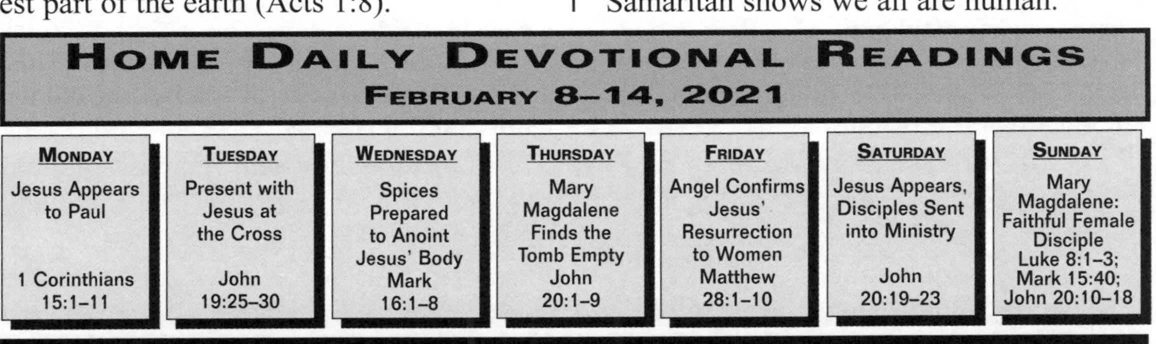

Home Daily Devotional Readings

February 8–14, 2021

Monday	Tuesday	Wednesday	Thursday	Friday	Saturday	Sunday
Jesus Appears to Paul	Present with Jesus at the Cross	Spices Prepared to Anoint Jesus' Body	Mary Magdalene Finds the Tomb Empty	Angel Confirms Jesus' Resurrection to Women	Jesus Appears, Disciples Sent into Ministry	Mary Magdalene: Faithful Female Disciple
1 Corinthians 15:1–11	John 19:25–30	Mark 16:1–8	John 20:1–9	Matthew 28:1–10	John 20:19–23	Luke 8:1–3; Mark 15:40; John 20:10–18

LESSON 11 FEBRUARY 14, 2021

MARY MAGDALENE: A FAITHFUL DISCIPLE

ADULT TOPIC:
SHOWING LOYALTY

BACKGROUND SCRIPTURE:
MARK 15:40; 16:1–9; LUKE 8:1–3; JOHN 20:10–18

LUKE 8:1–3; MARK 15:40; JOHN 20:10–18

King James Version

AND it came to pass afterward, that he went throughout every city and village, preaching and shewing the glad tidings of the kingdom of God: and the twelve were with him,
2 And certain women, which had been healed of evil spirits and infirmities, Mary called Magdalene, out of whom went seven devils,
3 And Joanna the wife of Chuza Herod's steward, and Susanna, and many others, which ministered unto him of their substance.

• • • Mark 15:40 • • •

THERE were also women looking on afar off: among whom was Mary Magdalene, and Mary the mother of James the less and of Joses, and Salome.

• • • John 20:10–18 • • •

THEN the disciples went away again unto their own home.
11 But Mary stood without at the sepulchre weeping: and as she wept, she stooped down, and looked into the sepulchre,
12 And seeth two angels in white sitting, the one at the head, and the other at the feet, where the body of Jesus had lain.
13 And they say unto her, Woman, why weepest thou? She saith unto them, Because they have taken away my Lord, and I know not where they have laid him.
14 And when she had thus said, she turned herself back, and saw Jesus standing, and knew not that it was Jesus.

New Revised Standard Version

SOON afterwards he went on through cities and villages, proclaiming and bringing the good news of the kingdom of God. The twelve were with him,
2 as well as some women who had been cured of evil spirits and infirmities: Mary, called Magdalene, from whom seven demons had gone out,
3 and Joanna, the wife of Herod's steward Chuza, and Susanna, and many others, who provided for them out of their resources.

• • • Mark 15:40 • • •

THERE were also women looking on from a distance; among them were Mary Magdalene, and Mary the mother of James the younger and of Joses, and Salome.

• • • John 20:10–18 • • •

THEN the disciples returned to their homes.
11 But Mary stood weeping outside the tomb. As she wept, she bent over to look into the tomb;
12 and she saw two angels in white, sitting where the body of Jesus had been lying, one at the head and the other at the feet.
13 They said to her, "Woman, why are you weeping?" She said to them, "They have taken away my Lord, and I do not know where they have laid him."
14 When she had said this, she turned around and saw Jesus standing there, but she did not know that it was Jesus.

MAIN THOUGHT: And it came to pass afterward, that he went throughout every city and village, preaching and shewing the glad tidings of the kingdom of God: and the twelve were with him, And certain women, which had been healed of evil spirits and infirmities, Mary called Magdalene, out of whom went seven devils. (Luke 8:1–2, KJV)

Luke 8:1–3; Mark 15:40; John 20:10–18

King James Version	*New Revised Standard Version*
15 Jesus saith unto her, Woman, why weepest thou? whom seekest thou? She, supposing him to be the gardener, saith unto him, Sir, if thou have borne him hence, tell me where thou hast laid him, and I will take him away.	**15 Jesus said to her, "Woman, why are you weeping? Whom are you looking for?" Supposing him to be the gardener, she said to him, "Sir, if you have carried him away, tell me where you have laid him, and I will take him away."**
16 Jesus saith unto her, Mary. She turned herself, and saith unto him, Rabboni; which is to say, Master.	**16 Jesus said to her, "Mary!" She turned and said to him in Hebrew, "Rabbouni!" (which means Teacher).**
17 Jesus saith unto her, Touch me not; for I am not yet ascended to my Father: but go to my brethren, and say unto them, I ascend unto my Father, and your Father; and to my God, and your God.	**17 Jesus said to her, "Do not hold on to me, because I have not yet ascended to the Father. But go to my brothers and say to them, 'I am ascending to my Father and your Father, to my God and your God.'"**
18 Mary Magdalene came and told the disciples that she had seen the Lord, and that he had spoken these things unto her.	**18 Mary Magdalene went and announced to the disciples, "I have seen the Lord"; and she told them that he had said these things to her.**

LESSON SETTING

Time: *circa* A.D. 27–30
Place: Galilee and Jerusalem

LESSON OUTLINE

I. **Introduction of the Women (Luke 8:1–3; Mark 15:40)**
II. **Mary, Alone at the Tomb (John 20:10–12)**
III. **Mary's Encounter with Jesus (John 20:13–16)**
IV. **Mary Follows Jesus' Command (John 20:17–18)**

Unifying Principle

Being a truly committed follower of someone often is difficult, but there are people who reveal consistent loyalty no matter what happens. How do you show your loyalty and faithfulness? Mary Magdalene demonstrated her unwavering discipleship and loyalty to Jesus through her actions.

Introduction

Throughout history, people, especially those in religious authority, have downplayed the role of women in ministry. The following narrative reflects the responsibilities a circle of devoted women had in the ministry of Jesus. Although several scriptural passages are used to support this missive, the conclusion can be reached that women have been called to the mission of Jesus Christ from its inception. This lesson will chronicle women such as Joanna, Susanna, Salome, Mary, and Mary Magdalene, whom Jesus first appeared to in all four Gospels.

Exposition

I. Introduction of the Women (Luke 8:1–3; Mark 15:40)

Prior to this scene, Jesus had dinner with a Pharisee named Simon and encountered an unnamed woman. She came in the house and began crying. She wet Jesus' feet with her tears and then anointed Him with perfume. When Simon scolded the woman, Jesus rose in her defense by noting He had not been offered by the household the customary treatment of water for His feet, neither a kiss of greeting. The woman had been the only one to provide these luxuries to Him. As Jesus sent the woman on her way, He forgave her sins, and Simon's guests began to question Jesus' authority to forgive sin.

Soon after this event, Jesus began to travel the region, preaching and proclaiming the Kingdom of God was at hand. Jesus was not alone in His journey, as Luke noted the twelve disciples were with Him. Some women also were present. One in particular was singled out, who was identified as Mary Magdalene.

Continuing the list of Jesus' companions, Luke noted two other women—Joanna, the wife of Chuza the steward of Herod Antipas, and Susanna. Mary Magdalene has forever been identified as the woman from whom Jesus exorcised demons. However, it would seem she was not alone in having been healed. Joanna was one of the women from Galilee who followed and provided assistance to Jesus. She was mentioned with Mary Magdalene, Susanna, and others as having been "cured of evil spirits and infirmities" (Luke 8:2–3, NRSV). Joanna also was among the women who brought spices to anoint Jesus' body and found the empty tomb. Along with Mary Magdalene and Mary the mother of James, she delivered the news of the resurrection to the apostles (Luke 24:10). Luke also noted that the women from Galilee saw the Crucifixion (Luke 23:49) and the placement of Jesus' body in the tomb (Luke 23:55).

The fact that Chuza's wife was among Jesus' followers suggests His message reached the aristocracy. Joanna's presence among Jesus' followers has led to speculations that either Chuza died before she began following Jesus or that he himself was also a convert, although neither is suggested by the text. Nonetheless, these women were identified as major donors who financially supported Jesus' ministry. This probably included meals, travel, and lodging for both Jesus and the disciples. When Jesus asked the fishermen to follow Him, there was a need to provide sustenance for the movement as well as for their families at home. Luke noted these blessed women gave freely from their possessions. What is important here is that these women were not typical Jewish women, who generally did not have ownership in property and wealth, but were women of financial acumen. How they acquired their wealth is not documented. However, Joanna and others were able to provide for Jesus.

It is impossible to know the exact number of women and all the identities of those who were supporters. In a period during which the contributions of women were viewed as unimportant, Jesus rejected the norms of society and committed what would have been considered an appalling act by allowing women to travel in His company and be counted among the disciples in His public ministry. Mark noted several unidentified women, who were obvious supporters, at the scene of the Crucifixion, noting they were looking on from afar, where they would be safe from Roman (and Jewish) reprisal. Mark recognized Mary Magdalene but also noted another Mary was present. This second Mary was recorded as the mother of James the Less (the Younger), Joses, and Salome. James the Less was not one of the Twelve. Mark was thought to have called him "the young" or "the small" in order to distinguish him from James the son of Zebedee. Nothing else is known of him. Joses, his younger brother, was called Joseph in Matthew 27:56.

Salome is not to be confused with the daughter of this Mary, the wife of Clopas. She was another female follower of Jesus who ministered to him in Galilee and traveled with him to Jerusalem. If Mark 15:40 and Matthew 27:56 are parallel accounts, Salome may have been the mother of James and John (the sons of Zebedee). Salome, along with the two Marys, brought spices for Jesus' burial (Mark 16:1). Nevertheless, Mark supported the Lukan record of the women, who were active supporters in Jesus' ministry.

II. Mary, Alone at the Tomb (John 20:10–12)

After the women brought Jesus' disciples to the empty tomb, John said the disciples went away again to their own homes. At face value, John's rendition of this action seems impossible because this would place them in Galilee, far removed from Jerusalem. Additionally, going to their own homes would have Mary going to Galilee instead of a closer location in Jerusalem to tell the disciples of a risen Jesus. The confusion may arise in the interpretation of the departure, which consists of an idiom, *ἀπῆλθεν ουν παλιν πρὸς αυτους,* that literally means "to return to oneself, to go back to one's place or abode," essentially to go back home. Luke 24:12 also says Peter went back home after looking inside the empty tomb and seeing the wrappings that had clothed the body of Jesus. Peter probably did not have a home in Jerusalem, so though it is possible to translate this phrase as "they went back home," it could be misleading. More likely, the disciples went back to where they were staying.

John noted that Peter and "the other disciple, the one whom Jesus loved" (John 20:2, NRSV) went to the tomb at Mary Magdalene's urging. Mary originally went with spices to anoint the body of Jesus but discovered the stone rolled away. She ran to tell Peter and the other disciple the disturbing news. After the men left, Mary Magdalene stood outside the tomb, probably facing toward the entrance. Although she was positioned outside, she was able to bend over to look into the tomb. These crypts were small underground chambers that would allow one to enter, but they would not have had enough room for a large gathering. Additionally, this interment served only as a first burial because Jewish bodies eventually would be placed in an ossuary box during the final stages of burial. Mary was so distraught, she was crying or weeping at the sight of the mausoleum. As she peered into the grave, she was astonished to see two angels dressed in white robes. One was seated at the place where Jesus' head would have been, while the other was sitting at the foot.

III. Mary's Encounter with Jesus (John 20:13–16)

Recognizing Mary was completely distraught, the angels sought to comfort her by asking why she was crying. She replied someone had taken Jesus from the tomb and she did not know where they had put His body. Mary did not yet realize Jesus was resurrected, although Jesus had assured them He would rise.

As soon as Mary replied to the angels, she turned around and saw Jesus standing there, but she did not recognize Him. This may not make good sense to us. How could she *not* recognize Jesus after being such a faithful follower? However, we must remember Mary was grief-stricken and likely was surprised and startled to see anyone else at the tomb at such an early hour. Also, although she had been assured of His resurrection, Mary was taught such during much happier times; now, during a period of anguish, she was not thinking rationally. The statement, "She … saw Jesus standing there" (John 20:14, NRSV), seems inconsistent with what follows. Since a literal translation of "she saw Jesus standing there" might imply she recognized who He was, it may better to render this verse as, "She saw a man standing there; it was Jesus, but she did not know it was Jesus."

As the angels did, Jesus also asked Mary why she was weeping, but He also asked whom she was seeking. Mary's mind seems to have been clouded and confused, as she thought Jesus was the gardener. In her incessant grief, Mary asked if He was the one responsible for removing Jesus' body from the crypt. Although she did not get a reply, Mary stated that if He would tell her where they placed Jesus, she would go and reclaim His body. The spirit of Mary's love for and dedication to Jesus was on full display!

Jesus did not allow Mary to continue—He called her name, "Mary!" At this point, she seemed to recover from her fog and responded by calling Him *Rabbouni*, which in Aramaic means "Teacher." As Mary recognized Jesus, she shifted from an intimate position of calling His name Jesus to that of a more formal stance of address as Teacher. This indicates Mary recognized the teaching of Jesus and confirmed the resurrection He predicted. She came out of her inconsolable state of grief because He indeed had risen!

IV. Mary Follows Jesus' Command (John 20:17–18)

In her excitement, John noted Mary reached out to embrace Jesus. This passage traditionally has been cited as Jesus telling Mary not to touch Him. The Greek word for touch is *ἅπτω* (*hapto*); however, it also means "to grasp or clench." The *Douay-Rheims Challoner* renders this translation as, "Do not touch me" (John 20:17), while the *New International Version* reads, "Do not hold on to me." Louw and Nida's *Greek-English Lexicon* reads *μή μου ἅπτου (me mou aptou),* "Do not hold on to me," which echoes the *English Standard Version*'s "Do not cling to me." According to these renderings, Mary actually touched Jesus before he continued, "I have not yet ascended to the Father" (John 20:17, NRSV). The KJV translation, "Touch me not," has caused many interpreters to wonder why Jesus could not be touched. The NIV translation is more accurate, for He certainly was not untouchable. Nonetheless, the *Lexham Greek-English* renders this portion of the verse as *μή ἐγώ ἅπτω (me ego apto),* meaning, "Do not touch or grasp me." The idea of Mary touching Jesus possibly may be overplayed to believe that by touching Jesus she somehow would contaminate Him. John seemed to indicate Jesus ascended to His Father somewhere between the time at the tomb and the time when Jesus did allow the disciples to embrace Him and, in the case of Thomas, even touch and examine His wounds. Nonetheless, we are given a perspective that Jesus did ascend to heaven. Mary was then given a command to go and tell the brothers about Jesus' plans.

This group, whom we would refer to as the disciples, are identified as the close associates of a group of people having a well-defined membership. *Brothers* referred specifically to fellow believers in Christ. Additionally, this term indicated both men and women believers. John concluded this section by reporting that Mary followed Jesus' command and told the brothers she had seen the Lord and all the things He said to her. Whether they chose to believe her or not is not the primary issue. Jesus appeared to Mary and granted her the honor of being the one who first preached the Good News of His rising!

The Lesson Applied

Mary Magdalene has been touted as a prostitute, but this is not found in Scripture. John 8:3–11 is one source used to label Mary as the woman who was caught in adultery. However, that woman was not named, and she was not a prostitute. She was an adulterer. The idea of Mary being a prostitute probably originated with Pope Gregory I (the Great), who served as pope from A.D. 590–604. This sort of proclamation by one of the holy fathers was not the first deterrent to women in ministry but continued to distort the rightful call of women. God is the only one who decides who is invited into His ministry.

Let's Talk About It

Who owned the house where the disciples were staying?

Some undocumented anecdotes identify Peter as the owner of the place where the disciples hid following the Crucifixion. Tradition has it they returned to the Upper Room in the house where they celebrated the Passover. It also served as a refuge in light of the fear they faced. Although, this residence would figure prominently with the coming of the Holy Spirit in Acts, the house was probably the home of one of Jesus' other disciples and supporters. The fact they were staying there means it was home, or, as some have put it, "Home is where the heart is!" We must remember the disciples were on a spiritual journey with Jesus. The things they learned from Him were to be taken into all the world.

Home Daily Devotional Readings

February 15–21, 2021

Monday	Tuesday	Wednesday	Thursday	Friday	Saturday	Sunday
Paul Reflects on His Ministry	Greetings to Saints in Jesus Christ	The Holy Kiss Strengthens Ministry Bond	Ministry Shifts from Jews to Gentiles	Roman Official Refuses to Settle Dispute	Greetings to All Sisters in Ministry	Priscilla: Key Outreach Minister
2 Timothy 4:9–18	Colossians 4:7–15	2 Corinthians 13:11–13; 1 Thessalonians 5:23–28	Acts 18:4–11	Acts 18:12–17	Romans 16:1–2, 6–7, 12–13, 16	Acts 18:1–3, 18–21, 24–26; Romans 16:3–4; 1 Corinthians 16:19; 2 Timothy 4:19

PRISCILLA: CALLED TO MINISTER

ADULT TOPIC: RISK TAKER

BACKGROUND SCRIPTURE: ACTS 18:1–26; ROMANS 16:3–4; 1 CORINTHIANS 16:19; 2 TIMOTHY 4:19

ACTS 18:1–3, 18–21, 24–26; ROMANS 16:3–4

King James Version

AFTER these things Paul departed from Athens, and came to Corinth;

2 And found a certain Jew named Aquila, born in Pontus, lately come from Italy, with his wife Priscilla; (because that Claudius had commanded all Jews to depart from Rome:) and came unto them.

3 And because he was of the same craft, he abode with them, and wrought: for by their occupation they were tentmakers.

• • • • • •

18 And Paul after this tarried there yet a good while, and then took his leave of the brethren, and sailed thence into Syria, and with him Priscilla and Aquila; having shorn his head in Cenchrea: for he had a vow.

19 And he came to Ephesus, and left them there: but he himself entered into the synagogue, and reasoned with the Jews.

20 When they desired him to tarry longer time with them, he consented not;

21 But bade them farewell, saying, I must by all means keep this feast that cometh in Jerusalem: but I will return again unto you, if God will. And he sailed from Ephesus.

• • • • • •

24 And a certain Jew named Apollos, born at Alexandria, an eloquent man, and mighty in the scriptures, came to Ephesus.

25 This man was instructed in the way of the Lord; and being fervent in the spirit, he spake and taught diligently the things of the Lord, knowing only the baptism of John.

New Revised Standard Version

AFTER this Paul left Athens and went to Corinth.

2 There he found a Jew named Aquila, a native of Pontus, who had recently come from Italy with his wife Priscilla, because Claudius had ordered all Jews to leave Rome. Paul went to see them,

3 and, because he was of the same trade, he stayed with them, and they worked together—by trade they were tentmakers.

• • • • • •

18 After staying there for a considerable time, Paul said farewell to the believers and sailed for Syria, accompanied by Priscilla and Aquila. At Cenchreae he had his hair cut, for he was under a vow.

19 When they reached Ephesus, he left them there, but first he himself went into the synagogue and had a discussion with the Jews.

20 When they asked him to stay longer, he declined;

21 but on taking leave of them, he said, "I will return to you, if God wills." Then he set sail from Ephesus.

• • • • • •

24 Now there came to Ephesus a Jew named Apollos, a native of Alexandria. He was an eloquent man, well–versed in the scriptures.

25 He had been instructed in the Way of the Lord; and he spoke with burning enthusiasm and taught accurately the things concerning Jesus, though he knew only the baptism of John.

MAIN THOUGHT: Greet Priscilla and Aquila my helpers in Christ Jesus: Who have for my life laid down their own necks: unto whom not only I give thanks, but also all the churches of the Gentiles. (Romans 16:3–4, KJV)

Acts 18:1–3, 18–21, 24–26; Romans 16:3–4

King James Version	*New Revised Standard Version*
26 And he began to speak boldly in the synagogue: whom when Aquila and Priscilla had heard, they took him unto them, and expounded unto him the way of God more perfectly.	**26 He began to speak boldly in the synagogue; but when Priscilla and Aquila heard him, they took him aside and explained the Way of God to him more accurately.**
• • • Romans 16:3–4 • • •	**• • • Romans 16:3–4 • • •**
GREET Priscilla and Aquila my helpers in Christ Jesus:	**GREET Prisca and Aquila, who work with me in Christ Jesus,**
4 Who have for my life laid down their own necks: unto whom not only I give thanks, but also all the churches of the Gentiles.	**4 and who risked their necks for my life, to whom not only I give thanks, but also all the churches of the Gentiles.**

LESSON SETTING

Time: *circa* A.D. 49–52
Place: Asia Minor

LESSON OUTLINE

I. **Priscilla, Aquila, and Paul at Corinth (Acts 18:1–3)**
II. **Priscilla, Aquila, and Paul to Syria (Acts 18:18–21)**
III. **Introducing Apollos (Acts 18:24–26)**
IV. **Paul's Gratitude (Romans 16:3–4)**

Unifying Principle

Encounters that bring together people with similar gifts and talents can lead to greater opportunities for service in other arenas. How can common traits or experiences lead to a meaningful engagement in ministry or service? Priscilla and Aquila shared their tent-making business with Paul, and Paul shared his ministry of the Gospel with them.

Introduction

Throughout the centuries, many women have been faithful servants of the Lord. Although recognizing women in ministry (especially those in high-profile positions) has been slow to acceptance, in contemporary society we find women actually dominate both numbers and service in the church. As we continue to highlight the women who were instrumental in scriptural history, we find Prisca (*Πρίσκα, Priska*), which is the Greek form of *Priscilla*, who along with her husband Aquila figured prominently in the ministry and life of Paul. This devoted couple and co-laborers accompanied Paul in his travels and trade of tentmaking and instructed Apollos in the disciplines of the Lord. This couple obviously was special, as Paul continuously showed his gratitude and thanksgiving for their friendship.

Exposition

I. Priscilla, Aquila, and Paul at Corinth (Acts 18:1–3)

Following his travels in Thessalonica, Berea, and Athens, Paul left these regions and departed for Corinth. Paul was leaving Athens, a city known for philosophy and learning, to enter a city that, although only approximately fifty miles apart, was rough and known for its commercial prowess and decadence. Paul was about to take on a considerable mission in this city, where the primary religions were pagan. Corinth was famous for its worship of Aphrodite, whose temple supposedly housed a thousand sacred prostitutes. Additionally, many of the residents prayed to Poseidon, the ruler of the sea, to deliver positive results from fishing and trade. There, Paul found a man by the name of Aquila, who was a Jew and a native of Pontius, which was a region in northeastern Asia Minor on the south shore of the Black Sea. While living in Rome, Aquila and his wife Prisca, or Priscilla, had been expelled by the Emperor Claudius because of their preaching of a certain Chrestus—Jesus Christ. Additionally, Claudius ordered that all Jews be expelled from Rome. The couple settled in Corinth, where it seems they were well-known and established, prompting Paul to come to them. Initially, it does not seem Paul sought their company as members of the Christian community. To describe their commonality, Luke used the term *ὁμότεχνος* (*homotechnos*), which means they were practicing the same trade as tentmakers (*σκηνοποιός, skenopoios*). Although it may seem Aquila was a laborer, he may have been a man of means to have owned a home large enough for church gatherings, travel, and relocation, as needed. Nonetheless, Paul stayed with them, and they shared in their labor. There have been people who have scoffed at the idea of Paul's entering into what may seem to have been a demeaning line of work. However, this trade would have provided them with a good income, as it was considered equal to a homebuilder in contemporary society.

II. Priscilla, Aquila, and Paul to Syria (Acts 18:18–21)

Paul was preaching in the synagogues and reasoning with the people in his attempt to convert them to Christianity. Silas and Timothy came to visit, and it seems at this point, Paul had left the tentmaking trade and completely devoted himself to the preaching of Jesus (Acts 18:5). He was, however, resisted and became angry and determined to forget the Jews and take the message to the Gentiles. Subsequently, in a vision, the Lord commanded Paul to continue to preach, spread the Gospel, and not be afraid, for God would protect him from any attack. Paul remained in the city for eighteen months (Acts 18:9–11), probably continuing to stay with Priscilla and Aquila. However, after this period of time, Paul gave his regrets and farewell to the brothers, as he left and put out to sea, sailing away for Syria. Among the passengers were Priscilla and Aquila, who abandoned their business to follow Paul. Notably absent were Silas and Timothy, who had come to visit him in Corinth but probably remained in Macedonia to oversee the churches there.

Paul originally was headed for Antioch, but before he left, he had his head shaved in Cenchrae, Corinth's southeastern port, because it seems he had made the vow of a Nazirite. It is not known when Paul made this vow, which is unstated. Remember, the law in Numbers implies that living as a Nazirite was a matter of personal choice, as supported by Amos, who implied living as a Nazirite was a divine *charism* rather than a personal choice (Amos 2:11). In other Old Testament texts, people such as

Samson (Judg. 13:4–14) and Samuel (1 Sam. 1:11) seem to have been selected by God. Therefore, in this section, the implication is that Paul participated in the rituals connected with the conclusion of Nazirite observance. Possibly because of his being like Jesus, Samson, and Samuel, he desired to have the status of a Nazirite, which would imply one who seeks an especially close relationship with God.

After a voyage of approximately two or three days, the group of travelers arrived at the city of Ephesus. At some point, Paul visited the synagogue and began his discussions about Jesus. It seems he was successful in his discussions and attempts of reasoning among these unnamed Jews of the city because, unlike some of his other experiences, they asked him to stay longer. The synagogue community embraced Paul and his teachings. Paul was a gifted and educated man whom Jesus had selected to become the Lord's chosen instrument or vessel. In this imagery, Saul (later known as Paul) became an unfinished jar or receptacle into which God would pour His Spirit and sense of direction. As the potter made and molded the raw and unfinished clay, God used Saul's education and his knowledge of Scriptures and the law to understand and preach the reality that the Messiah or the Christ had arrived. Jesus said Saul would be the one to bear or take His name to the Gentiles and kings and the sons of Israel. When the Ephesians asked Paul to stay longer, he did not commit that he would. However, as he began to leave them, Paul did promise he would return to them if God willed it to happen.

Paul's Second Missionary Journey originated from the city of Antioch, and after going through Galatia, Asia Minor, and Macedonia, he arrived in Achaia, a part of Greece, with the last two major cities of Athens and Corinth. Leaving Corinth, on his return, he set sail from Ephesus on the final leg of his journey and traveled to the major cities of Jerusalem and Damascus before reaching Antioch, the place where the expedition had originated.

III. Introducing Apollos (Acts 18:24–26)

In Ephesus, Paul left behind Priscilla and Aquila, who encountered an Alexandrian Jew named Apollos who had a reputation as being educated and quite eloquent in his knowledge of the Scriptures. Apollos was probably refined since he hailed from this city that bears the name of its founder, Alexander the Great. Being the second largest city in Egypt and the largest city on the Mediterranean, it was bustling with trade and commerce. Alexandria was a large Hellenistic center but was also home to probably the most populous Jewish community in the world. Alexandria also boasted of the world's largest libraries, one of the Seven Wonders of the Ancient World and the site of the Greek translation of the Hebrew Bible. Apollos could not have escaped the influences from his hometown. The fact Apollos was competent in the Scriptures probably means he was considered to be well-versed or powerful (mighty) in his presentation and expertise in the Old Testament and the law. There has been speculation that Apollos became a rival of Paul, as some in the Corinthian church regarded him as their teacher, and divisions were described to have occurred between those who followed Paul, Apollos,

Cephas (Peter), and even Christ (1 Cor. 1:12; 3:4). The evidence is revealed in both Paul's first and second letters to the church at Corinth. Paul addressed these major divisions. Additionally, there seems to have existed a power struggle, originating from several powerful persons of wealth and status, that challenged Paul's rightful position as leader of the church. Paul, however, did not blame Apollos for the difficulties in Corinth and depicted him as a valued partner in his ministry. The fault lay with those Corinthians who were divisive and played favorites for their personal and political gain.

Nonetheless, Apollos had been instructed in the way and manner of the Lord, and being enthusiastic, his excitement seemed to be contagious. Apollos, probably a natural leader, was a gifted speaker and teacher who accurately taught about Jesus. Luke used the term *ἐπίσταμαι* (*epistamai*), meaning "to understand or to know" about the baptism of John, reflecting that Apollos was lacking in his overall knowledge! S. D. Toussaint believes Apollos's doctrine regarding Jesus was accurate but deficient, meaning Apollos did not know about the Holy Spirit's baptism. John's baptism symbolized a cleansing by God because of repentance toward God. Christian baptism represents a union with Christ in His death, burial, and resurrection by the Spirit's baptism.

Armed with what he believed was precise and in order, Apollos began speaking out freely and boldly while teaching in the synagogue. Although well-versed in his concepts of Judaism and his understanding of the Messiah, Apollos may have been a sincere believer who could not adequately merge the principles of the law with the Messiah in the person of Jesus. Apollos preached the baptism of John, which was for repentance (Mark 1:4), but not Christian baptism for the gift of the Holy Spirit (Acts 2:38). Recall that Israel and the Jews were looking for the Messiah; however, it became difficult for many to reconcile this in the person of Jesus Christ. In his exuberance, Apollos was incomplete and needed further instruction. Therefore, when Priscilla and Aquila heard him, they sprang into action by taking him aside and explaining to him the way and concepts of God in a more accurate and precise manner. Rather than embarrassing him in public or destroying his confidence and message, the godly couple invited Apollos to their home and instructed him further in the doctrine of the way of the Lord and the focus on the mission of Jesus Christ. Because of their dedication to the spread of the authentic Gospel and the actual mandates of Jesus, Priscilla and Aquila served as a blessing to Apollos, who became a dependable disciple of the Lord.

IV. Paul's Gratitude (Romans 16:3–4)

Paul was writing from the bustling seaport city of Corinth, located in Greece. In this letter to the church in Rome, Paul wished to introduce his friends and fellow coworkers (*συνεργούς: synergous*) to his audience. However, Paul likely was also using their names for credibility given that he had never been to Rome. They were known and hosted a church in their home, and it was with their trust (and others') that Paul wrote this letter. They were given the highest praise Paul gave another

Christian, as he called them *coworkers*. This designation is associated with Timothy (Rom. 16:21), Titus (2 Cor. 8:23), Mark, Demas, Aristarchus, and Luke (Phlm. 24). Interestingly, Priscilla is the only woman listed as a *synergous* (coworker), and it seems likely this title was reserved only for those for were not only committed followers of the Way but served in major leadership capacities. Therefore, Paul recommended these members greet Priscilla and Aquila.

Paul spoke fondly of the couple, who had placed themselves in danger by looking out for Paul. Paul did not explain exactly what the couple did to protect him—there could have been issues during their travels—however, Paul did note they risked (*ὑποτίθημι, hypotithemi*) their lives to safeguard him. Literally saying, "They put their lives under mine," or "not valuing their lives above my own." Jesus said, "Greater love has no one than this: to lay down one's life for one's friends" (John 15:13, NIV).

During Paul's ministry, people tried to kill him; therefore, Priscilla and Aquila were special to him. Paul continued by explaining his gratitude and just how thankful he was for their friendship and the concern of all of the Gentile houses of worship. In the following verses, Paul continued to greet other believers and co-laborers in the Gospel at Rome.

The Lesson Applied

Prisca (Priscilla) and her husband Aquila played a major role in the ministry of Paul over several years and continents. From their days as tentmakers, as well as their being active in the discipleship of Jesus, this couple was devoted to the expansion of the Gospel. This became evident in the manner in which they put their lives (and possibly even their wealth) at risk as they traveled. Moreover, their commitment to providing Apollos continued instruction revealed they were not selfish but a generous and loving couple. Our contemporary churches would be strengthened today if we followed their example!

Let's Talk About It

Early believers were able to accomplish so much. How might we do the same?

Believers of Jesus Christ are able to find mutual support in the Christian community. Regardless of the issues we face, there remains a remnant of believers who refuse to wilt in the face of adversity. Despite that which may seem to be a sense of apathy from the general community at large, we can be secure in the knowledge we are blessed in the strength of our numbers. All believers, who are girded by the Holy Spirit, may be confident the Lord is with us!

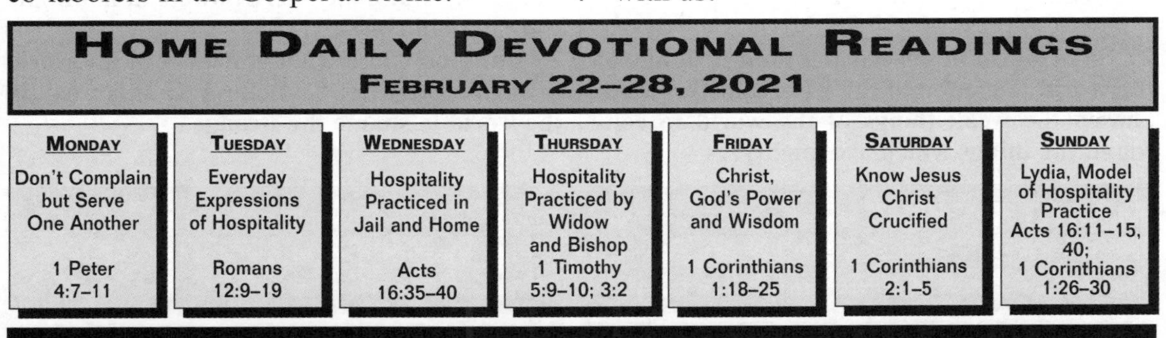

Home Daily Devotional Readings

February 22–28, 2021

Monday	Tuesday	Wednesday	Thursday	Friday	Saturday	Sunday
Don't Complain but Serve One Another	Everyday Expressions of Hospitality	Hospitality Practiced in Jail and Home	Hospitality Practiced by Widow and Bishop	Christ, God's Power and Wisdom	Know Jesus Christ Crucified	Lydia, Model of Hospitality Practice
1 Peter 4:7–11	Romans 12:9–19	Acts 16:35–40	1 Timothy 5:9–10; 3:2	1 Corinthians 1:18–25	1 Corinthians 2:1–5	Acts 16:11–15, 40; 1 Corinthians 1:26–30

LYDIA: CALLED TO SERVE

ADULT TOPIC:
SHOWING GENEROUS HOSPITALITY

BACKGROUND SCRIPTURE:
ACTS 16:11–15, 40; 1 CORINTHIANS 1:26–30

ACTS 16:11–15, 40; 1 CORINTHIANS 1:26–30

King James Version

THEREFORE loosing from Troas, we came with a straight course to Samothracia, and the next day to Neapolis;

12 And from thence to Philippi, which is the chief city of that part of Macedonia, and a colony: and we were in that city abiding certain days.

13 And on the sabbath we went out of the city by a river side, where prayer was wont to be made; and we sat down, and spake unto the women which resorted thither.

14 And a certain woman named Lydia, a seller of purple, of the city of Thyatira, which worshipped God, heard us: whose heart the Lord opened, that she attended unto the things which were spoken of Paul.

15 And when she was baptized, and her household, she besought us, saying, If ye have judged me to be faithful to the Lord, come into my house, and abide there. And she constrained us.

• • • • • •

40 And they went out of the prison, and entered into the house of Lydia: and when they had seen the brethren, they comforted them, and departed.

• • • 1 Corinthians 1:26–30 • • •

FOR ye see your calling, brethren, how that not many wise men after the flesh, not many mighty, not many noble, are called:

27 But God hath chosen the foolish things of the world to confound the wise; and God hath chosen the weak things of the world to confound the things which are mighty;

New Revised Standard Version

WE set sail from Troas and took a straight course to Samothrace, the following day to Neapolis,

12 and from there to Philippi, which is a leading city of the district of Macedonia and a Roman colony. We remained in this city for some days.

13 On the sabbath day we went outside the gate by the river, where we supposed there was a place of prayer; and we sat down and spoke to the women who had gathered there.

14 A certain woman named Lydia, a worshiper of God, was listening to us; she was from the city of Thyatira and a dealer in purple cloth. The Lord opened her heart to listen eagerly to what was said by Paul.

15 When she and her household were baptized, she urged us, saying, "If you have judged me to be faithful to the Lord, come and stay at my home." And she prevailed upon us.

• • • • •

40 After leaving the prison they went to Lydia's home; and when they had seen and encouraged the brothers and sisters there, they departed.

• • • 1 Corinthians 1:26–30 • • •

CONSIDER your own call, brothers and sisters: not many of you were wise by human standards, not many were powerful, not many were of noble birth.

27 But God chose what is foolish in the world to shame the wise; God chose what is weak in the world to shame the strong;

MAIN THOUGHT: And when she was baptized, and her household, she besought us, saying, If ye have judged me to be faithful to the Lord, come into my house, and abide there. And she constrained us. (Acts 16:15, KJV)

ACTS 16:11–15, 40; 1 CORINTHIANS 1:26–30

King James Version	*New Revised Standard Version*
28 And base things of the world, and things which are despised, hath God chosen, yea, and things which are not, to bring to nought things that are:	**28 God chose what is low and despised in the world, things that are not, to reduce to nothing things that are,**
29 That no flesh should glory in his presence.	**29 so that no one might boast in the presence of God.**
30 But of him are ye in Christ Jesus, who of God is made unto us wisdom, and righteousness, and sanctification, and redemption.	**30 He is the source of your life in Christ Jesus, who became for us wisdom from God, and righteousness and sanctification and redemption,**

LESSON SETTING

Time: *circa* A.D. 49–52 and 55–56
Place: Philippi and Ephesus

LESSON OUTLINE

I. The Macedonian Call (Acts 16:11–15, 40)
II. The Source of Your Calling (1 Corinthians 1:26–30)

UNIFYING PRINCIPLE

Many people have been recipients of generous hospitality or have been in a position to extend hospitality to someone. In what ways can openness and a listening ear provide opportunities to serve? Lydia was an attentive woman who responded to the Gospel message with faithfulness and generous hospitality.

INTRODUCTION

Today we will meet Lydia, one who served in the background but was able to ensure the work of Christ moved forward. Hospitality is born of a generous spirit and is not always linked to large material wealth. Rather, it comes from the willingness of the heart to be used by God and helps lead others to His side. God can use both the rich and highborn and the lowly to bring His purposes to pass. He simply needs those who are willing to serve.

EXPOSITION

I. THE MACEDONIAN CALL (ACTS 16:11–15, 40)

Verse 11 traces the route Paul and his companions—prominently among them, Silas (also called Silvanus), Timothy, and Luke—made as they set out from the port city of Troas, where they followed a straight course to Samothrace, an island without a natural harbor. On the following day, they proceeded to the city of Neapolis, a town in Thrace where Paul first landed in Europe. It was the seaport of the inland town of Philippi, which was a distance of about ten miles. Philippi was a prominent metropolis in the district of Macedonia. The city was a Roman colony, which became important later in this account. Paul and his companions spent several days in this city, which played a prominent role in their meeting certain interesting people, some of whom became important converts in this mission. On the Sabbath, Paul and his companions gathered outside the gate leading to the river, which was a place of prayer and contemplation. There they noticed a sizable group of women who had already gathered (*συνέρχομαι, synerchomai*). It is better to translate this location as "a place for prayer" rather than in the specific meaning of "synagogue," since Luke did use the word *synagogue* elsewhere and could have used it here, had he so desired. As Paul began to speak, the women earnestly listened to his words. It happened that a woman named Lydia was among this group of women.

Lydia hailed from the city of Thyatira, a city known for its commercial prowess in Asia Minor. By all accounts, Lydia was a wealthy and prosperous woman who was reported to have been an independent businesswoman. Luke used the term *πορφυρόπωλις* (*porphyrotolis*), which defines her as a merchant dealing in purple cloth or robes. Purple was a special color, as Solomon used it to array the new temple he was building, calling for skilled workmen who knew of its properties and beauty (2 Chron. 2:7). Sadly, the soldiers clothed Jesus in purple as they mocked him (Mark 15:17–20; John 19:2–5). Purple also was associated with the decadence of the future Babylon (Rev. 17:4; 18:12, 16).

Lydia was described as someone who had an acumen for business and trade, as she was also a broker of these fine goods. The fact she specialized in the color purple indicated she had acquired the knowledge of dying fabrics, which would afford her an upscale living, especially in the more urban centers of the region. Purple cloth was an expensive commodity that was valued and worn by the rich and would have given her access to a wealthy client base. Lydia was also someone who worshiped God by honoring and showing reverence for His principles, as is evident in the interest and attentiveness she showed to Paul. As the Lord opened her heart and mind, Lydia paid careful attention to and valued the words of Paul, which allowed her to have a positive response to his teaching. By the statement that she was a woman who worshiped God, Luke indicated she was a Gentile participant in Jewish worship. As a worshiper of God, she was likened to Cornelius (Acts 10:1–2) and those in Thessalonica (Acts 17:4) who were not proselytes to Judaism but did worship Yahweh. Even so, they were not initially a part of the Church. Lydia became a woman of action because her heart burned with the excitement of being part of the family of God. Here we are able to realize that the man of the Macedonian vision turned out to be a woman (Acts 16:9)!

Submitting to the will of the Holy Spirit and the observance of the visible acknowledgment of her commitment to the Lord, Lydia and all of her household were baptized. This reinforced the certainty she was wealthy, and the use of the phrase *all of her household* indicates her servants were baptized, as they would have followed the example of their master. If Lydia had children, generally, they would have followed the example of their mother and also submitted to baptism. Following the ceremony, she urged (*παρακαλέω, parakaleo*) and implored Paul and his companions to stay as guests in her house. She prayed they had seen her to be faithful to the Lord. Paul and his companions may have initially demurred Lydia's invitation; however, her personality must have convinced them to accept her hospitality and go into her residence. Her attempt to successfully host these guests was important because it served as yet another place of sanctuary for the believer. Luke used the same Greek term for *prevail* (*παραβιάζομαι, parabiazomai*) that described the urgings of the disciples who met Jesus on the road to Emmaus to stay with them in their homes (Luke 24:29). During this period, travelers stayed in private homes during their journeys. This was especially important during the movement of Christian missionaries such as Paul and his companions. During the days of persecution, the sign of the fish innocuously placed on a residence indicated a haven for believers. As Lydia opened her house to Paul, she became available to host a similar type of haven. Confirmation that she was a woman of considerable means was evidenced by the size of her house, as it would have had to be ample enough to house four men as well as her household without embarrassment.

Following the baptism of Lydia and her household, Paul and his companions were going to a place of prayer, which is probably the same one referenced in verse 13. While on the way, they encountered a slave girl who had the ability of divination. She should be more accurately identified as a fortune-teller, not a prophet. She was owned by what seemed to be more than one man, as verse 16 notes her "owners" were profiting from her trade (Acts 16:16). Although some people have assumed the owners were a man and his wife, the incidents that took place later seem to indicate several men were involved as the owners of this slave girl. The girl literally had a python spirit. *Python* was originally the name given to the snake that guarded the sacred place at Delphi, where divine oracles were given. Later, the word *python* was used of anyone who possessed the power to foretell the future. Nonetheless, the girl attached herself to Paul. When he exorcised the demon from her, her owners filed a complaint with the magistrates of the city. The magistrates, of course, found Paul and Silas guilty because the girl was a profit machine during a period when many people depended on the advice of a mystic.

Paul and Silas were beaten and thrown into the local prison, where they were shackled and their feet placed in stocks. Paul and Silas, however, kept their faith in the Lord and, while being held in the dungeons of the jail, witnessed to their fellow prisoners and sang and prayed! At some point, an earthquake occurred, destroying the prison (and the shackles) and freeing the inmates. When the jailer realized he was powerless to stop what was happening, he sought to kill himself because he knew he would be blamed and put to death by the authorities. Paul cried out to the jailer, telling him not to harm himself, and implored upon him to cast his fate on the Lord, to believe in Jesus, and he would be saved, including all of his household. Immediately, the jailer washed the wounds that had been inflicted upon Paul and Silas and saw his family baptized. The missionaries went into the house of the jailer, where they had dinner and celebrated the occasion. The following morning, the magistrates sent the police to drop the charges and release Paul and Silas. But Paul would not accept this release and cover-up. Because they had been arrested illegally, he decided to protest the magistrate's decision.

At this point, Paul invoked his Roman citizenship, which gave him certain rights. (Why he did not do this earlier is a mystery!) The authorities were frightened, and they begged Paul and Silas to leave the city. In only two places in Acts was Paul harmed or threatened by Gentiles—in Philippi and in Ephesus (19:23–41). In both instances, people were losing money in vested interests, and in each case, Paul was vindicated by a Roman official. After this, they probably went back to Lydia's house, where Paul and Silas met with fellow believers. With Paul's departure from Philippi, the first of the "we" sections in Acts ends, indicating Luke, the writer of Acts, may have remained on at Philippi (see 16:40).

II. The Source of Your Calling (1 Corinthians 1:26–30)

Paul returned to the city of Ephesus at the conclusion of his Second Missionary Journey (A.D. 52). While in Ephesus, he penned his first letter to the Corinthian church to address the divisions and spiritual and moral questions that had been plaguing the church. The initial focus of Paul's message, especially relating to the problems, was that the Corinthians had misunderstood God's message and the theme of the cross. Charles Ryrie notes that in these verses, Paul showed that worldly wisdom, so highly prized by the Corinthians, is the antithesis of the wisdom of God. Paul scolded them to consider and examine their calling unto God because not many people, in the natural state of humanity have the wisdom to challenge God. This includes those who may believe they are high or noble, especially the arrogant well-born. Paul implored them to reflect on the circumstances when they were called and the reason God chose the individuals in the first place, noting their calling was a gift *from* God, not a gift *to* God!

Continuing, Paul stripped the notion that the pseudo wise and powerful had the solutions to the issues faced by the Church. In a reverse manner of allegory, Paul exclaimed that God had chosen the foolish to shame and disappoint those who would place themselves above God. In this twist, God had selected the seemingly weaker things and people to do His will and disgrace those who oppressed the weak and the marginalized. In the imagery of Jesus' proclamation that "many who are first will be last, and the last first" (Mark 10:31, NIV), Paul implored these members to submit to the spirit of humility.

God has rejected the ignoble and sordid foundations of society, which He will not approve, in favor of the things that please Him. God chooses people who may seem insignificant or inferior in the eyes of the rich and powerful who do not have a relationship with God. The former will enter the Kingdom, while the latter may face an eternity of damnation. Life is filled with testimonies of individuals who have overcome poverty and the lack of resources to become successful in their careers because of their trust and dependence on the unlimited reserves of God.

Paul seemed to repeat his thoughts while noting the things that are socially acceptable will be rejected by the things that are not.

In his message of God's rejecting the values of the world, Paul remonstrated to the Corinthians against assimilating the values of their city and culture. It is impossible for humans to decipher the mind and will of God. Paul implored the believers to understand that the wisdom of the sensible is to understand His way, but the foolishness of fools is deceit (Prov. 14:8). Therefore, because of humanity's limited knowledge, especially about God, humans are unable to boast before God.

Concluding, Paul reminded the Corinthian church that it was by God's doing, or His will, that they were in the body of Jesus Christ. As a gift from God, Jesus provides all wisdom and righteousness, which includes justice and sanctification. It is this that leads to consecration in holiness where the act of redemption occurs. God also has put us right with Himself through Christ and has made us His people and set us free. An alternative translation model for this verse is that God has caused our lives to be completely linked with Christ Jesus, and through Christ, He gives us His own wisdom. Additionally, God also puts us right with Himself, and through Jesus Christ, we become His special people, free from sin.

The Lesson Applied

Believers who follow the will of God are subject to having their plans altered by the Lord. As an example, we are able to chronicle the cities and regions traveled by Paul during his journeys. However, prior to reaching the targeted city of Philippi, Paul and his companions passed through the Phrygian and Galatian regions but were forbidden by the Holy Spirit to speak the word in Asia. Additionally, the Spirit of Jesus did not permit them to go into Bithynia or Mysia. We as believers and ministers of the Gospel must remain flexible to put God's agenda ahead of what we may perceive as our sense of direction. We must continue to follow the course set by the Lord.

Let's Talk About It

Should we share only the Word or also material wealth to advance His Gospel?

This lesson is filled with sharing the Gospel and also the believers' homes and food. The joy of these households, including the children and servants, is implied in the constant reference to sharing. Sadly, many people today see the Church as a place where they can enrich themselves rather than working to supply their own needs. Although economic issues plague society (Jesus was sensitive to the plight of the poor), Paul provided an example of an authentic sense of joy through sharing, where no one was gripped by greed but received joy because the act of sharing is rooted in the Gospel and Spirit of Jesus. He met others' physical needs as well as their spiritual ones. As His disciples, we must do the same.

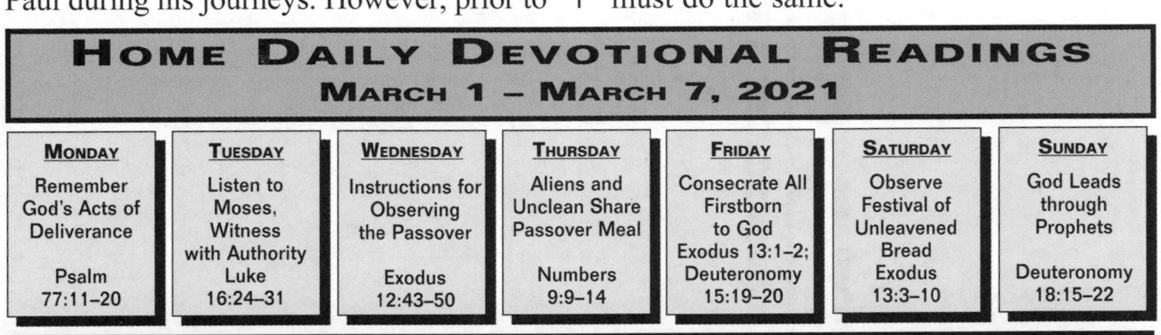

Home Daily Devotional Readings
March 1 – March 7, 2021

Monday	Tuesday	Wednesday	Thursday	Friday	Saturday	Sunday
Remember God's Acts of Deliverance	Listen to Moses, Witness with Authority	Instructions for Observing the Passover	Aliens and Unclean Share Passover Meal	Consecrate All Firstborn to God	Observe Festival of Unleavened Bread	God Leads through Prophets
Psalm 77:11–20	Luke 16:24–31	Exodus 12:43–50	Numbers 9:9–14	Exodus 13:1–2; Deuteronomy 15:19–20	Exodus 13:3–10	Deuteronomy 18:15–22

Third Quarter

March

April

May

MOSES: PROPHET OF DELIVERANCE

TOPIC:
FACING THE IMPOSSIBLE

BACKGROUND SCRIPTURE:
EXODUS 12:28–50; DEUTERONOMY 18:15–22

DEUTERONOMY 18:15–22

King James Version

THE LORD thy God will raise up unto thee a Prophet from the midst of thee, of thy brethren, like unto me; unto him ye shall hearken;

16 According to all that thou desiredst of the LORD thy God in Horeb in the day of the assembly, saying, Let me not hear again the voice of the LORD my God, neither let me see this great fire any more, that I die not.

17 And the LORD said unto me, They have well spoken that which they have spoken.

18 I will raise them up a Prophet from among their brethren, like unto thee, and will put my words in his mouth; and he shall speak unto them all that I shall command him.

19 And it shall come to pass, that whosoever will not hearken unto my words which he shall speak in my name, I will require it of him.

20 But the prophet, which shall presume to speak a word in my name, which I have not commanded him to speak, or that shall speak in the name of other gods, even that prophet shall die.

21 And if thou say in thine heart, How shall we know the word which the LORD hath not spoken?

22 When a prophet speaketh in the name of the LORD, if the thing follow not, nor come to pass, that is the thing which the LORD hath not spoken, but the prophet hath spoken it presumptuously: thou shalt not be afraid of him.

New Revised Standard Version

THE LORD your God will raise up for you a prophet like me from among your own people; you shall heed such a prophet.

16 This is what you requested of the LORD your God at Horeb on the day of the assembly when you said: "If I hear the voice of the LORD my God any more, or ever again see this great fire, I will die."

17 Then the LORD replied to me: "They are right in what they have said.

18 I will raise up for them a prophet like you from among their own people; I will put my words in the mouth of the prophet, who shall speak to them everything that I command.

19 Anyone who does not heed the words that the prophet shall speak in my name, I myself will hold accountable.

20 But any prophet who speaks in the name of other gods, or who presumes to speak in my name a word that I have not commanded the prophet to speak—that prophet shall die."

21 You may say to yourself, "How can we recognize a word that the LORD has not spoken?"

22 If a prophet speaks in the name of the LORD but the thing does not take place or prove true, it is a word that the LORD has not spoken. The prophet has spoken it presumptuously; do not be frightened by it.

MAIN THOUGHT: The LORD thy God will raise up unto thee a Prophet from the midst of thee, of thy brethren, like unto me; unto him ye shall hearken. (Deuteronomy 18:15, KJV)

LESSON SETTING

Time: *circa* 2000 B.C.
Place: Canaanite Wilderness

LESSON OUTLINE

I. The Promised Prophet of God (Deuteronomy 18:15–19)
II. The Authentication of a Prophet (Deuteronomy 18:20–22)

UNIFYING PRINCIPLE

Life often confronts us with situations that appear to offer only poor outcomes. How are we to respond when the seemingly impossible is asked of us? Following the command of God, the Hebrew people left Egypt under the leadership of a faithful prophet, Moses, who became a model for prophets to come.

INTRODUCTION

Today's lesson passage is part of a larger context from Deuteronomy 12:1–26:19 concerned with various laws for Israel. It also comes from the immediate scriptural context that includes Deuteronomy 16:18–18:22 and concerns the various officials who were to serve Israel in Mosaic days and for several generations following. The focus of the passage under discussion was the responsibilities of the officials to maintain pure worship life in the Promised Land and impartially administer justice.

As is true for much of what appears in the book of Deuteronomy ("Second Law"), what appears in this section is considered by many Old Testament interpreters as a sermon or address by Moses. He spoke to various leadership groups for the corporate and spiritual life of Israel and established some of the primary responsibilities for each group. He spoke to the role and responsibilities of judges in Deuteronomy 16:18–20. At one time, Moses administered judicial matters alone, until the task became overwhelming. Then he appointed leading men of the tribes as military leaders (commanders), officials, and judges (Deut. 1:15–18; Ex. 18). Most likely these men were the chief elders of each tribe. The judges appointed in each tribe probably were taken from that tribe's council. The judges were also to see that false worshipers were executed. The worship of false gods pulled the people of Israel away from rendering homage to the one true God, their source of life.

Moses summed up the requirements for the judges and officials by emphatically demanding them to follow justice exclusively. Apparently it was thought that impartial justice could be difficult to attain at times because of the weakness of human nature. Therefore it was absolutely essential that the standard set forth in the Law be followed precisely. Compliance with, and maintenance of, impartial justice would determine their lives and prosperity in the Promised Land (Deut. 16:18–20). But there was also a concern at the time for the maintenance of authentic worship of Yahweh. This theme is taken up specifically in Deuteronomy 16:21–17:1. These verses insisted the people must avoid incorporating anything from pagan worship practices into their worship of Yahweh. And they were to bring acceptable offerings—those without defect of any kind. Those who worshiped other gods deserved capital punishment because such an act threatened the nation's existence (17:2–7 prescribes capital punishment of false worshipers). After all, they were bound by a covenant with

Yahweh—a covenant that involved both privileges and responsibilities.

Discussion about the judges concludes in 17:8–13. Moses made a provision for future judges in Israel similar to that provided for judges in the time of the wilderness wanderings (1:17). Should a judge feel a case was too difficult for him to decide, he could refer it to a central tribunal of priests and the officiating chief judge to be established at the future site of the central sanctuary. The decisions of the tribunal would be final. Any rebellion against the tribunal was considered "contempt of court" and was a capital offense. Such a procedure placed priority on the rule of justice in the land and helped prevent lawlessness.

Moses turned his attention to matters related to the future kings of Israel, a topic he discussed in 17:14–20. When the time came that Israel could no longer tolerate its unique position of being without a king, the nation requested and received a king. Deuteronomy 17:14–15 speaks of the king's qualifications. His conduct is dealt with in verses 16–17. Then, verses 18–20 are concerned with his education.

Israel's king was required to meet two qualifications. First, he must be chosen by the Lord. The people could be certain God would not place someone on the throne whom He had not gifted to be king. Therefore, if a king failed, the reason for his failure would not lie in his lack of ability. Rather, his failure would be because of his moral life.

The second qualification of the king was that he must be an Israelite. A member of the Israelite community, reared from childhood in the traditions and the Scriptures of Israel, would be a much better choice than a foreigner to preserve and protect the purity of Israel's religion.

The king's primary purpose was to provide governmental leadership for the covenant people of God and help keep them loyal to that covenant relationship. His desires and objective always must be as God's servant. Therefore, it should be no surprise there were stringent requirements regarding the king's personal behavior. The prohibition against having multiple wives was given because many kings married foreign women to form political alliances. If the king followed the Lord, he would not need political alliances. Furthermore, foreign wives could influence the king to go astray and worship their idols. In terms of the king's education, it must consist of his copying, reading, and diligently following all the Law and decrees in the book of Deuteronomy.

Moses addressed matters relating to the spiritual leaders in the worship life of Israel—the priests and Levites—in 18:1–8. Only those who were descendants of Aaron could serve as priests (Num. 3:10). They generally were referred to as *the priests* or *the sons of Aaron* (Num. 10:8). The rest of the tribe, those not serving as priests, were designated as *Levites*.

The Levites served as ministers to the priests (Num. 18:1–7; 1 Chron. 23:28–32) and as teachers of the Law in Israel (Deut. 33:10; 2 Chron. 17:8–9). Priests officiated at the tabernacle and fulfilled duties. They functioned as judges (Deut. 17:8–9), as guardians of the scroll of the Law (17:18; 31:9), and as teachers of regulations concerning skin diseases (24:8). They also assisted Moses in the covenant renewal ceremony (27:9).

Exposition

The qualifications, role, and responsibilities of prophets are taken up in Deuteronomy 18:9–22. Interestingly, the discussion of authentic prophets and the "ultimate" prophet of Israel is set against the background of the practices of pagan prophets and paganism. Both were extensive among the various Canaanites whose land Israel would possess. The Old Testament exegete, John D. W. Watts, offers a helpful summary of the context in which the Israelites were to be cautious. Speaking of 18:9–22 he says: "A series of religious practices are pronounced unacceptable for Israel. The first refers to a practice sometimes called a part of the worship of Moloch. It apparently involved child sacrifice by fire and is understood to have been a part of Canaanite worship in various places including ancient Carthage which was settled by the Phoenicians.... It is cited as having been a problem for Israel at various times, but mainly in the later period with the peak at the time of Manasseh (cf. 2 Kings 2:6)" (Watts, "Deuteronomy," 254).

Then follows a variety of detestable ways in which pagans claimed to know God's will. Divination, from the Hebrew verb *qasam*, "to divide," means to give false prophecy or seek to determine the will of the gods by examining and interpreting omens. It was seeking to get secret knowledge, especially about future events. Divination was widely practiced in the ancient world in a variety of ways, including interpreting omens, consulting the stars, inspecting various animal organs, using divining rods, interpreting dreams, watching the movement of the water, and contacting the dead. *Qasam* also is used in Joshua 13:22; 1 Samuel 6:2; 28:8; 2 Kings 17:17; Isaiah 3:2; 44:25; Jeremiah 27:9; 29:8; Ezekiel 13:6, 9, 23; 21:21, 23, 29; 22:28; Micah 3:6–7, 11; Zechariah 10:2.

Sorcery ("casting spells") was an attempt to control people or circumstances through power given by evil spirits or demons. Interpreting of omens was to tell the future based on so-called "signs" in nature. Witchcraft (*kašap*) involved practicing magic by incantations. *One who casts spells* is literally from a term that means "one who ties knots," indicating someone who binds other people by magical mutterings. A spiritualist (necromancer) was one who supposedly communicated with the dead but who actually communicated with demons. These practices also are referenced in Leviticus 19:26; 2 Kings 21:6; Isaiah 2:6; and Micah 5:12.

All these practices were extremely common among the Canaanites. But they were forbidden to Israel and were detestable abominations—extremely offensive—to Yahweh. "Anyone who does these things is detestable to the Lord; because of these detestable practices the Lord your God will drive out those nations before you. You must be blameless before the Lord your God" (Deut. 18:12–13, NIV).

The desire to know and discern the will of God was not the issue here at all. It was the means by which Israel's contemporaries sought to do so that is discussed and condemned here. In the preface to his discussion of the authentic prophet in Israel, Watts suggests: "The desire to know the will of God, is declared legitimate. This prophet and his nature is then portrayed, not through a reference to the classic figures of Israel's prophets, but by pointing the way God provided for communication at Sinai. At that time the people feared the voice and the fire and asked for a mediator. Moses became this spokesman who stood between God and His people" (Watts, "Deuteronomy," 254).

I. The Promised Prophet of God (Deuteronomy 18:15–19)

In stark contrast to the pagan prophets and their practices among the Canaanites, God promised to provide His people with a prophet of His approval. Moses assured them in verse 15 (NIV): "The Lord your God will raise up for you a prophet like me from among you, from your fellow Israelites. You must listen to him." Watts asserts, "The prophet, then, is defined in terms of the covenant mediator with Moses as the supreme example. Through him Israel came into direct contact with the word and will of God.... This prophet is the 'mouth of God' for His people. He is required to pass on all that God gives him, but no more. That is all that is said about this high office. The picture can be filled out; however, in the full role of Moses in connection with covenant-making, it is used to fill in the details of the picture" (Watts, "Deuteronomy," 254).

Because the prophet like Moses would be chosen by the Lord, the Israelites were to hear and heed the prophet. The Israelites could be sure a line of prophets would follow in succession after Moses. This was based on their original request at Mount Horeb (Sinai) that the Lord speak to them through Moses as a mediator (Deut. 5:23–27). All the prophets God would raise up would be Israelites. And since the true prophet would speak only the words of the Lord, the people were obligated to live in compliance with those words.

There are two hermeneutical approaches to understanding the "prophet like Moses." Watts puts it in a clear perspective when he writes: "This promise to raise up a prophet like Moses has sometimes been understood to promise a succession in this position which assures the people of God of continual access to the word of God. Others understand it to refer to the one great figure who shall rise as a second Moses to establish a second covenant" (Watts, "Deuteronomy," 254). Over the centuries, Jewish scholars interpreted the promise of a prophet like Moses to refer to a special prophet who would appear before the Messiah came to establish His Kingdom. Based on Malachi 4:5, the Jews knew Elijah would return at the end of the age. Many wondered if it was John the Baptist, who dressed and ministered in ways similar to Elijah (Luke 3:1–9; Matt 3:4). John denied it and also denied he was the prophet whom Moses had promised (John 1:19–21). In one sense, John was an "Elijah" who prepared the way for Christ (Matt. 11:14; 17:12; Luke 1:13–17). However, John did not identify himself as the fulfillment of Malachi 4:5.

Moses certainly set the standard for all future prophets. Each prophet was to do his best to live up to the example of Moses until *the* Prophet came who would introduce the New Covenant. At the dawn of the age of the New Testament, the official leaders of Judaism were still looking for the fulfillment of Moses' prediction. The Apostle Peter said their search should have concluded with Jesus the Christ (Acts 3:19–26). Because the ultimate Prophet speaks for the Lord, He will hold accountable those who reject the words of the Prophet. "I will personally deal with anyone who will not listen to the messages the prophet proclaims on my behalf" (Deut. 18:19, NLT).

II. The Authentication of a Prophet (Deuteronomy 18:20–22)

"But a prophet who presumes to speak in my name anything I have not commanded, or a prophet who speaks in the name of other gods, is to be put to death" (Deut. 18:20, NIV). With these sobering words, the Lord Himself indicated the gravity and the seriousness of the integrity of a prophet. Two things are to be noted here. One is that prophets must speak *only* that which the Lord directs them to speak. Another is that a prophet must speak *only* on behalf of the Lord God. Otherwise, both that prophet and the message the prophet claims to announce are false.

A practical question inevitably arose from the people, given such detailed discussions about prophets and their message. *How would they know for sure a prophet was authentic?* There is a "time will tell" aspect to the response. That is, the validity of a prophet's message would be indicated by whether or not it came true.

The Lesson Applied

The New Testament contains much of the same concern for the message of God and the authenticity of those who claim to proclaim it as does the Old Testament. The matter is found in the epistles. First John 4:1 (NIV) warns: "Dear friends, do not believe every spirit, but test the spirits to see whether they are from God, because many false prophets have gone out into the world." John then provided a strategy for determining whether one is or is not a legitimate prophet. The proof is Christological—whether one affirms or denies the humanity of Jesus (as was common in the Johannine community). The truth or falsehood of everything rests on God's self-revelation in Jesus Christ.

Let's Talk About It

What are some identifiable sources of false religion in contemporary society?

A counterfeit gospel is one that denies the identity of Jesus Christ as the only begotten Son of God, who was born of a virgin woman, who was crucified on the cross at Calvary, and who was resurrected by God on the third day (1 John 4:2–5).

Home Daily Devotional Readings
March 8–14, 2021

Monday	Tuesday	Wednesday	Thursday	Friday	Saturday	Sunday
The Faith of Israelite Heroes	Jesus Heals Blind Man from Jericho	Enjoying the Manna and Local Produce	Marching around the City of Jericho	Rahab and Spies Confirm Rescue Plan	Rahab Saved While Jericho Is Destroyed	Joshua's Successful Conquest of Jericho
Hebrews 11:23–31	Luke 18:35–43	Joshua 5:10–12	Joshua 6:6–14	Joshua 2:15–24	Joshua 6:22–25	Joshua 5:13–6:5, 15–16, 20

Joshua: Prophet of Conquest

Topic:
Making Wise Choices

Background Scripture:
Joshua 5:13–6:27

Joshua 5:13–6:5, 15–16, 20

King James Version

AND it came to pass, when Joshua was by Jericho, that he lifted up his eyes and looked, and, behold, there stood a man over against him with his sword drawn in his hand: and Joshua went unto him, and said unto him, Art thou for us, or for our adversaries?
14 And he said, Nay; but as captain of the host of the Lord am I now come. And Joshua fell on his face to the earth, and did worship, and said unto him, What saith my Lord unto his servant?
15 And the captain of the Lord's host said unto Joshua, Loose thy shoe from off thy foot; for the place whereon thou standest is holy. And Joshua did so.

• • • Joshua 6:1–5, 15–16, 20 • • •

1 Now Jericho was straitly shut up because of the children of Israel: none went out, and none came in.
2 And the Lord said unto Joshua, See, I have given into thine hand Jericho, and the king thereof, and the mighty men of valour.
3 And ye shall compass the city, all ye men of war, and go round about the city once. Thus shalt thou do six days.
4 And seven priests shall bear before the ark seven trumpets of rams' horns: and the seventh day ye shall compass the city seven times, and the priests shall blow with the trumpets.
5 And it shall come to pass, that when they make a long blast with the ram's horn, and when ye hear the sound of the trumpet, all

New Revised Standard Version

ONCE when Joshua was by Jericho, he looked up and saw a man standing before him with a drawn sword in his hand. Joshua went to him and said to him, "Are you one of us, or one of our adversaries?"

14 He replied, "Neither; but as commander of the army of the Lord I have now come." And Joshua fell on his face to the earth and worshiped, and he said to him, "What do you command your servant, my lord?"
15 The commander of the army of the Lord said to Joshua, "Remove the sandals from your feet, for the place where you stand is holy." And Joshua did so.

• • • Joshua 6:1–5, 15–16, 20 • • •

1 Now Jericho was shut up inside and out because of the Israelites; no one came out and no one went in.
2 The Lord said to Joshua, "See, I have handed Jericho over to you, along with its king and soldiers.
3 You shall march around the city, all the warriors circling the city once. Thus you shall do for six days,
4 with seven priests bearing seven trumpets of rams' horns before the ark. On the seventh day you shall march around the city seven times, the priests blowing the trumpets.
5 When they make a long blast with the ram's horn, as soon as you hear the sound of the trumpet, then all the people shall shout

MAIN THOUGHT: And the Lord said unto Joshua, See, I have given into thine hand Jericho, and the king thereof, and the mighty men of valour. (Joshua 6:2, KJV)

JOSHUA 5:13–6:5, 15-16, 20

King James Version	*New Revised Standard Version*
the people shall shout with a great shout; and the wall of the city shall fall down flat, and the people shall ascend up every man straight before him.	with a great shout; and the wall of the city will fall down flat, and all the people shall charge straight ahead."
• • • • • •	• • • • • •
15 And it came to pass on the seventh day, that they rose early about the dawning of the day, and compassed the city after the same manner seven times: only on that day they compassed the city seven times.	15 On the seventh day they rose early, at dawn, and marched around the city in the same manner seven times. It was only on that day that they marched around the city seven times.
16 And it came to pass at the seventh time, when the priests blew with the trumpets, Joshua said unto the people, Shout; for the LORD hath given you the city.	16 And at the seventh time, when the priests had blown the trumpets, Joshua said to the people, "Shout! For the LORD has given you the city.
• • • • • •	• • • • • •
20 So the people shouted when the priests blew with the trumpets: and it came to pass, when the people heard the sound of the trumpet, and the people shouted with a great shout, that the wall fell down flat, so that the people went up into the city, every man straight before him, and they took the city.	20 So the people shouted, and the trumpets were blown. As soon as the people heard the sound of the trumpets, they raised a great shout, and the wall fell down flat; so the people charged straight ahead into the city and captured it.

LESSON SETTING

Time: *circa* **2000 B.C.**
Place: Gilgal, Jericho

LESSON OUTLINE

I. **Joshua Encounters the Divine Commander (Joshua 5:13–6:5)**

II. **Joshua and the People Experience Victory (Joshua 6:15–16, 20)**

UNIFYING PRINCIPLE

Individually and corporately, people face choices. How do we discern what choices are best and organize our actions? Joshua and the people of Israel chose to honor a covenant with God, obeying God's instructions perfectly.

INTRODUCTION

The passage under discussion is closely connected with some mighty acts of God as He prepared the people of Israel for the conquest of Jericho. That would have been an epic undertaking by any ancient people and was especially so for the people of Israel under the capable military and spiritual leadership of Joshua. The people camped at Gilgal prior to the military engagement against Jericho. Among the mighty acts of God they had witnessed before making camp at Gilgal was the miraculous crossing of the Jordan River (Josh. 3–4). That event included the Lord's instructions about the crossing, the stoppage of the flow of the Jordan River, and the memorialization of the crossing. From a combination of Joshua's leadership and by God's miraculous intervention, about two million soldiers and civilians crossed the Jordan. A beachhead was quickly established at Gilgal.

It would appear it was time to strike immediately at the strongholds of Canaan. The morale of the people of Canaan had utterly collapsed in the face of one old and two recent news items that had spread through the land. First, the God of Israel dried up the Red Sea. Then the Israelites defeated the powerful kings of the Amorites in the Transjordan (Josh. 2:10–11). Finally, Yahweh also dried up the waters of the Jordan River so the Israelites could cross over into Canaan (5:1).

Yet rather than proceed further with military activity, Israel had some unfinished business that was spiritual in character. It was time for renewal. Consecration must precede conquest. Before God would lead Israel to victory, He led them through three experiences. They renewed the rite of circumcision (5:2–9). The people celebrated the Passover (v. 10), and they ate from the bounty of the land's produce (vv. 11–12).

When the nations of the land were filled with terror, the Lord commanded Joshua to circumcise the sons of Israel. He obeyed, despite the fact it must have been difficult for him as a military commander to incapacitate his entire army in that hostile environment.

Following the circumcision of all the males, the Lord acknowledged the completed task by declaring, "'Today I have rolled away the shame of your slavery in Egypt.' So that place has been called Gilgal to this day" (5:9, NLT). Not only was the meaning of *Gilgal* "to roll" to remind Israel of the memorial stones (4:19–20), but now the related idea of "rolling" would commemorate Israel's act of obedience at the same site. In the act of circumcision, the people indicated the consecration of themselves to the Lord who would fight for them at Jericho.

The second significant ritual at Gilgal was the celebration of the Passover. Celebration of the Passover at Gilgal was only the third Passover the nation had observed. The first was observed in Egypt the night before their deliverance from bondage and oppression (Ex. 12:1–28). The second was observed at Mount Sinai just before the people broke camp and moved toward Canaan (Num. 9:1–5). It was important for the Israelites entering the Promised Land to recall the sprinkling of lamb's blood on the doorpost and lintel, and to imagine the awful death cries of the firstborn of the Egyptians, the excitement of the midnight departure, the terror of the Egyptian pursuit, and the thrill of walking between walls of water to escape Egypt. They needed to remember the mighty acts God already had done for them.

They were, in effect, reliving the first Passover. As the lambs were slain, they were assured that as the crossing of the Red Sea was followed by the destruction of the Egyptians, now the crossing of the Jordan would be followed by the defeat of the Canaanites. Their recollection of the past was an excellent preparation for the tests of the future.

Joshua 5:11–12 records the experience of the Israelites eating from extreme productivity of the land. This occurred the morning after they had eaten the Passover and were prepared for battle. Since they gave evidence of wanting to be fully obedient to the Law of God, it is likely they first brought the wave offering of a sheaf of grain, as required in Leviticus 23:10–14. Then the people ate freely of the harvest. Earlier God had promised to bring Israel into a land of abundance. "For the LORD your God is bringing you into a good land of flowing streams and pools of water, with fountains and streams that gush out in the valleys and hills. It is a land of wheat and barley; of grapevines, fig trees, and pomegranates; of olive oil and honey. It is a land where food is plentiful and nothing is lacking" (Deut. 8:7–9, NLT). At last the people of Israel tasted the fruit of the land and realized it was a foretaste of blessings to come.

Interestingly, the day following the enjoyment of the bounty of the land of Canaan, the manna stopped. The manna had continued for forty years, about an entire generation (Ex. 16:4–5). Now, however, it ceased just as suddenly as it had begun, which was an indication its provision was not a matter of chance but of special providence. God continued to give the manna until they grew and entered the land of promise. He stopped performing the miracle of the manna because natural food was available.

The stage was set for the theophany, the self-revelation of God, to Joshua in preparation for the taking of Jericho.

EXPOSITION

I. JOSHUA ENCOUNTERS THE DIVINE COMMANDER (JOSHUA 5:13–6:5)

It seemed obvious the next step would be the capture of Jericho. Prior to the crossing of the Jordan, a divine message of instruction was given to Joshua about how to proceed. Nothing similar had occurred prior to the assault against Jericho. Joshua, therefore, apparently went alone on a reconnaissance mission for the upcoming attack against the seemingly unassailable city. Perhaps he was concerned or even perplexed as he viewed the secure walls of Jericho. The spies reported at Kadesh Barnea that the cities of Canaan were "large, with walls up to the sky" (Deut. 1:28, NIV). Joshua possessed extensive and successful military experience. However, he had never led an attack on a fortified city that was prepared for a long siege. Jericho was probably the most invincible of all the Canaanite cities.

There was also the question of armaments. Israel's army had none of the equipment traditionally associated with conducting a campaign against such a well-fortified city. Mostly their weapons were slings, arrows, and spears—which would be of minimal effectiveness against Jericho. Joshua knew the battle of Jericho must be won because now that they had crossed the Jordan, Israel's troops had no place to which they could retreat. Additionally, they could not bypass the city because that would leave their women, children, goods, and livestock at Gilgal exposed to certain destruction.

During that time of deep pondering, Joshua saw "a man standing in front of him with a drawn sword in his hand" (Josh. 5:13, NIV). Joshua inquired if he were an ally of Israel or of the residents of Jericho. "Are you a soldier?" was essentially Joshua's question to the mysterious individual. Denying he was either, the individual told Joshua he was the commander of the Lord's army. Joshua immediately recognized he was in the presence of a divine messenger and indicated that by falling face down to the ground and asking, "What message does my Lord have for his servant?" (5:14, NIV). *Commander of the Lord's army* is a common motif in the Old Testament. In keeping with the Deuteronomist's historian's conception of the Lord fighting for Israel (cf. Deut. 1:30; 31:6), the host of His heavenly attendants or helpers (angels) are envisioned as an army (cf. Gen. 32:1–2; 2 Kings 6:15–17; Psalm 103:20–21). The commander of this heavenly host is the angel of the Lord, (cf. Exod. 3:2; Num. 22:22–23; Judges 6:11–24), who is not clearly distinguished in the Old Testament from the Lord himself.

In a theophany, a self-revelation of God, the recipient of such understood God to be present in an audible and visual experience. These features of the encounter were secondary to the revealing of the message of God to the recipient. "God often draws near to disclose His will to humanity and to exert a guiding hand in the history of His people. There are, of course, some similarities with the experience of Moses at the burning bush (Ex. 3:1–10). Both Moses and Joshua fell to the ground and were commanded to remove their shoes because the place on which they stood was holy ground. That is, it was a place (and experience) in which they uniquely and personally encountered God—one that would have a profound impact on their lives and the lives of God's people.

The author-editor of the Joshua narrative interrupted the encounter between Joshua and the commander of the Lord's army to give some significant information about the city of Jericho at 6:1 (NLT), "Now the gates of Jericho were tightly shut because the people were afraid of the Israelites. No one was allowed to go out or in." This description confirmed what Rahab the prostitute said to the spies in Joshua 2:11.

So there this impressive fortress stood, in full view of Joshua, whose conversation with the commander of the Lord's army continued. The commander, who was actually the Lord Himself, promised victory to Joshua and declared He had given Jericho into his hands. The city, its king, and its army all would fall to Israel. The tense of the Hebrew verb is prophetic perfect (*I have delivered*), describing a future action as if it were already accomplished. The victory was absolutely assured by the declaration of God.

The Lord then indicated the strategy Joshua and the people were to follow in the conquest of Jericho (6:3–5). Joshua and his armed men were to march around the city once a day for six successive days. During these marches, seven priests were to blow trumpets preceding the Ark of the Covenant. On the seventh day they were to circle Jericho seven times, at which time the walls of Jericho would collapse and the city would be taken. The whole experience was laced with significant theological symbolism. First, it shows God as purpose oriented. The march around the walls of Jericho may have been meaningless to some, but it revealed one has to only act in faith to the divine initiative to experience victory. Second, it shows that obedience to God is foundational to our success in life. In the end, only God could be credited for the victory and receive the glory.

II. Joshua and the People Experience Victory (Joshua 6:15–16, 20)

Verse 15 provides a summary of the actions of the people on the seventh day. They did just as they had been directed. "The seventh time around, when the priests sounded the trumpet blast, Joshua commanded the people, 'Shout! For the Lord has given you the city!'" (6:16, NIV). Joshua and the people completely complied with the unconventional instructions for military engagement the Lord had given. It was also a word of encouragement and confirmation of God's promise regarding victory.

The *New Living Translation* of verse 20 expresses the summary of the Jericho campaign: "When the people heard the sound of the rams' horns, they shouted as loud as they could. Suddenly, the walls of Jericho collapsed, and the Israelites charged straight into the town and captured it." The promises of God and the obedience of Joshua were thus shown to be true.

The Lesson Applied

Reflecting on multiple experiences of faith in the past, the author of Hebrews 11 said of the experience at Jericho: "By faith the walls of Jericho fell, after the army had marched around them for seven days. By faith the prostitute Rahab, because she welcomed the spies, was not killed with those who were disobedient" (Heb. 11:30–31, NIV). To be sure, faith played a major role in the victory at Jericho, and it was based on Israel's having repeatedly encountered the miraculous power of God in their past. At the same time, however, Hebrews 11 provides insight about an equally necessary component to experiencing God's mighty acts—obedience.

The narrative about the victory demonstrates in a dramatic way that at times what God demands of His people to achieve success sometimes defies human logic and comprehension. Nonetheless, it is always the combination of obedience and faith that results in our victory and most compelling contribution to seeing God's glory.

Let's Talk About It

What have been some impediments to obedience to God's directions?

Some of the impediments to faith have been self-pride and human determination to find its own way. The first sin humanity faced was the sin of pride that caused it to refuse to acknowledge God's way was the best and only productive choice. After human beings sinned, they aggravated their problems as they failed to express sorrow for their infringement against God. Our failure to repent will always doom us.

Home Daily Devotional Readings
March 15–21, 2021

Monday	Tuesday	Wednesday	Thursday	Friday	Saturday	Sunday
God Loves Covenant Keepers	Entering God's Promised Rest	New Covenant Made with the Israelites	Josiah Prepares to Repair the Temple	Josiah Seeks Guidance to Confront Disobedience	Josiah Leads in Covenant Renewal	Huldah Confirms Coming Judgment; Josiah Spared
Psalm 25:1–10	Hebrews 4:1–11	Deuteronomy 29:1–13	2 Kings 22:1–7	2 Kings 22:8–13	2 Kings 23:1–3	2 Kings 22:14–20

HULDAH: PROPHET OF WISDOM

TOPIC:
SEEKING WISDOM FOR THE FUTURE

BACKGROUND SCRIPTURE:
2 KINGS 22

2 KINGS 22:14–20

King James Version

SO Hilkiah the priest, and Ahikam, and Achbor, and Shaphan, and Asahiah, went unto Huldah the prophetess, the wife of Shallum the son of Tikvah, the son of Harhas, keeper of the wardrobe; (now she dwelt in Jerusalem in the college;) and they communed with her.
15 And she said unto them, Thus saith the LORD God of Israel, Tell the man that sent you to me,
16 Thus saith the LORD, Behold, I will bring evil upon this place, and upon the inhabitants thereof, even all the words of the book which the king of Judah hath read:
17 Because they have forsaken me, and have burned incense unto other gods, that they might provoke me to anger with all the works of their hands; therefore my wrath shall be kindled against this place, and shall not be quenched.
18 But to the king of Judah which sent you to enquire of the LORD, thus shall ye say to him, Thus saith the LORD God of Israel, As touching the words which thou hast heard;
19 Because thine heart was tender, and thou hast humbled thyself before the LORD, when thou heardest what I spake against this place, and against the inhabitants thereof, that they should become a desolation and a curse, and hast rent thy clothes, and wept before me; I also have heard thee, saith the LORD.

New Revised Standard Version

SO the priest Hilkiah, Ahikam, Achbor, Shaphan, and Asaiah went to the prophetess Huldah the wife of Shallum son of Tikvah, son of Harhas, keeper of the wardrobe; she resided in Jerusalem in the Second Quarter, where they consulted her.
15 She declared to them, "Thus says the LORD, the God of Israel: Tell the man who sent you to me,
16 Thus says the LORD, I will indeed bring disaster on this place and on its inhabitants—all the words of the book that the king of Judah has read.
17 Because they have abandoned me and have made offerings to other gods, so that they have provoked me to anger with all the work of their hands, therefore my wrath will be kindled against this place, and it will not be quenched.
18 But as to the king of Judah, who sent you to inquire of the LORD, thus shall you say to him, Thus says the LORD, the God of Israel: Regarding the words that you have heard,
19 because your heart was penitent, and you humbled yourself before the LORD, when you heard how I spoke against this place, and against its inhabitants, that they should become a desolation and a curse, and because you have torn your clothes and wept before me, I also have heard you, says the LORD.

MAIN THOUGHT: Because thine heart was tender, and thou hast humbled thyself before the LORD, when thou heardest what I spake against this place, and against the inhabitants thereof, that they should become a desolation and a curse, and hast rent thy clothes, and wept before me; I also have heard thee, saith the LORD. (2 Kings 22:19, KJV)

King James Version	*New Revised Standard Version*
20 Behold therefore, I will gather thee unto thy fathers, and thou shalt be gathered into thy grave in peace; and thine eyes shall not see all the evil which I will bring upon this place. And they brought the king word again.	**20 Therefore, I will gather you to your ancestors, and you shall be gathered to your grave in peace; your eyes shall not see all the disaster that I will bring on this place." They took the message back to the king.**

LESSON SETTING
Time: *circa* 620 B.C.
Place: Judah

LESSON OUTLINE
I. The Consultation with Huldah the Prophetess (2 Kings 22:14)
II. The Message of Huldah for Disobedient Judah (2 Kings 22:15–17)
III. The Message of Huldah for Humble Judah (2 Kings 22:19–20)

Unifying Principle

No one knows all the implications of what they learn. Who can help us understand what the future holds? King Josiah's advisers consulted the prophetess Huldah. She shared her God-given insights about the coming days of the nation and the king.

Introduction

Today's lesson belongs to what is designated the third and final part of the book of 2 Kings. This significant section of the book includes 18:1–25:30. Roy L. Honeycutt suggests this section should be titled "Decades of Renewal and Eventual Destruction: the Kingdom of Judah Alone" (Honeycutt, "2 Kings," 155). Second Kings 22:1–23:30 belongs to the period in Judah's history known as the period of Josiah's reforms. Several significant periods in Judah's history precede this decisive era in Judah. Second Kings 18–20 focuses on the renewal of Judah under prophetic influence and details Hezekiah's handling of an international crisis with Assyria. Relevant to this time was Hezekiah's reformation and independence (18); the ministry of Isaiah (19:1–20:19); and the evaluation of Hezekiah's reign (20:20–21).

Second Kings 21 portrays the widespread apostasy in Judah under two of its most infamous kings. Manasseh's evil reign is described in 21:1–18. He did evil in the eyes of the Lord, following the detestable practices of the nations the Lord had driven out before the Israelites (v. 2). He sacrificed his own son in the fire, practiced sorcery and divination, and consulted mediums and spiritists. He did much evil in the eyes of the Lord, provoking him to anger (v. 6). Manasseh led Judah astray so that they did more evil than the nations the Lord had destroyed before the Israelites (v. 9).

The evils of Amon are recorded in 2 Kings 21:19–26. The theological historian said of Amon: "He did evil in the eyes of the Lord, as his father Manasseh had done. He followed completely the ways of his father, worshiping the idols his father had worshiped, and bowing down to them. He forsook the Lord, the God of his ancestors, and did not walk in obedience to him" (21:20–22, NIV). Amon was assassinated by some of his courtiers.

The reasons Amon's own officials assassinated him are not made completely clear. However, it is not likely the reason was spiritual. While it's true the Mosaic Law declared idolaters should be slain (Deut. 13), in reality no one in the land possessed the authority to deal with an idolatrous king. The conspirators likely were more interested in and motivated by politics. Amon was probably pro-Assyrian. After all, they had released his father from prison. Conversely, the officials were pro-Babylonian, not realizing the rise of Babylon ultimately would mean the fall of Judah. Amon's son and successor, Josiah, was definitely pro-Babylonian and even died in battle trying to stop the Egyptian army from assisting Assyria against Babylon. The fact the people made Josiah the next king suggested they did not want a pro-Assyria king.

Josiah, whose name means "Yahweh heals or supports," was Judah's king from 640–609 B.C. Josiah became king at the age of eight following a two-year reign of Amon, his father. The people who avenged the death of Amon by killing his assassins made Josiah king (2 Kings 21:24). Josiah reigned as Judah's king for thirty-one years (2 Kings 22:1; 2 Chron. 34:1). It was said of his reign: "He did what was right in the eyes of the LORD and followed completely the ways of his father David, not turning aside to the right or to the left" (2 Kings 22:2, NIV). Josiah's loyalty to the ways of Yahweh and the spiritual reforms under his reign were paramount in the interest of the author(s) of 2 Kings. Honeycutt asserts: "The theological and religious interests of the Deuteronomic editor are clearly revealed in his minimal concern for historical events unrelated to the reform movement. Except for 23:1–2 and 23:28–30, the whole of his treatment of Josiah focuses on the reformation" (Honeycutt, "2 Kings," 155).

Josiah's reform was most notably associated with the discovery of the Book of the Law, which occurred *circa* 622 B.C. Historical data provided by the Chronicler, however, indicates Josiah had begun a series of reforms in Judah some six years prior to the discovery of the Book of the Law. Josiah began to purge the land of all traces of Canaanite Baal and Asherah fertility worship (2 Chron. 34:3–7). Beyond that, he had initiated a renovation of the temple. Second Chronicles 34:9–13 gives details of the renovation project. It was during this renovation that the Book of the Law was found (v. 14). The complete impact of this event on Judah in Josiah's time is indeterminable.

During the routine matters related to the renovation of the temple, Hilkiah ("Yah's portion") the high priest, reported to Shaphan, the scribe and treasurer, "I have found the Book of the Law in the temple of the LORD" (2 Chron. 34:15, NIV). Though some debate still accompanies the exact identity of the document discovered by Hilkiah, since the time of Jerome (*circa* A.D. 345–419), it has been identified as the book of Deuteronomy—or portions of it. At any rate, a major thrust of the book of Deuteronomy was to call the nation of Israel to exclusive loyalty to Yahweh. Such an emphasis is consistent with the escalated spiritual reforms and covenant renewal seen in Josiah's reign following the discovery of the Book of the Law.

Hilkiah gave the book to Shaphan. His first response was to read it. Shaphan then went to King Josiah to give him an update. He first reported on the progress of the temple refurbishment and gave a financial accounting (2 Chron. 34:16–17). He then told Josiah about the discovery of the book Hilkiah had given him and read it to Josiah. The immediate reaction of Josiah (2 Kings 22:11) inspired his personal and national responses in Judah.

Exposition

I. The Consultation with Huldah the Prophetess (2 Kings 22:14)

The response of King Josiah to the discovery of the Book of the Law is recorded in 2 Kings 22:11–13. When the king heard what was written in the Book of the Law, he tore his clothes in despair. This was the response of people in Jewish culture as an expression of emotional or spiritual distress (Gen. 37:29, 34; Josh. 7:6; 2 Kings 5:7; 6:30; 11:14; 19:1; Est. 4:1; Job 1:20; 2:12). King Josiah then commissioned several of his top officials to inquire of the Lord concerning the spiritual condition of Judah and how Judah should respond to what they discovered. He apparently feared the anger of the Lord and sought to turn it away from himself and all the people of Judah. The shock expressed by the king at the contents of the Law revealed Judah had not consulted the Law for a long time.

Josiah's anxious desire to know what to do in response to the discovery of the Law was confessional in nature, as 2 Kings 22:13 (NIV) reveals, "Go and inquire of the Lord for me and for the people and for all Judah about what is written in this book that has been found. Great is the Lord's anger that burns against us because those who have gone before us have not obeyed the words of this book; they have not acted in accordance with all that is written there concerning us." Honeycutt indicates the significance of Josiah's response in sending the officials to seek understanding, "The most significant response to the reading of the book of the law (sic.) was the delegation of messengers to seek a prophetic oracle concerning the welfare of himself, the people, and the whole of Judah. Thus, from its inception, the reform is directly related to prophetic foundations. Such prophetic emphasis is altogether consonant with the continuing exaltation of the prophetic office through the books of Kings" (Honeycutt, "2 Kings," 285).

Having received their assignment, the officials of Josiah traveled to Jerusalem to what was called the Second Quarter, where Huldah ("mole") the prophetess and her husband Shallum ("replacer," "the replaced") lived. At least fourteen men in the Old Testament are named Shallum. The Shallum under discussion was responsible for the royal or priestly wardrobe The Second Quarter was in the northern part of Jerusalem, the boundaries of which were extended during the monarchy. This part of the city was most open to enemy attack. The term *prophetess* appears only six times in the pages of the Old Testament. It is applied to Miriam, Deborah, Huldah, and Noadiah. They were the only women to function as prophetesses (Ex. 15:20; Judg. 4:4; 2 Kings 22:14; 2 Chron. 34:22; Neh.

6:14). This was also applied in a singular instance to the wife of Isaiah (Isa. 8:3). That instance, however, was probably in a metaphorical sense.

II. The Message of Huldah for Disobedient Judah (2 Kings 22:15–17)

Huldah's message was founded on the authority of Yahweh Himself. She indicated this by the statements: "This is what the Lord, the God of Israel says" (v. 15, NIV); "This is what the Lord says" (v. 16, NIV); "This is what the Lord, the God of Israel says concerning the words you heard" (v. 18, NIV). The formula appears again in verse 19 with, "I also have heard you, declares the Lord" (NIV). The first part of Huldah's message was addressed to "the man who sent you." Perhaps the intention here was to include Josiah with all the population of Judah as a common person and not in his identity as king. This seems to be supported by the fact Huldah's oracle was directed to the entire nation of Judah. Insofar as the nation was concerned, the Lord God certainly would send His wrath due to their repeated disobedience and disregard for the Law. This judgment, in the form of the invasion of Babylon, would come because they had forsaken Him and made idols and burned incense to them. Just as Josiah had perceived, God's anger burned against His people because they had forsaken His appointed way whereby they could experience blessing, enjoy life, and demonstrate to all other peoples how glorious it was to live under the Lord's leadership.

The Lord indicated His anger would burn against Judah and not be quenched. That is to say, the Lord's anger against rebellious Judah would not desist until it had accomplished what He intended—the destruction of Jerusalem, the temple, and much of the land of Judah and the deportation of the people by the Babylonians.

III. The Message of Huldah for Humble Judah (2 Kings 22:19–20)

Prophetess Huldah had an oracle—a divine response or pronouncement to Josiah's inquiry—of good news for him. Her message was specifically to the king of Judah. The good news for Josiah was the result of several aspects of his response to the discovery of the Book of the Law. One was a general statement about Josiah's responsive heart. That response motivated him to humble himself before God. He had taken seriously the pronouncement of God's coming wrath. Then Josiah expressed sorrow and penitence over the spiritual state of Judah, as evidenced by the tearing of his clothes and weeping. Josiah's sorrow was real. It was also spiritually enriching to the king and to Judah.

Huldah's words specifically for Josiah from the Lord were: "Therefore I will gather you to your ancestors, and you will be buried in peace. Your eyes will not see all the disaster I am going to bring on this place" (22:20, NIV). So they took her answer back to the king. Josiah died in battle (see Introduction) *circa* 609 B.C., about four years before Nebuchadnezzar's first attack on Jerusalem in 605 B.C.

The Lesson Applied

Josiah was preceded by his father Amon and his grandfather Manasseh. Both men are said to have forsaken the Lord and practiced idolatry. Under both men, the nation of Judah followed the same path. The historian gives this heart-wrenching summary of Manasseh's evil influence in Judah: "Moreover, Manasseh also shed so much innocent blood that he filled Jerusalem from end to end—besides the sin that he had caused Judah to commit, so that they did evil in the eyes of the LORD" (2 Kings 21:16, NIV). One legitimately can assume his son Amon had a similar sinister influence on the spiritual life of the nation. Despite his biological and spiritual roots, Josiah was true to the ways of Yahweh and sought how he could deepen his relationship with Him (2 Chron. 34:3). This was all the more remarkable when one recalls he started his reign at the age of eight. One can only speculate as to the source(s) of his spiritual nurture that put him on a path diametrically opposite to that of his father and grandfather. This part of lesson convincingly expresses the truth that the generational cycle of evil can be broken. The descendants of thoroughly evil people can be just as holy as their ancestors were unholy.

Josiah further demonstrated the unassailable truth that the person who sincerely seeks consecration to the Lord will discover that and further means to achieve sanctification (Deut. 4:29–31; Jer. 29:13). Early on, Josiah sought the Lord. The Book of the Law contained the Scriptures for that generation. It was their Bible. It contained God's laws, commandments, and promises. It prescribed what He required and specified the consequences of disobedience.

The follower of the Lord who would experience spiritual growth and an ever-deepening walk with Him must consistently study the Scriptures. Therein is nurture for the one who desires to be more Christlike (Acts 20:32; Col. 3:16; 1 Thess. 2:13; Heb. 4:12).

Let's Talk About It

To what extent does the spiritual life of a political leader affect the spiritual life of those whom he or she serves?

On the one hand, Manasseh negatively influenced his son Amon, and both negatively influenced the people of Judah. However, one can take the path of Josiah and turn to the Lord in humble submission. We are like clay in the fact that what we see, we often become. But we never should underestimate the strength of turning to better examples for living out our lives. We, like Josiah, can break generational cycles of evil in our lives.

Home Daily Devotional Readings
March 22–28, 2021

Monday	Tuesday	Wednesday	Thursday	Friday	Saturday	Sunday
Elijah with Moses and Jesus	John the Baptist, the New Elijah	Elijah Sent to King Ahab	Elijah Challenges Baal Prophets	Elijah in the Wilderness with God	God Commissions Elijah for New Work	King Ahab Meets Prophet Elijah
Mark 9:2–8	Mark 9:9–13	1 Kings 18:1–4	1 Kings 18:20–26, 30–33, 36–39	1 Kings 19:1–8	1 Kings 19:9–15	1 Kings 18:5–18

Elijah: Prophet of Courage

Topic:
The Bearer of Bad News

Background Scripture:
1 Kings 18–19; Matthew 17:1–13

1 Kings 18:5–18

King James Version

**AND Ahab said unto Obadiah, Go into the
land, unto all fountains of water, and unto all
brooks: peradventure we may find grass to
save the horses and mules alive, that we lose
not all the beasts.
6 So they divided the land between them
to pass throughout it: Ahab went one way
by himself, and Obadiah went another way
by himself.
7 And as Obadiah was in the way, behold,
Elijah met him: and he knew him, and
fell on his face, and said, Art thou that my
lord Elijah?
8 And he answered him, I am: go, tell thy
lord, Behold, Elijah is here.
9 And he said, What have I sinned, that thou
wouldest deliver thy servant into the hand of
Ahab, to slay me?
10 As the Lord thy God liveth, there is no
nation or kingdom, whither my lord hath not
sent to seek thee: and when they said, He is
not there; he took an oath of the kingdom and
nation, that they found thee not.
11 And now thou sayest, Go, tell thy lord,
Behold, Elijah is here.
12 And it shall come to pass, as soon as I am
gone from thee, that the Spirit of the Lord shall
carry thee whither I know not; and so when I
come and tell Ahab, and he cannot find thee, he
shall slay me: but I thy servant fear the Lord
from my youth.**

New Revised Standard Version

**THEN Ahab said to Obadiah, "Go through the
land to all the springs of water and to all the
wadis; perhaps we may find grass to keep the
horses and mules alive, and not lose some of
the animals."
6 So they divided the land between them to
pass through it; Ahab went in one direction by
himself, and Obadiah went in another direction by himself.
7 As Obadiah was on the way, Elijah met
him; Obadiah recognized him, fell on his face,
and said, "Is it you, my lord Elijah?"
8 He answered him, "It is I. Go, tell your lord
that Elijah is here."
9 And he said, "How have I sinned, that you
would hand your servant over to Ahab, to
kill me?
10 As the Lord your God lives, there is no
nation or kingdom to which my lord has not
sent to seek you; and when they would say,
'He is not here,' he would require an oath
of the kingdom or nation, that they had not
found you.
11 But now you say, 'Go, tell your lord that
Elijah is here.'
12 As soon as I have gone from you, the spirit
of the Lord will carry you I know not where;
so, when I come and tell Ahab and he cannot find you, he will kill me, although I your
servant have revered the Lord from my youth.**

MAIN THOUGHT: And he answered, I have not troubled Israel; but thou, and thy father's house, in that ye have forsaken the commandments of the Lord, and thou hast followed Baalim. (1 Kings 18:18, KJV)

1 Kings 18:5–18

King James Version

13 Was it not told my lord what I did when Jezebel slew the prophets of the Lord, how I hid an hundred men of the Lord's prophets by fifty in a cave, and fed them with bread and water?
14 And now thou sayest, Go, tell thy lord, Behold, Elijah is here: and he shall slay me.
15 And Elijah said, As the Lord of hosts liveth, before whom I stand, I will surely shew myself unto him to day.
16 So Obadiah went to meet Ahab, and told him: and Ahab went to meet Elijah.
17 And it came to pass, when Ahab saw Elijah, that Ahab said unto him, Art thou he that troubleth Israel?
18 And he answered, I have not troubled Israel; but thou, and thy father's house, in that ye have forsaken the commandments of the Lord, and thou hast followed Baalim.

New Revised Standard Version

13 Has it not been told my lord what I did when Jezebel killed the prophets of the Lord, how I hid a hundred of the Lord's prophets fifty to a cave, and provided them with bread and water?
14 Yet now you say, 'Go, tell your lord that Elijah is here'; he will surely kill me."
15 Elijah said, "As the Lord of hosts lives, before whom I stand, I will surely show myself to him today."
16 So Obadiah went to meet Ahab, and told him; and Ahab went to meet Elijah.
17 When Ahab saw Elijah, Ahab said to him, "Is it you, you troubler of Israel?"
18 He answered, "I have not troubled Israel; but you have, and your father's house, because you have forsaken the commandments of the Lord and followed the Baals.

LESSON SETTING

Time: ***circa*** **865 B.C.**
Place: Samaria

LESSON OUTLINE

I. Ahab and Obadiah Search for Water (1 Kings 18:5–6)
II. Obadiah and Elijah Meet (1 Kings 18:7–16)
III. Elijah and Ahab Meet (1 Kings 18:17–18)

Unifying Principle

People like to go their own way until faced with crises beyond their control. How shall we respond to the advice of those who have great wisdom and insight? In 1 Kings, God sent Elijah to warn Israel of impending disaster, and in Matthew, Elijah appeared with Jesus to affirm Jesus' mission.

Introduction

Today's lesson text belongs to the third major section of 1 Kings that includes 17:1–22:53 and can be viewed as the prophetic revolt against the worsening spiritual condition of the Northern Kingdom of Israel under its kings. More specifically, the lesson passage belongs to 1 Kings 17:1–22:40, which focuses on the prophets and King Ahab. Ahab, the son and successor of Omri, was the seventh king of Israel's Northern Kingdom. He reigned as king for twenty-two years from 874 B.C. to 853 B.C. He married Jezebel, the daughter of Ethbaal, a priest-king of Tyre (1 Kings 16:31). Jezebel was a devotee to the Tyrian god Melqart and openly endorsed the worship of Baal in Israel by supporting 450 Baal prophets and 400 prophets of the goddess Asherah (1 Kings 18:19).

As a result of Ahab's marriage to Jezebel and their subsequent plummet into idolatry individually and as a nation, this shameful summary is given: "Ahab son of Omri did more evil in the eyes of the LORD than any of those before him. He not only considered it trivial to commit the sins of Jeroboam son of Nebat, but he also married Jezebel daughter of Ethbaal king of the Sidonians, and began to serve Baal and worship him. He set up an altar for Baal in the temple of Baal that he built in Samaria. Ahab also made an Asherah pole and did more to arouse the anger of the LORD, the God of Israel, than did all the kings of Israel before him" (1 Kings 16:30–33, NIV).

Antithetical to the hypocritical instability and religious syncretism of Ahab stood the stalwart prophet Elijah the Tishbite. His name means, "my God is Yah" or "the Lord is my God." He held the distinction of being the grandest character Israel ever produced.

Elijah's ministry spanned the reigns of three kings of the Northern Kingdom of Israel—Ahab, Ahaziah, and Jehoram. He audaciously encountered and challenged the idolatry of kings, often visiting them without having been invited. Elijah's ministry was introduced dramatically: "Now Elijah the Tishbite, from Tishbe in Gilead, said to Ahab, 'As the LORD, the God of Israel, lives, whom I serve, there will be neither dew nor rain in the next few years except at my word'" (1 Kings 17:1, NIV). Because the Canaanite belief was only Baal could govern the dew and the rain, Elijah's pronouncement was as an immediate challenge: Who is really God, Baal or the Lord?

Elijah's audaciousness was further demonstrated in his challenge to the royal court in a time during which Jezebel had slaughtered several prophets of the Lord. She was attempting to eliminate them completely from Samaria (1 Kings 18:4). The survival of the prophetic community was mainly due to the loyalty to the Lord of a courtier of Ahab, Obadiah (18:3–4, 13).

Through Obadiah, Elijah arranged a meeting with Ahab after a three-year drought Yahweh had sent as punishment for Israel's apostasy. Ahab's attitude toward Elijah, certainly colored by his own defection from the covenant with Yahweh, was revealed in his greeting to Elijah: "Is that you, you troubler of Israel?" (18:17, NIV). However, Elijah placed the responsibility for the natural calamities of Israel squarely on the shoulders of the idolatrous king and his predecessors.

Exposition

I. Ahab And Obadiah Search for Water (1 Kings 18:5–6)

Today's lesson is set in the context of a punitive drought the prophet Elijah predicted would plague the Northern Kingdom of Israel during the reign of Ahab and Jezebel. Old Testament scholar M. Pierce Matheney Jr. says of the significance of Elijah, "The most important leader of the true worship of Yahweh since Moses was Elijah the Tishbite. He was an isolated figure, appearing to announce the drought" (Matheney, "1–2 Kings," 208). Elijah had been and was being prepared by the Lord to demonstrate to all Israel that Yahweh, not Baal, is still the only true God. Elijah's name, which means "my God is Yah/Yahweh," conveyed that truth! Elijah lived in Gilead east of the

Jordan River near a community called Tishbe. Perhaps as Elijah heard reports of Jezebel's increasing tactics to replace the worship of the Lord with Baal worship, his godly heart was stirred up. God gave him a mission. Armed with God's promise, he walked westward to Samaria. Bursting into the palace, he issued an ultimatum to King Ahab. He claimed the Lord is the God of Israel, He is alive, and that he, Elijah, was God's servant (17:1). Elijah could confidently declare there would be neither dew nor rain because God had promised to withhold these from the land if His people turned from Him to other gods (Lev. 26:18–19; Deut. 11:16–17; 28:23–24).

Having made his dramatic announcement, Elijah was told by the Lord to leave Samaria, return eastward, and hide in a ravine by the wadi Kerith, east of the Jordan River. Elijah had to hide because he soon would be hunted by the king (1 Kings 18:10). God promised to provide food and drink for His servant at this unlikely spot. Elijah obeyed the Lord, who miraculously provided for him as He had promised.

In the third and last year of the famine, God directed Elijah to present himself to King Ahab. Elijah had God's word that He soon would end the drought. The famine that resulted from the drought was particularly severe in the capital city of Samaria. God was directing this calamity especially at the guilty parties, Ahab and Jezebel. This situation prompted Ahab and his trusted servant Obadiah to go in different directions looking for some grass in the valleys or near the springs where the most necessary animals (horses and mules) might graze. Although Ahab wasn't especially concerned about the people of the land, he did want his army to be strong, just in case of an invasion.

II. Obadiah and Elijah Meet (1 Kings 18:7–16)

Obadiah recognized Elijah when they met somewhere outside Samaria. "Obadiah recognized Elijah perhaps by his hairy garment (2 Kings 1:8)" (Matheney, "1–2 Kings," 210). Upon their meeting, out of respect for the prophet, Obadiah bowed down to the ground. He could hardly believe he had found Elijah! Elijah, wanting to talk with Ahab, instructed Obadiah, "Go tell your master, 'Elijah is here'"(1 Kings 18:8, NIV). Obadiah, however, was afraid Elijah would disappear again. Obadiah explained to the prophet how Ahab had searched for him at home and abroad with no success. Obadiah affirmed that fact by the familiar words, "As surely as the Lord your God lives." (18:10; 17:1, 12). In those places where they had sought Elijah that reported he was not there, Ahab made them swear an oath they had not found Elijah. Obadiah knew the movements of the prophet were quite unpredictable,

To persuade Elijah his concern was sincere, Obadiah related proof that he was a devout believer in the Lord since his youth. Obadiah seemed to assume Elijah had heard about his hiding and feeding the prophets of the Lord during Jezebel's purge of the true prophets from the land. Obadiah had hidden one hundred of the Lord's prophets and provided them with food and water. Perhaps this was known among many of the faithful in Israel, especially the prophets. However, Jezebel or her supporters would not have been familiar with Obadiah's actions. Therefore, Obadiah's concerns for his own life were all the more intense. There was no real need for Obadiah to be concerned, however. Elijah assured Obadiah he would not disappear but would indeed appear before Ahab that same day.

III. Elijah and Ahab Meet (1 Kings 18:17–18)

When Ahab heard Obadiah's message, the king went to meet the prophet. Elijah maintained the initiative as God's spokesman to whom the king must submit. "The king brings a serious charge against the prophet when he labels him *troubler of Israel*. But the prophet boldly turns the accusation back upon the king. Ahab and Omri have abandoned the Lord and gone after the Baals, local manifestations of the Canaanite storm and fertility god" (Matheney, "1–2 Kings," 208). Therefore, Ahab and his ancestors were in fact the ones who troubled Israel and were responsible for the devastating drought.

The Lesson Applied

Moses, Joshua, and other subsequent leaders of ancient Israel strictly warned the Israelites against intermarriage or even strong social ties with the Canaanites. Israel was a unique people, called of God and consecrated to His divine purposes and plans, both for them and the rest of humanity. The fulfillment of that was contingent on their dedication to the covenant relationship between them and Yahweh.

Churches, communities and nations sometimes lose their spiritual moorings and tend to drift into disloyalty and disobedience toward God. There is always an Elijah who audaciously demonstrates who the true God is.

Today's lesson is an impressive reminder about the blinding effects of sin. Those outside the will of God have a tendency somehow to forget God always holds His people accountable for their actions. In reality, each person is his or her own "troubler" and must answer to God.

Let's Talk About It

In what ways was Elijah a model of godliness and service to the Lord?

Elijah was a prophet of God during some of the most troubling times in Israel's history. The nation was engulfed in idol worship and held Baal as its chief god. However, Elijah, though threatened with death, walked with God and delivered God's truth. His life was marked by complete devotion to serving God.

Home Daily Devotional Readings

March 29–April 4, 2021

Monday	Tuesday	Wednesday	Thursday	Friday	Saturday	Sunday
Isaiah Foretells the Suffering Servant	Jesus, the Suffering Servant	Jesus Foretells His Death and Resurrection	Jesus, Raised from Death	The Risen Christ Appears to Disciples	Christ Revealed in Breaking of Bread	Christ Suffered and Interceded for Sinners
Isaiah 52:13–53:3	Acts 8:26–35	Luke 18:31–34	Luke 24:1–12	Luke 24:13–27	Luke 24:28–35	Isaiah 53:4–11

The Suffering Servant Brings Salvation

Topic:
Finding Hope in the Midst of Oppression

Background Scripture:
Isaiah 52:13–53:12; Luke 24:1–35

Isaiah 53:4–11

King James Version

SURELY he hath borne our griefs, and carried our sorrows: yet we did esteem him stricken, smitten of God, and afflicted.

5 But he was wounded for our transgressions, he was bruised for our iniquities: the chastisement of our peace was upon him; and with his stripes we are healed.

6 All we like sheep have gone astray; we have turned every one to his own way; and the LORD hath laid on him the iniquity of us all.

7 He was oppressed, and he was afflicted, yet he opened not his mouth: he is brought as a lamb to the slaughter, and as a sheep before her shearers is dumb, so he openeth not his mouth.

8 He was taken from prison and from judgment: and who shall declare his generation? for he was cut off out of the land of the living: for the transgression of my people was he stricken.

9 And he made his grave with the wicked, and with the rich in his death; because he had done no violence, neither was any deceit in his mouth.

10 Yet it pleased the LORD to bruise him; he hath put him to grief: when thou shalt make his soul an offering for sin, he shall see his seed, he shall prolong his days, and the pleasure of the Lord shall prosper in his hand.

11 He shall see of the travail of his soul, and shall be satisfied: by his knowledge shall my righteous servant justify many; for he shall bear their iniquities.

New Revised Standard Version

SURELY he has borne our infirmities and carried our diseases; yet we accounted him stricken, struck down by God, and afflicted.

5 But he was wounded for our transgressions, crushed for our iniquities; upon him was the punishment that made us whole, and by his bruises we are healed.

6 All we like sheep have gone astray; we have all turned to our own way, and the LORD has laid on him the iniquity of us all.

7 He was oppressed, and he was afflicted, yet he did not open his mouth; like a lamb that is led to the slaughter, and like a sheep that before its shearers is silent, so he did not open his mouth.

8 By a perversion of justice he was taken away. Who could have imagined his future? For he was cut off from the land of the living, stricken for the transgression of my people.

9 They made his grave with the wicked and his tomb with the rich, although he had done no violence, and there was no deceit in his mouth.

10 Yet it was the will of the LORD to crush him with pain. When you make his life an offering for sin, he shall see his offspring, and shall prolong his days; through him the will of the LORD shall prosper.

11 Out of his anguish he shall see light; he shall find satisfaction through his knowledge. The righteous one, my servant, shall make many righteous, and he shall bear their iniquities.

MAIN THOUGHT: But he was wounded for our transgressions, he was bruised for our iniquities: the chastisement of our peace was upon him; and with his stripes we are healed. (Isaiah 53:5, KJV)

LESSON SETTING

Time: ***circa*** **518–465 B.C.**
Place: Judah

LESSON OUTLINE

I. The Vicarious Suffering of the Servant (Isaiah 53:4–6)
II. The Sacrificial Death of the Servant (Isaiah 53:7–9)
III. The Ultimate Triumph of the Servant (Isaiah 53:10–11)

UNIFYING PRINCIPLE

When life reaches its darkest depth, people wonder if there is still hope for the future. Where can we find the promise of joy that will overcome our deepest sorrow? Isaiah 52:13–53:12 reminds us of God's servant who suffered profoundly for others, and Luke 24 records the encounter of the Emmaus travelers with the resurrected Jesus.

INTRODUCTION

Today's passage is a brief excerpt from an extended passage that includes Isaiah 52:13–53:12. This text constitutes the fourth and final Servant Song in Isaiah and is, at the same time, undoubtedly, the most well-known of those songs. Consistent with the interpretive task in other passages, Old Testament scholars and serious students of the Scriptures exert diligent effort in attempts to identify the Servant in the first *Sitz-im-Leben* or life setting. To be sure, a word of comfort and encouragement were needed by the Jews who were reestablishing themselves and rebuilding their entire community in Palestine following the Exile. They were faced with how to construe the messages and missions of people from their own ranks, such as Zerubbabel, Haggai, Nehemiah, and Ezra. Even more challenging was how to interpret, especially in theological terms, the role of world leaders who directly impacted Jewish history. Understandably, the Jews anxiously inquired how leaders such as Cyrus, Cambyses, Darius, Xerxes and Artaxerxes—all kings of Persia, modern-day Iran—fit into Yahweh's plans for Israel.

Constant inquiry was conducted among the people concerning the identity of the prophesied Servant. Multiple identities of the Servant—all legitimate—had been made. The words of the prophet made it clear that at times the Servant was to be identified as the nation Israel (Isa. 49:3). In most cases the Servant was anonymous. But in a few situations, the Servant of Yahweh was a pagan king, such as Cyrus. Such an act was consistent with Israel's understanding of the sovereignty of Yahweh (44:24). Therefore, it was the Lord Himself who said of Cyrus, "He is my shepherd and will accomplish all that I please; he will say of Jerusalem, 'Let it be rebuilt,' and of the temple, 'Let its foundation be laid'" (44:28). Cyrus also was referred to as the *Lord's anointed* (messiah, christ) whose monarchy was directed by Yahweh and through whom the future of Israel would be directed (45:1).

Given such background, it is easily understandable why Old Testament exegetes seek the identity of the Servant in the original historical context of the passage. Many of the passages themselves identify the Servant, and the prophets were addressing a word of hope to their own generation. However, the nature of prophecy and of God's self-revelation contain a dynamism such that the Lord's word cannot be restricted to the particularity of one locale or epoch in time. Few passages of Scripture demonstrate this more clearly or convincingly than the Servant Song in Isaiah 52:13–53:12. A distinctive feature of the song is the extent to which the Servant is also a sufferer. Suffering had been associated with the Servant heretofore (Isa 50:6). The suffering of the Servant in the Isaiah 52:13–53:12, however, ascends to unique heights in both its intensity and character. The suffering here is vicarious. It is suffering of one for the benefit of many. So distinctive is the role of the Servant in the present passage that many speak of the Suffering Servant.

Can the Servant be identified or associated historically with Cambyses and/or Darius? Can the Suffering Servant be identified with Zerubbabel, whom many biblical historians identify as a martyr? Perhaps. Yet the prominence of Isaiah 52:13–53:12 in the New Testament indicates the passage is ultimately Christocentric and not strictly embedded in Israel's past. That all but one of the verses of Isaiah 53:1–12 appear in the New Testament is significant. Citations from Isaiah 53:1–12 appear in all four Gospels, Acts, Romans, Philippians, Hebrews, and 1 Peter. For the writers of the New Testament, the one whose suffering was portrayed in Isaiah 52:13–53:12 possibly could be identified with a figure four and a half centuries prior to Jesus. New Testament writers insisted, however, that the One who fulfilled the role of Suffering Servant and Savior was Jesus exclusively.

Exposition

I. The Vicarious Suffering of the Servant (Isaiah 53:4–6)

Old Testament interpreter Page H. Kelley has suggested the unit of Scripture that constitutes Isaiah 42:11–53:12 can be discussed under the general title "The Travail and Triumph of the Servant." Isaiah 52:13–15 proceeds from humiliation to exaltation. The Servant's unlikely beginnings are taken up in 53:1–3. Then verses 4–6 focus on the Servant's vicarious suffering done on the behalf of others. The Servant's sacrificial death is contained in 53:7–9. The Servant's ultimate triumph is found in 53:10–12.

A brief discussion of the unpromising prospects of the Suffering Servant helps put his ministry and ultimate victory in perspective. Kelley says of what he calls the Servant's "unlikely beginnings": "Almost all possible misfortunes are attributed to the servant in these verses. He grows up in a hostile environment, like a root out of dry ground. He is so unimpressive and unattractive that men are repelled by the sight of him. He is exposed to scorn, rejection, sorrow, grief, and the bitterness of loneliness.... How incredible that one who had such an unlikely beginning should accomplish such a glorious mission!" (Kelley, "Isaiah," 343.)

The suggestion has been made that Isaiah 53:4–6 constitutes the heart of Isaiah 53 and is simultaneously at the essence of the Gospel message. That is, the guiltless Suffering Servant dies as a sacrifice. Israel's religious system, specifically its understanding of atonement—how one was placed in a right relationship with

God—rested on the death of innocent animals dying for the guilty sinners (Lev. 16). Kelley effectively sums up the message and meaning of the Servant's vicarious suffering. "In v. 4 the speakers describe their initial reaction to the servant's suffering, a reaction they now acknowledge to be totally inaccurate. They supposed that he was being smitten by God for some unspeakable crime which he had committed. Their confession thus reveals that they shared the commonly held assumption that all suffering was the direct result of sin. What happened subsequently to this to change their minds is not stated, but it must have been a momentous experience. The outcome is that they now recognize that the servant's sufferings are not a consequence of his own sins but of theirs" (Kelley, "Isaiah," 342).

The vicarious nature of the suffering of the Servant is unveiled in the use of first-person plural pronouns throughout Isaiah 53:4–6. Verse 5 indicates he was "pierced," literally "pierced through," or wounded for our transgressions. *Transgression* (*peša*) is one of multiple Old Testament words for disobedience to God. It sometimes is translated *rebellion* and speaks of the intentional disobedience to a specific command of God. When Paul referred to the transgression of Adam (humanity) in Romans, he had in mind the rejection of the prohibition of partaking of the forbidden fruit. That the Servant was bruised for our iniquities speaks of his suffering for the twisted or perverse or crooked behaviors of people, which is what *iniquity* means. *Bruised* here has the implication of being crushed, as under the weight of a heavy burden. The punishment by way of chastisement the author spoke of in verse 5 probably refers to scourging with a whip, a common form of punishment in that culture. The wounding of the Servant is theological—it has a purpose or goal. It is by means of the wounds experienced vicariously by the Servant that others are healed. In this context, the healing is spiritual, not physical.

The author then provided the familiar and picturesque portrayal of the plight of human beings in terms of their relationship with God. The *New Living Translation* expresses it: "All of us, like sheep, have strayed away. We have left God's paths to follow our own. Yet the Lord laid on him the sins of us all" (Isa. 53:6). The tendency of sheep is to travel together. If the leading sheep turns aside from the path for grass, water, or some other purpose, all the sheep usually follow. Such had been the pattern for the people of Isaiah's day. Such is the pattern of people of all generations. Because of that tendency to go astray, the Lord laid on the Suffering Servant the sins of all people in order to bring them back to Himself.

II. The Sacrificial Death of the Servant (Isaiah 53:7–9)

Animal and other sacrifices were common in the Jewish community and were understood to be an indispensable part of maintaining or restoring their relationship with Yahweh. However, the sacrifice spoken of here in Isaiah was unique. Kelley calls attention to this when he states, "The servant's suffering eventually leads to his death, which is described here in sacrificial terms. There is a profound difference, however, between this sacrifice and those mentioned in the priestly legislation. It is a sacrifice offered outside the Temple, and the victim is a *blameless man* [emphasis added] rather than an unblemished animal. Furthermore, it is a sacrifice that makes all other sacrifices unnecessary" (Kelley, "Isaiah," 343).

This part of the passage places great stress on the passive, submissive, obedient response to that to which the Servant was subjected. He was the total antithesis of the straying sheep in the previous part of the passage. "He was oppressed and treated harshly, yet he never said a word" (53:7) is how the NLT states it. The author then turned his attention to the perfect sheep. In the balance of verse 7, the quiet, gentle nature of sheep is stressed. Having seen many sheep sheared for their wool or killed as sacrifices, the people of Israel were well aware of the submissive nature of sheep. Kelley comments here: "And unlike other victims led to the slaughter, he opened not his mouth. No word of accusation or self pity fell from his lips.... This statement alone is sufficient to exclude Israel from consideration as the suffering servant, for in her time of suffering she complained loudly and bitterly (cf. 40:27; 49:14)" (Kelley, "Isaiah," 343).

The author then turned his attention to the death and burial of the Suffering Servant. "Unjustly condemned, he was led away. No one cared that he died without descendants, that his life was cut short in midstream. But he was struck down for the rebellion of my people. He had done no wrong and had never deceived anyone. But he was buried like a criminal; he was put in a rich man's grave" (53:8–9, NLT). To be *led* or *taken away* actually means to be taken forcibly from one place to another. In this case, it was from life to death (Gen. 5:24; 2 Kings 2:3; Prov. 24:11).

The dramatic nature of the experience is enhanced by the following words about verse 9. "The text does not make it clear whether he died of some dread disease, was slain by a mob, or was executed after a farcical trial. In any event, he died the death of sinner and was buried with the wicked.... The verse ends with a ringing affirmation of the servant's innoncency [*sic*]" (Kelley, "Isaiah," 343–344).

III. The Ultimate Triumph of the Servant (Isaiah 53:10–11)

Everything the Suffering Servant underwent was part of the mysterious, sovereign plans of God, despite how horrific it was. "To say that it was the will of the Lord to bruise the servant (v. 10) means that the events leading up to his death were part of the diving plan to conquer sin. The Lord *permitted* [emphasis added] him to suffer, therefore, not out of anger toward, him, but out of love toward the sinner" (Kelley, "Isaiah," 344). The passion, or suffering, of the Servant was for purposes of salvation all along. Just as He always had been, God, through the experience of the Suffering Servant, was enacting another means by which His people could be brought back into right relationship with Him. Herein is the expression of an unconditional outlook on the sovereignty of God. He is able to do—and will do—that which is necessary and in keeping with His character of holiness and love to achieve His purposes. The life, suffering, and death of the Servant must not be viewed exclusively through human eyes. To do so is to see only unjust treatment, undeserved suffering, humiliation, senseless abuse, death, and misidentification for the Servant.

However, everything about the Servant hinges on the opening words of Isaiah 53:10, "Yet it was the LORD's will to crush him and cause him to suffer" (NIV). *The Message* translation suggests here: "Still, it's what GOD had in mind all along, to crush him with pain." Out of His sovereignty and plans, God brings resounding victory from what apparently is total defeat. "The revolutionary truth announced in these verses [10–12] is that the servant's vindication comes after his death. A great miracle takes place, therefore, for after his death and burial he is enabled to see his offspring, to prolong his days, and to witness the successful completion of his mission.... His death, therefore, is not his defeat, but his noblest achievement and the means by which many are reconciled to God" (Kelley, "Isaiah," 344).

The Lesson Applied

Suffering is an experience most people seek to avoid as much as possible. Some suffer because they are the victims of the actions of others. Others suffer as the result of their own choices and the consequences thereof. Still others suffer as the result of being caught in a cross fire of spiritual struggles. Today's lesson presents a different perspective on suffering. Though the Isaiah passage centers primarily on the suffering rejection of the Servant, additional details concerning the Servant reveal his suffering was redemptive. The agony of the Servant resulted in triumph for him and for people who turned to God in faith (Isa. 53:4–6; Acts 8:26–35). A part of what makes the Good News "good" is that the suffering of Jesus was part of God's redemptive plan. Jesus expressed God's love for creation in His suffering and provided a means for salvation. One recalls the words of the Apostle Paul in Romans 8:28 (NIV), "And we know that in all things God works for the good of those who love him, who have been called according to his purpose."

Let's Talk About It

How does the knowledge of Jesus' suffering for our salvation affect your faith?

Jesus' suffering is an example of how we can deepen our faith in God. He allowed His faith in God to guide Him through sufferings and challenges. His suffering was redemptive because it allowed Him to focus on God's will for His life. When we pattern our lives after Him, our suffering will likewise help us to channel our energies in the right direction. Furthermore, He has provided to us His Spirit to empower us to follow the example He set.

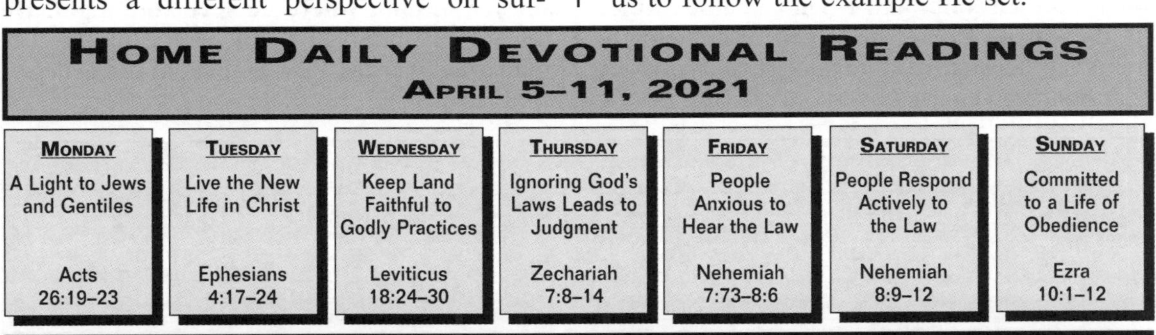

Home Daily Devotional Readings
April 5–11, 2021

Monday	Tuesday	Wednesday	Thursday	Friday	Saturday	Sunday
A Light to Jews and Gentiles	Live the New Life in Christ	Keep Land Faithful to Godly Practices	Ignoring God's Laws Leads to Judgment	People Anxious to Hear the Law	People Respond Actively to the Law	Committed to a Life of Obedience
Acts 26:19–23	Ephesians 4:17–24	Leviticus 18:24–30	Zechariah 7:8–14	Nehemiah 7:73–8:6	Nehemiah 8:9–12	Ezra 10:1–12

LESSON 6 APRIL 11, 2021

EZRA: FAITH AND ACTION PREACHER

TOPIC:
CONFESSION AND CORRECTION

BACKGROUND SCRIPTURE:
EZRA 9–10

EZRA 10:1–12

King James Version

NOW when Ezra had prayed, and when he had confessed, weeping and casting himself down before the house of God, there assembled unto him out of Israel a very great congregation of men and women and children: for the people wept very sore.

2 And Shechaniah the son of Jehiel, one of the sons of Elam, answered and said unto Ezra, We have trespassed against our God, and have taken strange wives of the people of the land: yet now there is hope in Israel concerning this thing.

3 Now therefore let us make a covenant with our God to put away all the wives, and such as are born of them, according to the counsel of my lord, and of those that tremble at the commandment of our God; and let it be done according to the law.

4 Arise; for this matter belongeth unto thee: we also will be with thee: be of good courage, and do it.

5 Then arose Ezra, and made the chief priests, the Levites, and all Israel, to swear that they should do according to this word. And they sware.

6 Then Ezra rose up from before the house of God, and went into the chamber of Johanan the son of Eliashib: and when he came thither, he did eat no bread, nor drink water: for he mourned because of the transgression of them that had been carried away.

New Revised Standard Version

WHILE Ezra prayed and made confession, weeping and throwing himself down before the house of God, a very great assembly of men, women, and children gathered to him out of Israel; the people also wept bitterly.

2 Shecaniah son of Jehiel, of the descendants of Elam, addressed Ezra, saying, "We have broken faith with our God and have married foreign women from the peoples of the land, but even now there is hope for Israel in spite of this.

3 So now let us make a covenant with our God to send away all these wives and their children, according to the counsel of my lord and of those who tremble at the commandment of our God; and let it be done according to the law.

4 Take action, for it is your duty, and we are with you; be strong, and do it."

5 Then Ezra stood up and made the leading priests, the Levites, and all Israel swear that they would do as had been said. So they swore.

6 Then Ezra withdrew from before the house of God, and went to the chamber of Jehohanan son of Eliashib, where he spent the night. He did not eat bread or drink water, for he was mourning over the faithlessness of the exiles.

MAIN THOUGHT: Then Ezra rose up from before the house of God, and went into the chamber of Johanan the son of Eliashib: and when he came thither, he did eat no bread, nor drink water: for he mourned because of the transgression of them that had been carried away. (Ezra 9:6, KJV)

Ezra 10:1–12

King James Version

7 And they made proclamation throughout Judah and Jerusalem unto all the children of the captivity, that they should gather themselves together unto Jerusalem;
8 And that whosoever would not come within three days, according to the counsel of the princes and the elders, all his substance should be forfeited, and himself separated from the congregation of those that had been carried away.
9 Then all the men of Judah and Benjamin gathered themselves together unto Jerusalem within three days. It was the ninth month, on the twentieth day of the month; and all the people sat in the street of the house of God, trembling because of this matter, and for the great rain.
10 And Ezra the priest stood up, and said unto them, Ye have transgressed, and have taken strange wives, to increase the trespass of Israel.
11 Now therefore make confession unto the LORD God of your fathers, and do his pleasure: and separate yourselves from the people of the land, and from the strange wives.
12 Then all the congregation answered and said with a loud voice, As thou hast said, so must we do.

New Revised Standard Version

7 They made a proclamation throughout Judah and Jerusalem to all the returned exiles that they should assemble at Jerusalem,
8 and that if any did not come within three days, by order of the officials and the elders all their property should be forfeited, and they themselves banned from the congregation of the exiles.
9 Then all the people of Judah and Benjamin assembled at Jerusalem within the three days; it was the ninth month, on the twentieth day of the month. All the people sat in the open square before the house of God, trembling because of this matter and because of the heavy rain.
10 Then Ezra the priest stood up and said to them, "You have trespassed and married foreign women, and so increased the guilt of Israel.
11 Now make confession to the LORD the God of your ancestors, and do his will; separate yourselves from the peoples of the land and from the foreign wives."
12 Then all the assembly answered with a loud voice, "It is so; we must do as you have said.

LESSON SETTING

Time: *circa* 365-300 B.C.
Place: Judah

LESSON OUTLINE

I. The People Respond to Ezra's Prayer (Ezra 10:1–4)
II. The Preparation for the Public Assembly (Ezra 10:5–8)
III. The Jerusalem Assembly and Its Work (Ezra 10:9–12)

Unifying Principle

Sometimes people can lose their sense of direction in life and turn away from the values they once held. How can we recapture the values we once cherished? Ezra led the returned exiles in prayer and repentance, and afterward he read the book of the Law, to which the people listened and then joyously worshiped the Lord.

Introduction

Two different personalities were used by the Lord to set Israel free from Babylonian captivity and return them to Israel. One was the king of a pagan nation who was the vessel of Yahweh and whose actions had been predicted by two of the classical prophets. The other servant whom the Lord used to effectuate Israel's liberation was a Jewish priest and scribe. As disparate as these men were, both were crucial to the fulfillment of Yahweh's promises and purposes.

Cyrus the Great was the third king of Anshan and assumed the throne around 550 B.C. Reliable ancient historians record that Cyrus was reared by a shepherd after his grandfather Astyages, the king of Media, ordered that he be killed. Such an unthinkable plot arose after Astyages dreamed Cyrus eventually would succeed him as king before Astyages's death. Rather than execute the young boy, the officer charged with the execution instead carried him into the hills to the shepherds. As an adult, Cyrus organized the Persians into an army and revolted against his grandfather and father, Cambyses I. He defeated them and claimed their throne.

Shortly after his ascension to the Medo-Persian throne, Cyrus held a vast empire stretching from the Aegean Sea to India. Following the defeat of the Babylonian army at Opis, Cyrus's troops took control of Babylon, considered an impossible task by all estimations. The people in the capital welcomed Cyrus with open arms, seeing him as a liberator rather than a conqueror. The only remaining world power was Egypt, which he left for his son Cambyses II to conquer. Cyrus rightfully carried the title "the Great."

Old Testament authors and prophets clearly understood that in His Sovereignty, Yahweh had ordained Cyrus for His purposes, just as He had ordained that Judah would be inhabited again by the emancipated exiles. One has merely to look to the premier prophet, Isaiah, for indications of this perspective: "'This is what the LORD says—your Redeemer, who formed you in the womb: I am the LORD, the Maker of all things, who stretched out the heavens, who spreads out the earth by myself, who foils the signs of false prophets and makes fools of diviners, who overthrows the learning of the wise and turns it into nonsense, who carries out the words of his servants and fulfills the predictions of his messengers, who says of Jerusalem, "It shall be inhabited," of the towns of Judah, "They shall be rebuilt," and of their ruins, "I will restore them," who says to the watery deep, "Be dry, and I will dry up your streams," who says of Cyrus, "He is my shepherd and will accomplish all that I please; he will say of Jerusalem, 'Let it be rebuilt,' and of the temple, 'Let its foundations be laid'" (Isa 44:24–28, NIV).

Today's lesson passage is inextricably connected with and flows from the previous major section of Ezra 8:1–9:1–15. Chapter 9 contains a focus on fasting and confession by Ezra. An extended prayer of repentance is found in 9:6–15. Emmett W. Hamrick says of the character of the prayer: "The prayer begins with a confession of guilt. The prayer has been classified as a 'doxology of judgment,' because it is both a confession of guilt and praise to God for the justness of punishment. In the first clause Ezra uses the first person singular but switches immediately to the first person plural. In this way he identifies himself with the corporate community and speaks in its behalf. Although he had not engaged in a mixed marriage, he must speak of our guilt because he cannot disassociate himself from the corporate body" (Hamrick, "Ezra–Nehemiah," 467).

Interestingly, Ezra's confession was multigenerational, in that he spoke of the sins of his forefathers, actually their *iniquities* (Deut. 5:3). This is a term that generally in the Old Testament connotes that which is "twisted, perverse, contorted." It was Ezra's perspective that these iniquities had resulted in the Exile (Ezra 9:7). The time of captivity was a method of purifying the people and reestablishing a close relationship between them and God. Apparently the Exile had not accomplished its purpose because of the people's tendency to stray from their obligations to the covenant. Previous generations, as well as his own, had been steeped in sin, according to Ezra.

Ezra's prayer accented the grace of Yahweh. It was the grace of God that allowed the people to return to the land. This was occasioned by the edict of Cyrus in 538 B.C., but it was the Lord's graciousness that allowed the kings of Persia to grant the Jews freedom to return to the land of Israel and rebuild the temple. Yet despite this grace, they were once again in bondage—bondage to sin.

Leaders reported to Ezra that some Israelites had been involved with their pagan neighbors' detestable practices (Ezra 9:11, 14) which meant they had married Gentiles. Marrying outside the community of Israelites was one of God's major prohibitions (Exod. 34:11–16; Deut. 7:1–4). This was not because of racial difference, for the peoples of the surrounding areas were of the same Semitic race. The reason was strictly religious. Should God's people married outside Israel, they would be tempted to participate in pagan idolatrous worship (1 Kings 11:3–5). Intermarrying with people who did not worship Yahweh was symptomatic of the way the people forsook other aspects of the Law of God.

Ezra's prayer had some specific objectives. Hamrick observes: "The prayer ends in a manner doubtless calculated to move the people to immediate confession and drastic action. The sins of the past had brought the Exile, but God had cut it short and had preserved a remnant. But now the remnant had sinned and no further mercy could be expected.... Ezra offers no word of hope. He can only confess that *we are guilty before thee*" (Hamrick, "Ezra–Nehemiah," 467).

Exposition

I. The People Respond to Ezra's Prayer (Ezra 10:1–4)

Many of the people acknowledged something had to be done about the situation. Apparently this sin had gone on and had been tolerated for some time. Many of those who had intermarried had children. No doubt some devout Jews were grieved because of this sin in the community. Perhaps they were afraid to speak up or had tried and were rebuffed. Nevertheless, since some leaders now joined Ezra in grieving the sin, these righteous people began to demand something be done. A large crowd of Israelites gathered with Ezra and wept bitterly. Shecaniah ("Yahweh has taken up dwelling") spoke for all the people who were weeping. He was a priest who had returned with Zerubbabel *circa* 537 B.C. He acknowledged the nation's unfaithfulness but believed there was still hope for Israel. "But tears alone were not enough. Shecaniah proposed that the foreign wives with their children be separated from their husbands and fathers" (Hamrick, "Ezra–Nehemiah," 467). He suggested: "Now let us make a covenant before our God to send away all these women and their children, in accordance with the counsel of my lord and of those who fear the commands of our God. Let it be done according to the Law" (Ezra 10:3, NIV).

Shecaniah assured Ezra the people would support him in such a decision. The priest was summoning the nation to do something distasteful and difficult. It could cause bitter division between family members and friends. However, he appealed on the basis of the Law of God that was supposed to be the people's rule of life. The Law also was a safeguard for this situation. An Israelite could marry a non-Jewish woman if she had become Jewish in faith. Perhaps that is why each marriage was investigated thoroughly, to determine if any women had become Jewish proselytes (Ezra 10:16–19).

To be sure, divorce was not the norm in Jewish culture (Mal. 2:16). However, it might have been preferable in this situation because if the intermarriages with pagans continued, such would lead the nation away from true worship of Yahweh.

II. The Preparation for the Public Assembly (Ezra 10:5–8)

The next step was for the people to indicate their sincerity in their confession and repentance. They did this by taking an oath before God. "So Ezra stood up and demanded that the leaders of the priests and the Levites and all the people of Israel swear that they would do as Shecaniah had said. And they all swore a solemn oath" (Ezra 10:5, NLT). Oath-taking was not a frivolous matter in Jewish culture. It obligated the oath-taker to do what he had promised. If he did not, he would be punished and incur the displeasure of God (Eccl. 5:4–6).

Meanwhile, Ezra sought some private time to fast and continue to grieve over the unfaithfulness of the people (Ezra 10:6). He found this privacy in the residence of Jehohanan ("Yahweh is gracious"), a priest. This Jehohanan is sometimes equated with the high priest of Nehemiah 12:22–23 who is considered then to be a grandson of the high priest Eliashib ("God repays or leads back"). Hamrick explains the importance of Ezra's time with Jehohanan beyond a time of personal and spiritual retreat: "There he not only spent the night fasting and mourning, but apparently conducting some very important business. Since Jehohanan was almost certainly the high priest at the time, it would have been judicious for Ezra to plan his strategy in consultation with him" (Hamrick, "Ezra–Nehemiah," 468). The partnership between these two religious leaders would prove to be extremely beneficial to the success of the renewal.

The next step in the process of the renewal was to send out a proclamation for all the exiles to assemble in Jerusalem within three days. Anyone who did not appear would lose his property and also be expelled from the assembly of the exiles. The leaders and elders could render such a decision (Ezra 10:8). Ezra possessed such authority to send out a proclamation with threat of punishment because of the edict of the king.

III. The Jerusalem Assembly and Its Work (Ezra 10:9–12)

Verse 9 establishes the setting of the assembly. The square to the east of the temple could accommodate thousands of people. The temple area was always the center of action in the book of Ezra. On the appointed day in November–December 458 or 457 B.C., as the people were gathering, a rainstorm was in progress. This was the rainy season (typically October–mid-April). However, because of the oath (v. 5) and because of the threat of punishment, the meeting went on as planned.

Hamrick says of Ezra's proclamation: "Ezra's speech was mercifully short and to the point" (Hamrick, "Ezra–Nehemiah," 468). *The Message* expresses it: "Ezra the priest stood up and spoke: 'You've broken trust. You've married foreign wives. You've piled guilt on Israel. Now make your confession to God, the God of your ancestors, and do what he wants you to do: Separate yourselves from the people of the land and from your foreign wives'" (Ezra 10:10–11). Ezra called the people to task and challenged them to remember the God who had brought them through.

The Lesson Applied

Members of contemporary society have a tendency to place much emphasis on personal rights and freedoms and that which is popular and trending. Such an approach to life, as well as many behaviors, come to be perpetuated from one generation of people to another. Sometimes even that which is immoral, unethical, or contrary to the clear teachings of the Scriptures continues to be prominent in the lives of people. When this persists, it is possible and even probable that what is absolutely unacceptable in the eyes of God becomes the norm in society. There is always the need for those who earnestly yearn for, seek, and help actualize a right relationship with God.

Let's Talk About It

Based on the ministry of Ezra, what would you consider to be prerequisites for effective spiritual leaders?

Effective spiritual leaders agonize over spiritual failures. They also acknowledge their shortcomings and repent of their sins and inability to maintain their faith. They also become more prayerfully aware of their need to get closer to God and lead their followers to imitate them. they exhibit courage to do what is right in terms of making God the center of their worship and praise.

Home Daily Devotional Readings

April 12–18, 2021

Monday	Tuesday	Wednesday	Thursday	Friday	Saturday	Sunday
Daniel Intercedes for Jerusalem	Nehemiah Orders Temple Cleansing and Restoration	Nehemiah Restores Ministries of Levites, Singers	Nehemiah Reforms Sabbath Observances and Practices	Nehemiah Sets Standards for Jewish Marriages	Nehemiah Sent to Rebuild Jerusalem	Nehemiah Inspires the People to Rebuild
Daniel 9:4–6, 15–19	Nehemiah 13:4–9	Nehemiah 13:10–14	Nehemiah 13:15–22	Nehemiah 13:23–27	Nehemiah 2:1–10	Nehemiah 2:11–20

NEHEMIAH: THE CAPTIVE CUPBEARER REBUILDS A NATION

TOPIC:
INITIATING RENEWAL

BACKGROUND SCRIPTURE:
NEHEMIAH 2:11–20; 13:1–22

NEHEMIAH 2:11–20

King James Version

SO I came to Jerusalem, and was there three days.
12 And I arose in the night, I and some few men with me; neither told I any man what my God had put in my heart to do at Jerusalem: neither was there any beast with me, save the beast that I rode upon.
13 And I went out by night by the gate of the valley, even before the dragon well, and to the dung port, and viewed the walls of Jerusalem, which were broken down, and the gates thereof were consumed with fire.
14 Then I went on to the gate of the fountain, and to the king's pool: but there was no place for the beast that was under me to pass.
15 Then went I up in the night by the brook, and viewed the wall, and turned back, and entered by the gate of the valley, and so returned.
16 And the rulers knew not whither I went, or what I did; neither had I as yet told it to the Jews, nor to the priests, nor to the nobles, nor to the rulers, nor to the rest that did the work.
17 Then said I unto them, Ye see the distress that we are in, how Jerusalem lieth waste, and the gates thereof are burned with fire: come, and let us build up the wall of Jerusalem, that we be no more a reproach.
18 Then I told them of the hand of my God which was good upon me; as also the king's words that he had spoken unto me. And they

New Revised Standard Version

SO I came to Jerusalem and was there for three days.
12 Then I got up during the night, I and a few men with me; I told no one what my God had put into my heart to do for Jerusalem. The only animal I took was the animal I rode.
13 I went out by night by the Valley Gate past the Dragon's Spring and to the Dung Gate, and I inspected the walls of Jerusalem that had been broken down and its gates that had been destroyed by fire.
14 Then I went on to the Fountain Gate and to the King's Pool; but there was no place for the animal I was riding to continue.
15 So I went up by way of the valley by night and inspected the wall. Then I turned back and entered by the Valley Gate, and so returned.
16 The officials did not know where I had gone or what I was doing; I had not yet told the Jews, the priests, the nobles, the officials, and the rest that were to do the work.
17 Then I said to them, "You see the trouble we are in, how Jerusalem lies in ruins with its gates burned. Come, let us rebuild the wall of Jerusalem, so that we may no longer suffer disgrace."
18 I told them that the hand of my God had been gracious upon me, and also the words that the king had spoken to me. Then they said,

MAIN THOUGHT: Then said I unto them, Ye see the distress that we are in, how Jerusalem lieth waste, and the gates thereof are burned with fire: come, and let us build up the wall of Jerusalem, that we be no more a reproach. (Nehemiah 2:17, KJV)

NEHEMIAH 2:11–20

King James Version	*New Revised Standard Version*
said, Let us rise up and build. So they strengthened their hands for this good work.	**"Let us start building!" So they committed themselves to the common good.**
19 But when Sanballat the Horonite, and Tobiah the servant, the Ammonite, and Geshem the Arabian, heard it, they laughed us to scorn, and despised us, and said, What is this thing that ye do? will ye rebel against the king?	**19 But when Sanballat the Horonite and Tobiah the Ammonite official, and Geshem the Arab heard of it, they mocked and ridiculed us, saying, "What is this that you are doing? Are you rebelling against the king?"**
20 Then answered I them, and said unto them, The God of heaven, he will prosper us; therefore we his servants will arise and build: but ye have no portion, nor right, nor memorial, in Jerusalem.	**20 Then I replied to them, "The God of heaven is the one who will give us success, and we his servants are going to start building; but you have no share or claim or historic right in Jerusalem."**

LESSON SETTING

Time: *circa* 445 B.C.
Place: Judah/Jerusalem

LESSON OUTLINE

- **I. Nehemiah's Inspection of Jerusalem (Nehemiah 2:11–16)**
- **II. Nehemiah's Challenge to the Local Officials (Nehemiah 2:17–18)**
- **III. Challenges from Neighboring Authorities (Nehemiah 2:19–20)**

UNIFYING PRINCIPLE

People often are contemplative before they make major decisions. How does one, or should one, react after careful consideration of a major decision? Nehemiah set out to rebuild the walls of Jerusalem after praying and surveying the ruins.

INTRODUCTION

Many readers naturally conclude the book was written by Nehemiah ("Yah comforts or encourages") because the opening words of the book declare they are the words of Nehemiah the son of Hachaliah ("wait confidently on Yahweh"). In fact, it is widely believed Nehemiah originated the following passages: 1:1–7:5; 12:27–43; 13:4–31. But there are two different views regarding the authorship of the rest of Nehemiah. Some believe Nehemiah wrote the whole book, relying on his own memories. Others believe Ezra wrote the book, using Nehemiah's memoirs for the passages listed above. As evidence for the second view, it is noted that Nehemiah 7:5–73 and Ezra 2:1–70 are almost identical.

The similarities of Nehemiah and Ezra can be explained partly by the fact they are only one book in the Hebrew Bible. In fact, many scholars argue that Chronicles, Ezra, and Nehemiah were compiled by the same person. All these books exhibit similar themes, such as a focus on the Levites, the temple, and extensive lists. With such priestly interests, the one who masterminded this long document may well have been a priest, like Ezra.

The historical setting of Nehemiah is the second half of the Hebrew book of Ezra-Nehemiah (458–420 B.C.). During this period, the Persian emperor Artaxerxes I

Longimanus allowed the Jews to return to their land and rebuild Jerusalem.

During that time, Nehemiah occupied a prominent position in the emperor's court. He served as the trusted cupbearer of Artaxerxes I. In his role as cupbearer to the king, Nehemiah was responsible for tasting the wine before serving it to the king to be certain it was not poisoned. This role afforded Nehemiah frequent access to the king. In Artaxerxes' twentieth year on the throne (444 B.C.), he allowed Nehemiah to go to Jerusalem and rebuild its walls. Nehemiah stayed in Jerusalem for twelve years and then returned to Persia in Artaxerxes' thirty-second year (432 B.C.). Around 425 B.C., Nehemiah left Persia and returned to Jerusalem for the last time (Neh. 13:6–7). Nehemiah's memoirs could not have been completed until after his second visit to Jerusalem. Thus, the earliest the book of Nehemiah could have been completed would be around 425 B.C.

Ezra returned in the seventh year of the reign of Artaxerxes (Ezra 7:8) while Nehemiah returned in the twentieth year (Neh. 2:1). However, based on the way the revival of Ezra appears in the middle of the story of Nehemiah (Neh. 8–10), many students of Scripture have argued that Nehemiah returned before Ezra.

The arguments for reversing Ezra and Nehemiah in this way are generally not convincing. Nevertheless, the inclusion of part of the Ezra story in the middle of the Nehemiah memoirs still needs explanation. It could be Nehemiah's rebuilding the walls of the city was only part of the reconstruction needed among God's people. Even more necessary was the reinstitution of the Law. Ezra certainly had used the Law previously in his dealings with the people. However, at this time the prominent priest and scribe, Ezra, partnered with Nehemiah in order to thoroughly teach the people God's Law (Neh. 8:9). Apparently, the compiler of Nehemiah wanted to show the walls of the city would mean nothing without the wall of the Law surrounding the people.

The book of Nehemiah records the restoration of Jerusalem under the leadership of Nehemiah. In the book, the returning Jews showed spiritual lethargy and a cold-hearted indifference toward God. It took a determined, godly leader like Nehemiah to motivate this group to act on God's promises and rebuild Jerusalem's walls.

However, the completion of Jerusalem's walls is only half the story of Nehemiah. The walls were rebuilt by chapter 6, but the book has seven more chapters. These last chapters record a revival and describe the repopulation of the city. The subject of the book is not merely the rebuilding of the walls, but the complete restoration of the people of Jerusalem.

The book of Nehemiah makes it clear God did not restore His people only one time. Instead, He repeatedly, constantly, and continually restored His people. He sent various prophets and leaders to teach, motivate, and guide the people into righteousness. Zerubbabel led a group of exiles to Jerusalem and began to rebuild the temple (Ezra 1–6). Then Ezra led a second group of exiles back to Jerusalem and helped restore the people to obedience to the Mosaic Law (Ezra 7–10). Nehemiah then returned and motivated the people to rebuild the walls of Jerusalem (Neh. 1–6). Finally, Nehemiah returned a second time and exhorted the people to adhere closely to God's Law (Neh. 13).

Exposition

I. Nehemiah's Inspection of Jerusalem (Nehemiah 2:11–16)

Nehemiah was on duty at his royal post in Susa, the capital. Hanani ("my grace" or a shortened form of "Yahweh is gracious"), whom some believe to have been the biological brother of Nehemiah and who was later put in charge of Jerusalem (Neh. 7:2), brought some distressing news to Nehemiah regarding the community in the homeland. The author/compiler of the book of Nehemiah shared the encounter in 1:2–3 (NIV): "Hanani, one of my brothers, came from Judah with some other men, and I questioned them about the Jewish remnant that had survived the exile, and also about Jerusalem. They said to me, 'Those who survived the exile and are back in the province are in great trouble and disgrace. The wall of Jerusalem is broken down, and its gates have been burned with fire.'" Nehemiah's response was one of great grief and worship: "When I heard these things, I sat down and wept. For some days I mourned and fasted and prayed before the God of heaven" (1:4, NIV). Nehemiah was typically in good spirits as he served the king. The news from Jerusalem, however, left him depressed and anxious. King Artaxerxes noticed a sadness of heart not associated with illness (2:2). Nehemiah raised the rhetorical question of why shouldn't he be sad when his ancestral home lay in ruins and the gates had been destroyed by fire. The king inquired as to what Nehemiah wanted. The king then asked Nehemiah when he would return. This question indicated the king would give him permission. Nehemiah responded immediately with a specific time frame, again indicating forethought on his part.

Aware he would face opposition from his enemies, Nehemiah requested letters of permission from the king to allow him to pass through the various provinces in the Trans-Euphrates, the large area west of the Euphrates River. He also asked the king to write a letter to Asaph, the man in charge of the king's forest. Nehemiah realized he would need access to timber for rebuilding the gates, the wall, and other parts of the city. Prepared in this way, he made the trip to Jerusalem.

Nehemiah knew there was no way he could share with the people in Jerusalem what God led him to accomplish without first doing some research and planning. Following what was apparently a customary three days (Ezra 8:32), probably devoted to customary Middle Eastern social amenities, Nehemiah started to formulate specific plans for rebuilding of the walls of Jerusalem. The three days likely also were spent thinking, praying, and getting acquainted with some people there. "Nehemiah, always a shrewd and practical administrator, did not wish to involve the local authorities in his plans until he himself had a clear idea about how he ought to proceed. Therefore, he inspected the city walls secretly by moonlight, accompanied only by a few personal servants" (Hamrick, "Ezra–Nehemiah," 472).

Nehemiah then made a careful survey of the walls to analyze the problem he faced. Under the cover of night and accompanied by a few select companions, he gained perspective. Then, as outlined in Nehemiah 3, he developed an effective plan to accomplish the task he had come to Jerusalem to perform. In his nighttime inspection, he rode his mount (donkey or mule) from the Valley Gate. Proceeding southward, he followed the slopes of the valley past the Jackal's Well. Then he went to the Dung Gate. The Fountain Gate was north of the Dung Gate on the eastern wall. Apparently the rubble there kept him from proceeding on his mount, so he went up the valley.

Nehemiah was faced with quite a daunting task, as the Old Testament interpreter Emmett W. Hamrick notes: "When Nebuchadnezzar destroyed the city, these terraces with the buildings constructed on them began to collapse down into the valley below. By the time of Nehemiah, the entire area along the east wall was an incredible mass of fallen stones. Nehemiah abandoned the pre-exilic line of the east wall altogether and constructed a new line along the eastern crest of the hill" (Hamrick, "Ezra–Nehemiah," 474). During this entire process, Nehemiah continued to maintain the secrecy of his work, as Nehemiah 2:16 indicates.

II. Nehemiah's Challenge to the Local Officials (Nehemiah 2:17–18)

Once Nehemiah decided on clear plan of action, he proceeded for the first time to reveal to others his intention to rebuild the wall. Then I said to them, "You see the trouble we are in: Jerusalem lies in ruins, and its gates have been burned with fire. Come, let us rebuild the wall of Jerusalem, and we will no longer be in disgrace" (2:17, NIV). Nehemiah noted the trouble the people were in. Part of the trouble he had in mind was the physical distress that had resulted from the inability of the Jews to defend themselves against hostile neighbors. On the other hand, there was also the disgrace brought about by the humiliation they had experienced from the invasion of Nebuchadnezzar as well as by other foreign leaders.

Nehemiah concluded his remarks with a personal testimony of how God's gracious hand was upon him. And he affirmed things King Artaxerxes had said to him. "The people responded with predictable enthusiasm when Nehemiah told them how God intervened to remove their frustrations and to make possible the restoration of the city. They volunteered to support the building operation and began immediately to make preparations for the good work" (Hamrick, "Ezra–Nehemiah," 474).

III. Challenges from Neighboring Authorities (Nehemiah 2:19–20)

Upon his arrival in Jerusalem, Nehemiah faced opposition. When Sanballat the Horonite and his associate Tobiah from Ammon heard Nehemiah had arrived to help Israel, they were displeased (2:10). Sanballat was the representative of the Persian (now Iran) government in Samaria. Tobiah was also a royal leader and deputy governor in the province. Immediately they began to plan how to stop Nehemiah from achieving his goal. Perhaps they were hoping to gain control of Judah. When it became known that Nehemiah planned to rebuild the walls of Jerusalem, Sanballat and Tobiah intensified their opposition to Nehemiah. The rebuilding of Jerualem's walls clearly indicated Nehemiah's intention to separate Judah from Samaritan administration. In that Nehemiah did not reveal any written authorization for his project, his detractors suggested he might be rebelling against the king. Otherwise, they mocked and ridiculed Nehemiah and his cohorts. Geshem the Arab (6:1–2, 6), an ally of the Persian king and ruler of a vast area from Arabia to Egypt, joined the opposition to Nehemiah. However, Nehemiah was resolute in his objectives and clear about the status of his challengers in regard to Israel: "The God of heaven will help give us success. We his servants will start rebuilding, but as for your, you have no share in Jerusalem or any claim or historic right to it" (2:20, NIV).

The Lesson Applied

Patriotism is a term that has emerged in fresh ways and with a new prominence in contemporary times in this country. Probably the majority of people identify patriotism with loyalty to one's country—including its history and heritage, place in the context of the rest of the world, and features that make the country unique—and a sense of the legacy the country has and will forge. Patriots, then, are people who have some sense of understanding of these things along with some appreciation of them and a commitment to preserve and perpetuate them. Symbols—such as flags, songs, poems, and the like—play an important role in the experience of patriotism.

By this depiction, Nehemiah was certainly a patriot. He had an emotional and historic attachment to his country and its heritage and history. Yet there was much more for him. He felt an irresistible urge to do all he could to help restore the brokenness of his country. He could not be content to experience success and security while his beloved homeland lay in ruins and was dominated by outsiders with no appreciation for the uniqueness of Israel. He was willing to make a difference for his homeland and his people, whatever sacrifices were involved. Inextricably connected with all that was a relationship with God that undergirded and guided his actions. All that is the profile of the consummate patriot.

Let's Talk About It

List and discuss the traits of Nehemiah that made him an effective leader.

Humility: Nehemiah was cupbearer to the king. Yet, he understood the stewardship of his role.

Organization: Nehemiah quickly assembled working teams to rebuild the wall with haste and had people working around the clock to finish the job.

Hands On: He took his place alongside of the people to do this great work.

Home Daily Devotional Readings
April 19–25, 2021

Monday	Tuesday	Wednesday	Thursday	Friday	Saturday	Sunday
Praise for God's Wonderful Works	God's Blessings Intended for All	The Lord, Our Sovereign	Plea for Mercy for Jerusalem	Mourn the Destruction of Zion	God's Mercy and Love Never End	Remember and Restore Us
Psalm 111	Zechariah 8:18–23	Psalm 102:12–22	Psalm 79	Jeremiah 9:17–22	Lamentations 3:22–33	Lamentations 5:1–22

A PLEA FOR RESTORATION

TOPIC: OVERCOMING LOSSES AND BROKENNESS

BACKGROUND SCRIPTURE: LAMENTATIONS 5

LAMENTATIONS 5

King James Version

REMEMBER, O LORD, what is come upon us: consider, and behold our reproach.
2 Our inheritance is turned to strangers, our houses to aliens.
3 We are orphans and fatherless, our mothers are as widows.
4 We have drunken our water for money; our wood is sold unto us.
5 Our necks are under persecution: we labour, and have no rest.
6 We have given the hand to the Egyptians, and to the Assyrians, to be satisfied with bread.
7 Our fathers have sinned, and are not; and we have borne their iniquities.
8 Servants have ruled over us: there is none that doth deliver us out of their hand.
9 We gat our bread with the peril of our lives because of the sword of the wilderness.
10 Our skin was black like an oven because of the terrible famine.
11 They ravished the women in Zion, and the maids in the cities of Judah.
12 Princes are hanged up by their hand: the faces of elders were not honoured.
13 They took the young men to grind, and the children fell under the wood.
14 The elders have ceased from the gate, the young men from their musick.
15 The joy of our heart is ceased; our dance is turned into mourning.
16 The crown is fallen from our head: woe unto us, that we have sinned!
17 For this our heart is faint; for these things our eyes are dim.

New Revised Standard Version

REMEMBER, O LORD, what has befallen us; look, and see our disgrace!
2 Our inheritance has been turned over to strangers, our homes to aliens.
3 We have become orphans, fatherless; our mothers are like widows.
4 We must pay for the water we drink; the wood we get must be bought.
5 With a yoke on our necks we are hard driven; we are weary, we are given no rest.
6 We have made a pact with Egypt and Assyria, to get enough bread.
7 Our ancestors sinned; they are no more, and we bear their iniquities.
8 Slaves rule over us; there is no one to deliver us from their hand.
9 We get our bread at the peril of our lives, because of the sword in the wilderness.
10 Our skin is black as an oven from the scorching heat of famine.
11 Women are raped in Zion, virgins in the towns of Judah.
12 Princes are hung up by their hands; no respect is shown to the elders.
13 Young men are compelled to grind, and boys stagger under loads of wood.
14 The old men have left the city gate, the young men their music.
15 The joy of our hearts has ceased; our dancing has been turned to mourning.
16 The crown has fallen from our head; woe to us, for we have sinned!
17 Because of this our hearts are sick, because of these things our eyes have grown dim:

MAIN THOUGHT: Turn thou us unto thee, O LORD, and we shall be turned; renew our days as of old. (Lamentations 5:21, KJV)

LAMENTATIONS 5

King James Version

18 Because of the mountain of Zion, which is desolate, the foxes walk upon it.
19 Thou, O LORD, remainest for ever; thy throne from generation to generation.
20 Wherefore dost thou forget us for ever, and forsake us so long time?
21 Turn thou us unto thee, O LORD, and we shall be turned; renew our days as of old.
22 But thou hast utterly rejected us; thou art very wroth against us.

New Revised Standard Version

18 because of Mount Zion, which lies desolate; jackals prowl over it.
19 But you, O LORD, reign forever; your throne endures to all generations.
20 Why have you forgotten us completely? Why have you forsaken us these many days?
21 Restore us to yourself, O LORD, that we may be restored; renew our days as of old—
22 unless you have utterly rejected us, and are angry with us beyond measure.

LESSON SETTING

Time: *circa* 580 B.C.
Place: Judah

LESSON OUTLINE

I. A Prayer for Remembrance Amid Details of Devastation (Lamentations 5:1–18)
II. A Prayer for Restoration (Lamentations 5:19–22)

UNIFYING PRINCIPLE

People seek restoration when their possessions are taken and relationships are broken. How does one cope with the loss of that which is important? The writer of Lamentations trusted God would reestablish a relationship with Israel.

INTRODUCTION

The book of Lamentations takes its name from mournful poems or songs of lament or sorrow over some significant loss. The twenty-fifth book of the Bible contains a series of laments pertaining to the destruction of Jerusalem in 587 B.C. Each of the five chapters of the book of Lamentations contains a poem of sorrow. Each of the first four chapters is an acrostic, in which successive verses begin with successive letters of the Hebrew alphabet, with some variations.

Since the time of the Septuagint, the Greek translation of the Old Testament (*circa* 250 B.C.), authorship of Lamentations has been attributed to Jeremiah. The Hebrew text of the book, however, does not make that claim. Several considerations favor Jeremiah as the author. Jeremiah was known as a composer of laments (2 Chron. 35:25). He was personally known as the prophet who mourned: "Oh, that my head were a spring of waters and my eyes a fountain of tears! I would weep day and night for the slain of my people" (Jer. 9:1, NIV). In Lamentations 3:1, the author seemed to identify himself with Jeremiah when he said, "I am a man who has seen affliction by the rod of the LORD's wrath" (NIV). Moreover, there is similarity in tone between Lamentations and portions of Jeremiah, and there are many linguistic affinities between both books as well.

Finally, a similar perspective exists in Lamentations and Jeremiah regarding the cause of the fall of Jerusalem (Lam. 1:2–18; 2:14; 4:13–17; Jer. 2:19; 14:7; 16:10–12; 23:11–40).

What can be asserted with certainty about the authorship of Lamentations is that its author was an eyewitness to the fall of Jerusalem. When all the evidence is taken together, tradition's assignment of authorship to Jeremiah seems the most plausible approach.

Chapter 1 of Lamentations mourns the misery resulting from the destruction of Jerusalem and provides a theological explanation for the desolation as God's judgment for Judah's sin. Verses 1–11 in chapter 1 set forward Jeremiah's lament over the devastation of Jerusalem. Verses 12–22 contain Jerusalem's cry for mercy.

Chapter 2 continues the lament over the ruin brought about by divine anger and calls the people to prayer. More specifically, 2:1–10 focuses on the Lord's anger. The grief of the prophet Jeremiah is in 2:11–19, and 2:20–22 has a plea from Jeremiah.

Chapter 3 moves from a combination of lament and hope in verses 1–24 to a psalm of praise for the compassion and faithfulness of the Lord in verses 25–39. This is followed by a confession in verses 40–54 and an accompanying prayer in verses 55–66.

Lamentations 4 vividly portrays the horrors of the siege and fall of Jerusalem and explains the spiritual leaders—the prophets and priests of the city—were partly to blame for the calamity.

Lamentations 5 summarizes the conditions associated with the Exile and concludes with a prayer for restoration. Herein is contained a prayer for remembrance from the remnants of the details of the devastation (5:1–18) and a prayer for restoration from the remnants (5:19–22).

Exposition

I. A Prayer for Remembrance Amid Details of Devastation (Lamentations 5:1–18)

Chapters 1–4 of the book of Lamentations sometimes are referred to in Old Testament studies as *dirges*, songs of deep sorrow often associated with funerals. Most of the material in those chapters is also rhetorically an acrostic. Each verse or main section of the passages begins with the first letter of the Hebrew alphabet (*aleph*) and proceeds to the last letter of the Hebrew alphabet (*taw*). The most notable example of acrostic is Psalm 119. Additional examples include Psalms 9–10; 25; 34; 37; 111–112; 145; and Proverbs 31:10–31. The acrostic is a mnemonic device, an instructional method for helping people memorize the poem, and expressed completeness of the subject matter.

Lamentations 5 departs from this pattern and is more liturgical (related to worship) than an instructional method. Although it has the character of a lament (a song of sorrow), it is properly a prayer. Verse 1 introduces the prayer. The remnant called on God to remember the indignities they had suffered and to look at their present disgrace. Jeremiah already had indicated God notices such atrocities (Lam. 3:34–36). Therefore the people's call was not just for God to see what had happened, for He sees everything according to Proverbs 15:3. They actually were seeking for God to see and act on their condition. Robert M. Laurin puts the prayer in perspective when he says of the prologue to the prayer: "The opening cry remember is common throughout the Old Testament for God to recall his promises (Ex. 32:13; Psalms 25:6; 74:2). It presupposes the faith that refuses to give up, even though it may be severely tested. So the people seek to stir up the Lord's loving action by graphically describing the carnage. The Promised Land (our inheritance; cf. Deut. 4:21) has been taken over by others. This is what brought special disgrace, since the land had been promised to the Israelites by the Lord (Gen 12:7; Deut. 6:18). What Israel forgot, of course, was that continued existence in the land had its conditions (Deut. 4:25–31). It did not belong to Israel, but to Yahweh. Israel was only permitted to live there as 'sojourners' (Lev 25:23), so long as they kept the commands of the Lord" (Laurin, "Lamentations," 221).

Verse 2 speaks more specifically of the Exile of the people of Israel and the occupation by the Babylonians: "Our inheritance has been turned over to strangers, our homes to foreigners" (NIV). This also served as an indication of their disobedience and shame. By means of the use of the first person *we, us, our*, the people described the general conditions of suffering caused by Babylon (vv. 2–10). Judah had been parceled out to foreigners. Babylon assumed dominion over the land, and its occupying forces were stationed there (Jer. 40:10; 41:3). Moreover, nations surrounding Judah appropriated or annexed some of her land for themselves (Ezek 35:10).

The suffering is portrayed in terms of the loss of the most basic of human relationships—that of parent and child (Lam. 5:3). The men were as defenseless as the orphans and fatherless and the women were as vulnerable as widows. Throughout the Old Testament, the concept of widowhood appears to depict a position of helpless despair. It often is linked with aliens and orphans as individuals who could not protect themselves (Ex. 22:22; Deut. 10:18; 24:19–21; 26:13; 27:19; Isa. 1:17). Under the rule of Babylon, Judah had no rights or means of protection. It was the crushed enemy, and Babylon its cruel overlord

Verses 4–5 speak of the desperation associated with the acquisition of the most basic needs for existence. "Because they are no longer God's tenants on the land but were vassals of aliens, they had to suffer the rigors of servitude. They had to pay for the water they drank, as well as for the wood they burned. The pathos of the situation is seen when the Hebrew is translated: 'our own water ... our own wood.' They bore the burden of unyielding forced service that demanded labor of even the very young (v. 13)" (Laurin, "Lamentations," 221).

Israel's problems were much exacerbated by the desperate yet tenuous political alliances they had made with Egypt and Assyria. Israel had submitted to Egypt and Assyria to get enough bread. The Hebrew words for *submitted to* literally mean "to give the hand to or to shake hands." The implication was establishing a pact or treaty (2 Kings 10:15) and frequently referred to a group surrendering or submitting to a more powerful entity as part of a treaty (1 Chron. 29:24; 2 Chron. 30:8; Jer. 50:15). In the past, Judah had pledged allegiance both to Egypt and Assyria for the sake of national security (Ezek 16:26–28; 23:12, 21). The fathers or past leaders of Judah shifted their allegiance between countries. Such fickleness ultimately destroyed them. Their sin brought their death, and their survivors bore their punishment. The current generation was not claiming to be suffering unjustly for their forebears' sins (Lam. 5:16). However, they saw their punishment as a logical conclusion to the foolishness of their ancestors.

The quest for food (bread) and the ravages of the lack of it among the people at the time are dramatically indicated in Lamentations 5:9–10. The severe conditions and scarcity of food prompted the people to take desperate means for survival. The scarcity of food and the resulting starvation caused a raging fever among the Jewish people (4:8). *The Message* graphically expresses their fevered condition.

Verses 11–14 portray the horrors inflicted upon various segments of Jewish society by the Babylonians. Something cruel and despicable occurred to every element of their society. The first group mentioned who suffered the horrors of foreign occupation were the women of Jerusalem and the virgins—women of marriageable age. Women who survived the Babylonian assault on their cities were mercilessly raped by the sadistic soldiers. The leaders of the nation were brutalized by the Babylonians. Princes were hung up by their hands. The elders also were treated contemptuously. The able-bodied young men were brutalized by the Babylonians. The young men who survived the Babylonian invasion were enslaved. These adolescent boys were reduced to the status of slaves.

Matters of justice and the resolution of judicial issues among the citizenry were discontinued. The elders, responsible for conducting these services, no longer met at the gate of the city to do so. Even the music, which the young men typically performed, had ceased being played.

Verses 15–16 express the pitiable plight of the remnant in Israel. The *crown* connotes the long-past independence of Israel and its glory and majesty (2:15). And the king who wore the crown of Israel was now in exile (4:20). The prayer then becomes confessional (5:16–18).

II. A Prayer for Restoration (Lamentations 5:19–22)

The song concludes with a haunting question that pervades the whole book and depicts the struggle of faith. Referring to the call to remember with which the poem began (5:1), the people affirm that in the midst of a changing and oft-destructive world, Yahweh's promises and rulership remain constant (Pss. 9:8; 93:2; 103:19). So how can He allow the desolation to endure? The people of Israel wrestled with a theological matter that multiple generations of believers have: *Why is there evil in the world overseen by a loving, powerful God?*

Israel ultimately did not (and could not) answer the question. They simply raised it and contended with it. Rather, they concluded the prayer—and the book of Lamentations—with what they needed and sought more than anything else—restoration (Lam. 5:21–22). The people wanted to be restored to the blessings of God's covenant, and that included being restored to the land of Israel (Lev 26:40–45). More than anything in the quest for restoration was God's faithfulness to His covenant promises. Unless God had utterly rejected the nation, the people could depend on Him to grant their request.

The Lesson Applied

From where and why do cataclysmic experiences in life originate? Why is there turmoil in the world—natural catastrophes, devastating diseases, economic crises, wars, and the like? To be sure, many such occurrences are unexplainable. Some have no answers. Others are not unilateral—they do not have a single source or explanation. Yet, evidenced in this lesson, the Bible is unmistakable in indicating some disasters are punitive acts of God.

For generations, Israel had been disobedient to the covenant requirements of God. Throughout that time, He warned them through prophets and others that He would call them into accountability. The invasion by Babylon and the Exile were frequently declared as coming punishment. Yet the people persisted in their rebellion. When they finally candidly confessed their waywardness, they began the journey to restoration. Such is always the case in one's relationship with God. Confession—agreeing with Him about our spiritual status—brings restoration to a right relationship. This is a fundamental truth of the Gospel (1 John 1:9).

Simultaneously, there is also the inescapable truth that some mystery attends many of the misfortunes of life. *Theodicy* is the area of Christian theology that addresses the tension between an all-powerful and loving God and the pervasiveness of calamity in the world. Believers have always and perhaps always will struggle with this tension and seek answers. Sometimes answers come. Frequently they do not. Some take the stand: *If God is the sovereign, loving God that is proclaimed, He would not allow evil to exist.* Wise counsel comes from the Old Testament exegete who says, "Do not let appearances deceive you. If God is God, then his ways must be mysterious; he is a God who 'hides himself' (Isa. 45:15). He may still be loving, and yet not act in ways we assume he should (Isa. 55:8)" (Laurin, "Lamentations," 221). That reality permits the quest for understanding and questions. More importantly, however, it calls for a commitment in faith and a respect for the sovereignty of God.

Let's Talk About It

Why do we place more emphasis on the love and grace of God than on His punishment of disobedience?

As humans, we tend to put more emphasis on the goodness of God because we do not like to be chastised or disciplined. However, we also must come to acknowledge God is the One who sets the standards for human life. He disciplines us when we fall away, in order to save us from our sins. His discipline is an act of love and grace.

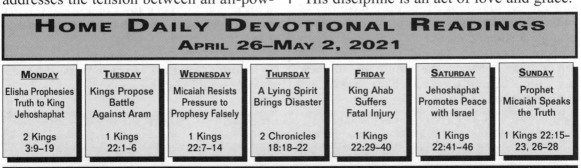

Home Daily Devotional Readings

April 26–May 2, 2021

Monday	Tuesday	Wednesday	Thursday	Friday	Saturday	Sunday
Elisha Prophesies Truth to King Jehoshaphat	Kings Propose Battle Against Aram	Micaiah Resists Pressure to Prophesy Falsely	A Lying Spirit Brings Disaster	King Ahab Suffers Fatal Injury	Jehoshaphat Promotes Peace with Israel	Prophet Micaiah Speaks the Truth
2 Kings 3:9–19	1 Kings 22:1–6	1 Kings 22:7–14	2 Chronicles 18:18–22	1 Kings 22:29–40	1 Kings 22:41–46	1 Kings 22:15–23, 26–28

MICAIAH: SPEAKING TRUTH TO POWER

TOPIC:
SPEAKING TRUTH BOLDLY

BACKGROUND SCRIPTURE:
1 KINGS 22:1–40

1 KINGS 22:15–23, 26–28

King James Version

SO he came to the king. And the king said unto him, Micaiah, shall we go against Ramoth-gilead to battle, or shall we forbear? And he answered him, Go, and prosper: for the LORD shall deliver it into the hand of the king.

16 And the king said unto him, How many times shall I adjure thee that thou tell me nothing but that which is true in the name of the LORD?

17 And he said, I saw all Israel scattered upon the hills, as sheep that have not a shepherd: and the LORD said, These have no master: let them return every man to his house in peace.

18 And the king of Israel said unto Jehoshaphat, Did I not tell thee that he would prophesy no good concerning me, but evil?

19 And he said, Hear thou therefore the word of the LORD: I saw the LORD sitting on his throne, and all the host of heaven standing by him on his right hand and on his left.

20 And the LORD said, Who shall persuade Ahab, that he may go up and fall at Ramoth-gilead? And one said on this manner, and another said on that manner.

21 And there came forth a spirit, and stood before the LORD, and said, I will persuade him.

22 And the LORD said unto him, Wherewith? And he said, I will go forth, and I will be a lying spirit in the mouth of all his prophets. And he said, Thou shalt persuade him, and prevail also: go forth, and do so.

23 Now therefore, behold, the LORD hath put a lying spirit in the mouth of all these thy prophets, and the LORD hath spoken evil concerning thee.

New Revised Standard Version

WHEN he had come to the king, the king said to him, "Micaiah, shall we go to Ramoth-gilead to battle, or shall we refrain?" He answered him, "Go up and triumph; the LORD will give it into the hand of the king."

16 But the king said to him, "How many times must I make you swear to tell me nothing but the truth in the name of the LORD?"

17 Then Micaiah said, "I saw all Israel scattered on the mountains, like sheep that have no shepherd; and the LORD said, 'These have no master; let each one go home in peace.'"

18 The king of Israel said to Jehoshaphat, "Did I not tell you that he would not prophesy anything favorable about me, but only disaster?"

19 Then Micaiah said, "Therefore hear the word of the LORD: I saw the LORD sitting on his throne, with all the host of heaven standing beside him to the right and to the left of him.

20 And the LORD said, 'Who will entice Ahab, so that he may go up and fall at Ramoth-gilead?' Then one said one thing, and another said another,

21 until a spirit came forward and stood before the LORD, saying, 'I will entice him.'

22 'How?' the LORD asked him. He replied, 'I will go out and be a lying spirit in the mouth of all his prophets.' Then the LORD said, 'You are to entice him, and you shall succeed; go out and do it.'

23 So you see, the LORD has put a lying spirit in the mouth of all these your prophets; the LORD has decreed disaster for you.

MAIN THOUGHT: And Micaiah said, As the LORD liveth, what the LORD saith unto me, that will I speak. (1 Kings 22:14, KJV)

1 KINGS 22:15–23, 26–28

King James Version	*New Revised Standard Version*
••••••	••••••
26 And the king of Israel said, Take Micaiah, and carry him back unto Amon the governor of the city, and to Joash the king's son;	**26 The king of Israel then ordered, "Take Micaiah, and return him to Amon the governor of the city and to Joash the king's son,**
27 And say, Thus saith the king, Put this fellow in the prison, and feed him with bread of affliction and with water of affliction, until I come in peace.	**27 and say, 'Thus says the king: Put this fellow in prison, and feed him on reduced rations of bread and water until I come in peace.'"**
28 And Micaiah said, If thou return at all in peace, the LORD hath not spoken by me. And he said, Hearken, O people, every one of you.	**28 Micaiah said, "If you return in peace, the LORD has not spoken by me." And he said, "Hear, you peoples, all of you!"**

LESSON SETTING

Time: *circa* 853 B.C.
Place: Israel

LESSON OUTLINE

I. Micaiah's Message of Doom (1 Kings 22:15–18)
II. Plan of the Divine Council (1 Kings 22:19–23
III. Indication of an Authentic Prophet (1 Kings 22:26–28)

UNIFYING PRINCIPLE

Telling the truth to those who are in power can be difficult. How does one give a difficult message to powerful people? Micaiah resolved that he would tell King Ahab only what the Lord said to him.

INTRODUCTION

First and 2 Kings, the eleventh and twelfth books of the Christian canon, were originally one book and formed a part of a larger history of Israel. A near consensus in Old Testament scholarship is that the division of the original work into two parts occurred in the Greek translation of the Hebrew Scriptures, the Septuagint. There, 1 and 2 Kings were known as 3 and 4 Kings. First and 2 Samuel were originally known as 1 and 2 Kings, and 1 and 2 Samuel were originally a single work. Tradition holds that the prophet Jeremiah is the author of 1 and 2 Kings. The final recorded incident in 2 Kings was the release of Jehoiachin from prison by Evil-merodach, *circa* 560 B.C. (2 Kings 25:27–30). There are some affinities between the theology contained in the books of Kings and that in the book of Jeremiah. Moreover, it is likely Jeremiah could have been alive at the time of the incident referred to above. The books of Kings give no indication as to their authorship, and there is no way of determining with certainty the authorship.

The author of 1 and 2 Kings reflected three concerns in Israel's theological history. With Deuteronomy 28 (esp. vv. 1–14) ever in mind, the author of the historical books was concerned to maintain consciousness of the fulfillment of God's word. Three concerns are evident in 1 and 2 Kings as the author made this evaluation. The author meticulously noted that every aspect of God's word would be fulfilled—

the promises, the blessings, the consequences of disobedience, and God's words of warning. The word of God had been clearly articulated in the Deuteronomic codes. It was just as clearly articulated by the classical prophets Nathan, Elijah, Elisha, Isaiah, and others. The emphasis on the dynamic character of *davar*, the word of God, could not be ignored.

The author also had great concern for the maintenance of the purity of Israel's liturgical life. Two aspects of this were emphasized. One was absolute loyalty to strict monotheism. The requirement of the daily recitation of the Shema (Deut 6:4–9) and its emphasis on the oneness of God was more than a thoughtless, automatic mouthing of words. It was, in effect, a confession of faith by which Israel acknowledged the One True God and His immutable commandments for them. Absolute loyalty to the One True God also expressed itself in worship offered only to Him in a place dictated by Him. Ultimately, this meant worship was centered in Jerusalem, which was distinguished from sites associated with paganism.

The author of 1 and 2 Kings also had a concern for hope for the future of Israel. This rested upon the authority of the oracles and commands of Yahweh and a sense of His salvific purposes through Israel. The foibles and failures of the patriarchs and kings of Israel did not dismantle God's purposes. The tragedies that befell Israel in retribution for their spiritual depravity did not dismantle God's purpose, neither would the divided kingdom of Israel, nor the Exile in Babylon. Through a faithful remnant and the Messianic Age, God would create a future.

First Kings 22 points to a major division of the book of 1 Kings that deals with what some Old Testament scholars refer to as the *prophetic revolt* and includes 1 Kings 17:1–22:53. Chapters 17–22 more specifically focus on King Ahab and the prophets. The story of Elijah and the drought is recorded in chapter 17. The contest between the prophet of Yahweh and the prophets of Baal is in chapter 18. Revelation at Mount Carmel is covered in chapter 19. War with Benhadad and Aram (Syria) is the concern of chapter 20. The narrative of the vineyard of Naboth in Jezreel appears in chapter 21. And today's lesson is part of the larger context that is chapter 22 and is concerned with the last battle of Ahab.

Exposition

I. Micaiah's Message of Doom (1 Kings 22:15–18)

M. Pierce Matheney Jr. provides a helpful overview of the larger context of today's lesson passage. "After his decisive victories over Benhadad II, Ahab joined the coalition of kings against Assyria at the battle of Qarqar on an equal basis with Benhadad. Evidently, Benhadad had not kept his agreement to return all the cities (20:34), and Ramoth-gilead was still in Aramean hands. The main interest of the story lies in the contrast between the victory oracle of the institutional prophets and the prediction of Ahab's death by Micaiah, son of Imlah, otherwise unknown. This is the first formal encounter between the true and false prophets. The correct name for these victory prophets is 'lying' prophets (22:22; cf. 13:18; Jer 23:25–26). Micaiah insists on speaking the true word of Yahweh, even though it spells doom for the king. Though Ahab commands that Micaiah be held in prison, and tries to avoid his fate, he is later mortally wounded by one of the archers" (Matheney, "1 Kings," 221). In effect, the battle into which Jehoshaphat and Ahab were about to engage against the Arameans was *cherem/herem*, the Hebrew concept of "holy war." These wars were fought in the name of Yahweh and usually at His direction (Deut. 2:24; 3:6; 20:16–18; Num. 21:2–3l; Josh. 6:21; 8:26; 10:28–43; 11:11). The basic intention of *herem* was to drive out nations or tribal peoples that occupied land that the Lord intended for His covenant people, Israel. That also involved the eradication of all traces of idolatry and paganism that often was common in those places. Thus, holy war required the destruction of all humans who practiced paganism, along with all their livestock and other possessions. The taking of any spoils of war from such places was strictly prohibited.

Before such a momentous undertaking, both militarily and in terms of the particular type of war it was, Jehoshaphat wanted divine counsel from the Lord before he and Ahab launched their mission. Apparently Ahab was quite indifferent regarding the matter. However, to placate Jehoshaphat, Ahab called for the prophets, about four hundred of them. These evidently were prophets of the Lord. Prophets of Baal, introduced to the Northern Kingdom by Jezebel, Ahab's wife (along with Baalism), would have been unacceptable to Jehoshaphat. However, the prophets who were consulted were apostate prophets. They had no concern about obtaining and relating the true word of the Lord. Their desire was to provide their king the type of advice they thought he wanted to hear. This would please him, and he would favor them. Their answer to Ahab's question somehow led Jehoshaphat to believe they did not have the mind of the Lord, so he requested a prophet true to the Lord of whom they could inquire (2 Kings 3:11).

Ahab replied there was one man of God remaining whom they could contact. However, that one always prophesied evil for Ahab. Therefore, Ahab indicated he hated him. Obviously Ahab was more concerned about feeling good than he was about knowing the truth. The prophet Micaiah was one of Elijah's proteges. His name means "Who is like Yahweh?" and he was one of the comparatively few faithful prophets in Israel in that day. Because of Jehoshaphat's continuing interest in hearing from Micaiah, Ahab sent for him.

Ahab's messenger to Micaiah urged the prophet to do the politically correct thing and concur with the statements of all the other prophets. "Look, the other prophets without exception are predicting success for the king. Let your word agree with theirs, and speak favorably" (1 Kings 22:13, NIV). "Micaiah objects with an oath to any human principle of control over his oracle. Yahweh himself is the only authority of the prophet's word. Once the prophet knows this word of the Lord, no human authority can keep him from delivering the message" (Matheney, "1 Kings," 221). Once in the presence of King Ahab, the king asked Micaiah if they should proceed with war or not. Micaiah's reply was sarcastic, But he likely did not deliver it in a sarcastic tone, which would have been inappropriate for a man of his character. Ahab recognized at once what Micaiah was doing. His own reply was equally sarcastic (v. 16). He probably had never told Micaiah to swear to tell him nothing but the truth before, as he did not need to. But Ahab's saying that probably sounded good.

The time for sarcasm was past. Micaiah related the burden of the Lord in all its devastating simplicity and force. Micaiah said he had seen, perhaps in a vision, all Israel scattered over the hills of Gilead like sheep without a shepherd. They were wandering and in need of leadership. The Lord had told the prophet these sheep had no master, obviously a reference to Ahab. After the death of the shepherd in battle, the sheep would return home without being pursued by the enemy, Aram. Ahab reacted to this sober warning offhandedly (v. 18), unwilling to consider it seriously.

II. Plan of the Divine Council (1 Kings 22:19–23)

Micaiah proceeded to explain the rest of what God had shown him. The explanation was not about the battle. Rather, it was about the advice both kings had been receiving from the four hundred court prophets. He called on the two kings to hear the word of the Lord. Micaiah saw the host of heaven, the angelic armies of God, assembled around the throne of God. In the vision, the Lord sought one of His heavenly beings to go forward to entice Ahab to go into war and meet his death. Various opinions were expressed among the host of heaven. Eventually, a spirit stepped forward and volunteered to fulfil the task. When asked by the Lord by what means this would be accomplished, the willing heavenly council member responded, "I will go out and be a lying spirit in the mouths of all his prophets" (22:22, NIV). Or, as *The Message* has it: "'Easy,' said the angel, 'I'll get all the prophets to lie.' 'That should do it,' said God. 'On your way—seduce him!'" Clearly the message was expressed in both a dramatic and creative method to achieve the maximum impact on the king and the prophets of spurious motives. That is evident in Micaiah's concluding words to Ahab in verse 23 (NIV): "So now the Lord has put a lying spirit in the mouths of all these prophets of yours. The Lord has decreed disaster for you."

III. Indication of an Authentic Prophet (1 Kings 22:26–28)

Ahab's reaction evidences the blindness and folly that overtake those who disregard the Lord's message. Instead of repenting, as he had done previously (21:27), now calloused in sin to the point of insensibility, Ahab ordered that Micaiah be given to Amon, the city mayor, and to Joash, the king's son. The term *king's son* was apparently a title of a royal official and was not intended to be taken to mean the actual son of Ahab (2 Chron. 28:7; Jer. 36:26; 38:6). Ahab instructed Amon and Joash to imprison the prophet who had warned him of impending doom. Micaiah had the final word, however, and it was another gracious but strong warning for Ahab, indicating the king would not return from battle safely. The prophet also called on all present to remember his words for they would prove the Lord had spoken through him when his prophecy came to pass.

"Ahab's treatment of Micaiah reveals that Jezebel was not the only source of persecution. The threat of perpetual prison or perhaps death is in Ahab's word, *until I come in peace.* But Micaiah accepts the test of all true prophecy, namely that it will come to pass (Deut. 18:20–22; Jer. 28:9)" (Matheney, "1 Kings," 223).

The Lesson Applied

Ahab's attitude and reaction to the prophet Micaiah and the word of the Lord through him to Ahab causes one to reflect on the admonition of the well-experienced pastor and mentor Paul to his understudy Timothy. He passionately wrote in 2 Timothy 4:1–5 (NLT): "I solemnly urge you in the presence of God and Christ Jesus, who will someday judge the living and the dead when he comes to set up his Kingdom: Preach the word of God. Be prepared, whether the time is favorable or not. Patiently correct, rebuke, and encourage your people with good teaching. For a time is coming when people will no longer listen to sound and wholesome teaching. They will follow their own desires and will look for teachers who will tell them whatever their itching ears want to hear. They will reject the truth and chase after myths. But you should keep a clear mind in every situation. Don't be afraid of suffering for the Lord. Work at telling others the Good News, and fully carry out the ministry God has given you."

The message is clear to all who serve in sharing the message of God, whether as a pastor, evangelist, teacher, or otherwise. Some people approach the message as if it is restaurant buffet line and they can choose some of it and reject other parts. Some receive only what is appealing to them. And they reject and often have disdain for God's messenger. The attitude and approach of Micaiah and Paul were alike. The messenger of the Lord must be certain the message comes from Him. Once that is established, the messenger is obligated to proclaim it, no matter how the recipient(s) respond to it. The validity of the message is not in their response. It is in the certainty that it accomplishes what the Lord sent it out to accomplish.

Let's Talk About It

What safeguard does the New Testament provide for distinguishing between true and false messengers of God?

"By this you know the Spirit of God: every spirit that confesses that Jesus Christ has come in the flesh is from God, and every spirit that does not confess Jesus is not from God" (1 John 4:2–3, NRSV). We must test the spirits to see whether or not they are of God. The Spirit of God will always confess Jesus is the Christ of God.

Home Daily Devotional Readings
May 3–9, 2021

Monday	Tuesday	Wednesday	Thursday	Friday	Saturday	Sunday
Discipline the Immoral Person with Respect	Uphold Justice for All Peoples	Seek and You Will Find Me!	Lip Service Is Not Enough	Jerusalem Punished and Rescued	Judah, Blind to God's Ways	Israel Will Enjoy a Bright Future
1 Corinthians 5:1–5	Exodus 23:1–9	Jeremiah 29:10–14	Mark 7:1–8	Isaiah 29:1–8	Isaiah 29:9–12	Isaiah 29:13–24

ISAIAH: OFFERING HOPE FOR THE FUTURE

TOPIC:
EMPTY RITUALS ARE USELESS

BACKGROUND SCRIPTURE:
ISAIAH 29

ISAIAH 29:13–24

King James Version

WHEREFORE the Lord said, Forasmuch as this people draw near me with their mouth, and with their lips do honour me, but have removed their heart far from me, and their fear toward me is taught by the precept of men:
14 Therefore, behold, I will proceed to do a marvellous work among this people, even a marvellous work and a wonder: for the wisdom of their wise men shall perish, and the understanding of their prudent men shall be hid.
15 Woe unto them that seek deep to hide their counsel from the LORD, and their works are in the dark, and they say, Who seeth us? and who knoweth us?
16 Surely your turning of things upside down shall be esteemed as the potter's clay: for shall the work say of him that made it, He made me not? or shall the thing framed say of him that framed it, He had no understanding?
17 Is it not yet a very little while, and Lebanon shall be turned into a fruitful field, and the fruitful field shall be esteemed as a forest?
18 And in that day shall the deaf hear the words of the book, and the eyes of the blind shall see out of obscurity, and out of darkness.
19 The meek also shall increase their joy in the LORD, and the poor among men shall rejoice in the Holy One of Israel.
20 For the terrible one is brought to nought, and the scorner is consumed, and all that watch for iniquity are cut off:
21 That make a man an offender for a word, and lay a snare for him that reproveth in

New Revised Standard Version

THE Lord said: Because these people draw near with their mouths and honor me with their lips, while their hearts are far from me, and their worship of me is a human commandment learned by rote;
14 so I will again do amazing things with this people, shocking and amazing. The wisdom of their wise shall perish, and the discernment of the discerning shall be hidden.
15 Ha! You who hide a plan too deep for the LORD, whose deeds are in the dark, and who say, "Who sees us? Who knows us?"
16 You turn things upside down! Shall the potter be regarded as the clay? Shall the thing made say of its maker, "He did not make me"; or the thing formed say of the one who formed it, "He has no understanding"?
17 Shall not Lebanon in a very little while become a fruitful field, and the fruitful field be regarded as a forest?
18 On that day the deaf shall hear the words of a scroll, and out of their gloom and darkness the eyes of the blind shall see.
19 The meek shall obtain fresh joy in the LORD, and the neediest people shall exult in the Holy One of Israel.
20 For the tyrant shall be no more, and the scoffer shall cease to be; all those alert to do evil shall be cut off—
21 those who cause a person to lose a lawsuit, who set a trap for the arbiter in the gate, and

MAIN THOUGHT: They also that erred in spirit shall come to understanding, and they that murmured shall learn doctrine. (Isaiah 29:24, KJV)

King James Version	*New Revised Standard Version*
the gate, and turn aside the just for a thing of nought.	**without grounds deny justice to the one in the right.**
22 Therefore thus saith the LORD, who redeemed Abraham, concerning the house of Jacob, Jacob shall not now be ashamed, neither shall his face now wax pale.	**22 Therefore thus says the LORD, who redeemed Abraham, concerning the house of Jacob: No longer shall Jacob be ashamed, no longer shall his face grow pale.**
23 But when he seeth his children, the work of mine hands, in the midst of him, they shall sanctify my name, and sanctify the Holy One of Jacob, and shall fear the God of Israel.	**23 For when he sees his children, the work of my hands, in his midst, they will sanctify my name; they will sanctify the Holy One of Jacob, and will stand in awe of the God of Israel.**
24 They also that erred in spirit shall come to understanding, and they that murmured shall learn doctrine.	**24 And those who err in spirit will come to understanding, and those who grumble will accept instruction.**

LESSON SETTING

Time: *circa* 705–701 B.C.
Place: Judah/Jerusalem

LESSON OUTLINE

- **I. Hypocritical Worship and God's Promised Remedy (Isaiah 29:13–14)**
- **II. Judah's Crafty Counselors (Isaiah 29:15–16)**
- **III. God's Transformation of Nature and Society (Isaiah 29:17–24)**

UNIFYING PRINCIPLE

Relationships suffer when humans lapse into immorality. What is the result when we or others have been immoral? Isaiah prophesied that God would punish the people of Judah but still be merciful and restore the nation.

INTRODUCTION

A general summary of Isaiah is essential to the hermeneutical, the interpretive, task. Isaiah is indisputably one of the more widely read and familiar books of the prophets and of the Old Testament in general. Isaiah the man was one of the stellar personalities of the Scriptures, almost without peer. The fact is, however, the Bible contains rather scant biographical and personal information about Isaiah. Isaiah 1:1 indicates he fulfilled his prophetic ministry during the reigns of four kings of Judah: Uzziah, Jotham, Ahaz, and Hezekiah. From this it can be concluded Isaiah lived and ministered to the nation of Judah in Jerusalem between *circa* 750 to 700 B.C.

The book bearing his name reveals that Isaiah was parent to two sons, both of whom were involved, either directly or indirectly, in his prophetic task. His son Shear-Jashub proclaimed God's message to King Ahaz in 734 B.C. concerning the downfall of Syria and Israel (7:1–25). Another son, Maher-shalal-hash-baz, bore a highly symbolic name, meaning "swift to plunder, quick to spoil," to foreshadow Assyria's invasion and destruction of Syria and Israel (8:1–4).

A few personal episodes in the life of Isaiah are recorded. Isaiah 20 reveals the prophet was divinely commissioned to travel naked and barefooted through Jerusalem for three years. This dramatic message condemned Judah's alliance with Egypt and told of the impending doom of Egypt and Ethiopia. Isaiah prophesied the deliverance of the city of Jerusalem from Sennacherib in 701 B.C. (Isa. 36–37; 2 Kings 18:13–19:37), and he witnessed Hezekiah's recovery from a life-threatening illness (Isa. 38; 2 Kings 20:1–11). Second Kings 20 also indicates Isaiah preached condemnation to Hezekiah for his hospitality to the emissaries of the Babylonian king Merodach-Baladan (Isa. 39; 2 Kings 20:12–19). His apocalyptic proclamation of Jerusalem as a place of peace, prosperity, and productivity (Isa. 2:1–4) and his detailed and dramatic description of the destruction of Babylon (Isa. 13) complete the personal information about the prophet.

Old Testament interpreters generally divide the book of Isaiah into two main divisions based upon the literary characteristics and content contained in them and upon the historical context reflected in the text. Isaiah 1–39, which includes the call and fifty-year ministry of Isaiah, is clearly from the preexilic period, prior to 587 B.C. Since the time of the work of the German scholar, J. C. Döderlein, in the late eighteenth century, near consensus exists among Old Testament exegetes that Isaiah 40–66 comes from the period of the Babylonian exile and during the time of restoration under the Persian king Cyrus. The contents of Isaiah 40–66, usually designated Deutero-Isaiah or Second Isaiah, includes a historical span from *circa* 586 B.C. to 438 B.C. Authorship of Deutero-Isaiah is attributable to people associated with Isaiah, the son of Amoz. Another scholar in the late eighteenth and early nineteenth centuries, Bernard Duhm, suggested Isaiah 56–66 should be considered a distinctive unit, Trito-Isaiah or Third-Isaiah. This commentary will refer to Isaiah and Deutero-Isaiah.

Today's lesson passage belongs to the larger scriptural context that is Isaiah 28:1–32:30, which focuses on divine wisdom versus human folly. Adequate discussion of the lesson passage cannot proceed apart from a brief consideration of 29:1–8, the immediate context of the passage to be discussed.

Exposition

I. Hypocritical Worship and God's Promised Remedy (Isaiah 29:13–14)

In regard to Isaiah 29:1–8, Old Testament interpreter Page H. Kelley writes, "This oracle probably belongs to the period between 705 and 701 B.C. It gives evidence of having been delivered during one of the religious festivals in Jerusalem. It falls naturally into two divisions, the first (vv. 1–4), describing the city's distress under siege, and the second (vv. 5–8), the sudden discomfiture of her foes. In the first division Yahweh appears as Jerusalem's enemy, but through a complete turnabout in events he appears in the second as her defender" (Kelley, "Isaiah," 274).

In this oracle the name *Ariel* appears for the first time in the book of Isaiah. "The city is referred to not its usual name, but as Ariel (vv. 1, 2, 7). This strange name comes from the Akkadian, arallu, meaning 'underworld,' 'ghost,' or 'mountain of the gods.' The Hebrew word ariel occurs also in Ezekiel 32:15–16, where it probably is translated 'altar hearth.' Ariel is probably to be interpreted, therefore, as 'altar of God,' a name especially appropriate for Jerusalem because of the presence in it of Solomon's Temple" (Kelley, "Isaiah," 274).

There is a focus on Jerusalem in 29:5–8. The protection described here refers to her deliverance from Assyria, recorded in chapter 37. It would have seemed impossible to hope the Assyrians would not take the city. Only by the Lord's sovereign intervention was Jerusalem spared. Though 29:5–8 refers to the Assyrian soldiers becoming like fine dust and chaff when they were slaughtered, these verses seem to have eschatological overtones as well. The foe of Israel, who assaults the nation with visions of conquering and looting Israel, will in reality go away as empty as a hungry man who dreams he is feasting but awakes to find it was only a dream. When the Assyrian soldiers were destroyed in Isaiah's day, no doubt the people of Jerusalem were delirious with joy. But shortly the difficulty of that situation subsided in their thinking, and life returned to normal. Rather than turning back to God, the nation got more deeply involved in sin.

Isaiah 29:9–14 is a self-contained unit of Scripture. Kelley says of it, "This passage describes the spiritual condition of the people of Jerusalem just prior to 701 B.C. They were blind people (vv. 9–12), whose only service to God was lip service (vv. 13–14). The description of their blindness reminds one of the words that were spoken to the prophet at the time of his call (cf. 6:9–10).... The condition of the people is like that of a man who is dazed, blind, and intoxicated—all at the same time! Their moral lethargy is compared to a deep sleep, a kind of hypnotic sleep like that of Adam (Gen 2:21), and of Abram (Gen 15:12), of Saul (1 Sam 26:12), or of Jonah (Jonah 1:5)" (Kelley, "Isaiah," 275).

The Lord condemned what the people had been offering as worship as mere lip service, apart from sincerity, and rituals that were essentially nothing more than rote responses (Isa. 29:13). *The Message* captures the impressiveness of that which would occur at the Lord's intervention (29:13–14).

II. Judah's Crafty Counselors (Isaiah 29:15–16)

These verses are a direct confrontation of political and military decisions some of the leaders of Judah had made attempting to protect themselves from other nations. "This brief oracle condemns the leaders of Judah who were attempting to form a secret alliance with Egypt (cf. 28:7–22; 30:1–7; 31:1–3). They boasted that their plans had been devised with such secrecy that not even the Lord himself knew what they had done. They thought that for once they had outwitted and outmaneuvered him and his meddling prophet" (Kelley, "Isaiah," 275). The leaders attempted to hide their plans from God by doing things at night. They were not thinking clearly. Although God can hide things from man, humanity cannot hide things from God. Such thinking twisted the facts and confused the potter with the clay. A jar, however, cannot deny the potter made it or say the potter is ignorant (Isa. 45:9; 64:8). In fact, according to the Lord's correction of the arrogant leaders, no created thing can deny it exists only because of the one who created it. Actually the people knew nothing of what was going on, but God always knows everything.

III. God's Transformation of Nature and Society (Isaiah 29:17–24)

Some interpretive challenges are associated with this part of the passage, particularly with verse 17. The *New International Version* states the verse: "In a very short time, will not Lebanon be turned into a fertile field and the fertile field seem like a forest?" The *New Living Translation* expresses it: "Soon—and it will not be very long—the forests of Lebanon will become a fertile field, and the fertile field will yield bountiful crops."

The primary message and intention seem to be that the prophet was calling upon the people to put their trust in Yahweh and His plans for the future of Jerusalem, Israel, and beyond. God had a future and a plan of redemption in mind. Kelley summarizes verses 18–21 as follows: "Verse 18 promises that in the golden age to come there will be a reversal of the situation previously described in vv. 9–12. The Lord's people, referred to as the meek and the poor of the earth, will find new joy in him (v. 19). The ruthless and arrogant, on the other hand, will cease to be, together with all those who pervert justice (vv. 20–21)" (Kelley, "Isaiah," 275). The essence of the message is that God would redeem the futile political wrangling of Israel's leaders that had led to frustration.

As the result of their political strategy, Judah's leaders had turned things upside down. God, however, would one day redeem everything exclusively according to His plans and by His power. The devastated land would become a paradise, the disabled would be healed, and the outcasts would be enriched and rejoice in the Lord. There would be no more scoffers or ruthless people practicing injustice in the courts. The founders of the nation, Abraham and Jacob, would see their many descendants all glorifying the Lord. Those who had been ignored—such as the needy and humble—would know rejoicing. On the other hand, the enemies of the humble and needy, the scoffers and arrogant, would be eliminated (vv. 20–21).

Kelley writes of verse 22–24: "Verses 22–24 describe the inner transformation that will take place among the people of Israel in the age to come. Jacob's shame and dismay will end when he sees his children, the work of God's hands, gathered around him. In that day, they will sanctify the Holy One of Jacob and stand in awe of the God of Israel. Even the confused in mind and the rebellious among them will come to an understanding of the meaning of true religion" (Kelley, "Isaiah," 275). The historical context of this, of course, was the Assyrian invasion under Sennacherib.

Despite the attempts Israel had taken to protect itself by its humanly inspired plans, the Lord had His own plans that would bring Him glory, both in that historical context and beyond. The attitude of the people of Jerusalem and Judah would completely change. The Lord promised Israel that, "No longer will Jacob be ashamed; no longer will their faces grow pale [from fear]." (v. 22, NIV). As their children grew up in safety, they would realize God had protected and generously blessed them. They would respond by standing in awe of Him. That is, they would worship Him. The Lord's delivering them from Sennacherib was a foretaste of the ultimate deliverance they would experience. People who were wayward and who complained would change and accept instruction (29:18). An inner change among the people would lead to a change of attitudes and behavior (v. 24).

The Lesson Applied

"Trust in the Lord with all your heart; do not depend on your own understanding. Seek his will in all you do, and he will show you which path to take. Don't be impressed with your own wisdom. Instead, fear the Lord and turn away from evil. Then you will have healing for your body and strength for your bones." So instructed the wisdom writer in Proverbs 3:5–8 (NLT) for those who desire to be wise and who want a meaningful and contented life. To trust in the Lord wholeheartedly means one should not rely or depend on one's understanding because human insights are never enough. God's ways are incomprehensible (Isa. 55:8–9; Rom. 11:33–34). All the wisdom a person may acquire never can replace the need for full trust in God's superior ways. *Heart* in Hebrew refers to one's emotions (Prov. 12:25; 13:12; 14:10, 13) but more often to a person's intellect—such as understanding (Prov. 10:8), discernment (15:14), reflection (15:28), or will (5:12). People who acquire wisdom always must remember they did not become wise by themselves. Wisdom comes from God (2:6). This reminder is similar to Proverbs 3:5. A heart awareness of and proper response to God help prevent the evil of pride. As a result, God gives health and vigor (4:22). Health in one's bones is mentioned several times in Proverbs (3:8; 12:4; 14:30; 15:30; 16:24; 17:22). This suggests, as is well known today, spiritual and physical health are related.

All this is to say that as Judah in Isaiah's day learned, it is equally true today: Those who know peace, contentment, and authentic prosperity are those who follow God's instructions. Following results in reverence for Him that produces both obedience and authentic worship toward Him.

Let's Talk About It

What are some reasons, like the leaders of Judah, God's people sometimes think they can hide things from God?

Because we are clever, we forget God sees beyond our actions. We forget God looks at our motives as they are revealed in the heart. We have been also been convinced by Satan that God only uses human beings as pawns for His own good. But when we come to see God as God, we respect Him as Creator and Lord of all.

Home Daily Devotional Readings
May 10–16, 2021

Monday	Tuesday	Wednesday	Thursday	Friday	Saturday	Sunday
Apostles Speak Truth to Council	Prophet Jeremiah Is Arrested and Imprisoned	Ebed-Melech's Trust in Jeremiah Honored	Jeremiah Reaffirms Prophecy of Zedekiah	Jeremiah's Last Days in Jerusalem	Jerusalem Destroyed; People Exiled	Zedekiah Must Submit to Babylonian Conquest
Acts 4:13–22	Jeremiah 37:11–16	Jeremiah 38:7–13; 39:15–18	Jeremiah 37:17–21	Jeremiah 38:24–28	2 Kings 25:1–12	Jeremiah 38:14–23

JEREMIAH: THE SUFFERING PREACHER OF DOOM

TOPIC:
THE CONSEQUENCES OF GIVING CHALLENGING ADVICE

BACKGROUND SCRIPTURE:
JEREMIAH 37–38

JEREMIAH 38:14–23

King James Version

THEN Zedekiah the king sent, and took Jeremiah the prophet unto him into the third entry that is in the house of the LORD: and the king said unto Jeremiah, I will ask thee a thing; hide nothing from me.
15 Then Jeremiah said unto Zedekiah, If I declare it unto thee, wilt thou not surely put me to death? and if I give thee counsel, wilt thou not hearken unto me?
16 So Zedekiah the king sware secretly unto Jeremiah, saying, As the LORD liveth, that made us this soul, I will not put thee to death, neither will I give thee into the hand of these men that seek thy life.
17 Then said Jeremiah unto Zedekiah, Thus saith the LORD, the God of hosts, the God of Israel; If thou wilt assuredly go forth unto the king of Babylon's princes, then thy soul shall live, and this city shall not be burned with fire; and thou shalt live, and thine house:
18 But if thou wilt not go forth to the king of Babylon's princes, then shall this city be given into the hand of the Chaldeans, and they shall burn it with fire, and thou shalt not escape out of their hand.
19 And Zedekiah the king said unto Jeremiah, I am afraid of the Jews that are fallen to the Chaldeans, lest they deliver me into their hand, and they mock me.
20 But Jeremiah said, They shall not deliver thee. Obey, I beseech thee, the voice of the LORD, which I speak unto thee: so it shall be well unto thee, and thy soul shall live.

New Revised Standard Version

KING Zedekiah sent for the prophet Jeremiah and received him at the third entrance of the temple of the LORD. The king said to Jeremiah, "I have something to ask you; do not hide anything from me."
15 Jeremiah said to Zedekiah, "If I tell you, you will put me to death, will you not? And if I give you advice, you will not listen to me."
16 So King Zedekiah swore an oath in secret to Jeremiah, "As the LORD lives, who gave us our lives, I will not put you to death or hand you over to these men who seek your life."
17 Then Jeremiah said to Zedekiah, "Thus says the LORD, the God of hosts, the God of Israel, If you will only surrender to the officials of the king of Babylon, then your life shall be spared, and this city shall not be burned with fire, and you and your house shall live.
18 But if you do not surrender to the officials of the king of Babylon, then this city shall be handed over to the Chaldeans, and they shall burn it with fire, and you yourself shall not escape from their hand."
19 King Zedekiah said to Jeremiah, "I am afraid of the Judeans who have deserted to the Chaldeans, for I might be handed over to them and they would abuse me."
20 Jeremiah said, "That will not happen. Just obey the voice of the LORD in what I say to you, and it shall go well with you, and your life shall be spared.

MAIN THOUGHT: Then Jeremiah said unto Zedekiah, If I declare it unto thee, wilt thou not surely put me to death? and if I give thee counsel, wilt thou not hearken unto me? (Jeremiah 38:15, KJV)

Jeremiah 38:14–23

King James Version	*New Revised Standard Version*
21 But if thou refuse to go forth, this is the word that the Lord hath shewed me:	**21 But if you are determined not to surrender, this is what the Lord has shown me—**
22 And, behold, all the women that are left in the king of Judah's house shall be brought forth to the king of Babylon's princes, and those women shall say, Thy friends have set thee on, and have prevailed against thee: thy feet are sunk in the mire, and they are turned away back.	**22 a vision of all the women remaining in the house of the king of Judah being led out to the officials of the king of Babylon and saying, 'Your trusted friends have seduced you and have overcome you; Now that your feet are stuck in the mud, they desert you.'**
23 So they shall bring out all thy wives and thy children to the Chaldeans: and thou shalt not escape out of their hand, but shalt be taken by the hand of the king of Babylon: and thou shalt cause this city to be burned with fire.	**23 All your wives and your children shall be led out to the Chaldeans, and you yourself shall not escape from their hand, but shall be seized by the king of Babylon; and this city shall be burned with fire."**

LESSON SETTING

Time: 587/86 B.C.
Place: Southern Kingdom (Judah)

LESSON OUTLINE

I. The Prophet Jeremiah Persecuted (Jeremiah 38:14–16)

II. The Prophet Jeremiah's Proclamation (Jeremiah 38:17–18)

III. The King's Response to the Prophet's Message (Jeremiah 38:19–23)

Unifying Principle

No one wants to be the bearer of bad news or challenging advice. How can we find courage to speak when what we have to say is likely to cause controversy or hard feelings? Jeremiah frankly discussed his concerns with King Zedekiah and then spoke with confidence that he was delivering a message from God.

Introduction

The name *Jeremiah* means "may Yahweh lift up." The Scriptures contain more personal information regarding Jeremiah than any other prophet. He was the son of Hilkiah, a priest from Anathoth, about three miles northeast of Jerusalem in the hill country of Benjamin (Jer 1:1). He was called to be a prophet in the thirteenth year of King Josiah, *circa* 627 B.C. (Jer. 1:2; 25:3; 36:2). Since his ministry extended from 626 to 586 B.C., Jeremiah was a contemporary of Zephaniah, Ezekiel, and Habakkuk.

Jeremiah's ministry occurred in a critical time in the history of the ancient Middle East. Upon the death of Josiah, the king of Judah, at the hands of the Egyptian army, Judah became subject to Egypt and its ruler Pharaoh Necho. The people of Judah chose Jehoahaz to succeed Josiah. Three months later, however, Necho appointed Jehoiakim (Eliakim) to rule as his vassal on the throne in Jerusalem. Having lost their freedom, the people of Judah forsook God and worshiped the idols they had worshiped in the days of Manasseh and Amon. This idolatry, Jeremiah proclaimed, was the reason for God's judgment.

In 605 B.C. Nebuchadnezzar defeated Pharaoh Necho at Carchemish, and Jehoiakim immediately submitted to the Babylonian king, who permitted him to remain on the throne as a vassal. Three years later, Jehoiakim rebelled against Nebuchadnezzar and was deposed (2 Kings 24:1–2). Jehoiachin replaced Jehoiakim on the throne for a brief period, but he was then exiled to Babylon by Nebuchadnezzar. Thousands of political and religious leaders were carried to Babylon with Jehoiachin in 597 B.C. (2 Kings 24:14–16).

Nebuchadnezzar made Zedekiah, Jehoiakim's brother, the new ruler of Judah. In 589 B.C., Zedekiah led a rebellion against Babylon, an action that brought a quick response from Nebuchadnezzar. His army entered Judah and destroyed all resisting fortified settlements. Nebuchadnezzar's army turned aside from besieging Jerusalem when the Egyptian army appeared in southwest Palestine in the summer of 588 B.C. When the Egyptians soon withdrew, Nebuchadnezzar resumed his siege. Several times during the siege of Jerusalem, Zedekiah consulted Jeremiah for counsel from the Lord. Though the prophet advised him to surrender, Zedekiah would not listen.

In the fourth month of 586 B.C., Jerusalem's walls were breached. One month later, the temple was burned, along with the palaces, houses, and other administrative buildings. An additional 4,600 of Jerusalem's residents were deported to Babylon.

Shortly after the destruction of Jerusalem by the Babylonians, Jeremiah, who had been imprisoned by Zedekiah, was released. Jeremiah then moved to Mizpah, the capital for Gedaliah, whom Nebuchadnezzar had appointed as the Jewish governor of the Babylonian province of Judah (Jer. 40:1–6). When Gedaliah was assassinated after only two months in office (41:1–3), Jeremiah was forcibly deported to Egypt by Jewish officers who had survived the catastrophes (42:1–43:7). In Egypt, he continued to preach oracles against the Egyptians (43:8–13) as well as against his own people (44:1–30).

The book of Jeremiah contains oracles, prose, sermons, laments, confessions, prayers, and dialogues. According to Jeremiah 36, Baruch, Jeremiah's scribe (secretary), wrote most of the book at the dictation of the prophet. This scroll was destroyed by Jehoiakim, but Jeremiah dictated a second, enlarged edition.

Jeremiah emphasized the provisions of the covenant between God and Israel. The covenant bound Israel to God in a special relationship of love, faithfulness, and hope. The covenant involved both privilege and responsibility. Faithfulness to the Lord and the covenant would bring blessing; disobedience would result in punishment, destruction, and exile (Deut 27:11–28:68). Jeremiah summoned the people to obey the words of the covenant and to turn from their idolatry and their unjust treatment of one another (Jer. 11:6–7). Contrary to the expectations of the religious and political authorities, and because of their apostasy, Judah and Jerusalem would experience the destruction of Jerusalem and deportation. Nevertheless, the experience of judgment was not God's last word. God promised to bring the people back from captivity and restore them to blessing (30:1–31:25). Israel's enemies would be defeated, and the people would sing joyfully of God's goodness.

Jeremiah personally suffered criticism, persecution, rejection, imprisonment, and placement in a muddy cistern where he was left to die. All this was because of his uncompromising proclamation of an unpopular yet divinely directed message of doom. The events of this lesson occurred *circa* 587/86 B.C., or just prior to that time, when the ever-increasing threat of Babylonian invasion became imminent. That invasion happened within a few months of the close of the chapter under discussion.

Exposition

I. The Prophet Jeremiah Persecuted (Jeremiah 38:14–16)

Today's lesson is the final of four pivotal encounters between the prophet Jeremiah and Judah's king, Zedekiah. A brief summary of the other encounters are helpful in understanding the current passage. Jeremiah's experience of persecution emerged from his prophetic preaching regarding the impending invasion by Babylon (the Chaldeans). Zedekiah, his court prophets, political advisers, and the general population of Judah had placed great confidence in the presence of and temporary military alliance with Egypt. In obedience to God's prompting of his message, Jeremiah declared something radically different: "Then the word of the LORD came to Jeremiah the prophet: 'This is what the LORD, the God of Israel, says: Tell the king of Judah, who sent you to inquire of me, "Pharaoh's army, which has marched out to support you, will go back to its own land, to Egypt. Then the Babylonians will return and attack this city; they will capture it and burn it down"'" (Jer. 37:6–8, NIV). He further warned that any withdrawal of Babylon would only be temporary. They would regroup and resume the attack against Jerusalem, eventually sacking and destroying the city.

As Jeremiah was leaving Jerusalem for Anathoth to receive his share of property there, the captain of the guard had Jeremiah arrested under the false accusation of desertion to the Babylonians. He was subsequently held in the house of Jonathan the secretary, which had been converted into a temporary prison. His overall circumstances were worsened by the fickleness and indecisiveness of King Zedekiah. Due to his concern over the opinion of his advisers, the king would not consult Jeremiah directly, even when he desperately wanted the prophet to pray for Judah (37:3). The messenger Zedekiah sent to request prayer, Jehucal, eventually urged the king to have Jeremiah killed (38:1, 4). Following Jeremiah's imprisonment (37:15–16), the king perceived an opportunity to consult Jeremiah directly and privately. Having brought Jeremiah to the palace, the king asked, "Is there any word from the LORD?" (37:17, NIV). The prophet gave him an immediate answer: The king would be handed over to the king of Babylon. Why say more? Jeremiah already had declared God's message many times only to see the message rejected. Jeremiah also exposed the false prophets as such during this encounter.

Infuriated because Jeremiah's words were hurting the war effort, four of Zedekiah's officials urged the king to kill the prophet. They accused Jeremiah of not seeking the welfare of the people, despite obvious evidence the welfare of the people was that to which he had dedicated his life. In his typical vacillation, Zedekiah conceded to Jeremiah's conspirators (38:5). Rather than killing Jeremiah, an act of shedding innocent blood, they imprisoned him in an old cistern, where he sank in the mire at the bottom. They hoped the prophet eventually would be forgotten there and die. God, however, provided a deliverer in the person of Ebed-Melech ("servant of the king), a man from Ethiopia.

Following his rescue from the abandoned cistern, the stage was set for the final encounter between Jeremiah and Zedekiah. The Old Testament interpreter James L. Green describes the setting of that encounter: "Zedekiah was now in deep distress. The siege was one of the most horrible in history, had lasted a long time. Provisions were low. People were dying of disease and starvation. Some were deserting. The king was desperate. He sent for Jeremiah" (Green, "Jeremiah," 172). As concerned as ever about the opinion of his court advisers, Zedekiah conducted the secret meeting in the third entrance to the temple of the Lord. This most likely was the king's private entrance to the temple. From the tone of the conversation and Zedekiah's requests that followed, it is evident he was seeking any vestige of hope. Zedekiah indicated he was going to ask Jeremiah something. And he indicated he wanted a candid response—full disclosure (38:14). This clearly placed Jeremiah in an awkward set of circumstances. Therefore, Jeremiah voiced two objections. First, if he answered with a message the king did not want to hear, there was no guarantee the king would not kill him. Second, any counsel Jeremiah gave likely was wasted because the king would not listen to him (38:15).

II. The Prophet Jeremiah's Proclamation (Jeremiah 38:17–18)

Again, as before, Jeremiah's message was a message from the Lord Himself, as verse 17 (NLT) indicates: "Then Jeremiah said to Zedekiah, 'This is what the Lord God of Heaven's Armies, the God of Israel, says: "If you surrender to the Babylonian officers, you and your family will live, and the city will not be burned down."'" The word of Yahweh, the Lord of the covenant with Israel, is superior to that of any and all other advisers or commanders.

In effect, Zedekiah inquired as he had earlier, "Is there any word from the Lord?" In reality, however, he actually sought a new word from the Lord. The only way for the lives of Zedekiah, his family, and the city to be spared was unconditional surrender to the Babylonians. Otherwise, the city would be captured and burned and Zedekiah would be killed (21:1–10; 37:17; 38:1–3).

III. The King's Response to the Prophet's Message (Jeremiah 38:19–23)

Heretofore, King Zedekiah had been known for indecisiveness and vacillation. He was much concerned that should he surrender, the Babylonians would hand him over to the Israelites who had already defected—surrendered to the Babylonians—and they would victimize him (38:19). Jeremiah reassured him such would not be the case. He then offered one fretful and final opportunity to Zedekiah: "You won't be handed over to them if you choose to obey the LORD. Your life will be spared, and all will go well for you" (38:20, NLT).

Zedekiah's compliance with the message of Jeremiah would bring deliverance to Zedekiah, the city, and the people and would avoid the Exile. Should he disobey, there would be negative and punitive consequences.

The Lesson Applied

Several requirements are placed upon the spokesperson of God. One is that the spokesperson of God must be motivated by an unmistakable sense of God's calling to such on his or her life. Despite his objections of his youth and/or inexperience, Jeremiah nonetheless overcame those due to the compelling calling of God on him. Similar experiences occurred to other Old Testament servants and prophets: Noah, Abraham, Moses, Gideon, Ezekiel, Isaiah, Amos and Hosea. The same is reflected in the New Testament in the experience of the Apostles and Paul. One's authority—the right to speak for God—is authenticated in one's calling by God.

The willingness to proclaim the message from God precisely as it is received is another requirement of the Lord's spokespeople. The message is not the message of the bearer of the message. It is the message of the sender, God Himself. Closely associated with this is the willingness to contend with the response of the hearers to the message. Sometimes the response will be positive. The hearers will be cordial and receptive to the message and messenger. At other times, the hearers will be uncordial, even hostile to the message and messenger. There might be attempts to discredit the messenger or even attempts to victimize him or her in some way. Still, the messenger must remain faithful to the task. Ultimately, the servant of the Lord must entrust all to the Lord.

Let's Talk About It

How would you characterize the contemporary climate in which God's servants must do their work for Him?

It is characterized by broad skepticism, subjectivism, and relativism; a general suspicion of reason; and an acute sensitivity to the role of ideology in asserting and maintaining political and economic power. People refuse to adhere to sound doctrine.

Home Daily Devotional Readings
May 17–23, 2021

Monday	Tuesday	Wednesday	Thursday	Friday	Saturday	Sunday
Treat Each Other Fairly	Taking Personal Responsibility	The Child Who Sins Suffers Punishment	The Righteous Child Is Rewarded	All Are Accountable for Their Sins	God Is Compassionate and Fair	Repent and Live Righteous Lives
Deuteronomy 24:14–18	Jeremiah 31:27–30	Ezekiel 18:10–13	Ezekiel 18:14–18	Ezekiel 18:19–24	Ezekiel 18:25–29	Ezekiel 18:1–9, 30–32

EZEKIEL: STREET PREACHER TO THE EXILES

TOPIC:
TAKE RESPONSIBILITY!

BACKGROUND SCRIPTURE:
EZEKIEL 18

EZEKIEL 18:1–9, 30–32

King James Version

THE word of the LORD came unto me again, saying,
2 What mean ye, that ye use this proverb concerning the land of Israel, saying, The fathers have eaten sour grapes, and the children's teeth are set on edge?
3 As I live, saith the Lord GOD, ye shall not have occasion any more to use this proverb in Israel.
4 Behold, all souls are mine; as the soul of the father, so also the soul of the son is mine: the soul that sinneth, it shall die.
5 But if a man be just, and do that which is lawful and right,
6 And hath not eaten upon the mountains, neither hath lifted up his eyes to the idols of the house of Israel, neither hath defiled his neighbour's wife, neither hath come near to a menstruous woman,
7 And hath not oppressed any, but hath restored to the debtor his pledge, hath spoiled none by violence, hath given his bread to the hungry, and hath covered the naked with a garment;
8 He that hath not given forth upon usury, neither hath taken any increase, that hath withdrawn his hand from iniquity, hath executed true judgment between man and man,
9 Hath walked in my statutes, and hath kept my judgments, to deal truly; he is just, he shall surely live, saith the Lord GOD.

New Revised Standard Version

THE word of the LORD came to me:

2 What do you mean by repeating this proverb concerning the land of Israel, "The parents have eaten sour grapes, and the children's teeth are set on edge"?
3 As I live, says the Lord GOD, this proverb shall no more be used by you in Israel.

4 Know that all lives are mine; the life of the parent as well as the life of the child is mine: it is only the person who sins that shall die.
5 If a man is righteous and does what is lawful and right—
6 if he does not eat upon the mountains or lift up his eyes to the idols of the house of Israel, does not defile his neighbor's wife or approach a woman during her menstrual period,

7 does not oppress anyone, but restores to the debtor his pledge, commits no robbery, gives his bread to the hungry and covers the naked with a garment,

8 does not take advance or accrued interest, withholds his hand from iniquity, executes true justice between contending parties,

9 follows my statutes, and is careful to observe my ordinances, acting faithfully—such a one is righteous; he shall surely live, says the Lord GOD.

MAIN THOUGHT: Behold, all souls are mine; as the soul of the father, so also the soul of the son is mine: the soul that sinneth, it shall die. (Ezekiel 18:4, KJV)

Ezekiel 18:1–9, 30–32

King James Version	*New Revised Standard Version*
• • • • • •	• • • • • •
30 Therefore I will judge you, O house of Israel, every one according to his ways, saith the Lord God. Repent, and turn yourselves from all your transgressions; so iniquity shall not be your ruin.	**30 Therefore I will judge you, O house of Israel, all of you according to your ways, says the Lord God. Repent and turn from all your transgressions; otherwise iniquity will be your ruin.**
31 Cast away from you all your transgressions, whereby ye have transgressed; and make you a new heart and a new spirit: for why will ye die, O house of Israel?	**31 Cast away from you all the transgressions that you have committed against me, and get yourselves a new heart and a new spirit! Why will you die, O house of Israel?**
32 For I have no pleasure in the death of him that dieth, saith the Lord God: wherefore turn yourselves, and live ye.	**32 For I have no pleasure in the death of anyone, says the Lord God. Turn, then, and live.**

LESSON SETTING

Time: *circa* 592–572 B.C.
Place: Babylon

LESSON OUTLINE

I. Retribution for Sin Comes to the Individual Sinner (Ezekiel 18:1–4)

II. Illustration: The Righteous Man (Ezekiel 18:5–9)

III. Divine Summons to Repentance (Ezekiel 18:30–32)

Unifying Principle

It is easy to blame our background or upbringing for the misfortunes we face. What is the role of personal responsibility? Ezekiel warned Israel that each person would answer for his or her own behavior and that all must repent of their sinful ways and obey God's commands to find favor with God.

Introduction

Ezekiel, the son of Buzi, whose name means "God will strengthen," was a prophet-priest of the sixth century B.C. In 597 B.C., he was taken captive during the first deportation to Babylon. King Nebuchadnezzar of Babylon deported King Jehoiachin, Ezekiel, and ten thousand others, including political and military leaders and skilled craftsmen (2 Kings 24:14–16). He lived in his own house at Tel-Abib near the river Chebar, which was an irrigation canal that channeled the waters of the Euphrates River into the surrounding arid region.

The prophet indicated his call in 593 B.C. was his thirtieth year, which probably indicated Ezekiel's age (Ezek. 1:1). It has, however, been interpreted in other ways: thirty years since the discovery of the Law book in 622 B.C.; thirty years since Jehoiachin's imprisonment; or a system of Babylonian chronology. Ezekiel was married, though there is scant additional information regarding his family life. His wife died suddenly during the siege of Jerusalem (24:15–18). Ezekiel continued to preach until about 571 B.C. (29:17). Ezekiel's ministry was one of diverse messages. Between 593 and 587 B.C., his ministry was characterized by warnings of impending judgment on Judah and Jerusalem. Messages of encouragement and hope for the future characterized his ministry from 587 B.C. to 571 B.C. The final year of his ministry contained a message on God's coming judgment upon Egypt at the hand of Babylon's King Nebuchadnezzar.

Ezekiel's ministry spanned some twenty-two years. The book bearing his name contains four clearly discernible periods of Babylonian-Judean history during which Ezekiel ministered.

Little is known about the end of Ezekiel's life. From an ancient Jewish tradition comes the belief that some of his own people killed him because his preaching was objectionable. In Kifl, south of ancient Babylon (now Iraq), a tomb is purported to be that of Ezekiel's. The dynamic, post-exilic prophet, whose ministry was characterized by dramatic portrayal of messages, visions, confrontational proclamation, and mysticism, rightfully holds a place as a premier prophet-priest in the Judeo-Christian tradition.

According to the chronological analysis suggested above, Ezekiel 18 belongs to the first period of the prophet's ministry, 593–588 B.C. Textually, Ezekiel 18 is a self-contained unit whose exclusive topic is individual responsibility for one's sins. Ezekiel boldly challenged conventional thinking about accountability for sin that had endured from Mosaic times. Ezekiel 18:1–4 sets the thesis that retribution for sin rests on the individual sinner. Verses 5–29 advance the notion that proofs of righteousness are discernible. This concept is supported by four major patterns of thought. Verses 5–9 present the first generation experience of sin and accountability, based upon the portrayal of a righteous man. Verses 10–13, the second generation, portrays a sinful son of a righteous man. The third illustration of the third generation, contained in 18:14–18, presents the righteous son of a wicked father. Elaboration on the main motif appears in verses 19–20. Ezekiel 18 concludes in verses 21–32 with the corollary to individual accountability for sin—individual redemption from sin.

Exposition

I. Retribution for Sin Comes to the Individual Sinner (Ezekiel 18:1–4)

The rhetorical style of Ezekiel 18 and much of the entire book of Ezekiel is something of a point-counterpoint approach. The prophet frequently engaged the prevalent and popular theology based on the theological roots of some concepts or the interpretation of them. He often cited these in a quotation and then proceeded to clarify and/or correct the erroneous incomplete interpretation. The people of Judah in Ezekiel's time sought answers or an explanation for their historical circumstances.

Judah sought an explanation in the sins of their ancestors, as reflected in the Lord's inquiry in 18:2. They questioned why righteous sons did not share in the guilt of the fathers (18:19). They questioned the justice of God while ignoring it was their own ways that were unjust, as in 18:25, 29.

The popular proverb about subsequent generations paying a price for the sins of the ancestors was a hermeneutical error. It was a faulty interpretation of a principle the Lord gave Israel in the days of Moses.

Their thinking was influenced by Exodus 20:5 and Numbers 14:18. Similar passages such as Exodus 34:6–7 and Deuteronomy 7:9–10 also were construed to explain current misfortunes on the basis of previous generations' sins.

Ezekiel challenged Judah's notions of one's negative circumstances or one's misfortunes resulting from the sins of previous generations. However, he did so strictly on the authority of God. He prefaced his challenge of the popular proverb about the children's teeth being set on edge by the sour grapes consumed by the fathers by saying: "The word of the LORD came to me" (Ezek. 18:1, NRSV).

"Know that all lives are mine; the life of the parent as well as the life of the child is mine: it is only the person who sins that shall die" (18:4, NRSV). Ezekiel's words in this text were a startling message on the theological landscape of post-exilic Judah.

None in his congregation would challenge the first proposition of his text. That Yahweh was the Creator-Owner of the cosmos was not debated among the Jews. Their book of beginnings, Genesis, had as its initial affirmation: "In the beginning God created the heavens and the earth" (Gen. 1:1, NIV). Frequent references to Yahweh as Creator appear throughout the sacred Scriptures of Israel (Pss. 8:3; 33:6, 9; 89:11–12; 96:5; 102:25; 104:24–25, 30; Isa. 37:16; 40:26, 28; 42:5; Jer. 10:12; 32:17). The writers of the New Testament also conveyed this crucial theological concept (Rom. 11:36; 1 Cor. 8:6; Eph. 3:9; Col. 1:16–17).

Moreover, none in Ezekiel's audience would challenge the concept that humanity owed its origins to Yahweh (Job 10:8–12; 35:10; Pss. 95:6; 100:3; 149:2; Isa. 64:8; Acts 17:26, 28–29; Eph. 2:10).

For the most part, Israel would have no quarrel with the second proposition of Ezekiel's message: The soul who sins is the one who will die. The interpreter of the passage must not isolate the verse from its context. Verse 4 stands as the bold proclamation of individual accountability for sin. Yet it also stands as a rejection of the doctrine of Israel proverbially expressed in Ezekiel 18:1–3. Yahweh Himself challenged the conventional wisdom in Israel regarding accountability for sin (18:2).

The Hebrew term translated as *set on edge* literally signifies something made dull (Eccl. 10:10). But it also can refer to a sour sensation. The point of the proverb is clear: Just as eating sour grapes produces a bitter taste, children are affected by their parents' behavioral choices. The truth of the proverb is yet intact. Judah, however, interpreted and applied this proverb incorrectly. Therefore, God said they should cease using it.

What was their hermeneutical error? Ezekiel's contemporaries actually were suffering the consequences of a history of rebellion against God. Rather than make the connection between *their own* spiritual unfaithfulness and their calamities, they resorted to blaming their ancestors for their circumstances. The bitter proverb about sour grapes and teeth set on edge became something of a slogan of resentment in the early post-exilic times.

Ezekiel actually clarified the matter of accountability. The person who sins will die (here, the physical consequences of sin per Ezek. 3:16–21; 33:12–20; Deut. 30:15–20). One will not die for the sins of another, but for her or his own sin. Guilt and accountability for sin is no more transferrable from one person to another than righteousness is (Ezek. 14:12–20).

II. Illustration: The Righteous Man (Ezekiel 18:5–9)

Ezekiel 18:5–29 constitutes a second major section of the entire chapter. The exegete John T. Bunn discusses the section under the heading, "Proofs of Righteousness are Discernable." He suggests the following method of approach to the interpretation of Ezekiel's message here. "As a method of setting forth this new idea Ezekiel uses three illustrations: that of the righteous man (vv. 5–9), that of the sinful son of the righteous man (vv. 10–13), and that of the righteous son of the wicked father (vv. 14–18). This is cast in the guise of hypothetical succeeding generations in the same family in order to combat the [misinterpreted] concept of Exodus 20:5 and 34:7. It is the intent of this teaching to eradicate forever an erroneous belief historically perpetuated in Israel (v. 3)" (Bunn, "Ezekiel," 282).

Ezekiel's message and the original intention of God's message to Israel was expressed clearly: "Suppose there is a righteous man who does what is just and right. … That man is righteous; he will surely live, declares the Sovereign Lord" (Ezek. 18:5a, 9b, NIV). The hypothetical individual under discussion here is, of course, a loyal Israelite who kept God's law and therefore was just and would not die because of sin. Death is frequently mentioned in this chapter (vv. 4, 13, 17–18, 20–21, 23–24, 26, 28, 32) and refers to physical death and not necessarily eternal punishment. Nonetheless, any Jew who did not express saving faith in the Lord would not be accepted by Him.

In portraying the righteous man, Ezekiel cited eight negative offenses along with eight positive characteristics. Among the negative behaviors the righteous man avoided were attending idol feasts in the mountains and worshiping idols in Israel. He did not commit adultery or incur ritual uncleanness during sex. He did not exploit people he had made loans to or exploit the poor. He did not lend with (high) interest rates or by demanding a profit (Exod. 22:25; 23:1–3, 6–8; Lev. 19:15, 35; 25:35–37).

On the positive side, he fed the hungry and clothed the naked (Deut. 15:7–11; Isa. 58:7; Matt. 25:35ff). He returned a debtor's pledge (Exod. 22:25–40). He lived justly and promoted justice. He lived by God's statutes, obeyed His ordinances, and lived with integrity. "Only when one is meticulous or careful, with the Hebrew reading v.9 'to deal truly,' can he be righteous. No halfhearted partial allegiance to the law will avail; it involves full commitment to the law" (Bunn, "Ezekiel," 282).

III. Divine Summons to Repentance (Ezekiel 18:30–32)

Based on the truths proclaimed above about the redemptive character of Yahweh and the insistence upon each person's accountability, Ezekiel's emphasis on repentance in this section should be expected. The power of these verses is well summarized by the Old Testament scholar John T. Bunn: "Yahweh has no desire to see even one of Israel condemned. Therefore a call to legalistic repentance, promise, and hope is extended. The condition which had created the inevitability of judgment was an attitude of rebellion against the law. Only repentance and return to the law would save life" (Bunn, "Ezekiel," 282).

Inherent in the experience of God's redemption is the requirement of repentance. *Shuv* (or *shub*), the Hebrew term for *repent*, connotes feelings of regret or a change of mind. In this sense, the term is applied to God in the Old Testament (Gen. 6:6–7; 1 Sam. 15:11, 35; Exod. 32:14). When applied to human beings, *shuv* most often denotes change of direction in one's behaviors or beliefs to the ways of God.

The call to repentance permeates Ezekiel 18:30–32, though it is variously expressed. The concept appears twice in verse 30: "Repent! Turn away from all your offenses; then sin will not be your downfall" (NIV). It appears twice in verse 31: "Rid yourselves of all the offenses you have committed, and get a new heart and a new spirit" (NIV). The passage concludes with the imperative to repent. That is balanced by the result of repentance—life. This concept also occurs in the pages of New Testament (2 Pet. 3:9).

The Lesson Applied

No individual ultimately is condemned or redeemed on the basis of someone else's behavior. In the Old Testament, Ezekiel declared: "The one who sins is the one who will die. … The righteousness of the righteous will be credited to them, and the wickedness of the wicked will be charged against them" (Ezek. 18:20, NIV). The accountability of each person is just as clearly declared in the New Testament. In fact, every instance of it there is gathered up in the familiar text of John 3:16–18.

From a sociological perspective, human beings live in community with other people. From a Christian theological perspective, believers are in a covenant relationship with each other. Every person is *affected* by the actions of others. Yet one is not *accountable* for the actions of others. Each person exclusively is accountable to God for his or her own behaviors.

Let's Talk About It

How do you explain the human tendency to blame others for one's plight?

Blaming others for our misdeeds and the consequences thereof is almost as old as creation itself. When the first parents sinned in the garden, they blamed each other and even the serpent. God did not fall for it. He dealt with each party for their trespass against Him. Rest assured we are responsible for our own individual failure to adhere to the Word of God. Each person is accountable for his/her own sins.

Home Daily Devotional Readings
May 24–30, 2021

Monday	Tuesday	Wednesday	Thursday	Friday	Saturday	Sunday
Jonah's Experience Foreshadows Christ's	Nineveh's Repentance: A Lasting Message	Jonah Turns Away from God's Call	Sailors Make Vows to the Lord	Jonah Resents God's Grace Toward Others	God's Compassion Overrides Jonah's Personal Comfort	God's Mercy Prevails
Matthew 12:38–42	Luke 11:29–32	Jonah 1:1–12	Jonah 1:13–16	Jonah 4:1–5	Jonah 4:6–11	Jonah 3

JONAH: FIERY HARBINGER OF DOOM

TOPIC:
CHANGING FOR THE BETTER

BACKGROUND SCRIPTURE:
JONAH 3

JONAH 3

King James Version

AND the word of the LORD came unto Jonah the second time, saying,
2 Arise, go unto Nineveh, that great city, and preach unto it the preaching that I bid thee.
3 So Jonah arose, and went unto Nineveh, according to the word of the LORD. Now Nineveh was an exceeding great city of three days' journey.
4 And Jonah began to enter into the city a day's journey, and he cried, and said, Yet forty days, and Nineveh shall be overthrown.
5 So the people of Nineveh believed God, and proclaimed a fast, and put on sackcloth, from the greatest of them even to the least of them.
6 For word came unto the king of Nineveh, and he arose from his throne, and he laid his robe from him, and covered him with sackcloth, and sat in ashes.
7 And he caused it to be proclaimed and published through Nineveh by the decree of the king and his nobles, saying, Let neither man nor beast, herd nor flock, taste any thing: let them not feed, nor drink water:
8 But let man and beast be covered with sackcloth, and cry mightily unto God: yea, let them turn every one from his evil way, and from the violence that is in their hands.
9 Who can tell if God will turn and repent, and turn away from his fierce anger, that we perish not?
10 And God saw their works, that they turned from their evil way; and God repented of the

New Revised Standard Version

THE word of the LORD came to Jonah a second time, saying,
2 "Get up, go to Nineveh, that great city, and proclaim to it the message that I tell you."
3 So Jonah set out and went to Nineveh, according to the word of the LORD. Now Nineveh was an exceedingly large city, a three days' walk across.
4 Jonah began to go into the city, going a day's walk. And he cried out, "Forty days more, and Nineveh shall be overthrown!"
5 And the people of Nineveh believed God; they proclaimed a fast, and everyone, great and small, put on sackcloth.
6 When the news reached the king of Nineveh, he rose from his throne, removed his robe, covered himself with sackcloth, and sat in ashes.
7 Then he had a proclamation made in Nineveh: "By the decree of the king and his nobles: No human being or animal, no herd or flock, shall taste anything. They shall not feed, nor shall they drink water.
8 Human beings and animals shall be covered with sackcloth, and they shall cry mightily to God. All shall turn from their evil ways and from the violence that is in their hands.
9 Who knows? God may relent and change his mind; he may turn from his fierce anger, so that we do not perish."
10 When God saw what they did, how they turned from their evil ways, God changed his

MAIN THOUGHT: And God saw their works, that they turned from their evil way; and God repented of the evil, that he had said that he would do unto them; and he did it not. (Jonah 3:10, KJV)

King James Version	*New Revised Standard Version*
evil, that he had said that he would do unto them; and he did it not.	**mind about the calamity that he had said he would bring upon them; and he did not do it.**

LESSON SETTING

Time: Eighth Century (700s) B.C. or *circa* 400 B.C.
Place: Nineveh

LESSON OUTLINE

I. Jonah Obeys the Lord's Call (Jonah 3:1–4)
II. Nineveh Believes God and Repents (Jonah 3:5–9)
III. God's Compassion on Repentant Nineveh (Jonah 3:10)

Unifying Principle

Change often is required in life if we are to live in peace with others. What can we do about life situations that threaten us harm? After hearing God's warning from Jonah, the people of Nineveh repented, and God forgave their sin.

Introduction

Scholars debate the time of the events recorded in the book of Jonah. There are two primary approaches to this matter. One is that the book was written by Jonah himself. Jonah, identified as the son of Amittai (Jon. 1:1; 2 Kings 14:25), served as a prophet in the eighth century B.C. Specifically, he was a prophet during the forty-year reign of Jeroboam II (786–746 B.C.). Those who follow this date believe the events of Jonah occurred in the first half of the eighth century, just after Jonah's return from Nineveh and prior to the reign of Tiglath Pileser.

If Jonah was the author of the book, one legitimately could question why he is referred to in the third person in most of the book. He is referred to in the first person only in Jonah 1:9; 2:2–9; and three verses in chapter 4. Moreover, the book is actually more *about* Jonah and not necessarily *by* him. Other reasons for questioning an early date for the book are Hebrew and Aramaic expressions more common to a much later period and reflecting some dependence on books such as Jeremiah and Isaiah and books from a time later than the eighth century. B.C.

The second approach to the date of Jonah focuses on the psalm in chapter 2. Scholars who follow this approach find a post-exilic (after 587 B.C.) setting for the passage and believe there is a parallel between the post-exilic Jewish community and the experience of Jonah. They suppose the historical setting of Jonah to be the time of Ezra and Nehemiah, approximately 450–400 B.C. This group also believes the book to be anonymous, reflecting authorship by someone of the prophetic school of Israel who understood God's concern for all peoples—not just for Israel.

To whichever date one subscribes, there is little legitimate debate as to the objectives of the book of Jonah. As A. J. Glaze observes: "It clearly exposes the narrow nationalism and shows the universal redemptive design of God for all mankind. Among the true worshipers there were those who understood that the nation had failed to fulfill her mission and that God was giving them another chance to be a true kingdom of priests (Ex. 19:5–6). They sought to awaken the national conscience.... The book of Jonah was held up before Israel as a summary of the message of her greatest prophets in order that she might understand God's world-embracing love. In this manner the narrative approaches the comprehensive attitude and message of Christianity" (Glaze, "Jonah," 156–157).

The book of Jonah, then, uniquely portrays the responsibility of a prophet named Jonah, the nation of Israel, and all Christians to understand God unconditionally loves all people. Beyond that, the book emphasizes the responsibility God's people have to communicate His love to all people and not to think of themselves as elitists.

Exposition

I. Jonah Obeys the Lord's Call (Jonah 3:1–4)

This part of the lesson reflects a second chance extended to Jonah, who had sought to avoid the Lord's call and commission to him to preach in Assyria. One will recall from earlier passages in the book of Jonah the riveting narrative of Jonah's calling and the equally riveting response he made to it. Yahweh summoned Jonah to cry out against Nineveh, to preach against it. He was to proclaim God's message of judgment to Nineveh. This unpopular message was made all the more difficult because he was an alien preacher declaring a message of condemnation to an audience on its native soil. That Jonah likely would be perceived as an interloper would be exacerbated by problems with language and threats to his personal safety. The Lord clarified the reason for the mission of Jonah and the message of judgment. The wickedness of Nineveh had come up before Him. God had taken notice of Nineveh's wickedness over a period of time. God's displeasure was over the general spiritual condition of Nineveh, not over specific sins.

The author of the book of Jonah provided a succinct yet riveting description of Jonah's response to Yahweh's call. He did arise, as the Lord commanded. Yet he did so to take refuge in Tarshish, away from the presence of the Lord. Motivated by the intimidation of the task before him or the unsavory thought to him personally that Nineveh might repent—or both—Jonah wanted to distance himself geographically from the task. The Lord had summoned Jonah to travel east, to Nineveh. Attempting to avoid the mission altogether, Jonah intended to travel west, to Tarshish. In Jonah's mind, Tarshish was the most distant, diametrically opposite port from Nineveh and his dreaded task. Having paid the cost for the trip, Jonah boarded the ship to Tarshish and sailed away from the Lord's presence.

One must read Jonah 1:4–2:10 to capture and fully appreciate the impact of both Yahweh's gracious second chance to Jonah and Jonah's obedience. Some would see in this event a form of coercion from God. The story makes it clear, however, that the emphasis is on the necessity of the proclamation of God's message, not on Jonah specifically as the messenger. Along the way, he came to experience the forgiving, restorative graciousness of God personally. He also witnessed something of the nature of prophecy and of the power of authentic repentance.

Jonah's commission was essentially the same the second time he received it. He was to go to Nineveh and declare God's message. The one distinctive feature of Yahweh's commission here was that Jonah was to declare "the message I give you" (Jon. 3:2, NIV). The message and mission must be done in strict compliance with the Lord's wishes.

In verse 3, the author turned from the monologue of Yahweh to Jonah to a narrative description of the prophet's reaction to the second summons. Jonah obeyed the word of the Lord and went to Nineveh. The author also provided a historical insight about the size of Ninevah: "Now Nineveh was a very large city; it took three days to go through it" (3:3, NIV). To this point in time, archaeologists have unearthed ruins of Nineveh indicating a circumference of approximately eight miles. An ancient historian reports the length of the city wall of approximately sixty miles. Nineveh in the present passage could very well include that city and several of its surrounding towns. Jonah had to carry the message over a city of such expanse or through individual streets over a three-day period.

The author indicated the obedience of Jonah. He began proclaiming the message immediately upon arrival in Ninevah. The *New Living Translation* expresses it: "On the day Jonah entered the city, he shouted to the crowds: 'Forty days from now Nineveh will be destroyed!'" (3:4). Some suggest this single sentence was the totality of Jonah's message, incessantly repeated. There were two aspects to the proclamation. One was the certainty of judgment on Nineveh. The original term, variously translated in English versions as *overturned, overthrown,* or *destroyed*, also appears in Genesis 19:29 in reference to Sodom and Gomorrah. The judgment was to be so thorough as to leave no hope. On the other hand, there was implicit in the message a condition. The Lord provided a period of forty days during which Nineveh could repent.

II. Nineveh Believes God and Repents (Jonah 3:5–9)

The reaction of the thoroughly pagan nation to Jonah's preaching is tersely, yet impressively stated in verse 5. By *belief*, the author definitely meant more than intellectual assent to the reality of God. *Belief* implies the people's recognition of the message of Jonah. They acknowledged impending destruction and wanted to avoid it. Their belief was validated by declaring a fast among all the people. They also put on sackcloth, clothing associated with mourning.

The impact of Jonah's message was even more impressively expressed by the governmental leader of the city of Nineveh. He removed his royal regalia, an expensive and highly ornamented upper garment. In its place, the king put on sackcloth, a garment of coarse material from camel or goat hair. It was either a loose-fitting sack placed over one's shoulders or it could be worn round one's midsection. The king also sat on a heap of ashes (Job 2:8; Isa. 58:5; Matt. 11:21). The actions of the king of Nineveh signified the all-inclusive call to repentance in the face of imminent judgment.

The king, along with all his courtiers, then issued a decree to all his subjects. He declared a citywide fast from all food and drink for both humans and animals. Furthermore, all the people and the animals were to be draped in sackcloth. Perhaps most importantly, he required: "Let everyone call urgently on God. Let them give up their evil ways and their violence" (Jon. 3:8, NIV). In other words, the city was called upon to repent—to change their behaviors. In calling upon the people to abandon their evil ways, the king spoke of general wickedness.

The lesson concludes at verse 9 with a rhetorical question of the king that expressed his hopes for his people and him. "Who knows? God may yet relent and with compassion turn from his fierce anger so that we will not perish" (NIV). The prayer was that God would honor the penitence of the people and respond in mercy rather than in judgment against Nineveh. The king's desire was that God would *exhale in compassion* toward Nineveh. The term *shub* (or *shubv*) appears in this verse in relation to God. The term in this context simply means that God would turn from His anger to compassion based on the repentance of the people.

III. God's Compassion on Repentant Nineveh (Jonah 3:10)

The author here indicated the Lord had taken as careful notice of the authentic repentance of the Ninevites as He had of their sinfulness. The authenticity of the Ninevites' repentance was demonstrated in the redirection of their lives (v. 10). The *New International Version* expresses it: "When God saw what they did and how they turned from their evil ways, he relented and did not bring on them the destruction he had threatened." The *New Living Translation* conveys the verse somewhat more captivatingly: "When God saw what they had done and how they had put a stop to their evil ways, he changed his mind and did not carry out the destruction he had threatened."

The NLT and NIV respectfully indicate the Lord had mercy and compassion on the people. The background of the synonymous terms *mercy* and *compassion* is the Hebrew term *hesedh* (or *chesed*). The term literally means "steadfast love." It is love that will not let go. Such love flows from the heart of God to all people based upon His divine nature. To be sure, *hesedh* is the Old Testament equivalent of the Greek *agapē*. This term generally is translated *unconditional love*. God's boundless, ever-abiding, unconditional love causes Him to act mercifully and redemptively toward those who turn to Him.

The text here speaks of a turning on the part of the people and God. As in the previous lesson, *shub* (or *shubv*) denotes the change in direction of the people. Likewise in the previous lesson, the Hebrew term *nacham*, translated as *relented* in the NKJV or *repented* in the KJV, describes the actions of Yahweh toward Nineveh. One exegete appropriates the meaning of this term by asserting the Lord was relieved of the necessity of punishing the Ninevites as He had promised. The Lord turned to compassion on the people based on their actions. In this way, the Lord achieved His redemptive purposes.

The Lesson Applied

One of the great tragedies of human society is that a sense of superiority or even elitism exists among some people. Their idea is the racial, cultural, or religious group to which they belong is more valued than others. Thus, they tend to minimize the value of those not in their group. Or they ignore them altogether. Such smugness too often invades religious ranks—even Christianity. When this happens, people come to erroneously think they have a monopoly on God's grace or salvation. They deceive themselves into believing they are sole heirs of truth. They delude themselves into believing God only cares for those of their ilk, that He has the same exclusionary attitudes they possess. Today's lesson calls attention to this.

God's love, mercy, salvation, and plans are boundless. Of necessity, the Lord works—and always has—in the confines of the particularity of people. He works with people of certain geographical, racial, religious, and cultural situations. Yet that does not mean He is limited to any of those. The Scriptures are unmistakable in their message that God's love and redemptive purposes extend to all of creation. He desires the entire cosmos be reconciled to Him. To this end, the Lord calls upon His people to take His message of redemption and reconciliation to others. He especially has a heart for the lost sheep whom some of His current sheep don't acknowledge. So He calls His people to rise above their narrowness and reach the unreached for Him. The failure or unwillingness to do so is also a failure to grasp what it means to be part of the family of God. His people cannot decide who can or cannot be one of His. Only God has that authority or prerogative.

Finally, today's lesson is a reminder of the Lord's displeasure with the sins of people. He stands to judge those who are in disobedience to Him. That is true wherever and whoever they are. Yet as certainly as the Lord will judge sin and sinners, He will just as certainly show mercy to those who sincerely turn to Him.

Let's Talk About It

Discuss the importance of obedience to God.

Obedience includes the humble and sincere acceptance of the authority and will of God. It's not only conforming, but also demonstrating our devotion through our thoughts, words, and deeds. Obedience conveys the idea of positioning oneself under God's rule because it is best. Obedience is also an act of faith. Believing in God means we are convinced God's way is the right way for us to live.

Home Daily Devotional Readings
May 31 – June 6, 2021
Monday
Worried? Seek God's Counsel
1 Samuel 9:5–10
Tuesday
God Cares for His People
Ezekiel 34:11–16
Wednesday
Rich? Set Your Hope on God
1 Timothy 6:17–19
Thursday
Enlarge Your Faith Practices
Matthew 17:14–20
Friday
Overcome Worry through Faith
Luke 12:22–34
Saturday
Serve God with Your Whole Heart
Matthew 6:19–24
Sunday
Live Worry-Free Every Day
Matthew 6:25–34

Fourth Quarter

June

July

August

Lesson 1 June 6, 2021

Why Do You Worry?

Adult Topic: No Worries

Background Scripture: Matthew 6:19–34

Matthew 6:25–34

King James Version

THEREFORE I say unto you, Take no thought for your life, what ye shall eat, or what ye shall drink; nor yet for your body, what ye shall put on. Is not the life more than meat, and the body than raiment?

26 Behold the fowls of the air: for they sow not, neither do they reap, nor gather into barns; yet your heavenly Father feedeth them. Are ye not much better than they?

27 Which of you by taking thought can add one cubit unto his stature?

28 And why take ye thought for raiment? Consider the lilies of the field, how they grow; they toil not, neither do they spin:

29 And yet I say unto you, That even Solomon in all his glory was not arrayed like one of these.

30 Wherefore, if God so clothe the grass of the field, which to day is, and to morrow is cast into the oven, shall he not much more clothe you, O ye of little faith?

31 Therefore take no thought, saying, What shall we eat? or, What shall we drink? or, Wherewithal shall we be clothed?

32 (For after all these things do the Gentiles seek:) for your heavenly Father knoweth that ye have need of all these things.

33 But seek ye first the kingdom of God, and his righteousness; and all these things shall be added unto you.

New Revised Standard Version

"THEREFORE I tell you, do not worry about your life, what you will eat or what you will drink, or about your body, what you will wear. Is not life more than food, and the body more than clothing?

26 Look at the birds of the air; they neither sow nor reap nor gather into barns, and yet your heavenly Father feeds them. Are you not of more value than they?

27 And can any of you by worrying add a single hour to your span of life?

28 And why do you worry about clothing? Consider the lilies of the field, how they grow; they neither toil nor spin,

29 yet I tell you, even Solomon in all his glory was not clothed like one of these.

30 But if God so clothes the grass of the field, which is alive today and tomorrow is thrown into the oven, will he not much more clothe you—you of little faith?

31 Therefore do not worry, saying, 'What will we eat?' or 'What will we drink?' or 'What will we wear?'

32 For it is the Gentiles who strive for all these things; and indeed your heavenly Father knows that you need all these things.

33 But strive first for the kingdom of God and his righteousness, and all these things will be given to you as well.

MAIN THOUGHT: (For after all these things do the Gentiles seek:) for your heavenly Father knoweth that ye have need of all these things. But seek ye first the kingdom of God, and his righteousness; and all these things shall be added unto you. (Matthew 6:32–33, KJV)

MATTHEW 6:25–34

King James Version	*New Revised Standard Version*
34 Take therefore no thought for the morrow: for the morrow shall take thought for the things of itself. Sufficient unto the day is the evil thereof.	**34 "So do not worry about tomorrow, for tomorrow will bring worries of its own. Today's trouble is enough for today.**

LESSON SETTING
Time: A.D. 29
Place: Mount of Beatitude

LESSON OUTLINE

I. God Cares for You! (Matthew 6:25–31)
II. Seek the Kingdom of God (Matthew 6:32–33)
III. Don't Worry about Tomorrow (Matthew 6:34)

UNIFYING PRINCIPLE

Life's uncertainties can lead people to worry about how to obtain their basic needs. Whom can we trust to meet all our needs? The gospel of Matthew points out that our God who is truly sovereign will fulfill our needs.

INTRODUCTION

A few years ago a popular song told us, "Don't Worry, Be Happy." That is the sentiment expressed by Matthew in this text. The writer recorded Jesus' Sermon on the Mount in Matthew 5–7. Chapter 6:25–34 is part of a smaller unit of the sermon that directs us to focus on pleasing God and doing the things that will assure His presence in our lives.

The sermon itself is the Matthean presentation of Jesus' supremacy over Moses and the Law. Jesus' teachings deal with a personal relationship with God rather than an enumeration of a set of rules to obey. Setting one's focus on an intimate relationship with the Creator will bring about joyful obedience to His requirements for one to enter into His Kingdom. The sermon itself has several parts.

First, Matthew 5:1–12 is called the Beatitudes. They are a series of blessings for those who embrace the divine-human relationship and maintain their focus to please God.

Second, Matthew 5:13–16 outlines the relationship of the disciples to the world. Disciples are to be both like salt and light to the world they are ministering to. Salt has two purposes. First, it changes the taste of food. Disciples, as salt, are to change their families, communities, and world toward God. Second, as salt preserves, they are to preserve goodness and righteousness and seek to expand them throughout all the world.

Third, in Matthew 5:17–20 Jesus taught that the new law of righteousness is actually the fulfillment of the old. He did not come to destroy the Law but to build upon it in terms of providing its true meaning and call upon people to adhere to its divine truths.

Fourth, Matthew 5:21–48 consists of contrasts between the old interpretation of the Law and the new interpretation that Jesus gave. Throughout this pericope of Scripture, Jesus elevated His teachings over those of Moses. He taught His disciples, "You have heard that it was said ... But I say unto you" (Matt. 5:21–22, 27–28, 31–34, 38–39, NRSV). These contrasts reveal their common understanding of the Law compared with Jesus' teaching of the text with its original divine intent.

Fifth, the sermon contrasts the old practice of Judaism with the new teachings of Jesus. Matthew 6:1–18 deals with the motive behind our religious inclinations and actions in alms-giving, prayer, and fasting. Jesus' religious expressions and practices are matters that emerge from the heart and are efforts to develop a closer relationship with God rather than something to be done for personal accolades.

The text from which our lesson comes is a part of the sixth section of Jesus' sermon. Matthew 6:19–7:12 addresses the right use of property, how to deal with issues of anxiety and trust, judging others from the proper perspective, the proper way to teach and pray, and an admonition to practice the golden rule. We will return to this section for a more detailed exegesis in the exposition.

Seventh, Matthew 7:13–23 consists of a group of general warnings about who to follow and the rendering of lip service. Jesus warned the disciples that following Him requires resisting the crowd and actual effort to keep His commandments.

The final section of the sermon, Matthew 7:24–29, concludes with a parable and a summary statement. Those who listen and do what Jesus commands are like those who build a firm foundation for their homes. Those who hear but do not put His words into practice live in homes without a firm foundation and will sink in the time of adversity. Matthew ended the sermon by pointing out that Jesus, unlike the scribes, taught with authority.

Taken as a whole, Jesus' purpose for delivering the Sermon on the Mount was to focus His disciples' attention on building a relationship with God. For Jesus, the Kingdom of God had come near in Him and each person possessed a unique opportunity to enter therein.

As noted previously, the sixth section of the sermon focused on trust in God. This pericope of Scripture has three major points. First, Jesus illustrated the loving care of the Father for His children. Second, He pointed them in the direction of God so they could discover His care. Finally, since one has discovered what a loving Father is, one should not worry about their physical needs.

Exposition

I. God Cares for You! (Matthew 6:25–31)

The hymn by Civilla D. Martin expresses the sentiments of this text. It encourages us to, "Be not dismayed whate'er betide, God will take care of you; Beneath His wings of love abide, God will take care of you. God will take care of you, Through ev'ry day, O'er all the way: He will take care of you, God will take care of you" (Martin, "God Will Take Care of You," 52). *The Interpreter's Bible* suggests the man who wishes to store up treasure in heaven (v. 20), have the guiding principle of his life straight (v. 22), and serve God rather than property (v. 24) must get free of worry.

Jesus issued a point blank imperative, "Do not worry about your life, what you will eat or what you will drink, or about your body, what you will wear" (6:25, NRSV). Jesus' point centered on the great gift of life and God's ability and willingness to provide for its sustenance. The word *therefore* connects this pericope of Scripture with the previous one.

Investing in heavenly treasure is more beneficial and profitable. When one makes this type of spiritual investment, it provides one with a sense of security that expands beyond human life. It connects one to the Creator, Sustainer, and Redeemer of the universe. When one bases or establishes one's life on God, there is no need for anxiety or worry. The fact of the matter is, God cares for humanity, and His caring reaches into every aspect of life—eating, drinking, clothing, shelter, and more. Jesus' message personalizes God. He is the God who dirtied His hands to make human beings from the soil of the earth. He is the God who stooped to breathe life into that clay body. Moreover, He is the God who made male and female in His own image and likeness (Gen. 1–2).

At first glance, it appears the Lord Jesus was uttering mere words of comfort and encouragement, but the intent of the Lord was not to offer pleasantries. Jesus was not concerned to pull the disciples through a single moment of despair. Rather His intent was to direct and govern a lifestyle. He addressed a way of life. Disciples must embark on a life of trust in God. They are to trust God in all aspects of their lives.

Jesus moved in verse 25 to elevate the disciples' concept and understanding of life. Life consists of more than going through the routine of eating, drinking, and wearing clothing. Human life was meant to be lived in close proximity with God, its Creator. Human life was to be closely associated with the God who called it into existence.

Verse 26 supports this interpretation. Jesus pointed out the condition of the birds of the air as an example. Birds do not work to develop their foods, yet they are fed. God feeds them. As the crown of God's created order, the ones who are made in God's image and likeness, Jesus pointedly asked, "Are you not of more value than they?" (Matt. 6:26, NRSV). By asking this rhetorical question, Jesus was trying to get the disciples to consider the importance of the divine-human relationship. It was not abstract and impersonal as was the case in Greek and Roman mythology. God did not use human beings as toys from which He obtained humor or entertainment. Jesus noted God's personal concern for each person. *You are worth more.*

Humanity's intrinsic value outweighed those of other members of the created order. All of the created order has value, but humanity's value as partner with God and as steward of creation, according to Jesus' use of the superlative, exceeds all others. Therefore, worrying about life's necessities that God supplies even to birds is counterproductive. It does not add value or time to life.

The examples Jesus used in this pericope actually are reminders of God's great care for humanity. God takes care of the birds of the air. He glorifies and beautifies the earth with grass and flowers that, comparatively speaking, Solomon with all of his riches could not compete with. This greenery beautifies the earth today but is used as fuel to heat our oven tomorrow. Yet the fact of the matter is, if God takes so much care in how He weaves the grass that is soon to be burned to provide heat, then how much more is He concerned for those who reflect His image and likeness? Jesus reassured the disciples they are in God's kind and all-competent loving hands.

Based upon the platform of trust in God, Jesus concluded there exists no need for anxiety. Some people disagree with the precepts of this text because it appears Jesus was simply saying, "Do nothing. All will be provided for you." But that is not what Jesus was alluding to at all. Jesus knew work is a part of the experience of life. That is why He pointed to the birds' resourcefulness. Jesus also commended the unjust steward for using his ingenuity for making a way for himself, even though He condemned his methods (Luke 16:1–12).

Earlier in Luke's Gospel, Jesus warned His disciples that life did not consist of the abundance of goods (Luke 12:15–21). Furthermore, the temptation narratives recorded in both Matthew and Luke warned that people cannot live by bread alone but by every word that comes from the mouth of God (Matt. 4:1–4; Luke 4:1–4). All that to say yes, we are to work to earn a livelihood. However, our lives should not be so focused on the accumulation of goods or on satisfying our physical needs that we forget God. Our lives should not be so focused upon ourselves and our needs that we minimize our need of God and of His loving care for us. Jesus insisted a relationship with our Lord and Creator should take preference over everything else.

II. Seek the Kingdom of God (Matthew 6:32–33)

The thrust of this pericope is to direct disciples to seek the Kingdom of God. Jesus illustrated this by providing a contrast between Jewish and Gentile life. The Jewish people as a whole possessed a solid religious inclination and were much aware of the need to build their lives on a foundation of trust in God. (The first four of the Ten Commandments direct the Hebrews to worship and acknowledge the Lord God as their Source of life and point of worship. See Ex. 20:1–11). Those who did not possess this inclination toward the God of Abraham—the Gentiles—were not aware of their need for God.

Gentiles in general did not possess a solid understanding of God. Their gods consisted of idols, riotous living, wayward lifestyles, and earthly ambitions of power and fame. Jesus warned His hearers to avoid seeking after these things. He knew human beings were created for a higher purpose. That purpose is to seek after God's presence. The word *seek* is important here. It means "to strive for, to search for, or to pursue after." Followers of Jesus are to seek after God. Recognition and acknowledgment of God as Creator and Lord are to be pursued before temporal blessings. In fact by putting first things first—seeking after the Kingdom of God and His righteousness—one will find God's gift of temporal blessings as a mainstay in their lives. When Solomon asked God for wisdom to rule the children of Israel effectively, God was pleased with his request and granted him the things he did not ask for: riches, honor, glory, and long life (1 Kings 3:5–14).The text makes it clear temporal blessings are automatic for those who seek God's presence. They are an outgrowth of a personal relationship with and trust in God.

III. Don't Worry about Tomorrow (Matthew 6:34)

The last verse to be examined in this passage expands the concept of trust in God beyond the supplying of basic necessities of life into the unknown and uncertain future. The providential care of God for humanity extends into eternity. Jesus affirmed the unknown future is known by God. Therefore, we should completely entrust our tomorrows into His loving hands. Again, He reissued the imperative or prohibition to not be anxious based upon relationship with God. The motif is if Jesus' followers seek God as a priority, they have a God who not only will provide for their temporal needs, but one who will assure their future prosperity. Jesus alerted His listeners that each day will have its own set of challenges, but He also assured them God can handle those challenges. Seeking first the Kingdom of God has its own set of benefits, one of which is to face the future and other obstacles with the confidence that Civilla D. Martin expressed so eloquently in her hymn—*God will take care of you.*

The Lesson Applied

What good is a sermon if it does not point us to God? Jesus' message in this text is simple: *Don't be anxious. Trust in God.* This trust is based on a personal relationship with God, our Creator, Sustainer, and Redeemer. The underlining purpose Matthew hoped to achieve in the development of the entire Sermon on the Mount, and of his book as a whole, was to emphasize dependency on God beyond the need for temporal blessings. Worship and total dependency on the providential care of God must be our major priority and objective.

Let's Talk About It

How does Jesus' Sermon on the Mount relate to Moses' giving of the Ten Commandments?

When Moses gave the Ten Commandments, God was viewed as an abstract figure who provoked fear into the hearts of the Hebrew people. Jesus' presentation of God in the Sermon on the Mount revealed Him as a personal Lord and Savior who loves His creation. He should be reverenced for who He is and what He does. He provides for the birds of the air and clothes the lilies of the field with incomparable beauty and glory. His human creations are much more valuable than both of those. Jesus' message was that the Kingdom of God has come near. It shows God is personal and He loves us both individually and collectively. The sermon is superior to the Law simply because it reveals God in a loving and a salvific perspective.

HOME DAILY DEVOTIONAL READINGS
JUNE 7–15, 2021
MONDAY
Do Not Fear the Storm
Mark 4:35–41
TUESDAY
Do Not Fear Persecution
Matthew 24:9–14
WEDNESDAY
No Separation from God's Love
Romans 8:31–39
THURSDAY
I Have Overcome the World
John 16:25–33
FRIDAY
Choose to Follow Me Now!
Matthew 8:18–22
SATURDAY
Jesus Delivers the Demon-Possessed
Matthew 8:28–34
SUNDAY
Jesus Stills the Stormy Seas
Matthew 8:23–27

WHY ARE YOU AFRAID?

Adult Topic: Calming the Storm

Background Scripture: Matthew 8:23–27; Mark 4:35–41; Luke 8:22–25

MATTHEW 8:23–27

King James Version

AND when he was entered into a ship, his disciples followed him.
24 And, behold, there arose a great tempest in the sea, insomuch that the ship was covered with the waves: but he was asleep.
25 And his disciples came to him, and awoke him, saying, Lord, save us: we perish.
26 And he saith unto them, Why are ye fearful, O ye of little faith? Then he arose, and rebuked the winds and the sea; and there was a great calm.
27 But the men marvelled, saying, What manner of man is this, that even the winds and the sea obey him!

New Revised Standard Version

AND when he got into the boat, his disciples followed him.
24 A windstorm arose on the sea, so great that the boat was being swamped by the waves; but he was asleep.
25 And they went and woke him up, saying, "Lord, save us! We are perishing!"
26 And he said to them, "Why are you afraid, you of little faith?" Then he got up and rebuked the winds and the sea; and there was a dead calm.
27 They were amazed, saying, "What sort of man is this, that even the winds and the sea obey him?"

LESSON SETTING
Time: A.D. 25
Place: Sea of Galilee

LESSON OUTLINE
I. Faith to Follow (Matthew 8:23)
II. Faith During the Storm (Matthew 8:24–26)
III. Faith in the One Who Will Deliver (Matthew 8:27)

UNIFYING PRINCIPLE

People often lose confidence amidst the storms of persecution, rejection, and poverty. Where can we find assurance when beset by the storms of life? Fearing they would not survive the windstorm, the disciples turned to Jesus to save them.

INTRODUCTION

Believers find assurance in knowing God cares about the issues that concern us and will respond to our earnest pleas. After Jesus spent a full day teaching on the shores of the Sea of Galilee, He told His disciples it was time to head to the other side of the lake. So they left the crowd, got into the boat, and started to cross over.

MAIN THOUGHT: And he saith unto them, Why are ye fearful, O ye of little faith? Then he arose, and rebuked the winds and the sea; and there was a great calm. (Matthew 8:26, KJV)

After awhile, a great and mighty storm arose on the sea. If we put ourselves in the disciples' shoes, we might empathize with them. They were tired! It had been a long day. They were trying to get their Teacher to the other side of the Sea of Galilee, and here comes a monster of a storm. Now, they had seen storms before. Some of them were fishermen and knew how to handle a boat in a storm. But this was different—the storm was more like a cyclone! The waves washed over the boat. The boat filled with water. They thought they were going to drown!

Sometimes we think that if we could see Jesus, touch Him, and talk to Him as the disciples did, our faith would be stronger. Yet they were within feet of Jesus and still had little faith. A person can get more faith by asking Jesus. He gladly will increase your faith when you face scary situations. The symbolism behind the story of Jesus calming the storm should bring encouragement and hope for anyone facing a storm in life.

Exposition

I. Faith to Follow (Matthew 8:23)

Scholars of the Synoptic Gospels suggest the emphasis of Matthew 8:18–9:8 is discipleship. The three miracles in this section speak of Jesus' power and authority. Discipleship, according to many, means submitting oneself to that power and authority. In the printed text of today's lesson (including the three preceding verses this writer will include), Matthew the Evangelist wanted his Jewish believing readers to know Jesus had authority over the powers of chaos (8:23–27). Matthew revealed even before the storm on the sea subtle hints of the chaos a disciple of Jesus might encounter. The Evangelist's record of Jesus having a conversation with a scribe who insisted he would follow Jesus wherever He went, for example, was the first hint. Jesus replied with a saying relative to discipleship. Many are familiar with His response, "Foxes have holes, and birds of the air have nests, but the Son of Man has nowhere to lay his head" (8:20, NRSV). This response to the scribe implied that those who commit themselves to following Jesus must be prepared to be rejected by family and friends with little expectation they will have various creature comforts. The next verse provides an additional clue. "Another of his disciples said to him, 'Lord, let me first go and bury my father.' But Jesus said to him, 'Follow me, and leave the dead to bury their own dead'" (8:21–22, NRSV). The burial of a parent, according to Jewish scholars was one of the highest duties in Jewish society, taking precedence over many other obligations dictated by the Mosaic Law. One commentary suggested it is not clear whether "the dead" who were to bury the disciple's father were spiritually dead or whether the expression was simply a hyperbolic way of saying, *Let others fulfill this obligation.* In any event, Jesus insisted that following Him must take precedence over even the highest of family responsibilities. As the skillful editor he was, Matthew combined these two discipleship sayings, or responses of Jesus, with the story about Jesus calming a storm by inserting the discipleship sayings into the sea narrative after the opening sentence. "Now when

Jesus saw great crowds around him, he gave orders to go on the other side" (8:18, NRSV). That is, in principle the journey had already begun. This was when the question of what it means to follow Jesus was raised. This impression is reinforced when the miracle story resumed in verse 23 (NRSV): "And when he got into the boat, his disciples followed him." In this way, scholars believe the storm narrative became an acted parable about what it means to follow Jesus. Faith in Jesus requires one must follow.

II. Faith During the Storm (Matthew 8:24–26)

Suddenly amidst what was calm, the northeasterly breeze stiffened, and along the horizon of the lake to the north and east the clouds thickened. The skies rapidly grew darker, and in no time a wild wind came down the gorge of the Jordon from the heights of Hermon on the north. The cyclonic storm was upon the lake.

The disciples attempted to rapidly adjust their sails, but with every moment the storm grew worse until it became a great tempest heaving the sea like an earthquake. The waves lashed furiously and broke over the sides of the boat so that it already was filling. Repeatedly the boat was buried amid the foam of the breakers that burst over the lower parts completely. They were in great danger. The Synoptic Gospels each portray the event as more than just a bad storm. The situation was life-threatening. In Hebrew thought, the sea symbolizes the forces of chaos arrayed against God, which God brings into subjection (Gen. 1:2; Pss. 93:3–4; 104:6–9). The disciples, seasoned fishermen, were familiar with bad weather and the dangers of the sea, yet in this instance they were deathly afraid. Meanwhile Jesus was laying on the seat of the stern steeped in the profound slumber of exhaustion. Jesus was asleep! There is no other biblical reference to Jesus' sleep.

They didn't want to awaken Him. But their situation was critical and growing more so every moment. All their efforts to bail out the water were to no avail, and the sails were beyond their management. Another wave might send their boat to the bottom and hurl them all into a hopeless struggle for life in the midst of the fury of the elements. They rushed and woke Him with a cry of anguish and fear. The repetition of *Master* (Luke 8:24) indicated the sense of urgency felt by the boat's occupants. Some believe Jesus responded to their pleas with a moment of hesitation and then a look of pity and rebuke. They added, "Master, carest though not that we perish?" (Mark 4:38, KJV). For a moment more He paused to calm their fears. "Why are ye fearful, O ye of little faith?" (Matt. 8:26, KJV). Jesus was still Master even if He was asleep, but they had not yet come to understand He was the Lord of nature. He stood forth now in the midst of the howling storm, calm and unruffled in his majesty. Not one tremor of alarm or one token of confusion. "Silence!" Jesus said, addressing the winds as human beings. "Be still!" He commanded the turbulent dashing waves as if they were animals (Mark 4:39, NLT). Instantly the winds hushed into peace and the waves subsided placidly. It was a miracle! Always after the storm the swell remains for a time after the winds have died down. But the lake in this case became calm at once. Again turning to the disciples with a chiding voice, Jesus asked: "Why are you afraid? You have so little faith!" (Matt. 8:26, NLT). They had witnessed many of Jesus' miracles. They should have recognized before His power over nature. "Where is your faith?" He asked in gentle rebuke. They feared exceedingly, and no wonder. Here was One who in the same day had cured a blind–mute lunatic, met the learned scribes and Pharisees in debate and defeated them, taught many wonderful things in parables, and now with a word made the cyclonic winds cease and calmed the raging sea. They were filled with amazement.

III. Faith in the One Who Will Deliver (Matthew 8:27)

The story ends with the disciples asking, "What sort of man is this, that even winds and sea obey him?" (8:27, NRSV). The answer is, of course, *the Messiah* who manifests divine power that was, according to the prophets, expected to be supernaturally endowed and therefore able to work miracles. The sea miracle raises the question, but the answer must await Peter's confession in 16:16. Until then the disciples would grow in their apprehension and comprehension of Jesus. However, they had much to learn yet, and they needed to grow in the knowledge of the Lord Jesus Christ, who Matthew wanted his readers to know had the divine power to rescue them in times of chaos.

This is not the only time in the canon that we have seen a violent raging sea. Recall the story of Jonah. Jonah was aboard a ship that was about to capsize due to his presence. Jonah nor any of his companion travelers had the power to either keep the sea from raging or steer the ship. Jonah's only recourse was to sacrifice himself by jumping overboard. The sea's rage was a punishment for Jonah's refusal to do God's bidding. His presence was needed to be rid of because of his iniquity (Jon. 1). Jesus, on the other hand, calmed the sea without self-sacrifice or the sacrifice of any of His crew. His ability to calm the sea was indicative of His righteous stature before the elements of the earth that are commanded before God. Matthew's question was rooted in the history of Israel.

Given the relative early position of this story in Matthew's Gospel, it was continuing to unfold who this Messiah was. Each story impacted the whole narrative of Jesus, and this story no less. This question, "What sort of man is this?" was the primary question Matthew continued to unpack for the duration of his Gospel. Given this was early in Jesus' ministry, we primarily have seen Him as a teacher at the Sermon on the Mount (chapters 5–7). He had completed a few healings, but this story points to the fact Jesus was so much more than a healer. Yes, He could command disease. Though special, that was not necessarily unique. Obviously, others in Scripture were able to heal through divine means (such as Elisha in 2 Kings 5:10–14), but only one momentarily controlled the chaos of the sea—Moses (Ex. 14:21). (Joshua held back parts of a river, but not the sea.) One of Matthew's objectives was to demonstrate Jesus was the new and improved Moses, a prophet who had not been seen in Israel since (Deut. 34:10–12). However, there was one major difference between Jesus' command of the sea and Moses'. Exodus makes it clear that Moses raised his hands and *the Lord* moved back the sea. In Jesus' case, the sea and wind obeyed *His* voice. This is the difference between derivative power and self-actualized power. Jesus' authority was inherent. Moses and others only acted as vessels through which the power of God worked. Certainly, Matthew was building his case—Jesus is the Messiah with whom no other can compare. Others had done miracles, but not on the level and through a demonstration of raw, yet gentle power. This Messiah was able to do it all. He controlled the sea and delivered His disciples.

The Lesson Applied

As followers of Jesus Christ, we have the opportunity to not only follow Christ but also to work where we see God already at work. Prior to getting on the boat, Jesus spent the day touching the lives of those with whom He came into contact. He was teaching. He was struggling with the Pharisees as well as dealing with the misunderstanding and interruptions of His family. Then there was the healing of the blind, mute lunatic and other miracles of cure. There was the intense work of parabolic teaching, and Jesus ended that day with a need for rest. So He went to sleep in the boat.

What does this mean for us? Like the disciples, as we observe what God is doing around us, He invites us to join Him in His work. We often act as though God tells us what He wants us to do and sends us off all by ourselves to try to do it. Then, anytime we may need God, we can call on Him and He will help us. What might be more accurate? When God is about to do something, He reveals what He is about to do to His people. Why? God wants to do it through His servants. Christ's followers are not, however, exempt from experiencing life's storm. This is true even more so when we find ourselves serving God. Like the scribe, we too may be rejected by family and friends. Most times it's not us personally who is being rejected, but our faith or beliefs or convictions we hold. Also, like the disciple who wanted to first bury his father and then follow Jesus, for the sake of one's values and calling, one must be willing to alienate even close relatives because of God's call. This does not by any means suggest we ignore God's command to honor our parents and love others. Rather, it implies we make it a priority to follow God for the sake of God's Kingdom.

One's faith can prepare him/her for hardship, ostracism, and alienation. This was the experience for Jewish Christian missionaries at the time the Gospel was written. It has been the experience of new Christians wherever the Gospel has been proclaimed in a non-Christian culture. This is also true for people of color.

Taking a stand on controversial social issues in Jesus' name can draw hostility from others. African American clergy are no strangers to being treated with contempt from other races and cultures for taking a stand for social justice. As Christ followers who believe in equality, our faith sometimes is buffeted by the storms of persecution, rejection, and poverty. Our circumstances as believers can become dire, even to the point of significant loss. In light of this, even seasoned believers can become fearful God is nonchalant toward their difficulties. God may not answer believers at the immediate sign of trouble in our lives. This, however, should not keep us from praying to God because survival of our storms is possible only by calling on the Master of the sea. We must trust God's timing while recognizing God's sovereign power over our lives and our world. When chaos enters our lives, we have the assurance of knowing only Jesus Christ has the divine power to rescue us. Despite our faith at times being weak and inadequate, we have confidence in our faith that God's love can lift us.

Let's Talk About It

How do you balance faith and well-being? Do faintness, weariness, and exhaustion dominate your physical, mental, emotional or spiritual being? What do you do to rejuvenate? How do you create an environment of care?

One could argue Matthew's mentioning Jesus being asleep on the ship was perhaps a lesson in self-care. Synoptic scholars paint the picture that on the boat a weary Jesus sank down on the seat placed near the stern of the boat and fell asleep. This might be the only time the Gospel records the sleep of Jesus.

Self-care is an integral part of our spiritual journey. Often people believe that to be spiritual we have to lay at the altar of self-sacrifice, running ourselves into the ground. The Gospels record Jesus sleeping, eating, drinking, and spending time with friends. Even as the Son of God, all work and no play made Jesus a dull Messiah! In addition to a regular interval prayer, this story helps show us that part of Jesus' regiment was sleep.

One of the ways the enemy is able to destroy and take down the people of God is by convincing us we do not need to take time for rejuvenation. We do! Especially for those who work in ministry, the work is arduous, time-consuming, and emotionally draining. This makes our minds, bodies, and spirits tired. It is easy to become overwhelmed. The good news is we have an example in Jesus to do something different than what others may impose on us.

Self-care is more than just the care for self. It also involves us being a part of a caring environment. An integral part of self-care is taking care of those we work with and creating an environment of self-care. Quick and easy examples include: Compliment people publicly. Ask people what they are looking forward to. Change your computer password to something you're looking forward to. Make eye contact and smile. Try not to frown while doing certain tasks or paperwork.

Home Daily Devotional Readings
June 14–20, 2021

Monday	Tuesday	Wednesday	Thursday	Friday	Saturday	Sunday
Fringes Aid Remembering God's Commandments	Disciples and Family Witness Girl's Healing	Woman Testifies to Jesus' Healing Touch	Jesus Opens Eyes of the Blind Men	Jesus Restores Speech to Mute Man	Join the Lord's Harvest Today	Faith in God Heals Many Ills
Numbers 15:37–41	Luke 8:40–42, 49–56	Luke 8:42–48	Matthew 9:27–31	Matthew 9:32–34	Matthew 9:35–10:1	Matthew 9:18–26

HEALED BY FAITH

Adult Topic:
A Healing Touch

Background Scripture:
Matthew 9:18–26; Mark 5:21–43; Luke 8:40–56

MATTHEW 9:18–26

King James Version

WHILE he spake these things unto them, behold, there came a certain ruler, and worshipped him, saying, My daughter is even now dead: but come and lay thy hand upon her, and she shall live.

19 And Jesus arose, and followed him, and so did his disciples.

20 And, behold, a woman, which was diseased with an issue of blood twelve years, came behind him, and touched the hem of his garment:

21 For she said within herself, If I may but touch his garment, I shall be whole.

22 But Jesus turned him about, and when he saw her, he said, Daughter, be of good comfort; thy faith hath made thee whole. And the woman was made whole from that hour.

23 And when Jesus came into the ruler's house, and saw the minstrels and the people making a noise,

24 He said unto them, Give place: for the maid is not dead, but sleepeth. And they laughed him to scorn.

25 But when the people were put forth, he went in, and took her by the hand, and the maid arose.

26 And the fame hereof went abroad into all that land.

New Revised Standard Version

WHILE he was saying these things to them, suddenly a leader of the synagogue came in and knelt before him, saying, "My daughter has just died; but come and lay your hand on her, and she will live."

19 And Jesus got up and followed him, with his disciples.

20 Then suddenly a woman who had been suffering from hemorrhages for twelve years came up behind him and touched the fringe of his cloak,

21 for she said to herself, "If I only touch his cloak, I will be made well."

22 Jesus turned, and seeing her he said, "Take heart, daughter; your faith has made you well." And instantly the woman was made well.

23 When Jesus came to the leader's house and saw the flute players and the crowd making a commotion,

24 he said, "Go away; for the girl is not dead but sleeping." And they laughed at him.

25 But when the crowd had been put outside, he went in and took her by the hand, and the girl got up.

26 And the report of this spread throughout that district.

MAIN THOUGHT: But Jesus turned him about, and when he saw her, he said, Daughter, be of good comfort; thy faith hath made thee whole. And the woman was made whole from that hour. (Matthew 9:22, KJV)

LESSON SETTING

Time: A.D. 25
Place: Capernaum

LESSON OUTLINE

I. **The Faith of a Bold Father and a Timid Woman (Matthew 9:18–20)**
II. **The Healing of a Daughter (Matthew 9:21–25)**
III. **Female Believers: Inheritors of the Kingdom of God (Matthew 9:26)**

Unifying Principle

People often look to others to help them with their health issues. Where does healing come from? Jesus told the woman with the issue of blood that she was healed because of her faith, and He told Jairus his daughter was healed and restored to life.

Introduction

Adults experience great illnesses or know someone who has. Perhaps you have been a caregiver to a sick loved one. Adults are willing to take bold action to obtain healing, and parents are willing to go to any length to save their child(ren). Some parents have experienced the pain of losing a child. Many adults know someone who once was gravely ill but has been healed. This was the reality last year when for months millions of people recovered from a serious illness that took the lives of hundreds of thousands. This time last year our world was in the midst of a pandemic. Pneumonia of unknown causes was detected in Wuhan, China in December 2019. The outbreak was declared a Public Health Emergency of International Concern in January 2020. In February 2020, the World Health Organization (WHO) announced a name for the new coronavirus disease: COVID-19. At the time of this writing there were almost 5 million confirmed cases worldwide, more than 300 thousand confirmed deaths, and 213 countries, areas, or territories with cases according to the WHO. In time it became apparent the virus could be of vast concern for those with certain preexisting health conditions. In this country that meant certain populations could become devastated, the African American population being a key one. Because of this concern, various congregations across the country tapped into medical, psychosocial, and religious resources to offer insight, prevention, and life-sustaining services to help their communities. One particular African American consortium of interfaith communities created resources for women of all ages to become informed and to seek treatment and prevention of not only COVID-19 but to liberate women from the various health disparities already among us that could exacerbate those who tested positive for the virus. In today's lesson we see the faith component of a Jewish man and a Jewish woman. Matthew showed how Jesus honored their faith, and he especially shined a light on how Jesus brought respect, dignity, and health to the female believers in the story.

Exposition

I. The Faith of a Bold Father and a Timid Woman (Matthew 9:18–20)

Jesus had calmed a storm (8:23–27). Then He expelled demons from two men

(8:28–34). This showed His power over nature and the world of evil spirits. After these miracles took place in Gadarenes, Jesus returned by boat to Capernaum. The news of His return drew a great multitude that gathered about Him at the site where He landed. A man among the crowd boldly came to Jesus. The man was Jairus, the chief ruler of the synagogue (Mark 5:21–43). He told Jesus his twelve-year-old daughter (Luke 8:42) had died, and he requested Jesus come to his home and raise his daughter from the dead. The leader of the synagogue may have witnessed Jesus or another rabbi doing this previously, for it was customary for the Jewish prophets, in dispensing blessings, to lay hands on a person. This, however, was a father whose daughter was in need of being resurrected. As he knelt down before Jesus hoping in faith for Him to intervene, Jesus, feeling sympathy, knelt beside this father without saying anything. Jesus offered a comforting presence before He got up and followed Jairus as he led Jesus in the direction of his home.

In the midst of the crowd following Jesus was a woman who had been suffering for twelve years from a chronic hemorrhage. The woman's condition involved ritual uncleanliness. Thus she was a source of shame as well as physical discomfort. Though timid, she became motivated in her thinking, believing if only she could touch Jesus' garment she would be made well. Instead of spreading her uncleanliness to Jesus, her trusting touch would invite Jesus to impart healing and transformation. Trembling, she made her way with difficulty through the crowd. Creeping upon Jesus, she touched what scholars say was the blue-fringed border of His cloak or cape. Jesus was careful of His dress. Various references indicate the seamless robe and the cape or cloak was of fine material and fringes were attached to the four corners of His cloak. This was indicative of His vocation as a teacher. The hemorrhaging woman touched the tassel of Jesus' prayer shawl, a symbol of God's commandments and a reminder to be holy (Num. 15:37–39). Her touch expressed the woman's faith in the power of Israel's God to heal as well as her faith in Jesus as one sent from God. Immediately she felt different in her body and knew she was healed of the malady. In her timidity, she hoped to escape detection, but at the same time she rejoiced in her healing. Jesus knew power had gone out from Him, so He looked around searching to see the one who had done this. The woman, afraid and trembling, conscious of what had happened to her, knowing she was not hidden, came and fell down before Jesus and told Him in the presence of all the whole truth. She shared the motivation that led her to touch Him, the pitiable tale of years of the chronic misery and her present joyful experience of immediate cure. Jesus' reply to her was empowering and liberating: "Daughter, your faith has made you well. Go in peace. Your suffering is over" (Mark 5:34, NLT). She found healing for her body and with it, sympathy and pardon for her sins. She would not have obtained the latter had she been allowed to slip away and disappear into the crowd without confession.

II. The Healing of a Daughter (Matthew 9:21–25)

When Jesus finally arrived at Jairus's house, He found musicians and a large crowd gathered (Matt. 9:23). The musicians were playing melancholy tunes to stir up the grief and mourning of those in attendance. "Go away; for the girl is not dead but sleeping," stated Jesus (Matt. 9:24, NRSV). But His words were met with a scornful laugh and derision, for they knew she was dead. Jesus then asserted His authority and expelled them all from the house. Taking only three disciples and the parents of the little girl, Jesus entered the chamber where the little girl lay dead. He took the child by the hand and said: "Little girl, get up!" (Mark 5:41, NRSV). Instantly her spirit returned into her and she rose up and walked around. There was no convalescence. Her recovery was immediate and complete. The parents were beside themselves with amazement. They could hardly believe their eyes.

News spread quickly of the miracles Jesus did on that day. Jesus' power continued to magnify in Matthew's Gospel. Recall in the previous chapter Jesus healed some people, cast out some demons, and calmed the sea. With this story He raised the dead. The narrative was building Jesus' resume so that by the end of the story its readers should have no doubt Jesus was the Messiah of God.

Death in the ancient world was the last most menacing enemy. It had not been conquered nor could it be controlled. In a world in which children and young people died regularly, death was capricious and fearful. Also, given ancient beliefs of life after death, there was hardly a category of "good death." It was the unknown and to be feared. Jesus in this story took death by the hand and led it back to life.

III. Female Believers: Inheritors of the Kingdom of God (Matthew 9:26)

The theme that unites these two stories is *faith*. Matthew allowed us to see the faith of a Jewish leader and that of a woman compared and contrasted. According to Synoptic scholars, Matthew compared and contrasted the situation of a Jewish woman who was handicapped by a permanent state of uncleanliness with that of a male Jew who could approach Jesus directly. This man's faith is bold in Matthew's Gospel (Matt. 9:18) whereas in other accounts of the story, Jesus had to reassure the desperate father (Mark 5:36). On the other hand, Jesus had to offer exhortation to the woman in Matthew's account. He said, "Take heart" (Matt. 9:22, NRSV), the equivalent of *Be confident!* Jesus wanted the woman to be confident in God's readiness to save. From this trust, faith in herself as the object of God's loving care transformed her inner spirit along with her body. The question has been explored as to why this woman was depicted as so much more timid than the man. Scholars believe it was because she was a woman and because of the nature of her illness. Her medical condition rendered her unclean at all times, according to Leviticus 15:25. Anyone who touched her would contract her uncleanness and not be able to take part in religious activities. However, her condition had an additional emotional and spiritual side effect that made her shrink from approaching Jesus directly. She was unlike Jewish men who were even sicker than her but willing to boldly approach Jesus because they could. (Matt. 8:2). It wasn't a matter of her faith. She was convinced she could obtain healing from Jesus. Her timidity was probably due to her gender. Most biblical scholars agree that in Jewish society women ranked just a little ahead of children and slaves. Her inferior status prevented her from approaching Jesus with the confidence that He would treat her as a human being of equal dignity. Jesus' words to her were words of affection and not to be interpreted as paternalistic. His designation for her, *daughter*, assured her Jesus regarded her as worthy of respect.

Likewise, the fact Jesus troubled Himself to restore a girl to life may have been significant to early believers. Girls generally were not highly prized by their fathers. Male children were heirs and able to carry the name of the family. Female children were considered a burden because they were not given the same kind of societal freedom and were not understood to have a worthy contribution to the legacy and forward moving of the family. But Jesus' message through Matthew was that Jesus regarded female believers as equal inheritors of the Kingdom of God (1 Pet. 3:7).

The Lesson Applied

In times of health crisis, African -American women have been known to utilize their faith and spirituality. Research done on women of color suggests this has been a pattern for decades. One research journal reported that in 2001 a national survey of 3,172 women, aged 18 and older, was conducted in four languages, with over-sampling among African, Mexican, and Chinese Americans. Respondents were asked about their use of religion/spirituality for health reasons as part of a larger study on the prevalence of complementary and alternative medicine use among women. This paper focused on the subsample of 812 African-American women. The results were that overall 43 percent of African-American women in the study reported using religion/spirituality for health reasons in the past year. African-American women utilized religion and spirituality most often for serious conditions such as cancer, heart disease, and depression. The research concluded that religion and spirituality were associated with health-seeking behaviors of African-American women. Not only should churches of color help men with specific health prevention and treatment, but churches should help women and children as well. John said in his epistle that he wished above all things that we prosper and be in good and abundant health (3 John 1:2). Jesus is indeed not only our doctor but our healer!

Let's Talk About It

Are you familiar with the health disparities of women of color?

Do any of the following run in your family or have they run in generations of the past: obesity, diabetes, heart disease, cancer, and mental illness? Women of color are vastly affected by many health conditions in disproportionate numbers. Many of these health issues are due to the disparities in the healthcare system. People of color are less likely to seek preventative care and expert advice early on in illnesses. This is a complex issue because it entails the changing of some habits and ways of thinking but also structural changes that affect the manner in which women of color are treated in a hostile society.

Women of color are more likely to die in childbirth. They continue to rank as the highest number of new HIV cases. They are three times as likely to die in a pregnancy-related death than Caucasian women. There is probably no higher profile case to exhibit than tennis star Serena Williams. The tennis great began to experience discomfort after having her child. Initially, her health complaints were written off by her doctors and nurses. Eventually, by advocating for herself, she was able to get the care she needed for an embolism she had developed. If it had not been for her dogged perseverance, she likely would have died.

This Bible story demonstrated Jesus' care for women. There are no disparities in Jesus, only equality. Jesus' work demands we be not only informed about the issues that plague the population of more than half of our communities but we work to be agents of healing. None of us has the power to heal from the touch of our clothing, but through clear advocacy and personal interest in health, we can see some of those gaps in health and well-being begin to close.

We are able to do things collectively and individually. One is to stay abreast of health-related disparities for women of color. We must first acknowledge there is a problem to be a part of the solution.

Advocate for women of color for equal pay and benefits. One area to fight health disparities is through economic empowerment. Our system is based on money. Those who have money and good insurance have access to the best care. Lack of insurance often means no preventative care, which means ailments and diseases are discovered later, when the damage often is already done.

Beyond health insurance, it is important to advocate for benefits such as short-term disability and paid Family Medical Leave Act (FMLA) leave. Without it, many women are forced to return to work after a serious illness or giving birth long before they are ready. This leads to possible complications due to incomplete healing.

Lastly, participate in our own healthcare and awareness. Churches have the ability to hold forums on health, organize blood drives, prepare healthy fellowship meals, provide group exercise programs, and create networks of health professionals who are sensitive to the needs of women of color.

Jesus healed, and we can be His agents of healing in a sick and broken world.

HOME DAILY DEVOTIONAL READINGS
JUNE 21–27, 2021

MONDAY	TUESDAY	WEDNESDAY	THURSDAY	FRIDAY	SATURDAY	SUNDAY
Let's Sing of the Lord's Faithfulness	The Baptist Dies for the Faith	The Crowd's Hunger Satisfied	Believe the One Sent to You	The Sick Are Healed	Speak Confidently to Civil Authorities	Savior of the Fearful, Doubter, Needy
Isaiah 38:16–20	Matthew 14:1–12	Matthew 14:13–21	John 6:22–29	Matthew 14:34–36	Mark 13:9–12	Matthew 14:22–33

LESSON 4 JUNE 27, 2021

WHY DO YOU DOUBT?

Adult Topic:
An Amazing Feat

Background Scripture:
Matthew 14:22–33

MATTHEW 14:22–33

King James Version

AND straightway Jesus constrained his disciples to get into a ship, and to go before him unto the other side, while he sent the multitudes away.

23 And when he had sent the multitudes away, he went up into a mountain apart to pray: and when the evening was come, he was there alone.

24 But the ship was now in the midst of the sea, tossed with waves: for the wind was contrary.

25 And in the fourth watch of the night Jesus went unto them, walking on the sea.

26 And when the disciples saw him walking on the sea, they were troubled, saying, It is a spirit; and they cried out for fear.

27 But straightway Jesus spake unto them, saying, Be of good cheer; it is I; be not afraid.

28 And Peter answered him and said, Lord, if it be thou, bid me come unto thee on the water.

29 And he said, Come. And when Peter was come down out of the ship, he walked on the water, to go to Jesus.

30 But when he saw the wind boisterous, he was afraid; and beginning to sink, he cried, saying, Lord, save me.

31 And immediately Jesus stretched forth his hand, and caught him, and said unto him, O thou of little faith, wherefore didst thou doubt?

32 And when they were come into the ship, the wind ceased.

33 Then they that were in the ship came and worshipped him, saying, Of a truth thou art the Son of God.

New Revised Standard Version

IMMEDIATELY he made the disciples get into the boat and go on ahead to the other side, while he dismissed the crowds.

23 And after he had dismissed the crowds, he went up the mountain by himself to pray. When evening came, he was there alone,

24 but by this time the boat, battered by the waves, was far from the land, for the wind was against them.

25 And early in the morning he came walking toward them on the sea.

26 But when the disciples saw him walking on the sea, they were terrified, saying, "It is a ghost!" And they cried out in fear.

27 But immediately Jesus spoke to them and said, "Take heart, it is I; do not be afraid."

28 Peter answered him, "Lord, if it is you, command me to come to you on the water."

29 He said, "Come." So Peter got out of the boat, started walking on the water, and came toward Jesus.

30 But when he noticed the strong wind, he became frightened, and beginning to sink, he cried out, "Lord, save me!"

31 Jesus immediately reached out his hand and caught him, saying to him, "You of little faith, why did you doubt?"

32 When they got into the boat, the wind ceased.

33 And those in the boat worshiped him, saying, "Truly you are the Son of God."

MAIN THOUGHT: And immediately Jesus stretched forth his hand, and caught him, and said unto him, O thou of little faith, wherefore didst thou doubt? (Matthew 14:31, KJV)

LESSON SETTING

Time: A.D. 26
Place: Sea of Galilee

LESSON OUTLINE

I. **Faith and Discernment (Matthew 14:22)**
II. **Faith in Crisis (Matthew 14:23–27)**
III. **Faith for an Amazing Feat that Leads to Worship (Matthew 9:28–33)**

Unifying Principle

In the depth of crisis, people often are caught between trust and doubt. Will one trust that help will come? Jesus, by walking on water to save His disciples, demonstrated His divine empowerment to be the Savior of all.

Introduction

Have you ever been in a situation where you were experiencing a crisis? Then, after you were able to draw upon needed insights and resources to cope with your crisis, were you led to assist someone in their own crisis? Adults have experiences of being extremely fearful when undertaking life's ventures. In all phases of our lives, until we go to heaven, we undertake all sorts of worthwhile and notable ventures, and hopefully as a result experience success and impact the lives of those in our circles of influence. Adults may undertake a risky venture with zeal only to lose heart at a later time. Many adults in such a situation have needed someone to save them from a bad situation and have been fortunate enough to have a person or two fill this role in their situation. It is a blessing when adults can trust someone whom they respect and admire. Many of those people are supportive because they see potential in the person who desires to undertake a worthwhile and noble task. Because some of these undertakings are not just a notion, many adults who undertake them have experienced the power of a dangerous storm. Fortunately many of them have had a friend whom they could trust in difficult times.

In today's lesson, Synoptic scholars refer to this time in Jesus' ministry as the *Galilean crisis*. This was the beginning of signs the Jewish religious establishment would begin to turn on Jesus after He refused to be the king they perceived He could have been. He fed them bread in the wilderness, and they wanted to use Him to continue the food supply in the desert, but they didn't see Him as the Messiah or as John's Gospel put it, the Bread of Life. From Matthew's point of view, the final verses of the previous miracle in the wilderness (Matt. 14:13–21), Jesus dealt with this internally through prayer to His Father. Then He discovered the disciples were in their own crisis that Jesus would have to deal with and save them from.

Exposition

I. Faith and Discernment (Matthew 14:22)

The command by Jesus for the disciples to get into the boat and go before Him to the other side of the lake presupposed the fact that unusual circumstances existed. The result of the previous miracle—the feeding of the five thousand—was what some have described as a swelling tide of enthusiasm rising to its full height and thus moved the multitude to form a foolish and dangerous plan. This crowd wanted to crown Jesus and make Him their king. They were on the verge of coming and taking Jesus by force in order to do so. Because of these unusual circumstances, the most natural explanation, according to scholars, is that Jesus wanted to remove both Himself and His disciples from the foolish enthusiasm of the crowd. For that reason, He arranged for them to sail away at dusk across the sea while He dispersed the crowd. Because Jesus got the disciples out of the political atmosphere of revolutionary excitement, it was easier now to dispatch the crowd than it would have been with them present. Jesus understood the mind of the crowd. He hastened to prevent the revolt's purpose, which was precipitated by the recent death of the loved prophet John. The result of the miracle in the wilderness did not take Jesus by surprise. It was what He expected. Or perhaps, in a sense, it was what He had purposed to happen! It was time for the thoughts of many hearts to be revealed. And at least one of the reasons the miracle was performed was to help reveal people's hearts. Jesus provided a table for the people in the wilderness, gave them the grain of heaven, and sent them food until they were full (Ps. 78:19, 24–25). Some suggest He did this in order to test them and know what was in their hearts (Deut. 8:2). Did they love Him for His own sake or only because they expected worldly advantage? He knew beforehand that many followed Him for secret purposes, but He desired to bring the fact home to their own consciences. The miracle gave Him the opportunity and enabled Him to say, without fear of contradiction, "You are looking for me, not because you saw signs, but because you ate your fill of the loaves" (John 6:26, NRSV). It was a searching word. It put all of His followers who professed His name in a position where they had to examine their thoughts and ask themselves the question, *Why do I follow Jesus?*

II. Faith in Crisis (Matthew 14:23–27)

What's referred to as the Galilean crisis had come at last, and the remainder of Jesus' ministry was destined to be thorny as He suffered the alienation of the popular Jewish crowds and heard those who had been praising Him soon express disappointment and bitterness against Him. Knowing this led Him to go up on the mountain and pray (Matt. 14:23). Thoughts of the death of John the Baptist and His own day of death approaching on Calvary had left his soul in anguish. Meanwhile, with the second watch of the night came one of those sudden storms characteristic of this sea surrounded by mountains. The wind caused the sea to rise up more and more. In the previous storm encounter on the sea by night, Jesus was with the disciples and saved them when the waves were threatening to engulf their boat (8:23–27). Now they were in the midst of sea, distressed in rowing, making little headway with all their efforts because the wind was against them (Mark 6:48), and Jesus was not there. Nine hours of fearful struggle brought them but little over three miles to about the middle of the lake. They didn't attempt to approach the shore lest their boat be cast upon the rocks and destroyed and they were carried by the waves into the sea. Jesus, alone on the land and in prayer on the mountain, could see them in the midst of the strenuous pull of the oars as they sought to drive their boat on the face of the adverse wind. Despite what was going on in the inner spirit of Jesus' humanity during prayer, He knew His Father was with Him, and He thus began to focus on the disciples who were in the peril of the sea.

The storm was as violent as the first they had experienced and lasted longer. Their strength had been put to a severe test. Perhaps this storm was a preparation for a greater one to follow on the next day when the fickle crowd would turn away from their Master—the gale of a tornado of apostasy, said F. F. Bruce. The trial of faith in an absence of the Lord in the storm at sea would strengthen them to meet the tempest of temptation. Jesus left them for a while in the midst of that affliction to prepare them for the victory of their faith and for years of service ahead, stated William Taylor, author of *Miracles of Our Savior*.

According to scholars, the *fourth watch night* implied the Roman division of the night into four watches, as in Mark 13:35. This would be sometime between 3:00 a.m. and 6:00 a.m. They believed the night had three watches. It was during these hours when the disciples saw Jesus coming toward them, walking on the sea. As He got closer and closer, they didn't recognize the figure to be Jesus and became afraid. Several attempts have been made by textual critics to explain Jesus' walking on the water. It has been proposed, for example, that what happened was nothing more than an optical illusion. In the dim light of the fourth watch of the night, the figure of Jesus was seen as if walking on the water when actually walking through the surf in the shallows of the Northern Lake. While this is credible in theory, others write that the disciples would have quickly discovered their error, and the incident would not have been preserved for posterity. A different belief is that this story is from a resurrection experience that was erroneously transferred to the days of Jesus' ministry. Some scholars believe this story is a theophany: Jesus revealed Himself to His disciples as a divine being or as God. It is alleged that Jesus' statement to the terrified disciples in Matthew 14:27 (NRSV)—"Take heart, it is I; do not be afraid"—may reflect what's called the theophanic formula of Exodus 3:14 (NRSV), "I AM WHO I AM."

For many, this seems to be reading into the passage far more than Matthew intended. Furthermore, Peter understood the phrase in its normal sense: "Lord, if it is you …" (Matt. 14:28, NRSV). The words were meant to identify the walker on the sea as Jesus, not God. The figure walking the waves was, for Matthew, not a divine being but the Messiah whom God had endowed with supernatural power. Essential to Matthew's telling of this miracle is the fact that at the time of Jesus' appearance on the lake, the boat was far from land and being tortured by the waves.

This story sits in a continuum of narratives in which rulers were understood to have been divinely chosen to govern and even rule over the elements. As an example, Julius Caesar was shown by Lucan in his work *Pharsalia* in a similar light as Jesus. A storm came up while Julius Caesar was on a boat and was then convinced the boat would not submerge because nature knew who he was (W. Cotter, 170). Although this story about Caesar is fictional, the point is the same. The ruler did not simply govern people but even the elements of nature. Matthew's story has the same effect, and when it is considered that this story is placed between two other miracle stories, Jesus is shown to have supreme power. In the context of Matthew 14, Jesus was a provider, a ruler of nature, and a healer.

For Matthew, Jesus' miracle of walking on the sea was to aid the threatened disciples. As Messiah, He is the one charged and empowered by God to shepherd and care for God's people. Jesus immediately spoke to the terrified disciples with words of peace and reassurance (Matt. 14:27). He came to them in their hour of dire need and relieved their distress. Jesus' temporary absence earlier was a preparation for His perpetual absence to come later.

III. Faith for an Amazing Feat that Leads to Worship (Matthew 14:28–33)

Matthew alone recorded the episode of Peter walking on the water. According to *The Interpreter's Bible,* Peter's resolution to come to Jesus required great courage, and although his faith wavered, Christ strengthened him before it was too late. This passage, therefore, foreshadowed Peter's denial of Jesus and His restoration after the Crucifixion (John 21:15–10). Matthew thought of Peter as a type of Christian disciple whose teaching could be followed with confidence. Matthew concluded the story with the disciples' response, which is different than Mark's Gospel. Matthew agreed with Mark on theological perspective, but his literary purpose required that the later faith be foreshadowed during the earthly ministry. Just as the Gentile Magi worshiped Jesus at his birth long before the Gentile mission began, so those in the boat worshiped Jesus even though they did not yet know it would be only through a shameful death and subsequent resurrection that Jesus would enter fully into His Lordship. And yet, Peter and the other disciples responded to this miraculous happening properly with their limited understanding. Their worship reinforced Matthew's point that Jesus is the Anointed One of God worthy of worship. Though they did not understand fully, they understood enough to understand they were in the presence of one greater than they and whom God was with.

The Lesson Applied

In the times we currently live, it's not beyond temptation to become enthusiastic about values and convictions we hold. While this is not a problem in and of itself, it can become such that our discernment is clouded and we are so caught up in our causes that we may not become aware just what we are emotionally getting ourselves into that may not be of God's will. In the current political environment in which this writer writes, Christians seem to be easily held hostage by various political circles without seeking God's discernment as opposed to committing to party lines.

Jesus had discernment for the crisis that was before Him. On the other hand, the disciples escaped being a part of the wrong cause because Jesus knew the hearts of the people around Him. In time the apostles also would have discernment, but that would come after Pentecost. When we find ourselves in crisis, it is easy to not see the Lord's hand in the midst. But in fact, He has ordered our steps regardless of the crisis we find ourselves in. To be sure, our Christ knows what lies before us and can allow even the most tragic of circumstances to grow our faith in Him.

As in the earlier story of Jesus calming the sea while in the boat with the disciples, the boat here seems to represent the Church, buffeted by temptations, trials, and persecutions. In both, Jesus appears as the Church's champion who is strong to save those who call on Him in faith. Peter walking on the water depicts what it means to be a Christian caught midway between faith and doubt. Peter represents all who dare to believe Jesus is Savior, take their first steps in confidence that He is able to sustain them, and then forget to keep their eyes fixed on Him instead of on the towering waves that threaten to engulf them. Peter also represents the risk-taking of faith. Christians learn to live with uncertainties. The knowledge of faith speaks of realities that are of more importance than the things we can see and touch. To believe in the saving power of Jesus is to take a risk. We can worship our Lord even now before our life and troubles will be no more. The Gospel songwriter put it this way, "Don't' wait till the battle is over to shout, for we know in the end we're going to win."

Let's Talk About It

The boat could symbolize the Church. How can we as the Church hold onto certain faith during uncertain times? What are some specific things congregations can do to demonstrate faith? How can we share this faith with others?

As the Church, we are to be the demonstrable presence of God in the world. That is difficult to do if we are not filled with faith. Congregations during moments of crisis must commit themselves to the practice of intentional communal prayer so God might reveal what steps to take. The Church is then able to display its faith by continuing in its message and constant ministry to the glory of God. The Church shares its faith by being constant. There is a saying, "Never let them see you sweat." In other words, even in the midst of turmoil, as people of faith we have committed ourselves to be a peaceful and light-filled presence. If we are consistent in this, our faith will be shared and we will survive any storm. Jesus has built His Church on a rock, and the gates of hell will not prevail (Matt. 16:18).

HOME DAILY DEVOTIONAL READINGS
JUNE 27–JULY 4, 2021

Monday	Tuesday	Wednesday	Thursday	Friday	Saturday	Sunday
God Welcomes Foreigners	Naomi's Sorrow Turns to Joy	Symptoms and Treatment of Leprosy	Lepers Share Their Good News	Many Samaritans Believe in the Savior	Doing What Needs to Be Done	Cultivate Gratefulness for Acts of Healing
Isaiah 56:1–8	Ruth 4:3–6,13–15	Leviticus 13:1–8	2 Kings 7:3–11	John 4:39–42	Luke 17:1–10	Leviticus 13:45–56; Luke 17:11–19

AN ATTITUDE OF GRATITUDE

Adult Topic:
Expressing Thanks

Background Scripture:
Leviticus 13–14; Luke 5:12–16; 17:11–19

LEVITICUS 13:45–46; LUKE 17:11–19

King James Version

AND the leper in whom the plague is, his clothes shall be rent, and his head bare, and he shall put a covering upon his upper lip, and shall cry, Unclean, unclean.
46 All the days wherein the plague shall be in him he shall be defiled; he is unclean: he shall dwell alone; without the camp shall his habitation be.

• • • Luke 17:11–19 • • •

AND it came to pass, as he went to Jerusalem, that he passed through the midst of Samaria and Galilee.
12 And as he entered into a certain village, there met him ten men that were lepers, which stood afar off:
13 And they lifted up their voices, and said, Jesus, Master, have mercy on us.
14 And when he saw them, he said unto them, Go shew yourselves unto the priests. And it came to pass, that, as they went, they were cleansed.
15 And one of them, when he saw that he was healed, turned back, and with a loud voice glorified God,
16 And fell down on his face at his feet, giving him thanks: and he was a Samaritan.
17 And Jesus answering said, Were there not ten cleansed? but where are the nine?
18 There are not found that returned to give glory to God, save this stranger.
19 And he said unto him, Arise, go thy way: thy faith hath made thee whole.

New Revised Standard Version

THE person who has the leprous disease shall wear torn clothes and let the hair of his head be disheveled; and he shall cover his upper lip and cry out, "Unclean, unclean."
46 He shall remain unclean as long as he has the disease; he is unclean. He shall live alone; his dwelling shall be outside the camp.

• • • Luke 17:11–19 • • •

ON the way to Jerusalem Jesus was going through the region between Samaria and Galilee.
12 As he entered a village, ten lepers approached him. Keeping their distance,
13 they called out, saying, "Jesus, Master, have mercy on us!"
14 When he saw them, he said to them, "Go and show yourselves to the priests." And as they went, they were made clean.
15 Then one of them, when he saw that he was healed, turned back, praising God with a loud voice.
16 He prostrated himself at Jesus' feet and thanked him. And he was a Samaritan.
17 Then Jesus asked, "Were not ten made clean? But the other nine, where are they?
18 Was none of them found to return and give praise to God except this foreigner?"
19 Then he said to him, "Get up and go on your way; your faith has made you well."

MAIN THOUGHT: And one of them, when he saw that he was healed, turned back, and with a loud voice glorified God. (Luke 17:15, KJV)

LESSON SETTING

Time: A.D. 26
Place: The region between Galilee and Samaria

LESSON OUTLINE

I. **Leprosy (Leviticus 13:45–46)**
II. **Healing Elements (Luke 17:11–14)**
III. **Gratitude Leads to Salvation (Luke 17:15–19)**

UNIFYING PRINCIPLE

People often receive mercy but do not acknowledge the one who helped them. Do you show appreciation? Ten lepers, isolated by their skin diseases, were healed. Only one, who was a foreigner, was saved by his faith and offered thanks.

INTRODUCTION

In today's lesson we're going to experience a story of gratitude. Unfortunately, where there is gratitude, there is also ingratitude lurking nearby. During the COVID–19 global pandemic, there was a flood of appreciation for many people who were on the front lines of either dealing with the science, caring for those diagnosed and providing resources for those who were affected, and those who were responsible for leading us in the scientific, medical, economical, and essential services. A vast majority were filled with gratitude while others desperate for the laws to lift were ready to get back to business as usual. What was gleaned most from this unprecedented time was an insight that comes from our printed texts in both the Old and New Testaments. In the Leviticus text, the dreaded condition of leprosy was a reality. On the other hand, In Luke's Gospel, the reality of leprosy was unchanged, but hopes for healing and salvation through Jesus were available. Our New Testament text is reminiscent of *sunshine* and the Old Testament text is reminiscent of *rain*. Thus the insight gained is: It takes sunshine and rain to cultivate gratitude. Sunshine represents Jesus' complete healing of one, and rain represents the dreaded leprosy by which the ten were affected. The difference is that one was healed totally, but the other nine who were healed of their leprosy were diagnosed with something far worse—ingratitude. How does one overcome ingratitude? The cure for ingratitude is a demonstration of God so clear we can't deny either His power or His love.

EXPOSITION

I. LEPROSY (LEVITICUS 13:45–46)

Two full chapters of Leviticus are given to a description of leprosy, its diagnosis (Lev. 13), and the cleansing of the leper (Lev. 14). *Leprosy* was a generic term assigned to a range of maladies from mildew in houses and on clothes to skin diseases in humans. (Read the article on leprosy in *Harper's Bible Dictionary.*) The disease was so mysterious and so threatening that it was met with fear and ignorance. Jewish law demanded the diseased persons be removed from sight, isolated from all domestic contact (Lev. 13:45–46). According to Pentateuch scholars, there was a threefold ritual in which the leper had to partake in order to remove the uncleanliness if the leper were to be reintroduced to the community. There was the ceremony for the first day (14:2–8). The purpose of this ritual was not to cleanse the disease, but was a witness to the fact that the disease was already healed. The ritual was symbolic and religious, not therapeutic. There was also a second ceremony for the seventh day (14:9), and a third ceremony for the eighth day (14:10–32) where the focus was on offering the appropriate sacrifices.

It may be that leprosy in the Old Testament differed somewhat from leprosy in New Testament times. Keep in mind the laws had to do with the detection of the disease and its terrible results. Thus, it might miss the mark to conclude the Old Testament considered leprous diseases to be the result of sin. (To be sure, stories like the one about Miriam in Num. 12 show leprosy to be a manifestation of divine judgment.) A period of absence from the community was mandated for those with blemishes on their bodies. The offering of sacrifices allowed readmittance into the community activities. Ostracism was replaced by fellowship.

Leviticus says leprosy is like sin, but is not itself sin or a sign of sin. It is like sin in that it bars a person from cultic fellowship with God. Like sin, it is insidious, progressive, pervasive, benumbing, and loathsome. Several of Christ's miracles involved lepers. Interestingly, the blind were healed, the crippled were healed, but the lepers were *cleansed*. In Greek, this verb takes on a distinct moral nuance as demonstrated in the following passages: Acts 15:9; 2 Corinthians 7:1; Ephesians 5:26; James 4:8; 1 John 1:7, 9.

II. Healing Elements (Luke 17:11–14)

In these verses we see Jesus outside a village near the border of Samaria ministering to a group of people with a social disease. Nine of them were probably Jews, and the village was likely a Jewish village. Fellow sympathy in misery had broken down the barriers of race, and the one Samaritan stood up with the others, who were probably Jews, and joined with them in their plea for pity. The lepers' sheer misery brought them together despite their religious and ethnic differences. In this light, the fact that Jesus found them on the borderlands between Samaria and Galilee was evocative of their liminal state: They literally were marginalized by their disease and forged their own unclean community on the borderlands. Luke said they kept distant from non–lepers (Luke 17:12; Lev. 13:45–46; Num. 5:2). They formed their own colonies (2 Kings 7:3), and they positioned themselves near travelways in order to make appeals for charity. Showing themselves to a priest after healing was done according to the law (Lev. 14:2–32).

Thus, for Luke's readers, the first part was a healing story with the usual elements: The lepers cried for help; Jesus responded; the healing occurred in their act of obedient faith. They cried for help! They were miserably afflicted with this malady that was itself a living death. They spent their days in hopelessness, waiting for the end. They begged for pity and left it up to Jesus. At first Jesus didn't see them because of their social distancing, but when He did, He responded. He heard their cry. Jesus showed no reservation regarding His proximity to the ceremonially unclean men. Nor did He show any racial favoritism—He healed all ten lepers. His openness is a testimony to those who follow Jesus to extend ourselves to those who are rejected by society.

Jesus did not hesitate, but He ordered them to go at once and show themselves to the priest according to the instruction of their ceremonial law. The purpose of showing oneself to the priest was to have the priest certify the leper had been cleansed (Lev. 13:6) and thus cleared to be restored to the community. Each would go to the priest nearest his home, and the Samaritan would go to the temple on Gerizim. This command for them to show themselves to the priests proved Jesus came to fulfill the law, not to destroy it. He built on the old regime a new and better order.

Now it happened that in the lepers' going, they were cleansed. Their confidence in obeying the order of Jesus proved the occasion of immediate cure. One Synoptic scholar painted the picture of the immediate en–route–to–the–priest healing as such: The dry scales fell off from them, the white spots disappeared, a healthy color returned to their flesh, their disfigured members were restored, a thrill of new life coursed their veins, and with exceeding joy they perceived they were made whole.

III. Gratitude Leads to Salvation (Luke 17:15–19)

Surely all of the lepers were thrilled and were grateful to Jesus. Not so. Nine hurried to put an end to their social isolation, thinking only of themselves, in anticipation of being reunited with their families and friends. Only one remembered with gratitude Him who had made possible the cure, hastily turned back, praising God with a loud voice, and fell down beside the feet of Jesus, thanking Him. Luke inserted the significant explanation that this man who came back was a Samaritan. Thus, the second part for the sake of Luke's readers was the story of the salvation of a despised foreigner.

When Jesus said, "Your faith has made you well" (Luke 17:19, NRSV), the blessing certainly referred to some benefit other than that which all, including the other nine, had received earlier. The verb translated *made well* is the same word often translated *to be saved.* According to some, what we have here then is a story of nine being healed and one being saved. Luke, the physician, treated favorably the marginalized. The man was a Samaritan and hence an outcast and a religious heretic, and he had leprosy. But as already implied, in leper colonies, the common problem rendered Jew/Gentile distinctions unimportant. This was true not only in leper colonies but also in the presence of Jesus. However, only the foreigner received the full blessing of Jesus' ministry.

Jesus was disappointed because the nine had been received and healed. He did not find gratitude where it should have been expected. But it was gratifying to find it where it would not be expected. Jesus concluded the incident with the commanding affirmation: "Get up and go on your way" (17:19, NRSV). In essence, He told the Samaritan, "Your faith has saved you and made you well."

The Lesson Applied

Ten received the blessing. Only one returned to give thanks. Often the stranger in the church is the who sings heartily the hymns we have long left to the choir, who expresses gratitude for blessings we had not noticed, who listens attentively to the sermon we think we have already heard, who gets excited about our old Bible, and who becomes actively involved in acts of service to which we send small donations. Must it always be so?

Believers of all races and creeds seek God's presence to heal and restore them. One has to wonder if there would have been a Samaritan among a group of Jews if not for their common misery. In leper houses of today, racial and creedal prejudices are forgotten, for misery loves company. Wars are forgotten in desolation. Bickering dies in common disasters. Is that one reason why suffering comes? Such is our stubbornness, truths we refuse to learn from joy we learn from pain. Believers express gratitude to those who help them. They realize no one has to do anything for them. The least one can do is to show genuine gratitude. God looks for a response of gratitude.

Let's Talk About It

What people groups do religious communities tend to treat like lepers today?

In most cases, we do not treat people with diseases like leprosy in the same manner as in the days of old. We have come to understand through science that many of the diseases that were scary for preindustrial societies are no longer fearful. We have an understanding of germs, viruses, and bacteria that helps us treat others more humanely. However, as a society we tend to keep certain groups of people outside of the proverbial city gates.

As an example, consider people who have gained a felony conviction. Often after paying a debt to society, they are kept from the most meaningful integrations into society. Felons are kept from applying or being hired for many jobs, receiving federal financial aid for college education, voting, and applying for many housing situations. Their record also precludes them from receiving small business loans and other financial help to be entrepreneurs. Like the lepers, they live in a minimal space or experience a kind of social death that often relegates them to living outside the city gates.

The Church's goal must be to reach out to the disenfranchised and the troubled to bring them into the Christian fold. Our motto must be, "Everything old has passed away; see, everything has become new!" (2 Cor. 5:17, NRSV). We must proclaim that Jesus heals our brokenness and dysfunction. He welcomes us into the family of God.

Home Daily Devotional Readings

July 5–11, 2021

Monday	Tuesday	Wednesday	Thursday	Friday	Saturday	Sunday
Apollos and Paul, Builders	Entrusted to Take Gospel to Gentiles	Grace and Peace to All	God's Righteous Wrath	God's Actions Are Fair and Just	God's Righteous Actions for Saints, Sinners	The Gospel Changes Jews and Gentiles
1 Corinthians 3:1–11	Galatians 2:1–10	Romans 1:1–7	Romans 1:18–23	Romans 1:24–32	2 Peter 2:4–9	Romans 1:8–17

THE POWER OF THE GOSPEL

Adult Topic:
A Gift to Strengthen You

Background Scripture:
Romans 1

ROMANS 1:8–17

King James Version

FIRST, I thank my God through Jesus Christ for you all, that your faith is spoken of throughout the whole world.

9 For God is my witness, whom I serve with my spirit in the gospel of his Son, that without ceasing I make mention of you always in my prayers;

10 Making request, if by any means now at length I might have a prosperous journey by the will of God to come unto you.

11 For I long to see you, that I may impart unto you some spiritual gift, to the end ye may be established;

12 That is, that I may be comforted together with you by the mutual faith both of you and me.

13 Now I would not have you ignorant, brethren, that oftentimes I purposed to come unto you, (but was let hitherto,) that I might have some fruit among you also, even as among other Gentiles.

14 I am debtor both to the Greeks, and to the Barbarians; both to the wise, and to the unwise.

15 So, as much as in me is, I am ready to preach the gospel to you that are at Rome also.

16 For I am not ashamed of the gospel of Christ: for it is the power of God unto salvation to every one that believeth; to the Jew first, and also to the Greek.

17 For therein is the righteousness of God revealed from faith to faith: as it is written, The just shall live by faith.

New Revised Standard Version

FIRST, I thank my God through Jesus Christ for all of you, because your faith is proclaimed throughout the world.

9 For God, whom I serve with my spirit by announcing the gospel of his Son, is my witness that without ceasing I remember you always in my prayers,

10 asking that by God's will I may somehow at last succeed in coming to you.

11 For I am longing to see you so that I may share with you some spiritual gift to strengthen you—

12 or rather so that we may be mutually encouraged by each other's faith, both yours and mine.

13 I want you to know, brothers and sisters, that I have often intended to come to you (but thus far have been prevented), in order that I may reap some harvest among you as I have among the rest of the Gentiles.

14 I am a debtor both to Greeks and to barbarians, both to the wise and to the foolish

15 —hence my eagerness to proclaim the gospel to you also who are in Rome.

16 For I am not ashamed of the gospel; it is the power of God for salvation to everyone who has faith, to the Jew first and also to the Greek.

17 For in it the righteousness of God is revealed through faith for faith; as it is written, "The one who is righteous will live by faith."

MAIN THOUGHT: For I am not ashamed of the gospel of Christ: for it is the power of God unto salvation to every one that believeth; to the Jew first, and also to the Greek. (Romans 1:16, KJV)

LESSON SETTING

Time: A.D. 56–58
Place: Corinth

LESSON OUTLINE

I. **Paul, His Gospel and God's People (Romans 1:8–13)**
II. **Paul, His Evangelism and God's People (Romans 1:14–17)**

Unifying Principle

People often look to be in a relationship that provides them with strength and stability. Where do you find your strength? The Gospel is the power of God that can save all those who believe.

Introduction

At the time of Paul's correspondence to the believers in Rome, Rome had a population of at least one million comprised of people derived from all walks of life and every socioeconomic demographic. Although Judaism had been declared a legal religion by both Julius Caesar and Octavius, the Jews in Rome still endured negative perceptions and acute mistreatment. The two expulsions of Jews from Rome in A.D. 19 and 49 seem to affirm the existential difficulties of the Jews living in Rome during this time.

In A.D. 54 after the death of Claudius, Nero allowed the Jews to return to Rome. With great anticipation and excitement, Paul wrote to introduce himself to the church at Rome believing he would encounter a strong congregation upon his arrival. After delivering the alms gifts to the church at Jerusalem, Paul desired to go to Spain and also minister in the western Mediterranean region. So he wrote to clarify his understanding of the Gospel to the Gentiles and challenged the inappropriate attitudes and actions among Jews and Gentiles in the church.

John R. W. Stott called the epistle to the Romans "a kind of Christian manifesto of freedom through Jesus Christ." The letter to the Romans addressed the contextual complexities and conditions that Paul and the church of necessity were facing. John Harvey notes that Paul's epistle to the Romans had several interlacing purposes that addressed missionary, theological, and pastoral concerns.

Paul asserted we are not born free. Rather, humanity is born in sin and bondage. The Good News is that Jesus came to set humanity free. Stott further notes this freedom purchased by Jesus is freedom from the holy wrath of God upon ungodliness, freedom from alienation into reconciliation, freedom from what Malcolm Muggeride once called "the dark little dungeon of our own ego," freedom from death, freedom from ethnic conflict in the family of God, and freedom to give oneself to the loving service of God and others.

The book of Romans has had an important impact on the Church and its ministers. Martin Luther, the reformer, noted that Romans was the "chief part of the New Testament, and … truly the purest gospel." William Tyndale, the father of English Bible translators, noted that "Romans was the principal and most excellent part of the New Testament, and most pure Evangelion (Gospel)…. a light and a way into the whole Scripture." Augustine, the greatest Latin Father of the early church, upon reading Romans 13:13–14 noted that all the shadows of doubts were dispelled.

Ernst Kasemann asserts that Romans 1 looks to provide Paul's introduction by giving us the prescript (1:1–7), the proem (preface) (1:8–15), and the theme (1:16–17). Paul saw that both Jews and Gentiles were sinners and in need of God's righteous saving grace. This salvation received by faith would lead to the redefinition and reconstitution of the people of God as both having equal value and importance in the plan and economy of God. Paul stressed two emphases here: the integrity of the Gospel committed to him and the unity of the Jews and the Gentiles in the community of faith.

Exposition

I. Paul, His Gospel and God's People (Romans 1:8–13)

The backdrop of these verses hinge on the understanding that for Paul, the Gospel is just that—Good News to all who accept and access it by faith. Paul did not conceive of faith as just intellectual assent nor astuteness. Paul's faith required obedience. This obedience was undergirded by surrender and trust in the God who wrote the Gospel and Christ Jesus who is the content of the Gospel. Ernest Best trumpeted the truth when he noted, "obedience is the true measure of a person's faith."

Paul began this section by listing the priority of thanking God and his reasons for such exuberant praise. The *J. B. Phillips New Testament* reads, "I must begin by telling you how I thank God" (Rom. 1:8). Why was Paul thankful? His thankfulness was a common feature in his writings (1 Cor. 1:4; 2 Cor. 1:11; Phil. 1:3; Col. 1:3; 1 Thess. 1:2; 2 Thess. 1:3; 2 Tim. 1:3; Phlm. 1:4). Paul's thankfulness was rooted in "my God." Paul lifted the intensely personal aspect of his relationship with God. Paul's praise was "through Jesus" and for the believers in Rome. Through the redemptive sacrifice of Jesus on the cross and its results, Paul was able to give God praise. There was a direct praise for the believers in Rome and the report of their praiseworthy faith. The whole Roman Empire had been made aware of the faith these believers in Rome possessed. The important note here is that Paul expressed to the believers his thankfulness for them and saw that their faith was a direct work of God through Christ Jesus' atoning sacrifice for sinners, which includes both Jews and Gentiles.

The next important aspect of the text is Paul's prayer life. Paul advised the believers in Rome that although he had never met them nor greeted them in person, he interceded for them. Paul, in order to disavow this language as common rhetoric, called on God to be his witness that this prayer work for the Roman believers had been a legitimate pursuit in his ministry. John Stott reminds us here that in Paul's apostolic ministry, praying and preaching went together. There had been prayer for these unknown believers constantly.

Another facet of this plea for the Roman believers was that Paul may, if it was God's will, soon go to them, or that the way may be provided for him to see and fellowship with them. Paul's humility showed here in that he wouldn't impose his desires upon the will of God. Rather, he submitted his desire and will to God's plan and sovereignty.

Verses 11–13 provide us with the motivation of Paul. R. Kent Hughes suggests Paul's motivation here was mutual encouragement. Paul desired to impart some spiritual gift (*charisma*) to edify the Roman believers. His desire was to exhort, teach, and encourage them. Stott helps us here in that he notes the spiritual gifts (*charismata*) described in 1 Corinthians 12, Romans 12, and Ephesians 4 are bestowed by God, Christ, or the Spirit exclusively and therefore could not be given by Paul. The main idea here is that Paul's motivation was not to receive something from the church but rather to enhance and strengthen the church through the gift of encouragement. Paul was not selfish in his motivation and reasoning for visiting Rome.

Verse 12 seems as though Paul recognized the need to explain this motivation and bring balance to his earlier statements. Note his phraseology: "So that we may be mutually encouraged by each other's faith" (Rom. 1:12, NRSV). Paul's faith would be stimulated by these young believers and the young believers would be matured by exposure to a more experienced soldier. There is power in the reciprocal intertwining of mutuality, and Paul was not too proud to acknowledge and accept his need for it.

Verse 13 presents the reasons for Paul's delay in visiting the church at Rome. He said he had often been prevented from coming to them. Paul did not provide exactly what kept him from visiting, but he passionately related that visiting them had been a major priority in his mind and heart. (One might posit that Paul's work in Greece and other places had not been completed.)

We discover another motivation for his desire to come to Rome—"in order that I may reap some harvest among you" (1:13, NRSV). *Harvest* can be translated *fruit*. John Murray interprets this idea as Paul desiring to visit Rome in order to *gather* fruit, not to *bear* fruit. The apostle to the Gentiles would be visiting the capital city of the Gentiles to engage in an evangelistic reaping of Gentiles.

II. Paul, His Evangelism and God's People (Romans 1:14–17)

In this section, Paul made three relational statements: "I am obligated" (v. 14, NIV); "I am so eager" (v. 15, NIV); and "I am not ashamed" (v. 16, NIV). We see in verses 14 and 15 a glimpse of Paul's second motivation for ministry in Rome—He was under obligation. Paul saw evangelism as an obligation, not an option.

Paul declared he was a debtor (NRSV). How? Paul understood he had been entrusted with the Gospel by Christ Jesus and was under obligation to "pay" his Gospel debt. Stott asserts this language is really stewardship language as opposed to the language of indebtedness. Stott also notes the word picture here is still the same. Christ Jesus made Paul a debtor by committing the Gospel to his trust. Therefore, Paul was in debt to the Romans.

Paul utilized two phrases that encapsulate the entire Gentile population. The first, "to Greeks and non-Greeks" (NIV), pointed to those in the Greco-Roman culture and those outside of it. The second, "the wise and the foolish" (NIV), pointed to those who had intelligence and education and those who did not. Paul used these couplets of contrasting groups to show his debt to all the Gentile population. R. Kent Hughes makes a fantastic observation that Paul's debt was to God, but the payment was to men.

Verse 16 and 17 contain the fundamental tenet of the Christian faith. The heart of saving power rests only in the Gospel, and salvation is initiated and actualized by God. There is a dynamic aspect to the Gospel. It is not just lifeless words about piestitic religious truths. It is God at work. God lives and moves through the proclamation of His redemptive work through Christ Jesus. Robert Mounce asserts the Gospel is not simply a display of power but the effective operation of God's power leading to salvation. Mounce notes the Gospel has purpose and direction.

Paul declared in verse 16 that he was "not ashamed of the gospel" (NIV). The question is why would he have a reason to be ashamed of the Gospel?

First, the Gospel was identified with a poor Jewish carpenter who was crucified as a common criminal. Second, Jerusalem was under Roman captivity, and most Christians were commoners and slaves. This epoch of Christians identified themselves as brothers and sisters, and the countercultural aspects of what Christians practiced made the tentmaker's Gospel hard to swallow. Yet, Paul declared he had confidence in the Gospel of the Christ.

C. K. Barrett says Paul's figure of speech is called *litotes* (a rhetorical device in which an affirmative is expressed in its negative). What Paul really was suggesting was that he gloried in the Gospel and counted it a high honor to proclaim it. This was actually Paul's positive confession on the Gospel and could also be rendered, "I am proud of the Gospel."

Paul's reasons for being unashamed of the Gospel are linked by clauses. Paul was proud of the Gospel; Paul was eager to preach; the Gospel meditates God's saving power to everyone who accepts and accesses it by faith.

Gospel in the first century was a bit of a loaded term. It was used by Roman emperors as an apparatus of the empire. It simply means "good news." Thus Roman citizens paid attention to any message handed down by Caesar. In that same way, Paul understood his message (Gospel) was greater than that of Caesar's, and he had no reason to be ashamed because he knew from whence his message came and he knew the content of his message was Christ Jesus.

Paul's message was Gospel or Good News. It is the power of God. This shows us how the Gospel operates. The word *power* here is the word δυναμις (*dunamis*). We derive our English word *dynamite* from this Greek word translated as *power*. This power is saving power expressed in our reconciliation back to God, the forgiveness of sins, adoption into the family of God, receiving of His Holy Spirit, and the transformation of our minds.

Paul was proud of the Gospel because it is the saving power for all who accept and access it by faith. This is the outreach of the Gospel according to Warren Wiersbe. This saving power is received by any Jew and Gentile who will simply believe. Paul asserted there can be no difference in how one is saved. All people are saved the same way—by faith through grace.

Verse 17 provides Paul's logic about what is contained in the Gospel. Paul utilized the word *righteousness* over sixty times in this epistle. This righteousness is from faith to faith. Another translation might be a righteousness that is from first to last. Anders Nygren says, "'the righteousness of God' is a righteousness originating in God, prepared by God, revealed by God, and therein offered to us" (Hughes, 32).

The Lesson Applied

Gifts are wonderful things when they are given from the heart and appreciated. Today's lesson emphasizes Paul's willingness to share a gift with the church at Rome because he recognized the gift he had received from God in Christ.

Paul's excitement and anticipation were shown in that he expressed his thankfulness for the church at Rome and their well-known faith. He shared with them that although he had never met them, he prayed for them and desired to come to them that he may be a gift to them. Paul recognized the importance of mutuality in the sharing of gifts and expressed his hope in coming to greet and fellowship with them.

Like Paul, we are under divine obligation to share not only who we are, but also what God has given to us. Freely we received and freely we should give. Stewardship is not just about managing what we have materially, but also what we have spiritually.

Good news has to be shared. We share that God's Good News, the Gospel, is God's activity of transforming lives with His power. We share that God wants all to be saved because all have sinned and missed the mark. We share that this Gospel can be accessed and accepted by faith and all who believe will be saved.

Let's Talk About It

What are some creative ways to share the Good News?

One of the most creative ways to share the Good News is social media. Facebook, Instagram, and Twitter all serve millions of people. Consider using these mediums to bring the gift of the Gospel and encouragement to others.

As the world continues to evolve, it is of the utmost importance that churches and believers alike build their digital footprints. Various platforms have the ability to share Sunday services, virtual Bible studies, and other ministry opportunities that traditionally have been reserved for the church building. However, with technology the world is literally at our fingertips through the devices we use each day. The Church must make a concerted effort to gain mastery over these formats for Kingdom use.

Home Daily Devotional Readings

July 12–18, 2021

Monday	Tuesday	Wednesday	Thursday	Friday	Saturday	Sunday
God's Covenant with Abraham	All World's Families Blessed Through Abraham	Promise Realized by Faith Not Law	For All Who Share Abraham's Faith	Abraham Believed Despite Impossible Odds	In Christ, Believers Share Abraham's Faith	Abraham, Father of the Faithful
Genesis 15:1–5	Genesis 12:1–9	Romans 4:13–15	Romans 4:16–18	Romans 4:19–21	Romans 4:22–25	Romans 4:1–12

THE FAITH OF ABRAHAM

Adult Topic:
Seeking Assurance

Background Scripture:
Romans 4

ROMANS 4:1–12

King James Version

WHAT shall we say then that Abraham our father, as pertaining to the flesh, hath found?
2 For if Abraham were justified by works, he hath whereof to glory; but not before God.
3 For what saith the scripture? Abraham believed God, and it was counted unto him for righteousness.
4 Now to him that worketh is the reward not reckoned of grace, but of debt.
5 But to him that worketh not, but believeth on him that justifieth the ungodly, his faith is counted for righteousness.
6 Even as David also describeth the blessedness of the man, unto whom God imputeth righteousness without works,
7 Saying, Blessed are they whose iniquities are forgiven, and whose sins are covered.
8 Blessed is the man to whom the Lord will not impute sin.
9 Cometh this blessedness then upon the circumcision only, or upon the uncircumcision also? for we say that faith was reckoned to Abraham for righteousness.
10 How was it then reckoned? when he was in circumcision, or in uncircumcision? Not in circumcision, but in uncircumcision.
11 And he received the sign of circumcision, a seal of the righteousness of the faith which he had yet being uncircumcised: that he might be the father of all them that believe, though they be not circumcised; that righteousness might be imputed unto them also:

New Revised Standard Version

WHAT then are we to say was gained by Abraham, our ancestor according to the flesh?
2 For if Abraham was justified by works, he has something to boast about, but not before God.
3 For what does the scripture say? "Abraham believed God, and it was reckoned to him as righteousness."
4 Now to one who works, wages are not reckoned as a gift but as something due.
5 But to one who without works trusts him who justifies the ungodly, such faith is reckoned as righteousness.
6 So also David speaks of the blessedness of those to whom God reckons righteousness apart from works:
7 "Blessed are those whose iniquities are forgiven, and whose sins are covered;
8 blessed is the one against whom the Lord will not reckon sin."
9 Is this blessedness, then, pronounced only on the circumcised, or also on the uncircumcised? We say, "Faith was reckoned to Abraham as righteousness."
10 How then was it reckoned to him? Was it before or after he had been circumcised? It was not after, but before he was circumcised.
11 He received the sign of circumcision as a seal of the righteousness that he had by faith while he was still uncircumcised. The purpose was to make him the ancestor of all who believe without being circumcised and who thus have righteousness reckoned to them,

MAIN THOUGHT: For what saith the scripture? Abraham believed God, and it was counted unto him for righteousness. (Romans 4:3, KJV)

Romans 4:1–12

King James Version	*New Revised Standard Version*
12 And the father of circumcision to them who are not of the circumcision only, but who also walk in the steps of that faith of our father Abraham, which he had being yet uncircumcised.	**12 and likewise the ancestor of the circumcised who are not only circumcised but who also follow the example of the faith that our ancestor Abraham had before he was circumcised.**

LESSON SETTING

Time: A.D. 56–58
Place: Corinth

LESSON OUTLINE

I. ***Sola Fide* for Abraham (Romans 4:1–5**
II. ***Sola Fide* for David (Romans 4:6–8)**
III. ***Sola Fide* for Gentiles (Romans 4:9–12)**

Unifying Principle

People often look to those older than they are for assurance. Who is an example one can trust? Through faith, Abraham, the father of all who believe, proved he was in right relationship with God.

Introduction

Although we love to sing songs such as "Amazing Grace," "I Need Thee Every Hour," "Just As I Am," and "Hold to God's Unchanging Hand," we often feel that if we can just do enough good, the Lord will understand and we will make it to heaven somehow. Salvation by and through our own works is the tenor of the times, for many people either don't fully understand justification by faith or they are extremely hostile toward it. One writer has said humanity is more comfortable with this motto: "We get our salvation the old-fashioned way. We earn it!"

This mentality is endemic to humanity and has characterized much of religious tradition for quite a while. Paul, using rabbinic polemic, sought to clarify the meaning of *justification by faith* and did so by supplying Old Testament precedent and examples. Paul utilized Abraham, David, and the Gentiles. Each one was justified by faith alone or *sola fide*. Both are Latin terms. *Sola* means "alone" or "only," and *fide* means "faith." They were used by the sixteenth century reformer Martin Luther as he considered the doctrine of justification by faith.

Paul asserted this idea of justification by faith wasn't a new concept or phenomenological occurrence because it was present in the Old Testament. Paul also desired that the Gentiles understand and appreciate the spiritual history and heritage of faith they had gained by adoption.

Exposition

I. *Sola Fide* for Abraham (Romans 4:1–5)

In making his argument, Paul used a method much different than Peter at the Day of Pentecost (Acts 2:14–36). Peter quoted the Old Testament and then provided an explanation repetitively. Paul, however, connected with his readers by examining the desperate condition of humanity's plight without God and then expounded that the Gospel has the answer to humanity's problem.

After expositing God's method of salvation by the gift of grace through faith in 3:21–31, Paul turned his attention to proving his argument by using two great Old Testament Jewish witnesses: Abraham and David. In Romans 1:2 and 3:21, Paul asserted salvation through the gift of God's righteousness, as witnesses by the law and prophets. Paul argued God's gift is apart from the law and suggested it was the only way people in the Old Testament and his era could be saved.

Chapter 4 begins with a question: "What then shall we say that Abraham, our forefather according to the flesh, discovered in this matter?" (4:1, NIV). Paul's response was antithetical to his real answer, which was that Abraham was justified by his own works. Paul denied this assertion for a couple of reasons. First, it would give Abraham and the nation of Israel a reason to boast. If justified by his own works, then Abraham could commend himself. Paul took aim at this implication by asserting there can be no boasting before God because this would qualify as self-righteousness. It's implausible to think a sinner can establish his or her own righteousness before God.

The word translated as *flesh* is *σαρξ* (*sarx*). In Pauline thought, this was a complex and somewhat convoluted word as it is nuanced in many ways. In Paul's writings, *flesh* often took on a negative connotation. At this point, σαρξ was referring to the totality of his humanity—mind, body, and spirit. We should think of the use of σαρξ similarly to John 1:13, which states the children of God are not born of blood or the will of the flesh. In other words, the totality of his humanness had nothing to do with this. It was done by grace through his faith.

The use of *flesh* in the case of Abraham moves on multiples levels. Paul established that Abraham's flesh could not have earned his righteousness because righteousness was imputed prior to circumcision. When we are introduced to Abraham in Scripture, his flesh was utterly powerless. He was unable to produce children. His wife Sarah laughed and said, "After I have grown old, and my husband is old, shall I have pleasure?" (Gen. 18:12, NRSV). The point is made that Abraham's σαρξ, his body, his flesh was impotent. The same held true in regard to circumcision and righteousness. He stood powerless.

Second, Paul denied Abraham was justified by works based upon the Scripture. Paul asked, "For what does the scripture say?" (Rom. 4:3, NRSV). Note the following ideas lifted by Paul's question. The singular form of the word *Scripture* implied Paul recognized the unified body of inspired writings. Second, Paul drew no distinction between what the Scripture says and what God says through it. Third, because of the use of the present tense, Paul asserted that through the written text the living voice of God can be heard. Finally, Scripture has complete authority. In every concern, Scripture was acknowledged as the final authority.

Abraham believed God, and it was credited to him as righteousness. In verses 4–5, Paul pressed the significance of the word *credited*, *λογιζομαι* (*logizomai*), which he used five times in the six verses. Chapter 4 contains eleven occurrences of this word. *Credited* means to be "counted, imputed, considered, or reckoned."

In financial terms, it can suggest something being placed in one's account. Paul noted there were two different means of money being placed in your account—either by labor, *οφειλεμα* (*opheilema*), or gift, *χαρις* (*charis*). Paul deduced the language of *work, wages, debt*, or *obligation* would be the wrong language to use. To the person who trusts in God, it is God crediting his faith as righteousness.

Interestingly, this word *χαρις*, *gift*, is that same word translated as *grace* in other passages. Translation is an imperfect act, but the linguistic connection is clear. In Greek a gift is defined as an act of grace. Abraham's righteousness was a gift given in grace by God.

What did Paul assert here? Paul destroyed the incorrect use of Abraham, their model of salvation by works. Paul achieved this feat by utilizing the sacred text of the Torah. Salvation for Abraham was *sola fide* or only faith by grace.

II. *Sola Fide* for David (Romans 4:6–8)

Jewish Romans would have been interested in knowing how Paul's doctrine was relative to both their past and their present. Paul, no doubt accounting for this challenge, reinforced his logic by including David as a witness. He quoted Psalm 32:1–2, which is linked to Genesis 15:6.

Mounce sees this as a contrast in showing that all stand unworthy before God. While Abraham was known for obedience and David for adultery and murder, neither deserved God's favor. David wrote out of his own experience of forgiveness and relief of guilt.

Interestingly, Psalm 32:1–2 gives two important aspects to Paul's defense of justification by faith. First, God forgives sins and imputes righteousness. In Psalm 32, a penitential psalm, David expressed the blessedness of those whose sins have been put away. This idea is also noted in Luke 7:47 when Jesus said of the woman who wept at His feet, "Her sins, which were many, have been forgiven" (NRSV). In both of these examples, there is a central idea of repentance. Grace was given to David as well as the weeping woman. Both exhibited a contriteness that preceded the granting of grace. Their faith was demonstrated in that they understood their powerlessness in the presence of a righteous God. Their choice was to recognize their faults and beg for grace.

Second, God does not impute our sins. God imputes righteousness. Mounce suggests that we not miss the profundity of the statement because of its simplicity. Those who trust in God to handle their sins are completely forgiven. Nothing can be brought back for which provision has not been made. The question of the sins of the believers has been settled forever. Psalm 103:12 (NRSV) says, "As far as the east is from the west, so far he removes our transgressions from us."

God knows all of our sins, but God does not charge us with those sins. The blood of Jesus literally brings us into right standing before God so that our sins have no bearing on God's judgment. This is how Jesus' righteousness is imputed to believers by faith. David was the perfect example, for he had more mistakes on public record than most people in the Bible. Even with all of that of which he was guilty, he was regarded as righteous before God through faith.

III. *Sola Fide* for Gentiles (Romans 4:9–12)

Paul concluded this portion of his logic on justification by faith by showing that God's salvation is not only for the Jews but also includes the Gentiles. The first question was whether or not Abraham was justified by faith or works. The next formal question was to whom is the blessedness of justification extended. Is it only for the circumcised (the Jews), or is it also for the uncircumcised (the Gentiles)?

Verse 10 looks to answer the supplemental question of when Abraham was justified, before or after circumcision. Mounce instructs the reader that Abraham was declared righteous before he was circumcised. According to Jewish reckoning, there were several years between the time Abraham was accepted by God (Gen. 15:6) and his actual circumcision (Gen. 17:23–27).

The purpose of circumcision was raised as the next concern, and the response was that circumcision was both a *sign* and *seal*. As a sign, circumcision pointed beyond itself to something greater than it represented. Circumcision suggested an outward sign of inward things. As a seal, it legitimized the righteousness by faith that Abraham had while he was still uncircumcised. The idea of a seal was also one of ownership, confirmation, or attestation. The seal confirmed the reality of the righteous status in which Abraham stood by virtue of his faith.

God imputed righteousness to Abraham prior to circumcision. Therefore Abraham is the father of the uncircumcised who walk by faith as Abraham did prior to circumcision. It is important to note the covenant was maintained by obedience, not circumcision. Circumcision had no magical powers. It simply was a ceremony that witnessed covenant between God and humanity. Circumcision was but a sign of Abraham's obedience.

For Paul, circumcision was only as good as the one who is circumcised in heart, not necessarily body. He wrote in Romans 2:29 (NRSV), "Rather, a person is a Jew who is one inwardly, and real circumcision is a matter of the heart—it is spiritual and not literal." Literal circumcision is not something to be aspired for. Paul spoke disparagingly about it if it was relied upon as a badge of righteousness. He wrote, "I wish those who unsettle you would castrate themselves" (Gal. 5:12, NRSV). This statement was for those who preached that circumcision was necessary for Gentiles to become full members of the household of God. Circumcision was never to be the center, as he demonstrated in this passage and in Galatians. It was merely to be a sign of the distinctiveness of Abraham (and Israel) and a seal of Abraham's righteous status before God. For Gentiles, instead of being that seal and sign, it was a hindrance to the primacy of the Gospel and the faith born therein.

Paul completed this section by asserting that there is only one way to be justified—the path of faith. God is the Father of all who will place their trust in Him, regardless of their religious background or ethnicity. We must not elevate doctrine over behavior but understand that true faith survives in obedience.

True faith can exist only in obedience. As human beings, we only act on those things that we believe. If we believe God fully, it will result in obedience.

The Lesson Applied

This section of the book of Romans gives some strong pointers for what it means to be in or out of the family of God and how Christians should view their experience of faith.

Paul asserted his case for justification by faith by calling on a Scripture (singular). He did not attempt to convince the Jewish Romans on his own thinking or conjecture, and it should be noted by the grammar and phraseology of the text that Paul considered Scripture as living, life-giving, and authoritative in every concern. Therefore, for every issue, Paul sought the Scripture. The challenge for us in 2021 is to be as "on the Scripture" as we are on social media or other passionate pursuits of our lives.

Another application of Romans 4 is to remember the hopelessness we find in attempting to work for justification when it can only be imputed or credited to us by God's own grace. We work not to *be* saved, but rather because we *are* saved by God. Our efforts are in faithful response to what He has done.

Let's Talk About It

Is there a way to determine if one is trying to earn righteousness or resting in the assurance of salvation by grace in faith?

Truthfully, this is only something that can be determined by each person, for it has everything to do with the motivations of the heart. Those who are trying to earn salvation will produce righteous acts out of fear of punishment. In other words, *I do this because if I don't God will get mad at me.* Many people attend church, give tithes and offerings, and join ministries for this reason. On the other hand, if one's motivation comes from the fact that one has been given much by way of salvation and wants to freely give in return, then that is proper motivation.

The song "O, How I Love Jesus" may say it best: "O, how I love Jesus, because He first loved me." Works of righteousness are beautiful when they are done in response to the beauty and magnanimity of God's grace. Our works are to be a response of obedience to God's Word and our way of saying thank you to the One who has saved us. Our obedience must be an act of deliberate faith in the goodness and power of God. We believe in God and act out this belief in what we say, think, and do. Our faith is the positive response to God's loving action.

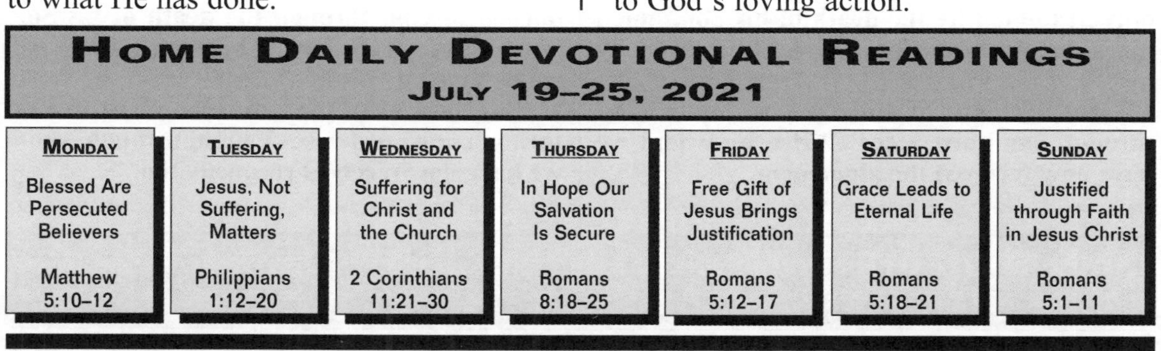

Home Daily Devotional Readings

July 19–25, 2021

Monday	Tuesday	Wednesday	Thursday	Friday	Saturday	Sunday
Blessed Are Persecuted Believers	Jesus, Not Suffering, Matters	Suffering for Christ and the Church	In Hope Our Salvation Is Secure	Free Gift of Jesus Brings Justification	Grace Leads to Eternal Life	Justified through Faith in Jesus Christ
Matthew 5:10–12	Philippians 1:12–20	2 Corinthians 11:21–30	Romans 8:18–25	Romans 5:12–17	Romans 5:18–21	Romans 5:1–11

Lesson 8 July 25, 2021

Justification through Faith

Adult Topic:
Seeking Reconciliation

Background Scripture:
Romans 5:1–11

Romans 5:1–11

King James Version

THEREFORE being justified by faith, we have peace with God through our Lord Jesus Christ:

2 By whom also we have access by faith into this grace wherein we stand, and rejoice in hope of the glory of God.

3 And not only so, but we glory in tribulations also: knowing that tribulation worketh patience;

4 And patience, experience; and experience, hope:

5 And hope maketh not ashamed; because the love of God is shed abroad in our hearts by the Holy Ghost which is given unto us.

6 For when we were yet without strength, in due time Christ died for the ungodly.

7 For scarcely for a righteous man will one die: yet peradventure for a good man some would even dare to die.

8 But God commendeth his love toward us, in that, while we were yet sinners, Christ died for us.

9 Much more then, being now justified by his blood, we shall be saved from wrath through him.

10 For if, when we were enemies, we were reconciled to God by the death of his Son, much more, being reconciled, we shall be saved by his life.

11 And not only so, but we also joy in God through our Lord Jesus Christ, by whom we have now received the atonement.

New Revised Standard Version

THEREFORE, since we are justified by faith, we have peace with God through our Lord Jesus Christ,

2 through whom we have obtained access to this grace in which we stand; and we boast in our hope of sharing the glory of God.

3 And not only that, but we also boast in our sufferings, knowing that suffering produces endurance,

4 and endurance produces character, and character produces hope,

5 and hope does not disappoint us, because God's love has been poured into our hearts through the Holy Spirit that has been given to us.

6 For while we were still weak, at the right time Christ died for the ungodly.

7 Indeed, rarely will anyone die for a righteous person—though perhaps for a good person someone might actually dare to die.

8 But God proves his love for us in that while we still were sinners Christ died for us.

9 Much more surely then, now that we have been justified by his blood, will we be saved through him from the wrath of God.

10 For if while we were enemies, we were reconciled to God through the death of his Son, much more surely, having been reconciled, will we be saved by his life.

11 But more than that, we even boast in God through our Lord Jesus Christ, through whom we have now received reconciliation.

MAIN THOUGHT: Therefore being justified by faith, we have peace with God through our Lord Jesus Christ. (Romans 5:1, KJV)

LESSON SETTING

Time: A.D. 56–58
Place: Corinth

LESSON OUTLINE

I. Peace and Hope (Romans 5:1–7)
II. Reconciliation and Hope (Romans 5:8–11)

Unifying Principle

People often struggle with fractured relationships that they may or may not have caused. How can these relationships be reconciled? Only justification by faith in Jesus Christ reconciles the ultimate ruptured relationship between God and humanity.

Introduction

Life can be a difficult exercise and enterprise even when we are encountering few storms. We often are too focused on the garnish of life as opposed to life's meaning and content. What makes life meaningful and fulfilling? What gives purpose and passion to life? When we reflect on our journey and accomplishments, what will be our measure or ruler of our success?

In today's lesson, Paul reminded us of several essential aspects of the Christian life that propel our lives to meaning, fulfillment, and purpose. As social beings, we need people who genuinely care for us and stand with us in difficult times. Often we are required to work our way through various disagreements or misunderstandings, and we are grateful for the forgiveness and reconciliation we receive when someone sacrifices to restore the relationship. The end result is we exist and live in peace.

Paul helped us discover not just the benefits of being pronounced *guiltless*, but also what it means to live life in a state of peace before God and others. We receive this state of life only by faith and not of our own righteousness. *Peace* is not the absence of storms, stress, disaster, pain, sorrow, or heartache. *Peace* is the state of mind that lives through the calamity and still says *my soul is content*. This is the blessed assurance of hope we have because of the sacrifice of Jesus' blood and body for sinners.

Exposition

I. Peace and Hope (Romans 5:1–7)

Paul completed his discussion asserting the need for justification (1:18–3:20) and the means and method of justification (3:21–4:25). He then turned his focus toward what John R. W. Stott calls the "bliss consequences" of justification by faith. This act of unmerited love is an absolute act of God in dealing with His people. William Newell calls this portion of the passage "the glorious results of justification by faith." C. K. Barrett describes this section as the "results of God's gracious act of redemption." Warren Wiersbe describes this section as "the blessings of our justification." Wiersbe notes that Paul was accomplishing two purposes in detailing these blessings. First, Paul expressed the wonderful reality of being a Christian here and now and not just in heaven.

Second, Paul assured his readers that justification isn't a temporary thing but a lasting reality. Paul listed seven spiritual blessings that assure the believer that the believer can never be lost. Once God has declared the believer righteous in Christ Jesus, the believer is kept in and by the power of God.

Scholars see another important implication for this section. Paul was crafting this section as a beginning point for his discussion on the security in Christ that results from a believer's justification. Note Paul's utilization of the phrase, "hope of sharing the glory of God" (Rom. 5:2, NRSV). In Romans 8:18–39, Paul worked through the idea of hope in God's glory in more detail. We are justified and move from reconciliation to hope and from hope to glory.

The complete paragraph (5:1–11) depends on the introductory words: "Therefore, since we are justified [declared righteous] by faith" (NRSV). This statement begins this new section by providing six radical statements for those whom God has justified by faith and summarizes the entire argument of chapters 1–4. The Greek form of the verb *declared righteous* or *justified* is the equivalent to *having been declared righteous*. Paul was saying that those who have believed are declared righteous by God and the deal is fully done. God will never change His mind (4:8). C. K. Barrett notes that we could translate this portion as, "Therefore, let us have peace since we have been declared righteous."

We have peace with God. Don't confuse this peace *with* God and the peace *of* God found in Philippians 4:6–7. The peace *of* God refers to personal peace we receive by asking God for it. Whenever we experience hardships, we can ask for the peace of God to be evident for us. This, however, is not peace *with* God. Peace *with* God notes that sinners had been in war with God because of our sins, and God's weapon was His wrath. Christ Jesus took our judgment upon Himself. As a result, the war between God and the sinner is over, and we now have peace with God.

As humans we quickly discover nothing we work for on the outside of us can procure or provide peace for us. Money, status, careers, nor any physical accouterments are able to provide peace. Paul told the church at Rome that the peace, ειρηνη (*eirene*), that is given by God is different from the peace given by the world or material possessions.

This peace is a consequence of Christ's death and resurrection (Rom. 4:24–25). This word *peace* is rooted in Paul's understanding of the Old Testament word *shalom,* which translates as "positive well-being" and "holistic health." Paul did not use the term primarily to refer to a state of inner tranquility, but to an external and objective one. To receive peace from God is to be in a relationship with God in which all hostility caused by sin is removed.

The locus of God's salvation, atoning, and wrath-averting work is non other than Christ Jesus. Romans 3:25–26 declares the sinner can receive justification only "through" or "in" Jesus. This is a consistent theme in Romans 5–8. All that God has for the believer can be located exclusively in Christ Jesus (5:1; 5:11; 5:21; 6:23; 8:39). Although there is not a prolonged Christological discussion here, one should note there does exist a definite Christological focus with the repeated emphasis that all the believer's experiences of God's blessings derive exclusively through Christ Jesus.

Romans 5:2 tells us we have grace, which here does not translate as *unmerited love* (*favor*). Paul used the word *grace* χαπις (*charis*) to indicate we have a privileged position of acceptance. Through Christ, we have obtained our introduction into this grace in which we have taken our stand. Two verbs help make the point of the passage clear. The word *access*, *προσαγωγη* (*prosagoge*), "taking the initiative to enter," is better translated *introduction*. The idea is that someone has to bring us in or that of a person being brought into God's presence or of a person being brought to meet a king.

Secondly, Paul noted that justified believers have taken their stand firmly in or on this grace into which they have been introduced. Justified believers are graced to live in the presence of God and have constant, continuous, and secure blessings from the Father.

We rejoice in our hope of the glory of God. Paul said there are three reasons believers should rejoice in Christian hope. This hope is a joyful and confident expectation built upon the foundation of God's promises. The glory of God is the object of this hope. Believers hope first in the coming of Jesus with great glory and power. Second, believers will not only see the glory, but also be transformed into it and will become His holy people. Lastly, creation will be freed from its struggle and bondage to decay and be renewed and experience God's glory.

Paul turned from rejoicing in the hope of God's glory to the rejoicing in tribulations. The word utilized for *afflictions* is Θλιψις (*thlipsis*). It is a technical word used in several aspects in Scripture. One usage refers to opposition and persecution from a hostile world. Another usage is for the suffering God's people should expect in the last days prior to the end. The root here means "to press" and that which may afflict the believer in life—distress, famine, nakedness, peril, or the sword (Rom. 8:35).

What is the believers' response? Paul said believers answer with *confidence and rejoicing*—*καυχαομαι* (*kauchaomai*). Why? Stott says first, suffering is the one and only path to glory. It was so for the Christ and so it is for those who follow Him. Second, suffering leads to glory in the end and maturity in the meanwhile. Suffering can be productive if we respond to it positively. Third, suffering is the best context in which to become assured of God's love.

A believer can rejoice under pressure because they know, *οιδα* (*oida*), that affliction produces endurance, *υπομονη* (*hypomone*), and endurance produces tested character, *δοκιμη* (*dokime*), and this takes us back to hope. This same pattern of linked values encouraging believers to face struggle with joy is found in two other places (1 Pet. 1:6–7; James 1:2–4).

As a result of possessing tested character, the believer who responds positively to suffering will discover their hope has been empowered. Douglas Moo is correct in his assertion that hope, like a muscle, will not be strong if it goes unused. The constant reaffirming and repeating of hope in the midst of apparently hopeless situations will bring ever-deepening conviction of the reality and assurance of that for which we hope. Hope never disappoints, *καταισχυνω* (*kataischuno*). Paul was saying the Christian should not fear the judgment will put them to shame in the sense that the foundation on which he has built his life and hope for eternal life should prove inadequate before God.

This is true because the believer has a means by which to be assured—God has poured out, *εκχεω* (*ekcheo*), His love in our hearts by the Holy Spirit whom He has given us. The believer has incomprehensible love and the awareness of the Holy Spirit assisting the believer in understanding what it means to be filled with God's love. Romans 5:5–6 forms a single statement that solidifies God's love for believers. These verses show that Paul was grounding the subjective experience of God's love in the objective atoning of Christ Jesus' work on the cross. Christ Jesus died for sinners at just the right time (Gal. 4:4).

The thesis of Romans 5:7 is the grandness and greatness of God's love for the ungodly as shown by the emphasis placed on the importance of Jesus' dying for the them. Paul announced the sacrifice of Jesus by asserting that seldom will a person give his life for a good person or organization. Yet, Jesus died for the ungodly (1 Pet. 3:18; 1 John 3:16).

II. Reconciliation and Hope (Romans 5:8–11)

John A. T. Robinson says verses 6–8 represent the charter of the Christian's salvation—the incredible basic fact upon which all the boundless benefits of the new life rest. We see in verse 8 the adversative *but*, which points the reader to the boundless grace of God and His love as a contrast to the self-oriented style of love of even the best in human love. God proved His own love for us in demonstrating Christ's death for sinners. Thus, now that we are His children, surely He will come to us more while we hope for the promise to be fulfilled.

Verse 9 brings together the important parts of verses 1–8 and provides a synthesis that repeats and even expands Paul's main idea—the assurance of Christian hope. Paul used part of a format here that would be familiar to the people. The rabbis called it *light to heavy* or *lesser to greater* (*a minori ad maius*). However, Paul's utilization of the phrase *how much more* signaled Paul was working from *major to minor*. Paul was arguing that if God has already completed the most difficult aspect—to reconcile and justify unworthy sinners—how much more can we depend on Him to fulfill the easier task of saving those who belong to Him from eschatological wrath.

The second parallel premise, again *greater to lesser*, is that while we were sinners, we were reconciled to God by the death of His Son. The word *atonement* means "reconciliation" or "to be brought back into fellowship with God." This word, *καταλλασσο* (*katallasso*), derives from the world of personal relationship. It refers to the bringing together of people or the making of peace between people. This "being brought back" happened while we were in a state of hostility toward God. Paul reminded us God took the initiative for the sinners' reconciliation (2 Cor. 5:19–20). Thus, sinners are transferred from being enemies of God to becoming God's children.

In Romans 5:11, Paul concluded this portion by rehearsing the earlier listed aspects and saying the believer should boast in them (5:2–3). Paul said this boasting and reconciliation are through the Lord Jesus Christ (5:1–2, 6–10). Paul reminded the believer to boast in the benefits that are through the Lord Jesus Christ.

The Lesson Applied

Chapter 5 identifies the blessings of justification and reconciliation. Paul noted several benefits related to the "here and now" existential life of the believer and the eschatological hope of the believer—peace with God, stance in grace, the hope of glory, the meaning of suffering, the meaning of love of Christ, and the relationship between law, sin, and grace.

Believers must become acquainted and fully invested in knowing the foundation of their blessings in Christ Jesus. Paul clearly showed in his epistle that all the benefits of Christianity are derived through Jesus Christ. This is antithetical to our present culture because we often seek meaning and purpose outside of our faith walk.

One of the overlooked and crucial aspects of this lesson may be the vital importance Paul placed on the concept of relationship. We move from judicial acquittal in a law court to the idea of the believer being introduced and brought into the sanctuary or presence of the King. Relationships are important and what one invests in a relationship indicates the worth of the relationship to them.

Let's Talk About It

What should a firm relationship with God be built upon?

Although believers are tempted to try to justify and reconcile themselves to God through various means of human ability and effort, Paul reminded us in Romans 5 that the benefits we possess in relationship to God are provided not by our merit, not by our perfection, not by our public standing or private intentions. Our benefits are based and founded only through Christ Jesus our Lord. Believers must be hungry to know upon what foundation their relationship has been built. This is why we sing "The Solid Rock"—"My hope is built on nothing less, than Jesus blood and righteousness ... On Christ the solid Rock I stand, all other ground is sinking sand." Thus, this relationship has to be one of faith and trust in the reality of God's love for humanity. Based upon the deliberate self-sacrificial act of intentional goodwill of toward humanity, Jesus offers salvation to all through the modem of faith. Without faith it is not only impossible to please God, but it is also impossible for eliminate the rift that stands between us and our Creator. Faith in Jesus is our security.

Home Daily Devotional Readings

July 26–August 1, 2021

Monday	Tuesday	Wednesday	Thursday	Friday	Saturday	Sunday
Obey God with Heart and Voice	God's Salvation Announced	Call on the Name of the Lord	Gentiles Believe by Faith	For the Salvation of the Gentiles	Regret for Not Hearing Christ's Word	Salvation Is for All People
Deuteronomy 30:6–14	Isaiah 52:1–10	Joel 2:28–32	Galatians 3:6–14	Romans 10:1–4	Romans 10:18–21	Romans 10:5–17

SALVATION FOR ALL WHO BELIEVE

Adult Topic:
Seeking Confidence

Background Scripture:
Romans 10:5–17

ROMANS 10:5–17

King James Version

**FOR Moses describeth the righteousness which
is of the law, That the man which doeth those
things shall live by them.
6 But the righteousness which is of faith speaketh on this wise, Say not in thine heart, Who
shall ascend into heaven? (that is, to bring
Christ down from above:)
7 Or, Who shall descend into the deep? (that
is, to bring up Christ again from the dead.)
8 But what saith it? The word is nigh thee,
even in thy mouth, and in thy heart: that is, the
word of faith, which we preach;
9 That if thou shalt confess with thy mouth
the Lord Jesus, and shalt believe in thine heart
that God hath raised him from the dead, thou
shalt be saved.
10 For with the heart man believeth unto righteousness; and with the mouth confession is
made unto salvation.
11 For the scripture saith, Whosoever believeth on him shall not be ashamed.
12 For there is no difference between the Jew
and the Greek: for the same Lord over all is
rich unto all that call upon him.
13 For whosoever shall call upon the name of
the Lord shall be saved.
14 How then shall they call on him in whom
they have not believed? and how shall they
believe in him of whom they have not heard?
and how shall they hear without a preacher?**

**15 And how shall they preach, except they be
sent? as it is written, How beautiful are the feet
of them that preach the gospel of peace, and
bring glad tidings of good things!**

New Revised Standard Version

**MOSES writes concerning the righteousness
that comes from the law, that "the person who
does these things will live by them."
6 But the righteousness that comes from
faith says, "Do not say in your heart, 'Who
will ascend into heaven?'" (that is, to bring
Christ down)
7 "or 'Who will descend into the abyss?'"
(that is, to bring Christ up from the dead).
8 But what does it say? "The word is near
you, on your lips and in your heart" (that is, the
word of faith that we proclaim);
9 because if you confess with your lips
that Jesus is Lord and believe in your heart
that God raised him from the dead, you will
be saved.
10 For one believes with the heart and so is
justified, and one confesses with the mouth and
so is saved.
11 The scripture says, "No one who believes in
him will be put to shame."
12 For there is no distinction between Jew and
Greek; the same Lord is Lord of all and is generous to all who call on him.
13 For, "Everyone who calls on the name of the
Lord shall be saved."
14 But how are they to call on one in whom
they have not believed? And how are they to
believe in one of whom they have never heard?
And how are they to hear without someone to
proclaim him?
15 And how are they to proclaim him unless
they are sent? As it is written, "How beautiful
are the feet of those who bring good news!"**

MAIN THOUGHT: For whosoever shall call upon the name of the Lord shall be saved. (Romans 10:13, KJV)

ROMANS 10:5–17

King James Version	*New Revised Standard Version*
16 But they have not all obeyed the gospel. For Esaias saith, Lord, who hath believed our report?	**16 But not all have obeyed the good news; for Isaiah says, "Lord, who has believed our message?"**
17 So then faith cometh by hearing, and hearing by the word of God.	**17 So faith comes from what is heard, and what is heard comes through the word of Christ.**

LESSON SETTING

Time: A.D. 56–58
Place: Paul's Third Missionary Journey from either Corinth or Cenchrea (Acts 20:2–3)

LESSON OUTLINE

I. Christ as Lord (Romans 10:5–13)
II. Christ the Gospel to Israel (Romans 10:14–17)

UNIFYING PRINCIPLE

Many people lack confidence in addressing life's circumstances. How can one gain trust? Salvation comes to all who confess Jesus Christ as Lord and believe in their hearts.

INTRODUCTION

In this text, Paul continued his discussion of Israel's inability to acknowledge Jesus as the Messiah and as the necessary means of its righteousness. Israel's failure was not the failure of God. It was Israel's rejection of God and its insistence on making the nation right with God by keeping the law. Israel's pursuit of right-standing with God fell short because, according to Paul, it did not seek it through faith. Thus, we discover the Israel that God rejected was the Israel that had rejected God.

In Romans 9:30–10:4, we see Israel's wrong focus, its pursuit of the law and works for righteousness. Paul argued that as a result of the people's actions, they stumbled over the fact of Jesus as the Messiah. This is a common occurrence today as well. Many of the essential things we miss are directly tied to our own actions or inability to act.

Romans 10:1–4 provides Paul's discussion of Israel's wrong approach to righteousness. Paul asserted that Israel's rejection of the Messiah was for several reasons. Israel was not receptive to the Messiah because the nation possessed a zeal, but not according to knowledge. Second, because of the people's ignorance of God's righteousness and their pride that sought their own righteousness, they didn't submit themselves to the righteousness of God. Lastly, they misunderstood their own law. In short, Israel failed to see Christ as the end of the law.

EXPOSITION

I. CHRIST AS LORD (ROMANS 10:5–13)

Paul continued his assertion in verses 5–9 that Christ is the end of the law. He contrasted two kinds of righteousness. The first is righteousness that has its beginning in the law. (He quoted Lev. 18:5; Gal. 3:12.) Paul referred to Moses, showing both the Levitical perspective and the Deuteronomic perspective. This helped Paul show that those who kept the law would have life. However, the trouble was that no one was able to keep the law. Although the law pointed one in the correct ethical and moral direction, it was powerless to provide the necessary assistance to achieve the completion of the law.

This law is contrasted with the law of faith. This law does not require great exploits (for example bringing Christ down from above or descending into hell—*Gehenna*—to bring Christ up). Why? Because Christ has already come amongst humanity, and He has already risen from the dead. Paul interpreted the law in terms of his understanding of the incarnation and Resurrection.

In Romans 10:9–10, Paul addressed the Jewish audience. Paul said to confess Jesus to be Lord and believe in their hearts that this risen Jesus, rejected by Israel, is the Messiah and Lord over all—and be willing to so confess Him as their own Christ and Lord before others. Douglas Moo noted, "This confession, Jesus is Lord, refers to the lordship which Jesus exercises in virtue of his exaltation This lordship presupposes the incarnation, death, and resurrection of Christ and consists in his vestiture with universal domination" (Moo, *The Epistle to the Romans*, 55–65). This confession probably may be thought of as an initial confession made in Christian baptisms—the pledge of a good conscience toward God (1 Pet. 3:21). This is the earliest Christian confession of faith (1 Cor. 12:3; Phil. 2:11).

Paul ascribed to Jesus a word that is used over six thousand times in the LXX, or Greek Old Testament (Septuagint), for *Yahweh.* The Hebrew *Yahweh* was deemed to be too holy to speak, so *Adonai* or *Lord* was used as a substitute. The implication of this fact cannot be taken for granted. Jesus is Lord. This asserts that Jesus' authority is absolute, unlimited, and universal. Those who come to Him acknowledge that they put themselves completely under His authority and that He may do with them whatever He wills without their hesitation. Outward confession stems from a profound inward conviction. Those who come to the Messiah must believe in their hearts that Jesus was raised from the dead by God and His resurrection is the center or core of Christian confession.

The confessional continued. One must also believe in one's heart that God raised Jesus from the dead. Moo continued here by further noting that saving faith is resurrection faith (1 Cor. 15:17). Paul explained in Romans 10:10. He said that with the heart the man believed unto righteousness, while confession with the mouth resulted in salvation. We should note there is a connection between believing and confessing. It is also the order of faith and action. Note we have two clauses in this text, *believing and confessing*, and *justification and salvation.* These are inseparable. Faith justifies one before God and acting out one's faith through confession leads to salvation.

In verses 11–12, Paul quoted Isaiah 45:17 from the Greek Old Testament to contrast the Jews' inability to locate the correct way to God by faith as opposed to the simple idea of believing. What does the true believer expect?

First, that in believing, they are going God's way. Second, that in believing by walking God's path, they never will be put to shame or guilt. The Hebraic phrase *to be put to shame* or *put to shame* or *ashamed* is to flee in fear. Paul was suggesting that those who believe in Jesus shall possess boldness and never have to flee in fear before Him at His appearing in the Day of Judgment (1 John 2:28; 4:17).

Romans 10:12 continues to strengthen Paul's message with, "There is no distinction between Jew and the Greek" (NRSV). This is the same repetitive phrase used by Paul to point to universal sinfulness (3:22). Paul utilized the phrase to refer to the confession of salvation that Jesus is Lord, and Jesus is rich unto all that call upon Him. Emphasis rests here on the fact that all were convicted of sin whether Jew or Gentile, and therefore, no distinction can exist regarding God's saving mercy. It is available to all and is given overflowingly to those who call upon Jesus. The universal availability of salvation is so gloriously open to all because it is rooted in the universal lordship of Christ Jesus.

In verse 13, Paul quoted from Joel 2:32 and affirmed the renewal of the covenant. Joel 2 sits in agreement with Deuteronomy 30 concerning how God will restore the fortunes of Israel after terrible judgment. Note how Romans 10:13 is linked to Romans 9–11 as a whole. If "those who call on the name of the Lord" is a regular biblical understanding of the people of Israel, then verse 13 is the functional equivalent of 11:26 (NRSV): "All Israel shall be saved." This verse connects to Paul's concern in 10:1 and points to the correct understanding of 11:26. The universal scope of this verse points to a Messiah who desires that all be saved, but He will not force anyone to come to Him.

Moo implied that verse 13 has several components to be discussed. First, in this verse salvation is promised. Second, it is the Lord who will do the saving. Third, He does it for all who will call on His name. Lastly, He does it for the whomevers or anybodies. Moo further stated that Paul preached a finished work, not for adherence to the law, but for any and all who would call on the name of the Lord and believe the good news of Jesus' death, burial, resurrection, and ascension.

II. Christ the Gospel to Israel (Romans 10:14–17)

In verses 14–15, we see another logical inference here—if everyone who calls on the name of the Lord will be saved, then it is crucial and necessary that all people have the opportunity to hear the Good News. Without the opportunity to hear, no one can believe. People cannot believe in what they have not heard. Therefore, it is vital that someone be dispatched to share the Good News. John Stott, in *Between Two Worlds*, advised looking at these verses and their verbs in reverse order: Christ sends heralds, heralds preach, people hear, hearers believe, believers call, and those who call are saved.

Paul quoted from Isaiah 52:7 to note how welcomed are those who come bearing the Gospel of Jesus. He understood the Isaiah passage referred to those who brought the good news of imminent release from Babylonian captivity, and Paul applied this verse to the heralds of the Gospel. The idea here is that Christ is present in the heralds, and in hearing the heralds, one hears Christ.

Although the good news had been proclaimed universally, not all had responded to it. Unfortunately, few Israelites had given the Good News a serious response.

Paul used Isaiah 53:1 to note his concern or even grief—who has believed our report? Who could believe the announcement of the Suffering Servant's exaltation? One idea raised here is that Paul was affirming his assertion from another angle. The Isaiah passages link with previous verses to show that his mission was to embody the prophetic task of announcing the Messiah to the world. Isaiah used the Hebrew word *akoe* for the word *message*. So the translation might read as, *Faith comes from the message, and the message happens through the word* (rhema) *of the Messiah*. So, we see here Paul's complete logic—preaching of the word through the message of faith. It is the word of faith because it awakens its hearers.

The Lesson Applied

In applying this lesson, some points are helpful to emphasize. As Christians, there is an obligation to understand the simplicity of righteousness by faith. We must understand it is not the righteousness based on the law, but on foundational and practical faith.

Second, there is a crucial need to understand the dynamics of righteousness by faith. The cause requires that we believe in our hearts, which will result in evidence and the confession of our mouth. The subject of our confession is the Lordship and resurrection of Christ Jesus. The result of this confession results in salvation.

Third, we must understand the universal scope of righteousness by faith. God desires to save all who would call upon the name of Christ Jesus. God desires that His love and mercy be received by all and that no distinction be made for those to receive His grace. This divine generosity should be shared and trumpeted through the world.

Let's Talk About It

What can we do to spread the great good news of the Gospel?

We must be believers in Jesus Christ to the extent we do all we can to learn about Him. Then we must seek to incorporate His teachings and life into our own lives. This is a lifelong quest. Yet it is one wherein we should get closer to Him on a daily basis. People would rather see a sermon than hear one. Actions do speak louder than words. Whatever we teach and preach, they must be reinforced and supported by our deeds if they are to be effective. James encourages us to also be doers of the Word. As we learn about Him, the more we must seek to learn so we can impart our knowledge and experience with the Lord to others. Finally, we must adopt a regular program of worship and study of His Word.

Home Daily Devotional Readings

August 2–8, 2021

Monday	Tuesday	Wednesday	Thursday	Friday	Saturday	Sunday
Love of Money, Root of Evil	Control Your Own Body	Abraham, Father of the Faithful	Worthy Examples of the Faithful	Actions of Faith in Daily Life	Like Jesus, Offer Sacrifices to God	The Living Actions of Faith
1 Timothy 6:6–10	1 Thessalonians 4:1–7	Acts 7:2–7	Hebrews 11:4–7, 17–27	Hebrews 13:1–9, 17–19	Hebrews 13:10–16	Hebrews 11:1–3, 8–16

LESSON 10 AUGUST 8, 2021

MEANING OF FAITH

Adult Topic:
The Example of Heroes

Background Scripture:
Hebrews 11; 13:1–19

HEBREWS 11:1–8, 13–16

King James Version

NOW faith is the substance of things hoped for, the evidence of things not seen.

2 For by it the elders obtained a good report.

3 Through faith we understand that the worlds were framed by the word of God, so that things which are seen were not made of things which do appear.

4 By faith Abel offered unto God a more excellent sacrifice than Cain, by which he obtained witness that he was righteous, God testifying of his gifts: and by it he being dead yet speaketh.

5 By faith Enoch was translated that he should not see death; and was not found, because God had translated him: for before his translation he had this testimony, that he pleased God.

6 But without faith it is impossible to please him: for he that cometh to God must believe that he is, and that he is a rewarder of them that diligently seek him.

7 By faith Noah, being warned of God of things not seen as yet, moved with fear, prepared an ark to the saving of his house; by the which he condemned the world, and became heir of the righteousness which is by faith.

8 By faith Abraham, when he was called to go out into a place which he should after receive for an inheritance, obeyed; and he went out, not knowing whither he went.

• • • • • •

13 These all died in faith, not having received the promises, but having seen them afar off,

New Revised Standard Version

NOW faith is the assurance of things hoped for, the conviction of things not seen.

2 Indeed, by faith our ancestors received approval.

3 By faith we understand that the worlds were prepared by the word of God, so that what is seen was made from things that are not visible.

4 By faith Abel offered to God a more acceptable sacrifice than Cain's. Through this he received approval as righteous, God himself giving approval to his gifts; he died, but through his faith he still speaks.

5 By faith Enoch was taken so that he did not experience death; and "he was not found, because God had taken him." For it was attested before he was taken away that "he had pleased God."

6 And without faith it is impossible to please God, for whoever would approach him must believe that he exists and that he rewards those who seek him.

7 By faith Noah, warned by God about events as yet unseen, respected the warning and built an ark to save his household; by this he condemned the world and became an heir to the righteousness that is in accordance with faith.

8 By faith Abraham obeyed when he was called to set out for a place that he was to receive as an inheritance; and he set out, not knowing where he was going.

• • • • • •

13 All of these died in faith without having received the promises, but from a distance

MAIN THOUGHT: Now faith is the substance of things hoped for, the evidence of things not seen. (Hebrews 11:1, KJV)

Hebrews 11:1–8, 13–16

King James Version	*New Revised Standard Version*
and were persuaded of them, and embraced them, and confessed that they were strangers and pilgrims on the earth.	**they saw and greeted them. They confessed that they were strangers and foreigners on the earth,**
14 For they that say such things declare plainly that they seek a country.	**14 for people who speak in this way make it clear that they are seeking a homeland.**
15 And truly, if they had been mindful of that country from whence they came out, they might have had opportunity to have returned.	**15 If they had been thinking of the land that they had left behind, they would have had opportunity to return.**
16 But now they desire a better country, that is, an heavenly: wherefore God is not ashamed to be called their God: for he hath prepared for them a city.	**16 But as it is, they desire a better country, that is, a heavenly one. Therefore God is not ashamed to be called their God; indeed, he has prepared a city for them.**

LESSON SETTING

Time: A.D. 60–90
Place: Rome

LESSON OUTLINE

I. What Faith Is! (Hebrew 11:1)
II. Accomplishments of the Faithful (Hebrews 11:2–8)
III. The Destination of the Faithful (Hebrews 11:13–16)

Unifying Principle

People enduring life's miseries hopelessly plod along the way of life. What can enliven this emptiness of existence? Faith in God provides the assurance of hope and conviction of certainty.

Introduction

Hebrews 11 often is called the *Heroes of Faith* or the roll call of the *Champions of Faith*. Others have called it the *Church's Hall of Fame*. The reason for this labeling is clear. Christians see it, especially the latter portion of this chapter (Heb. 11:17–40), as a list of those who trusted in God in spite of the tremendous challenges to their faith. Simply stated, the general depiction of the text is that they overcame *because* of their faith. Faith was the connecting conduit to the One who possessed the awesome ability to provide abundant and replenishing resources to these human creatures. That is why the pericope begins with an assessment or declaration of what faith is. To be sure, the first verse is not actually a definition of faith but a declaration of what faith is composed of. Its twin sister is hope, or at the least it is made up of the things that build hope in the reality of the unseen.

Three things are important as we examine this text. First, we must examine what faith is. The writer declares "Faith is the substance of things hoped for, the evidence of things not seen" (Heb. 11:1, KJV). But what does that mean? How does it work? What are the components that make up the substance of faith? Second, we will analyze the first part of the list of these faithful inherents—who they were, what they accomplished, and how they persevered. Finally, we will explore the objective of their faith. What did they see that gave them the ability to endure? What were their goals, and how were they able to keep them in view in the vastness of the challenges they faced? What we will discover is these warriors could envision a prize in the distance, a pearl of great price, a city like no other, that gave them the desire and the ability to pursue it beyond all others. We call it *faith*.

Exposition

I. What Faith Is! (Hebrews 11:1)

Hebrews 11:1 is not a definition of faith, even though it tells us what faith is. The definition of faith is contextual (see *The New Interpreter's Bible: Volume 12,* 132–133). The Greek word used for *faith* (*pistos*) could mean "trust, believe, loyalty, or assurance," depending of the context. Hebrews 11:1 refers back to the previous text of Hebrews 10:36–39. The writer's emphasis in that text is that "the just shall live by faith" (v. 38, KJV). It is a repeat of Romans 1:17.

The Apostle Paul, and later the great reformer Martin Luther, used this text to declare and support the Christian doctrine of justification by faith. Paul extrapolated the passage from Habakkuk 2:4, where it means essential trust in the providential care and judgment of God. This type of trust in God is what is needed to enable and propel believers to minister effectively as noted in the roll call of heroes of the faith in Hebrews 11:4–35.

Faith is the substance used to erect our spiritual fortitude and hope. That substance is the reality of the presence and power of the invisible God. It is the established Word of God that the writer of Genesis was much aware of (see "And God said" throughout Gen. 1). The Word of God called creation into existence out of nothing (*creation ex nihilo*). The Greek word used here to show God's Word as the undergirding of faith is *hypostasis*. It means "under, to prop something up." Belief has no power in and of itself. Its power derives from God's Word, which gives it its divine foundation and thrust.

Our faith must reside in God. God is the structural root of Christian faith. The writer of Hebrews recognized this in the opening verses (Heb. 1:2–3, 10, 3:3–4; 11:3). God is the subject even in the closing benediction (Heb. 13:20–25) as well as throughout the story of Christian redemption sandwiched in between Hebrews 1 and 13.

God is the One who called Jesus into service and the Church into being to fulfill the redemptive covenants He made with Israel (Heb. 9:24–28; 10:1–18; 12:22–24). Additionally, He is the Promise Issuer and Promise Keeper who exhibits an unimaginable love to believers (Heb. 11:10, 13-16). The writer's point in Hebrews 11:1 is, therefore, well taken and the book and scriptural texts have been carefully constructed on the Person and power of God as noted in the various textual references previously given.

Hebrews 11:1 is right to attribute faith as emerging out of the three-part *omni*-ness of God (omnipotence, omniscience, and omnipresence). That is where all bases for human hope must begin. God is the foundation and springboard of human hope, of human aspirations, of human progress. God is the Substance of things hoped for. Hebrew theology held to the concept that everything, whether good or bad, came from God.

Job confirmed this theological understanding after he experienced several calamities almost simultaneously. In response to them, he said, "Naked came I out of my mother's womb, and naked shall I return thither: the LORD gave, and the LORD hath taken away; blessed be the name of the LORD" (Job 1:21, KJV). In chapter 42, Job confessed God could do everything. He also experienced overwhelming restoration of his losses. The conclusion of Job's life said it all. He was a man of strong faith in God. His faith was resilient in both the good and bad times of his life. Job 42 confirms God as the One who undergirds human hopes and provides assurance that He is the Wind beneath our wings.

Not only is God the foundation of human hope and faith, the text points to His life and creative Word as the unseen evidence behind the things that are seen and experienced. That is to say, Hebrews 1:1 falls in line with Genesis 1; John 1:1–4; Colossians 1:15–19; and Hebrews 1:2–4; 11:3. (See Gen. 1 to discover the pluralities of divine activities, such as *God moved*, *God said*, *God divided*, *God saw*, *God called*, and *God made*, along with a group of "let there be" imperatives.) These Scriptures and activities cite God as the unseen reality behind all that is seen and that exists.

As forestated, Genesis 1 repeatedly declares God called creation into being. God was present when the beginning began. The writer of Genesis was careful to provide the emergence of a planned world and universe only after declaring the reality of God behind it.

Faith displays God in a radical way. It depicts God as the One behind the created order. Hence for the believer, the created order itself is a clear demonstration of the reality of the invisible God. The Johannine passage, which to a large degree mimics Genesis 1, also points to God as the Creator and adds *the Word* (*Logos*) of God as the preexistent Son (John 1:1–14). God as the foundation of our faith sent the preexistent Son into the world to enliven our faith and to use it as a springboard to eternal salvation, the object of our faith and hope (John 3:16; Rom. 8:24).

It is this God upon which our faith and hope is built. Our belief is that God made this world and the things that are seen emerged from the things that are not seen. Thus the believer is thoroughly convicted, even persuaded, that this is God's world and He is in control of it, despite things looking dismal at times. Faith in the God of creation provides a steady and sure conviction that our success belongs to God and is promised by Him.

II. Accomplishments of the Faithful (Hebrews 11:2–8)

Hebrews 11:2–8 builds off of Hebrews 11:1 and Hebrews 10:36–39. Since God is the foundation upon which faith is erected or built, one cannot help but reach great heights of success when they exercise it. That is why the elders were able to obtain a strong testimony. The word *elder* suggests the ancient believers of old. In other words, this truthful testimony has been around a long time. It is not something conceived of spontaneously. That is to say, world history itself validates the life of God and His power to empower human life and human activities. The elders are our biblical ancestors who refused to succumb to the challenges they faced. Their faith in God empowered and strengthened them to overcome their obstacles, and they were commended for their faith (v. 2). What better commendation could they have than to be included in the scriptural roll call of the faithful. That is to say, God Himself testified to their apparent faithfulness.

Verses 4–8 describe the divine approval of four people whose faith pleased God. They are the ancients: Abel, Enoch, Noah, and Abraham. Sandwiched in between the faith activities of these loyal adherents is a summary statement that shows faith as a necessary component if one is to be successful in pleasing God (v. 6). The key words of the roll call are "By faith."

The roll call begins with Abel. Abel was the second son of Adam and Eve. His story is recorded in Genesis 4:1–15. Abel was a sheep herder and at the appropriate time brought "of the firstlings of his flock and of the fat thereof. And the LORD had respect unto Abel and to his offering" (Gen. 4:4, KJV). The text does not explicitly tell us why Abel's offering was accepted or why his brother Cain's offering was rejected.

Hebrew theology contains the belief that the most precious possession a person has is life itself. Blood stands for life. Abel's offering of the firstlings of his flock was the offering of life. The blood of the sheep represented the giving of life to God. Hence his offering was sacrificial whereas Cain's was not. Nonetheless, Abel is the first person mentioned in the roll of honor and commended by God for his great faith. Because of his faith, Abel's voice continues to speak after his death. It is a commentary of Revelations 14:13, which says, "And I heard a voice from heaven saying unto me, Write, Blessed are the dead which die in the Lord from henceforth: Yea, saith the Spirit, that they may rest from their labours; and their works do follow them" (KJV).

Hebrews 11:5 recounts the one deed of Enoch. He walked with God. *Walked* as used here means "conversation." It also means "alignment" or "in step with." Enoch's life consisted of an enduring conversation with God. His brief story is told in Genesis 5:21–24, a mere four verses. Yet his faith accomplishment is resounding. He walked with God, and God was well-pleased with him. Nothing else mattered. The NRSV nails it clearly. Enoch did not experience death because God took him. His major objective was to align himself in the will of God.

However, the ultimate commendation of divine approval is recorded in all four Gospel accounts in relationship to Jesus. "This is my beloved Son, in whom I am well pleased" (Matt. 3:17, KJV; Mark 1:11; Luke 3:22). The Greek word for *pleased* is *eudokesa.* Here it is used in the aorist tense, which indicates timeless pleasure. The actual verb means "to think well of, to be pleased with, or to take delight in."

The Johannine account of Jesus' baptism differs slightly (John 1:29–34). John the Baptist acknowledged the presence and power of God as he saw the Spirit of God in the form of a dove descend upon Jesus. In John's Gospel, Jesus is one with the Father. The declaration of His life and coming into the human frame of reference to reveal the Father confirmed God's approval of Jesus as the Lamb of Salvation (John 1:1–3, 14, 18, 36).In other words, Jesus is the definitive revelation of God

Hebrews 11:6 builds off of God's testimony concerning Enoch. He pleased God. Pleasing God is a matter of expressing faith in Him. It is personal ratification that God lives. Jesus told His disciples to "believe in God, believe also in me" (John 14:1, KJV). Anyone approaching God must believe that He is. This belief must be a focused faith that continually seeks God's presence and does His will. God rewards those who seek out His presence and do His bidding.

Verses 7 and 8 describe Noah as an heir of righteousness and Abraham as one who has come into an inheritance. Both of these words, *heir* and *inheritance*, come from the Greek root word *kleros*, which means "one to acquire or to obtain," as in an allocation. Noah's faith propelled him to build an ark simply based on God's warning (Gen. 6–9). Noah preached a message of repentance, although the ears of his fellows were closed against him. Noah's righteousness was the act of faith he displayed in building the ark. He trusted God's Word that it would rain despite the weather conditions at that time. Abraham's faith led him to seek out a land without any prior knowledge of where he was going or what he was getting himself into (Gen. 12–25). Because of their faithful actions, they are called heirs of righteousness, respectively.

III. The Destination of the Faithful (Hebrews 11:13–16)

The aspect of divine promise is the subject of verses 13–16. Their faith allowed them to envision God's promise and to some extent experience it from afar, although its total fulfillment was yet to come. Their faith changed their perception of themselves. They no longer saw themselves as citizens of this world, but as sojourners and pilgrims in a strange land. They believed that their relationship with God destined them to true greatness.

The Lesson Applied

Faith emerges from the reality of God. God is the structure and foundation of our faith. Therefore, those who seek God will be rewarded with the ability to overcome obstacles and challenges to their faith. His reward is not always fulfilled during their lifetime, but they are convinced it is forthcoming because of God's promise. God is a Promise Keeper.

Let's Talk About It

Is faith blind hope?

Faith is not blind. The Christian faith is based upon God's truth. The biblical record confirms that believers see and receive God's promises. His promises will ultimately come to pass.

Home Daily Devotional Readings

August 9–15, 2021

Monday	Tuesday	Wednesday	Thursday	Friday	Saturday	Sunday
Save Your Life by Losing It	Respond to Abusers with Blessings	Be Faithful Until Death	Sanctified by Christ's Sacrifice	The Inner Life of New Believers	Approach God with a Pure Heart	Act in Ways That Preserve the Faith
Mark 8:31–37	1 Peter 3:9–18	Revelation 2:8–11	Hebrews 10:1–10	Hebrews 10:11–18	Hebrews 10:19–22	Hebrews 10:23–36

Lesson 11

August 15, 2021

A Persevering Faith

Adult Topic:
Keep Going

Background Scripture:
Hebrews 10:19–39

Hebrews 10:23–36

King James Version

**LET us hold fast the profession of our
faith without wavering; (for he is faithful
that promised;)
24 And let us consider one another to provoke
unto love and to good works:
25 Not forsaking the assembling of ourselves
together, as the manner of some is; but exhort-
ing one another: and so much the more, as ye
see the day approaching.
26 For if we sin wilfully after that we have
received the knowledge of the truth, there
remaineth no more sacrifice for sins,
27 But a certain fearful looking for of judgment and fiery indignation, which shall devour
the adversaries.
28 He that despised Moses' law died without
mercy under two or three witnesses:
29 Of how much sorer punishment, suppose
ye, shall he be thought worthy, who hath
trodden under foot the Son of God, and hath
counted the blood of the covenant, wherewith
he was sanctified, an unholy thing, and hath
done despite unto the Spirit of grace?
30 For we know him that hath said, Vengeance
belongeth unto me, I will recompense, saith
the Lord. And again, The Lord shall judge
his people.
31 It is a fearful thing to fall into the hands of
the living God.
32 But call to remembrance the former days,
in which, after ye were illuminated, ye endured
a great fight of afflictions;**

New Revised Standard Version

**LET us hold fast to the confession of our hope
without wavering, for he who has promised
is faithful.
24 And let us consider how to provoke one
another to love and good deeds,
25 not neglecting to meet together, as is the
habit of some, but encouraging one another, and all the more as you see the Day
approaching.
26 For if we willfully persist in sin after having
received the knowledge of the truth, there no
longer remains a sacrifice for sins,
27 but a fearful prospect of judgment, and a
fury of fire that will consume the adversaries.
28 Anyone who has violated the law of Moses
dies without mercy "on the testimony of two or
three witnesses."
29 How much worse punishment do you think
will be deserved by those who have spurned the
Son of God, profaned the blood of the covenant
by which they were sanctified, and outraged
the Spirit of grace?
30 For we know the one who said, "Vengeance
is mine, I will repay." And again, "The Lord
will judge his people."
31 It is a fearful thing to fall into the hands of
the living God.
32 But recall those earlier days when, after
you had been enlightened, you endured a hard
struggle with sufferings,**

MAIN THOUGHT: Let us hold fast the profession of our faith without wavering; (for he is faithful that promised;). (Hebrews 10:23, KJV)

King James Version	*New Revised Standard Version*
33 Partly, whilst ye were made a gazingstock both by reproaches and afflictions; and partly, whilst ye became companions of them that were so used.	**33 sometimes being publicly exposed to abuse and persecution, and sometimes being partners with those so treated.**
34 For ye had compassion of me in my bonds, and took joyfully the spoiling of your goods, knowing in yourselves that ye have in heaven a better and an enduring substance.	**34 For you had compassion for those who were in prison, and you cheerfully accepted the plundering of your possessions, knowing that you yourselves possessed something better and more lasting.**
35 Cast not away therefore your confidence, which hath great recompence of reward.	**35 Do not, therefore, abandon that confidence of yours; it brings a great reward.**
36 For ye have need of patience, that, after ye have done the will of God, ye might receive the promise.	**36 For you need endurance, so that when you have done the will of God, you may receive what was promised.**

LESSON SETTING

Time: A.D. 65
Place: Rome

LESSON OUTLINE

I. Be Prepared (Hebrews 10:23–25)
II. Do Not Fall Away (Hebrews 10:26–31)
III. Stay the Course (Hebrews 10:32–36)

Unifying Principle

People lacking self-assurance can feel overwhelmed by life's challenges. What can enable one to face life confidently? Believers in Jesus Christ, who persevere in hope and encourage others in love and good works, develop in faith.

Introduction

The authorship of Hebrews has been long debated. Some believe it was written by Paul. However, its language and theology are inconsistent with Pauline letters that were written by his own hand or at least dictated by him. Without this bit of information, readers are left with the question: Who wrote the book of Hebrews? It was written anonymously, so we don't know who actually wrote it. This is also a point of difference from Pauline epistles—he always identified himself as the author.

Hebrews' anonymous authorship does not have any bearing on its importance. Though listed as an epistle, the book is structured more like a sermon than a first-century letter, which would have followed a specific format. As such, it builds its arguments surrounding the superior status of Jesus and faith through a variety of rhetorical devices. One of those devices is repetition. While reading Hebrews, when a phrase is similar to an earlier phrase, it is designed to jog the memory of the reader so the two passages are linked even if not close in physical proximity. Consider Hebrews 10:19: "Therefore, my friends, since we have confidence to enter the sanctuary by the blood of Jesus" (NRSV). This verse invokes 4:14, "Since, then, we have a great high priest who has passed through the heavens, Jesus, the Son of God, let us hold fast to our confession" (NRSV). It is invoked again in verse 21: "and since we have a great priest over the house of God" (NRSV). The invocation is a telling link between the tenth and fourth chapters. The author was pointing at once to the supremacy of Jesus the Christ, the confidence believers should have in Him, and his current subject—a warning against apostasy or falling away from the faith.

Our passage, 10:23–36, is situated as an encouragement and reminder to the immense stakes of the faith. It is placed right before the famous legends of the faith passage of chapter 11. The writer was rounding into the climax of the faith exemplars as a further encouragement to his readers that persevering faith is possible and necessary. The contingency of his argument, as always, rests on the superiority and faithfulness of Jesus, who is the object of our faith and also subject of our faith. He is our hope and guarantor that endurance to the will of God has great reward even in the face of great cost, which should give us overwhelming confidence.

Exposition

I. Be Prepared (Hebrews 10:23–25)

Hebrews 10:23 continues to build a foundation that segmentally begins in verse 19. The phrase *let us* is a signal that what is being mentioned has its basis in earlier argumentation. *Let us* is to be a proper response to that which has been previously acknowledged.

The intended response, of course, is an unwavering confession of faith during what are perceived as insurmountable circumstances. Its rationale is based in the faithfulness of God and God's High Priest, Jesus. Through their faithfulness, the reader of the text is to be spurred to faithfulness.

Ray Stedman, biblical scholar, notes the following about the *let us* statements in verses 19–31: "Twice in verses 19–31 the writer uses the phrase *we have*. Following these, there is thrice repeated the words *let us*. The *we haves* mark provision; *let us* indicates privilege" (Stedman, *Hebrews*). Verse 23 is a statement of privilege in as much as the believer is advantaged by the faithfulness of God. The privilege, therefore, is not derived within the individual believer. Rather, it is imbued by connection to the Faithful One. The advantage is by connection only without the status of the individual being of question.

This provides interesting fodder in the interpretation of this text as it moves the emphasis from responsibility or compulsion to the notion of privilege or a right that one enjoys exercising. The confession of faith is that which cannot and should not be taken away, as an unalienable right. This points to the agency of the believer to exercise choice in how and to what measure he or she will comply with the will of God, and in what spirit.

The *let us* of verse 23 is followed by another in verse 24. Continuing this frame of thought, the emphasis is moved from the individual to the individual within the context of the greater community of faith. The faithfulness of each person is measured in part of the provocation of good works and love in others. That is to say, God protects the faithful.

The word used here is *παροξυσμος* (*paroxysmos*) which means "provocation, irritation, or sharp disagreement." The NRSV is a good interpretation of the word, but we may be tempted to soften its meaning through substitutionary words like *encourage* or *embolden*. It seems likely the writer wanted his readers to push each other until all are committed to the work of love and deed. This is not simply a few kind words but invokes the image of one who will not stop until something happens. The text could rightly read, "Let us irritate each other until each one is committed to love and deeds." In other words, let no one among you get overly comfortable.

Clearly, this was the intention as we move into the next verse. There were some in their community who had become lax in regular meetings for presumed worship and rituals. It is here they were to encourage one another to continue in the Lord's work, for the Day was near.

At this point our writer used the imagery of the Day of Judgment. He simply used "the Day" because there was no need to go into detail. The varied eschatology of the early church is well-documented, as is the hope and anxiety surrounding the return of Jesus. The provoking and encouragement that were needed reemphasized the unknown nature of the Day. Believers are to be prepared whenever it might take place. To this effect, Jesus told the Parable of the Ten Bridesmaids (Matt. 25:1–13). Our author's reference to "the Day" would have been easily decrypted by the first readers without hesitation. It is the Day of the Lord where both the quick and dead will be judged. His message: Be prepared.

II. Do Not Fall Away (Hebrews 10:26–31)

Moving into the next few verses, Hebrews appeals to the emotions of its readers after appealing to their reason. The main thrust of its emotional appeal is fear. In the next few verses, fear is the largest motivator. Specifically, the fear of falling into judgment and being deemed necessary of punishment.

The sheer power of God and the respect that He demands of His Son's sacrifice is highlighted. The notion of sin after confessing Jesus' lordship is disrespectful. To do so is to trample the sacrifice of Christ under feet. At play is a moral code the believer is to abide by that points to their sanctification by the blood of sacrifice. The writer did not detail the moral code, but given his understanding of Moses and the Law as a prefiguring type, it can be surmised the moral code at the least holds to truths expressed in the Mosaic Law (10:28–29; 9:15–22). If Hebrews holds consistent to much of the New Testament, particularly Jesus in Matthew's Gospel, then one can make an educated guess that Hebrews strengthens the moral codes of the Old Testament. Its beginning and final witness is love with ultimate allegiance to Jesus Christ, His teachings, and His community of believers.

Hebrews is not envisioning a type of moral perfection in which one does not sin at all. Rather, the opening verse of this passage points at the continual nature of this kind of sin. There are two words of focus here: *εκουσιως* (*ekousios*) and *αμαρτανω* (*hamartano*). The first means "intentionally" and the second "to sin." *εκουσιως* obviously points to the will, as in one's ability for decision and bringing that decision into existence. Secondly, *αμαρτανω* is a present-tense participle, meaning it is descriptive of an action that is continuous in nature. Essentially, Hebrews describes one who sins without ceasing even though he or she has confessed Christ. To live as if one has not been introduced to the truth of Christ is to degrade His perfect sacrifice and leave one open to the judgment of God. In this way, verses 26–30 are reminiscent of Paul's argument in Romans 6:1–4. Though grace is available, it can be rejected, even by those who in word have accepted it.

Rejection of grace drives fear because it is a spurning of God Himself and His Son. As it stated in Hebrews 10:31, "It is a fearful thing to fall into the hands of the living God" (NRSV), for vengeance does indeed belong to our God.

This is one more reminder within Hebrews that apostasy is not to be entertained. As stated in the "Articles of Faith," "We believe the Scriptures teach that such only are real believers as endure to the end; that their preserving attachment to Christ is the grand mark that distinguishes them from superficial professors" (*The New National Baptist Hymnal,* 608). Falling away from the faith is to be avoided at the cost of eternity.

III. Stay the Course (Hebrews 10:32–36)

This final section of our passage highlights the various trials the Hebrews' readers had undergone. One assumes the abuse and persecution were due merely to their profession of Christ and what that may have meant in their daily lives and their participation in normal activities.

First-century persecution was not as widespread as many of us would assume. Often abuse and persecution was localized and reactionary to both imaginary xenophobic fears and the ways in which Christians pulled out of mainstream culture. Consider two stories in Acts 16 and 19. In both stories Paul was persecuted because of his actions. In Acts 16 he cured a girl from a demon, resulting in her masters' financial ruin. In Acts 19 he preached that the people of the city should no longer buy idols. Paul disrupted the local economy. Christians who were Gentiles would no longer buy household gods, affecting artisans' bottom line. Christians who were Jews may have no longer contributed to local synagogues. In both instances, the economic well-being of local people was at stake. The persecution of Christians was so much more than doctrinal and religious in nature.

This understanding of Christian persecution is important to note in light of this particular text, given Hebrews' exhortation to endurance in their confidence. The confidence in the promise is not as much about the promise itself but the One who made the promise. This obviously circles back to earlier portions of the text (v. 23). The Hebrews evidently had their possessions plundered and were forced to watch as some of them were imprisoned. In the face of these kinds of obstacles, it would be tempting to walk away from a nascent faith and developing community, but the writer encouraged them to stay the course with the understanding God has something better prepared for them. It was his goal, as it should be for all Christians, for them to succeed in performing the will of God.

The Lesson Applied

As modern Christians who live in a state of religious freedom, we do not know true persecution and suffering for the name of Christ. However, we too can fall victim to falling away from the practice of true Christianity—following the will of God—by which we are committing apostasy. We never may be called upon by a tribunal, stand in front of a judge, or endure a group of angry people calling for our denouncement of the faith. However, we must be careful we do not live in ways that denounce the faith in our daily routines.

Furthermore, as Christians we must regularly meet with other Christians. This is how we gain strength for the journey. There is power in being surrounded by people of like minds. It is also where we might be irritated and irritate others to good works and the fullness of love.

Quite simply, through the fellowship of the saints we are taught through their example of what it means to be a Christian, to love as God loves, and to serve the people of the world without accepting the value systems of the world. Let each one of us be encouraged to continue on in faith, not losing the hope that we have professed in the Lord Jesus Christ! Even living in a digital age, we must constrain ourselves to live in fellowship with one another and to hold one another accountable.

Let's Talk About It

How is it possible to cheerfully accept the plundering of one's possessions?

Hebrews gives us some insight to this by noting they understood a greater reward is in store for those who endure to the end. At times, our motivations can be short-lived and short-sighted. To be a Christian is to play the long game. In other words, it is about realizing the loss of possessions, while horrific, is not the end all be all. Possessions, of course, can be replaced, and we can bounce back as history teaches us, but a falling away from grace is eternal and has far-reaching ramifications that cannot be rectified.

Another passage that is helpful in moments when we are concerned about our existential needs is Matthew 10:28: "Do not fear those who kill the body but cannot kill the soul; rather fear him who can destroy both soul and body in hell" (NRSV). Though the loss of material goods is destructive and hurtful, it does not have eternal consequences unless one chooses to fall away from God. Only through our clinging to what we know is pure and right can we endure even the most horrific circumstances. Our faith in God is enduring and strong enough to persevere. Job's faith experience helped Him to see that God has the final world over life's circumstances. Hold on to your faith.

Home Daily Devotional Readings
August 16–22, 2021

Monday	Tuesday	Wednesday	Thursday	Friday	Saturday	Sunday
Testing Our Love for God	Love God by Keeping His Commandments	Discerning the Spirit of Truth and Error	Knowing God, We Can Love Others	Faith Is the Victory	Believers in Jesus Have Life	Faith That Loves Overcomes Obstacles
Deuteronomy 13:1–4	John 14:15–24	1 John 4:1, 4–6	1 John 4:7–12	1 John 5:1–3	1 John 5:6–12	1 John 4:2–3, 13–17; 5:4–5

A CONQUERING FAITH

Adult Topic:
Perfect Love

Background Scripture:
1 John 4–5

1 JOHN 4:2–3, 13–17; 5:4–5

King James Version

HEREBY know ye the Spirit of God: Every spirit that confesseth that Jesus Christ is come in the flesh is of God:

3 And every spirit that confesseth not that Jesus Christ is come in the flesh is not of God: and this is that spirit of antichrist, whereof ye have heard that it should come; and even now already is it in the world.

• • • • • •

13 Hereby know we that we dwell in him, and he in us, because he hath given us of his Spirit.

14 And we have seen and do testify that the Father sent the Son to be the Saviour of the world.

15 Whosoever shall confess that Jesus is the Son of God, God dwelleth in him, and he in God.

16 And we have known and believed the love that God hath to us. God is love; and he that dwelleth in love dwelleth in God, and God in him.

17 Herein is our love made perfect, that we may have boldness in the day of judgment: because as he is, so are we in this world.

• • • 1 John 5:4–5 • • •

4 For whatsoever is born of God overcometh the world: and this is the victory that overcometh the world, even our faith.

5 Who is he that overcometh the world, but he that believeth that Jesus is the Son of God?

New Revised Standard Version

BY this you know the Spirit of God: every spirit that confesses that Jesus Christ has come in the flesh is from God,

3 and every spirit that does not confess Jesus is not from God. And this is the spirit of the antichrist, of which you have heard that it is coming; and now it is already in the world.

• • • • • •

13 By this we know that we abide in him and he in us, because he has given us of his Spirit.

14 And we have seen and do testify that the Father has sent his Son as the Savior of the world.

15 God abides in those who confess that Jesus is the Son of God, and they abide in God.

16 So we have known and believe the love that God has for us. God is love, and those who abide in love abide in God, and God abides in them.

17 Love has been perfected among us in this: that we may have boldness on the day of judgment, because as he is, so are we in this world.

• • • 1 John 5:4–5 • • •

4 for whatever is born of God conquers the world. And this is the victory that conquers the world, our faith.

5 Who is it that conquers the world but the one who believes that Jesus is the Son of God?

MAIN THOUGHT: And we have known and believed the love that God hath to us. God is love; and he that dwelleth in love dwelleth in God, and God in him. (1 John 4:16, KJV)

LESSON SETTING

Time: A.D. 90–95
Place: Ephesus

LESSON OUTLINE

I. Pass the Test: Choose Jesus (1 John 4:2–4, 13–17)
II. Believers Are Victorious (1 John 5:4–5)

UNIFYING PRINCIPLE

Faced with the world's allure, people contend with its many appeals. How can one resist this unhealthy allure? Believers through faith in Jesus overcome the world and its seductions with the hope of victory.

INTRODUCTION

First John is a part of the Johannine Scripture (the Gospel of John, 1, 2, 3 John, and Revelation). The book is ascribed to the Apostle John, although some scholars attribute it to an unknown author. Its theme is to warn the church to be on the lookout for those who were against the proclamation of Jesus as the Christ of God and to encourage the congregation to conduct itself within the boundaries of God's love. In fact, the writer was quite explicit in describing God's love as the transforming agent of life that sealed the congregants' salvation. His readers were affectionately called "my little children."

Prominent in first-century Christianity was staunch opposition from Judaizers, Gnostics, and others who argued against Jesus as the anointed Messiah. They were vehemently against the idea that Jesus came in the flesh. Paul also faced this kind of opposition in the church at Corinth and Thessalonica (1 Cor. 14–15; 1 Thess. 4).

This pericope of Scripture is part of a larger unit that completes the last third of the book (1 John 3:1–5:12). The first two units address the issue of the historical contribution of Jesus to human salvation. First John 4:2–3, 13–17; 5:4–5 deals with the confession of faith of Jesus as the Son of God and as the expiation for human sin and point to the victory of faith in His great sacrifice. These are highly situated Christological arguments that answer the questions of divine salvation and how it is accomplished.

First John was written to a congregation in conflict. Indeed, most of the New Testament churches reveal evidence of conflict either theological or ecclesiastical. The church at Corinth, for example, encountered retribution from the Apostle Paul for bringing pagan practices into the church (1 Cor. 1; 5; 15). He also fought against those in the congregation who denied the bodily resurrection. James, the Lord's brother, penciled his epistle to rebuke false teachers and those who claimed to accomplish their ministries simply through verbal acclamations (James 1–2). Peter addressed the conflict by reminding his adherents they were a peculiar people (1 Pet. 1).

The writer of 1 John approached the issue of internal church conflict by calling for believers to test the spirits. This testing is actually a test of faith for the believer. Two things are important here. The writer called for an examination. The spiritual must not be accepted by the believer simply because it is spiritual.

One must test the spirit to ascertain whether or not it is the Spirit of God. This examination must be the demand of those who possess the Spirit of God. First John has a formula that assures the right spirit will be selected by the believer. Second, the text declares those who possess the Spirit of God are victorious through the expiation of Jesus Christ. The writer of 1 John argued quite effectively that the way to a conquering faith is to be observant and vigilant in approaching the spiritual realm. Evil influences seek to mute believers' testimonies and destroy their faith. These evil forces must not be allowed to succeed in their heresy. They are the Antichrist.

Exposition

I. Pass the Test: Choose Jesus (1 John 4:2–4, 13–17)

First John 4:1 starts with a term of endearment. The writer affectionately called out to His readers using the term *beloved* to demonstrate pastoral concern and care. Three times the writer used this term to address his readers (1 John 4:1, 7, 11). The word is a form of the Greek word *agapeo*. Used here in the vocative sense, it carries the weight of loving oversight, as in a father using his close alignment with his children to warn them of the dangers that lie ahead. The writer continued with an imperative, "Do not believe every spirit" (v. 1, NRSV). This admonition is moderated because of the writer's use of the word *beloved.* However, the urgency of his message comes through the command for them to not entertain the message of error that had resulted in the splintering of the congregation.

The evidence of the evil workings was there for all to see. It was a distortion of the person and work of the Lord Jesus. What the writer was referring to are the heretical messages of Corinthian Gnostics and practitioners of Doceticism. These heretical groups argued that Jesus was not human. To them, human matter was sinful flesh. Being holy, Jesus could not be human but was merely an apparition or a divine spark that provided the knowledge (*gnosis*) for redemption. (For a full discussion on Gnosticism, see "Gnosticism" in *The Interpreter's Dictionary of the Bible* and Kurt Rudolph's *Gnosis: The Nature and History of Gnosticism.*)

This type of theology, though appearing initially to glorify God, actually was destructive to the faith. It denied the historical Jesus in terms of Him being a real person born in the flesh. If this heresy were allowed to go unchallenged, it would undermine the Christian Gospel and also Jesus' own words to the disciples after His resurrection, challenging them to put their hand in His side and to touch His hands (John 20:26–29). In fact, if Jesus was not human, there was no need for His resurrection from the dead, and neither could He be the sacrifice for human sin. The writer of 1 John saw the danger of this type of false teaching and set out to warn believers of its invasion into the church. He commanded believers to test the spirit in order to determine whether or not it was of God.

In that day, false prophets were a dime a dozen and worked feverishly to lure many away from the faith. Jesus warned the disciples in Matthew 7:15 to be aware of false prophets. In his classic *Word*

Pictures in the New Testament, John A. T. Robertson said, "Credulity means gullibility and some believers fall easy victims to the latest fads in spiritual humbuggery" (Robertson, *Word Pictures in the New Testament*, 229).

The true test of prophecy is whether or not the prophet acknowledges that Jesus Christ came as a real person. If that person confesses Jesus Christ, then that person has the Spirit of God (1 John 4:2). The key word here is the full and designated proper name of the Lord. *Jesus* is the name Joseph was told by the angel to call the new born Savior. Matthew 1:21 says, "And she shall bring forth a son, and thou shalt call his name JESUS: for he shall save his people from their sins" (KJV). The name *Jesus* means "Yahweh saves or will save" and is the Greek form of the Hebrew word *Joshua,* or more fully, *Yehoshauh*. Paul's reference to Jesus being born of a woman (Gal. 4:4–5) emphasized not only the virgin birth, but also, and more importantly, that "Jesus was born of flesh and blood and not a phantom redeemer who appeared only to disappear and leave behind him a collection of esoteric doctrines" ("Jesus Christ," *The Interpreter's Dictionary of the Bible,* 868–896). (Also see Heb. 2:14.)

That is to say, Paul presupposed the Jesus of the Gospel narratives as the fulfillment of Old Testament prophecy and built on the information contained in them to develop his doctrine for the Church. The central force of the Corinthian correspondence points to the resurrection of Jesus as God's supreme act of salvation for believers of the faith. The resurrection itself points to the historical facts contained in the Gospel narratives of Jesus' birth, life, and death. There was no need for the resurrection of a spark or phantom, one who did not actually live in the human sense. The four Gospel accounts, along with Paul and Peter, all agree that Jesus was born in the form of humanity (Matt. 1:21; Luke 2:6–7; John 1:14; Phil. 2:5–11; Gal. 4:4; Heb. 2:9–11, 14–18).

Not only did the writer of 1 John declare Jesus was born of a woman and was therefore fully human, but he also argued this same Jesus is the fulfillment of Old Testament prophecy, which designates Him as the Christ of God. The name *Christ* is the Greek word for *Messiah* or "God's anointed" (*Christos*). Hebrew theology held that God would send Someone who would deliver Israel from oppression (Isa. 9:6–7). This Deliverer or Messiah would come in the order of King David and restore Israel, bringing about justice, righteousness, peace, and renewed fellowship with God. The Servant Songs in the latter part of Isaiah widely broadcasted God's ability and promise to restore Israel to prominence (Isa. 40–66). Jesus as God's anointed was revealed in the Gospels of Matthew and Luke through special revelation to Mary, Joseph, the Magi, and the shepherds in the field. He not only came in human form, but His birth was a miraculous event orchestrated by none other than God Himself (Matt. 1:16–25; Luke 1:26–38; 2:1–11).

In the Gospel of John, Jesus is the preexistent Son (Word, *Logos*) who revealed the gracious presence and power of God to eliminate the darkness of sin from human life (John 1:1–6, 14, 17–18). John's Gospel account actually identified Jesus with God and as the One who the Father sent from above (14:1–12).

All four Gospel writers observed the Spirit landing on Jesus after His baptism as a sign of His divine anointing and approval (Matt. 3:16–17; Mark 1:10–11; Luke 3: 21–22; John 1:33–34). The supreme human testimony of Jesus as the Christ came in Peter's confession in answer to Jesus' question: "But whom say ye that I am? And Simon Peter answered and said, Thou art the Christ, the Son of the living God. And Jesus answered and said unto him, Blessed art thou, Simon Barjona: for flesh and blood hath not revealed it unto thee, but my My Father which is in heaven" (Matt. 16:15–17, KJV).

The New Testament is quite clear that proof of the spirit is the acknowledgment that Jesus is the One designated by God to be the atonement for human sin. Faith in Him justifies the believer before God and creates a new fellowship with Him. The Spirit of God possesses the believer and the believer becomes one with the Father through the work of the Son (John 14:1–17).

II. Believers Are Victorious (1 John 5:4–5)

When believers hold fast to their faith in Jesus Christ, they are victorious through the activity of Jesus on the cross of Calvary. They have been born anew in God and automatically through their faith in Him attach themselves to His power to overcome. Paul said we are conquerors through Him who loves us (Rom. 8:37). The Greek word for *conquer* is *nikao*. It means "to prevail or to overcome." First John assures believers that just as Jesus conquered death, He will fortify believers to prevail over sin and false prophets.

The Lesson Applied

Christ has conquered the greatest enemy facing humanity—death. He is the Mediator of our faith as well as the One God who has chosen to redeem humanity. No other person or doctrine can supply human salvation. Believers are victorious when they exercise their faith in Jesus.

Let's Talk About It

Why is Jesus central to salvation?

Jesus is central to salvation because He is fully human and fully God. The Synoptic Gospels (Matthew, Mark, and Luke) portray His humanity, whereas John's Gospel portrays His divinity. As the God-man, Jesus is the propitiation for human sin. He rose from the dead, and those who profess faith in Him are justified and set right with God. Without Jesus Christ, humanity remains dead in its sins.

Home Daily Devotional Readings

August 23–29, 2021

Monday	Tuesday	Wednesday	Thursday	Friday	Saturday	Sunday
From Death to Life in Christ	Strengthening the Inner Being	Every Deed, Good or Evil, Judged	God's Judgment of Human Behavior Impartial	Paul, Confident in the Ministry	Entering the Presence of Jesus	Live the Faith with Confidence
1 Corinthians 15:16–23	Ephesians 3:14–21	Ecclesiastes 12:9–14	Romans 2:4–11	2 Corinthians 4:1–6	2 Corinthians 4:7–15	2 Corinthians 4:16–5:10

HOPE ETERNAL

ADULT TOPIC:
BE CONFIDENT

BACKGROUND SCRIPTURE:
2 CORINTHIANS 4:16–5:10

2 CORINTHIANS 4:16–5:10

King James Version

FOR which cause we faint not; but though our outward man perish, yet the inward man is renewed day by day.
17 For our light affliction, which is but for a moment, worketh for us a far more exceeding and eternal weight of glory;
18 While we look not at the things which are seen, but at the things which are not seen: for the things which are seen are temporal; but the things which are not seen are eternal.

• • • 2 Corinthians 5:1–10 • • •

1 For we know that if our earthly house of this tabernacle were dissolved, we have a building of God, an house not made with hands, eternal in the heavens.
2 For in this we groan, earnestly desiring to be clothed upon with our house which is from heaven:
3 If so be that being clothed we shall not be found naked.
4 For we that are in this tabernacle do groan, being burdened: not for that we would be unclothed, but clothed upon, that mortality might be swallowed up of life.
5 Now he that hath wrought us for the selfsame thing is God, who also hath given unto us the earnest of the Spirit.
6 Therefore we are always confident, knowing that, whilst we are at home in the body, we are absent from the Lord:
7 (For we walk by faith, not by sight:)

New Revised Standard Version

SO we do not lose heart. Even though our outer nature is wasting away, our inner nature is being renewed day by day.
17 For this slight momentary affliction is preparing us for an eternal weight of glory beyond all measure,
18 because we look not at what can be seen but at what cannot be seen; for what can be seen is temporary, but what cannot be seen is eternal.

• • • 2 Corinthians 5:1–10 • • •

1 For we know that if the earthly tent we live in is destroyed, we have a building from God, a house not made with hands, eternal in the heavens.
2 For in this tent we groan, longing to be clothed with our heavenly dwelling—
3 if indeed, when we have taken it off we will not be found naked.
4 For while we are still in this tent, we groan under our burden, because we wish not to be unclothed but to be further clothed, so that what is mortal may be swallowed up by life.
5 He who has prepared us for this very thing is God, who has given us the Spirit as a guarantee.
6 So we are always confident; even though we know that while we are at home in the body we are away from the Lord—
7 for we walk by faith, not by sight.

MAIN THOUGHT: For we know that if our earthly house of this tabernacle were dissolved, we have a building of God, an house not made with hands, eternal in the heavens. (2 Corinthians 5:1, KJV)

2 Corinthians 4:16–5:10

King James Version	*New Revised Standard Version*
8 We are confident, I say, and willing rather to be absent from the body, and to be present with the Lord.	**8 Yes, we do have confidence, and we would rather be away from the body and at home with the Lord.**
9 Wherefore we labour, that, whether present or absent, we may be accepted of him.	**9 So whether we are at home or away, we make it our aim to please him.**
10 For we must all appear before the judgment seat of Christ; that every one may receive the things done in his body, according to that he hath done, whether it be good or bad	**10 For all of us must appear before the judgment seat of Christ, so that each may receive recompense for what has been done in the body, whether good or evil.**

LESSON SETTING
Time: A.D. 57
Place: Unknown

LESSON OUTLINE

I. **Eternal Glory Will Follow Brief Affliction (2 Corinthians 4:16–18)**
II. **The Hope to Receive Eternal Glory Before Death (2 Corinthians 5:1–4)**
III. **Being Ready Always for the Judgment (2 Corinthians 5:5–9)**

Unifying Principle

People fear the fragility of life and the meaning of death. In weakness and death, where can any assurance be found? God gives believers in Jesus Christ an eternal, unseen place in Him that is guaranteed by the Spirit.

Introduction

As adults grow older, they give more consideration to their mortality. Many of them have become the matriarchs and the patriarchs of their families. They have fond memories. Their legacy probably has been established and they have few regrets. But one thing they are aware of now more than ever is that they are closer to their mortality than ever before. Probably not a day goes by when one doesn't reflect on one's mortality. Aging causes many adults to endure the loss of physical and mental vitality that negatively impacts their quality of life. While on the one hand longevity is a gift, on the other hand, the gift of having been given many years of life often comes with physical and mental challenges.

Moses wrote in Psalm 90:10, 12: "The days of our life are seventy years, or perhaps eighty, if we are strong; even then their span is only toil and trouble; they are soon gone, and we fly away. … So teach us to count our days that we may gain a wise heart" (NRSV). It appears the gifting aspect of aging—the attitude, outlook, or one's spirituality—allows one to cope as best as one can with the other side of aging—the aches, pains, and emotional toll.

One aspect of the emotional toll is losing loved ones or close friends and longing to see them again. On top of this is the curiosity of what happens after death. Senior adults may have an idea based on their faith traditions, but as one ages, curiosity resurges due to the fact they are now reflecting more on their mortality than any other time in their life.

Last but not least, older adults may contemplate life's overall behaviors and the possibility of good works being rewarded and sin being punished. In today's lesson, as we continue our discussions relative to faith giving us hope, we can be confident in our hope that is eternal in Jesus Christ, despite what years bring upon our fragile bodies and minds.

Exposition

I. Eternal Glory Will Follow Brief Affliction (2 Corinthians 4:16–18)

According to the *The New Interpreter's Bible,* the main idea of this section of our text (4:16–18) is that eternal glory will follow brief affliction. "So, (Paul says, in view of the faith and hope expressed in 4:13–15), we do not lose heart. Though our outer self, (i.e., the physical person that undergoes the wearing and continual afflictions…) is wasting away, (Paul feels the drain on his physical vitality) yet the inward person (the redeemed and Spirit-supported self), is being renewed every day" (*The New Interpreter's Bible: Volume 12,* 132–133).

The context of Paul's second letter to the Corinthians needs to be considered before going any further. Chapters 1–7 discuss the reconciliation of Paul and the Corinthians. Apparently Jewish "super apostles" turned members of the church against Paul, and he felt an urgent need to pen a letter (a portion of 2 Cor.) to defend his apostleship.

Paul's ministry caused him to age, thus considering more and more his mortality. In verse 16 the point was that the daily wasting away of physical life is counteracted by the daily renewal of inner spiritual life and strength. To that thought he added the assurance that in spite of the affliction mentioned in verse 17—"For our light momentary trouble are achieving for us an eternal glory that far outweighs them all" (NIV)—Paul and others who serve Christ in the ministry of the church know affliction that is present and real can also be light and temporary in view of the blessing involved. *Weight* may suggest that when afflictions are put on one side of the scale and the glory, blessings, and privileges on the other, the latter will far outweigh the trials.

In verse 18, Paul pointed out we are not looking at the things that are seen but at the things that are unseen. The things that are seen are transient. The things that are unseen are eternal. For Paul, the things seen are the physical trials and sufferings he had to endure. Things unseen include the realities of faith, Christian fellowship, and the life of the Spirit. These things will endure eternally. The world eternal does not say these realities belong to a timeless sphere, but that they will continue everlastingly.

To sum up this section, Paul cautioned the Corinthians to remain vigilant because the things they had to endure presently were only temporary. Instead, they should keep focused on their true and eternal destiny with Christ in glory.

II. The Hope to Receive Eternal Glory Before Death (2 Corinthians 5:1–4)

For Paul, when believers rise again, they leave all that is earthly behind. Their bodies are renewed as a spiritual body fashioned by God—permanent, indestructible, and celestial. The body is the earthly tent we live in. It is the temporary habitation of the person's spirit on this earth, where we live like desert dwellers, as "strangers and foreigners" (Heb. 11:13, NRSV). The body, like the tent, is frail and insecure. The spirit of a person who inhabits the tent is real and abiding. Though the body and the spirit have influence on each other, the spirit survives the death of the body. In other words when this earthly tent is destroyed and we enter through death the heavenly region, we shall need—and receive—another home. This time it will not be feeble, unsubstantial, and temporary. It will be a building from God, a house not made with hands, eternal in the heavens. It will be beyond the reach of death and decay. This spiritual body is incorruptible and immortal (1 Cor. 15:44, 53). It will correspond to heavenly conditions and environment. This is the *unseen* that Paul preferred the Corinthians focus upon. Until we fully transition, it is natural even as believers to reflect on that which is *seen*.

In 2 Corinthians 5:2–4, Paul's anxiety in the face of death begins to appear. He looked forward to being clothed with his spiritual body. But he was anxious the change from the earthly tent to the heavenly dwelling should take place with no intermittent stage of disembodiment, which was one of the Jewish conceptions of the state of the dead preceding the Resurrection. This may have struck Paul with dismay. The coming of Christ before the hour of death arrived would prevent it. Paul longed for the Lord's return to transform his body before his death, for it would mean the immediate change from the earthly tent to the spiritual body. It would have been surprising if he had not looked forward to leaving the frail and ragged tent that was his earthly body. His victory over physical handicaps was a miracle of grace, but time and again he must have chafed at the limitations these imposed. He longed for a life so full and overwhelming that what was mortal would be swallowed up by it, like trampled sand by the incoming tide. This process had already begun, as was evident by the way in which the vitality of his spirit overcame the frailty of his body. When the light of God is flooding a man's soul, it shines the more through a physical envelope that is torn. God's strength is made perfect through weakness (2 Cor. 12:9).

III. Being Ready Always for the Judgment (2 Corinthians 5:5–9)

Believers are guaranteed a glorious future because God has created us for a purpose, working in us to will and do God's good pleasure in ways beyond our understanding (Phil. 2:13). The Holy Spirit serves as a guarantee of a future promise, a foretaste of the glory believers shall one day know. Death in such a case is only the final destruction of the envelope, a change physically so insignificant it may scarcely be noticed. *He died into glory as the stars die into the sunrise.* Though the physical process of death may be as natural as falling asleep, it should be noted death ushers in a crisis for the spirit that the New Testament takes seriously. It confronts us with the Judgment; it introduces us to a world that will make demands we cannot meet save through the grace of God. Therefore, we need His presence with us.

The Lesson Applied

As believers grow in faith, our focus shifts from physical and material things to things that are spiritual and eternal. Like Paul's ministry of service, believers live for the glory of God, serving others. Raising families likewise may wear down our physical existence (*seen*), but like Paul, the renewing grace and power of God (*unseen*) has kept our faith, loyalty, and will to serve at a high level. As believers grow and mature in the faith, we become more willing to relinquish the cares of this world and prepare to embrace a heavenly home. While the lyrics are true, "only what you do for Christ will last," the vessel we have had the honor of serving in does not last.

Believers grow to understand God is a God of love, grace and mercy, but also a God of judgment. We learn to trust God's sovereign authority regarding the distribution of both eternal reward and punishment. The judgment seat is like the reward position at the Olympic Games. Those who belong to the family of God will receive the reward for good things done in the body and experience the sadness of rewards lost because of useless things, because of their failure at times to be fit enough (1 Cor. 3:10–15; 4:4; Rom. 14:10–12). Christians know that some matters of faith will remain a mystery until we meet God face-to-face. Songwriter Alison Krauss wrote in "I Know Who Holds Tomorrow":

I don't know about tomorrow
I just live from day to day
I don't borrow from the sunshine
For the skies they turn to gray
And I don't worry for the future
For I know what Jesus said
And today I'll walk beside him
For he's what lies ahead.
Many things about tomorrow
I don't seem to understand
But I know who holds tomorrow
And I know who holds my hand.

Let's Talk About It

What does eternal life really mean for the Christian believer?

In John 3:16 we have Jesus' rationale for His coming into the world—to provide salvation to believers. Salvation is eternal life and fellowship with God. It is not something that happens after a believer passes away—eternal life is a current possession. Believers possess fellowship with God in the here and now. Paul said in 1 Corinthians 15 our hope is based on the resurrection of Jesus. He confirmed our hope is indeed assured through the sacrifice of Jesus. God raised Him and will raise us up too.

Home Daily Devotional Readings

August 30–September 8, 2021

Monday	Tuesday	Wednesday	Thursday	Friday	Saturday	Sunday
God Hardens Pharaoh's Heart	Don't Just Do Something; Stand There!	Victory by the Sea	Blessed Be God Our Savior	Victory in Jesus	Moses Sings of God's Triumph	Moses and Miriam Praise God
Exodus 14:1-9	Exodus 14:10-20	Exodus 14:21-31	Luke 1:67-75	1 Corinthians 15:51-58	Exodus 15:1-10	Exodus 15:11-21

*PARTIAL BIBLIOGRAPHY

Achtemeir, Paul J., ed. *Harper's Bible Dictionary*. New York: Harper and Row, 1985.

Akin, D. L. *The New American Commentary: 1, 2, 3 John*. Nashville: Broadman and Holman Publishers, 2001.

Anderson, G. P. "Hospitality." *Lexham Theological Wordbook*. Edited by D. Mangum, D. R. Brown, R. Klippenstein, and R. Hurst. Bellingham: Lexham Press, 2014.

Augustine of Hippo. "The City of God." *St. Augustin's City of God and Christian Doctrine, Vol. 2*. Edited by P. Schaff. Translated by M. Dods. Buffalo: Christian Literature Company, 1887.

Barbieri, L. A., Jr. "Matthew." *The Bible Knowledge Commentary: An Exposition of the Scriptures, Vol. 2*. Edited by J. F. Walvoord and R. B. Zuck. Wheaton: Victor Books, 1985.

Barclay, William. *The New Daily Study Bible*. Westminster: John Knox Press, 2004.

Barry, J. D., D. Bomar, D. R. Brown, R. Klippenstein, D. Mangum D., C. Sinclair Wolcott, and W. Widder, editors. "Right Hand." *The Lexham Bible Dictionary*. Bellingham: Lexham Press, 2016.

Black, M. C. *Luke*. Joplin: College Press Publishing Company, 1995.

Blum, E. A. "John." *The Bible Knowledge Commentary: An Exposition of the Scriptures, Vol. 2*. Edited by J. F. Walvoord and R. B. Zuck. Wheaton: Victor Books, 1985.

Borchert, G. L. *The New American Commentary: John 12–21*. Nashville: Broadman and Holman Publishers, 2002.

Bratcher, R. G. and E. A. Nida. *A Handbook on the Gospel of Mark*. New York: United Bible Societies, 1993.

Brown, F., S. R. Driver, and C. A. Briggs. *Enhanced Brown-Driver-Briggs Hebrew and English Lexicon*. Oxford: Clarendon Press, 1977.

Bunn, John T. "Ezekiel." *Broadman Bible Commentary: Jeremiah–Daniel*. Edited by Clifton J. Allen. Nashville: Broadman Press, 1969–1972.

Butler, T. C. *Holman New Testament Commentary: Luke*. Nashville: Broadman and Holman Publishers, 2000.

Buttrick, George Arthur, *et. al.*, ed. *The Interpreter's Bible: Volume 7*. Nashville: Abingdon-Cokesbury Press, 1952.

Carson, D. A. *The Gospel According to John*. Grand Rapids: Eerdmans Publishing Company, 1991.

Dictionary of Biblical Imagery. Downers Grove: InterVarsity Press, 1998.

Easton, M. G. *Easton's Bible Dictionary*. New York: Harper and Brothers, 1893.

Ellingworth, P. and E. A. Nida. *A Handbook on the Letter to the Hebrews*. New York: United Bible Societies, 1994.

Ellingworth, P. and H. Hatton. *A Handbook on Paul's First Letter to the Corinthians*. New York: United Bible Societies, 1995.

Evangelical Dictionary of Theology. Grand Rapids: Baker Books, 1996.

Francisco, C. T. "Genesis." *The Teacher's Bible Commentary*. Edited by H. F. Paschall and H. H. Hobbs. Nashville: Broadman and Holman Publishers, 1972.

Freedman, D. N., A. C. Myers, and A. B. Beck, eds. *Eerdmans Dictionary of the Bible*. Grand Rapids: W.B. Eerdmans, 2000.

Gangel, K. O. *Holman Old Testament Commentary: Joshua*. Nashville: Broadman and Holman Publishers, 2000.

Gesenius, W. and S. P. Tregelles. *Gesenius' Hebrew and Chaldee Lexicon to the Old Testament Scriptures*. Bellingham: Logos Bible Software, 2003.

Gill, John. *An Exposition of the Old Testament, Vol. 1*. London: Mathews and Leigh, 1810.

Glaze, A. J. "Jonah." *Broadman Bible Commentary: Hosea–Malachi*. Edited by Clifton J. Allen. Nashville: Broadman Press, 1969–1972.

"Gnosticism" in *The Interpreter's Dictionary of the Bible, Volume E-J*. Nashville, Abingdon Press, 1998.

Grassmick, J. D. "Mark." *The Bible Knowledge Commentary: An Exposition of the Scriptures*. Edited by J. F. Walvoord and R. B. Zuck. Wheaton: Victor Books, 1985.

Green, James L. "Jeremiah." *Broadman Bible Commentary: Jeremiah–Daniel*. Edited by Clifton J. Allen. Nashville: Broadman Press, 1969–1972.

Hamrick, Emmett W. "Ezra–Nehemiah." *Broadman Bible Commentary: 1 Samuel–Nehemiah*. Edited by Clifton J. Allen. Nashville: Broadman Press, 1969–1972.

Honeycutt, Roy L. "2 Kings." *Broadman Bible Commentary: 1 Samuel–Nehemiah*. Edited by Clifton J. Allen. Nashville: Broadman Press, 1969–1972.

Hughes, R. K. *Acts: The Church Afire*. Wheaton: Crossway Books, 1996.

Hughes, R. K. *Hebrews: An Anchor for the Soul, Vol. 1*. Wheaton: Crossway Books, 1993.

Hughes, R. K. *Luke: That You May Know the Truth*. Wheaton: Crossway Books, 1998.

Isaacs, M. E. *Reading Hebrews and James: A Literary and Theological Commentary*. Macon: Smyth and Helwys Publishing, 2002.

Jaffe, Eric, "The Complicated Psychology of Revenge," *Observer* 24, no. 8 (October 2011).

"Jesus Christ" in *The Interpreter's Dictionary of the Bible, Volume E-J*. Nashville, Abingdon Press, 1998.

Keck, Leander, ed. *The New Interpreter's Bible, Vol. 12, Hebrews*. Nashville: Abingdon Press, 1988.

Kelley, Page H. "Isaiah." *Broadman Bible Commentary: Proverbs–Isaiah*. Edited by Clifton J. Allen. Nashville: Broadman Press, 1969–1972.

Kelly, B. R. "Oaths" in *Holman Illustrated Bible Dictionary*. Edited by C. Brand, C. Draper, A. England, S. Bond, E. R. Clendenen, and T. C. Butler. Nashville: Holman Bible Publishers, 2003.

King, Martin Luther, Jr. "I've Been to the Mountaintop." Memphis: Mason Temple, April 3, 1968.
King, Martin Luther, Jr. "Letter from a Birmingham Jail." 1963.
Kissling, Paul. *Genesis, Vol. 2.* Joplin: College Press Publishing Company, 2009.
Kittel, Gerhard. *Theological Dictionary of the New Testament.* Grand Rapids: Wm. B. Eerdmans Publishing Co., 1964.
Laurin, Robert M. "Lamentations." *Broadman Bible Commentary: Jeremiah–Daniel.* Edited by Clifton J. Allen. Nashville: Broadman Press, 1969–1972.
Lea, T. D. *Holman New Testament Commentary: Hebrews & James.* Nashville: Broadman and Holman Publishers, 1999.
Levine, Amy-Jill. *Short Stories by Jesus: The Enigmatic Parables of a Controversial Rabbi.* New York: Harper One, 2015.
Louw, J.P. and E. A. Nida. *Greek-English Lexicon of the New Testament: Based on Semantic Domains, Vol. 1,* electronic 2nd ed. New York: United Bible Societies, 1996.
Martin, Civilla D. "God Will Take Care of You." *The New National Baptist Hymnal, 21st Century Edition.* Nashville: Triad Publications, 2001.
Martin, J. A. "Luke" in *The Bible Knowledge Commentary: An Exposition of the Scriptures, Vol. 2.* Edited by J. F. Walvoord and R. B. Zuck. Wheaton: Victor Books, 1985.
Matheney, M. Pierce, Jr. "1 Kings." *Broadman Bible Commentary: 1 Samuel–Nehemiah.* Edited by Clifton J. Allen. Nashville: Broadman Press, 1969–1972.
Matthews, Kenneth A. *New American Commentary: Genesis 11–50.* Nashville: Broadman and Holman Publishers, 2005.
Moo, Douglas. *The New International Commentary on the New Testament, The Epistle to the Romans.* Grand Rapids: Eerdman's Publishing Company, 1996.
Mote, Edward. "The Solid Rock." *The New National Baptist Hymnal, 21st Century Edition.* Nashville: Triad Publications, 2001.
Newman, B. M. and E. A. Nida. *A Handbook on the Acts of the Apostles.* New York: United Bible Societies, 1972.
Newman, B. M. and E. A. Nida, *A Handbook on the Gospel of John.* New York: United Bible Societies, 1993.
Newman, B.M. and P. C. Stine. *A Handbook on the Gospel of Matthew.* New York: United Bible Societies, 1992.
Paffenroth, K. "Chuza" in *Eerdmans Dictionary of the Bible.* Edited by D. N. Freedman, A. C. Myers, and A. B. Beck. Grand Rapids: W.B. Eerdmans, 2000.
Polhill, J. B. *The New American Commentary: Acts.* Nashville: Broadman and Holman Publishers, 1992.
Robertson, John A. T. *Word Pictures in the New Testament, Vol. VI, The General Epistles and the Revelation of John.* Nashville: Broadman Press, Nashville, 1933.
Rudolph, Kurt. *Gnosis: The Nature and History of Gnosticism.* Edinburgh: T. T. Clark Limited, 1984.
Ryrie, Charles C. *The Ryrie Study Bible.* Chicago: Moody Press, 1986.
Shields, M. A. and R. K. Hawkins. "YHWH" in *The Lexham Bible Dictionary.* Edited by J. D. Barry, D. Bomar, D. R. Brown, R. Klippenstein, D. Mangum, C. Sinclair Wolcott, and W. Widder. Bellingham: Lexham Press, 2016.
Smith, J. E. *1 & 2 Samuel.* Joplin: College Press Publishing Company, 2000.
Stallings, J. W. *The Gospel of John,* 1st ed. Edited by R. E. Picirilli. Nashville: Randall House Publications, 1989.
Stedman, Ray C. *Hebrews, The IVP New Testament Commentary Series, Vol. 15.* Edited by Grant R. Osborne. Downer's Grove: IVP Academic, 2010.
Stein, R. H. *The New American Commentary: Luke.* Nashville: Broadman and Holman Publishers, 1992.
Stott, John. *Between Two Worlds—the Art of Preaching in the Twentieth Century.* Grand Rapids: Eerdman's Publishing Company, 1982.
Swann, J. T. "Priest" in *The Lexham Bible Dictionary.* Edited by J. D. Barry, D. Bomar, D. R. Brown, R. Klippenstein, D. Mangum, C. Sinclair Wolcott, and W. Widder. Bellingham: Lexham Press, 2016.
Swanson, J. *Dictionary of Biblical Languages with Semantic Domains: Greek (New Testament),* electronic ed. Oak Harber: Logos Research Systems, Inc., 1997.
Taylor, William D. *Miracles of Our Savior.* Athens: Guardians of Truth Foundation, 2004.
The New Interpreter's Bible: Volume 12, Hebrews. Nashville: Abingdon Press, 1998.
The New National Baptist Hymnal, 21st Century Edition. Nashville: Triad Publications, 2001.
Toussaint, S. D. "Acts" in *The Bible Knowledge Commentary: An Exposition of the Scriptures, Vol. 2.* Edited by J. F. Walvoord and R. B. Zuck. Wheaton: Victor Books, 1985.
Watts, John D. W. "Deuteronomy." *Broadman Bible Commentary: Leviticus–Ruth.* Edited by Clifton J. Allen. Nashville: Broadman Press, 1969–1972.
White, Deborah Gray. *Freedom On My Mind: A History of African Americans.* Boston: Bedford: St. Martin's, 2013.
Wright, P. H. *Rose Then and Now Bible Map Atlas with Biblical Background and Culture.* Torrance: Rose Publishing, 2012.

* See Full Bibliography online at R. H. Boyd.com.